CW00405998

COASTAL DAWN

COASTAL DAWN

BLENHEIMS IN ACTION FROM THE PHONEY WAR
THROUGH THE BATTLE OF BRITAIN

ANDREW D BIRD

Grub Street • London

Published by
Grub Street
4 Rainham Close
London
SW11 6SS

Copyright © Grub Street 2012
Copyright text © Andrew D. Bird 2012

British Library Cataloguing in Publication Data

Bird, Andrew D
    Coastal Dawn: Blenheims in action from the phoney war
    through the Battle of Britain.
    1. World War, 1939-1945–Aerial operations, British.
    2. Blenheim (Bomber)–History.
    3. World War, 1939-1945–Campaigns–Great Britain.
    I. Title
    940.5'44'941-dc22

    ISBN-13: 9781906502690

All rights reserved. No part of this publication may be reproduced,
stored in a retrieval system, or transmitted in any form or by any
means electronic, mechanical, photocopying, recording or otherwise, without the prior permission of the copyright owner.

Cover design by Sarah Driver
Book design by Roy Platten roy.eclipse@btopenworld.com
Edited by Hannah Stuart

Printed and bound by MPG Ltd, Bodmin, Cornwall

Grub Street Publishing only uses
FSC (Forest Stewardship Council) paper for its books.

CONTENTS

ACKNOWLEDGEMENTS

The Battle of Britain was mythologized before it was even over and those who took part in it were bathed in the glow of legend like the knights at *King Arthur's Round Table*, but only now can we justifiably embrace the heroes we have left behind.

This book has been a long time in the making and a number of people have given me considerable help. My sincere thanks go to John Davies at Grub Street whose support and patience is invaluable. Thanks to Hannah Stuart for her editing, and getting a glimpse of my creative soul. Any mistakes that remain are mine alone. Thanks are also extended to Sarah Driver, Sophie Campbell, and Emer Hogan at Grub Street for their guidance in getting this project to fruition. As ever, it has been a pleasure to work with such a knowledgeable team and I look forward to future projects.

Special acknowledgement and thanks to series producer Michael Wadding of *War Hero In My Family*, a Channel 5 TV Series, and the 360 production team. My thanks also to actress Lisa Faulkner whose grandfather William 'Lelly' Day served with 235 Squadron throughout the Phoney War and the Battle of Britain. Initially I was unaware that I had written about Lisa Faulkner's grandfather. I was then asked to work on the first episode filmed in the winter of 2011, which was the start of Lisa's journey of discovery. I am extremely humble to have been involved.

Also, Dryden Goodwin, internationally acclaimed artist, for including me in his acclaimed Open project, a composite portrait of a diverse urban community connected to, working near and living alongside the focal landmark building of Carnegie's Battle Library in Reading. I was one of the twenty-six people drawn and the project was accompanied by animated video and soundtrack vignette in which I talked about 254 Squadron, Pilot Officer 'Bill' Baines and *Coastal Dawn*.

Inevitably a number of people have given me a considerable amount of help and guidance along the way. Firstly I would like to thank Group Captain Patrick Tootal OBE DL RAF (Ret'd), Secretary of The Battle of Britain Memorial Trust Capel-le-Ferne, Kent for his tireless dedication and work ethic. He was a great help putting me in touch with the handful of veterans of the 'trade protection' Blenheim squadrons who fought from the Phoney War through the Battle of Britain.

Particular gratitude must be given to the Jesuit Priesthood, for their hospitality and allowing me the generous access to Brother Norman, who in 1940 was a young nineteen-year-old pilot officer on one of the Blenheim fighter squadrons. His assistance in countless ways has been invaluable during the typing of the manuscript.

I have drawn heavily on the memories, knowledge and understanding of those dark days which Brother Norman shared with me and also on the conversations I had with Roger Morewood on the telephone to his Scottish home. To both I am extremely grateful. Our conversations have been both of harrowing experiences and fun times and have been absolutely fascinating.

To the families around the world who have given their time and help; Simon Woddy, Peter Manwaring, Jim Inniss, John Sise, John Wakefield, Philip Pardoe-Williams, Phil Lloyd, John Cronan, Jill Heistein, Noelle 'Twiz' Spence, Marion Bullen (niece of George Keel), Sue Kenworthy, Derek Ryan, Paul Wickings-Smith, Robert Hook, Ray Bullen, Malcolm Spiers, Nigel Pittman, Dr. Donal Lowry, cousin of Leading Aircraftman/Air Gunner Thomas Lowry, Pat Woodger, David Wright's family, Paul Emery, and Sally Goldsworthy for sharing her late father Group Captain 'Sam' McHardy's diary notes which he began making in 1990. I'm grateful to Katy Iliffe of Sedbergh School, for providing details on former pupil Herbert Capstick, the only Jamaican to fight in the Battle of Britain, and John Baird a former Sedbergh 100 yard runner and 1st XV rugby team player.

I wish to thank the Bundersarchiv-Militärarchiv in Freiburg, Germany, and the Operation Dynamo War Museum, Dunkirk, France. Special thanks to all the staff at The Aircraft Restoration Company, Duxford for their priceless knowledge, and for allowing me to use the original Bristol Aeroplane Company drawings of the four 0.303 machine-gun belly-pack mountings for the Blenheim fighter Mk IVF. I am indebted to Graham Warner for his definitive research contained in *The Bristol Blenheim – A Complete History*.

I owe a debt to a number of dedicated people who have given assistance beyond what could be reasonably expected in the various archives in Britain, Holland, France and Canada. My thanks to Richard Hughes in the sound archive at the Imperial War Museum and their former stalwart Brad King for his guidance and medal specialist Tony Coleman; and to the Department of National Defense, Ottawa, Ontario, Canada, for your incredibly helpful advice.

To all the staff at the Department of Research and Information Services at the Royal Air Force Museum, London, for your time, knowledge and enthusiasm for this untold story. I am also grateful to the staff in the photographic archive, The Air Historical Branch staff, and Wyb Jan Groendijk at Vredenhof Schiermonnikoog War Grave Cemetery, in the Netherlands.

To my unofficial librarian Marjorie McClure and her staff at Battle Library, Reading for your generous time and help searching the Reading borough council's library archive for military aviation books no longer on the shelves. Thanks to the staff at Oxfam Bookshop in Reading and particularly Richard Way Books, Henley-on-Thames for their helpfulness in searching for rare and secondhand books relating to Coastal Command.

I would also like to thank a number of aviation historians who have been brilliant and helpful along the way: Chris Goss for the loan of his unit papers, and hard-garnered archive photographs and other material. Peter Cornwell who has an encyclopedic knowledge of allied and Luftwaffe losses. Ross McNeill, John Weal, Martin Bowman, Andy Saunders, Martin Gleeson, Paul McMillan, Brian Bines, and Steve Darlow. In Norway: Kjell Sørensen, Morten Moe, Linzee Druce, Andreas Brekken. In Holland: Hans Nauta, John van der Maas, Harn van der Laan, Peter Hasselgren and Theo Boiten for his guidance and photographs. And in Canada, Dutchman Bob van Wye.

The last acknowledgement should really have come first. My eternal gratitude, Carol, Jessica and Nicholas for your support and – how shall I put this – tolerance.

"Those Blenheim fighter boys of Coastal Command were the real heroes. We fighter boys at least had a pretty deadly aeroplane in our hands, and then the consolation of chalking up a score once in a while. But those boys had little of the thrill or glamour, so to speak, and twice the danger. They knew, as pilots, observers and gunners, that every time they took to the skies they did not stand much chance of returning; but they never shirked a job and never hesitated. We 'fighter boys' should have taken our hats off to those boys instead of basking in our own glory."

P/O Tom Neil, August 1940.
Gun Button to Fire
(Reproduced by kind permission of Amberley Publishing)

INTRODUCTION

The newcomers took some ragging when they walked into the dining room. All were given a mug full of hot sweet tea and as many slices of freshly baked bread and butter and plum or strawberry jam as they wanted. Then the bomb exploded. Simultaneously, as the lights went out, the glass burst from their sash window frames, spraying slivers of glass everywhere. Knife-edged fragments sliced through the air as the walls transmitted the blast like a ripple through water, flaying those that stood in their path. Falling blue shreds of uniform cloth fluttered like confetti onto already butchered bodies of airmen and women.

The devastation was appalling, one hangar had taken a direct hit. Aircraft had been damaged, the workshops, squadron dispersal hut and mess hall made uninhabitable, all electricity, water and gas mains cut. With an unknown number injured, airmen and women clawed with bare hands at bricks and rubble.

Airborne above the aerodrome, Pilot Officer Douglas Wordsworth in T1805 saw a lorry topple into the sky like a wooden skittle, landing one hundred feet away from their dispersal hut. This was surreal, like the First World War Biggles stories he'd read which now seemed a lifetime ago. Yet, from the moment he'd read *Biggles Learns to Fly* Douglas Wordsworth's path was charted. His efforts to persuade his parents that he should join the regular Royal Air Force lasted until the late summer of 1938, when at the height of the Munich crisis Douglas was accepted on a short service commission.

Reluctance by members of Parliament to take action with uncertain events taking place in Europe had a detrimental effect on the Royal Air Force. The Air Ministry had no sense of urgency either. Then in 1934 an expansion programme was passed in the House of Commons, in preparation for the RAF to fight another war. Hundreds of young able-bodied young men began to be recruited. In the inter-war years between 1935 and 1938 the estimated intake was 4,500 aircrew and 40,000 airmen and apprentices. New modern methods in recruitment were devised which saw striking and appealing advertisements in flying magazines and daily and regional newspapers together with Air Ministry officials talking directly to the public, targeting both grammar and state schools and thereby capturing all social classes. In 1938's issue of *Flight* one advert ran: 'Royal Air Force – Skilled, semi-skilled and unskilled men may improve their prospects – Apply to any RAF Volunteer Reserve Recruiting Depot'. Tom Wilkinson aged seventeen, reported:

"I saw the advertisement, it sparked my imagination but being under twenty-one, parental permission was required. Over dinner I talked my father and mother into allowing me to join. Everyone was like-minded. I immediately began learning a trade as an aircraft apprentice."

Whatever their differences of background, all these young boys were children of their time. Norman Jackson-Smith escaped Liverpool aged fourteen for a career aboard a luxury liner before circumstances afforded him the means to learn to fly in a flimsy de Havilland Moth at Liverpool Aerodrome:

> "It was sheer enjoyment. I had found my freedom by becoming airborne. On January 14 1939 I was issued with an aviator's certificate, No. 16,895. On completion of my flying training I applied to the RAF and was granted a permanent commission in September 1939."

It was an immense occasion, Jackson-Smith thought, as his two sisters looked on while he stepped forward to receive his wings.

Victor Ricketts was an air correspondent for the London *Daily Express*, in his mid-twenties. He approached Arthur Clouston, a New Zealander who flew as a test pilot at Farnborough and in his spare time air raced. Ricketts arranged backing for a record-breaking attempt to Australia and back in a de Havilland Comet G-ACSS if Clouston took him along as second pilot. The first attempt had to be aborted after coming to grief in Turkey. Ricketts and Clouston's second attempt on a revised route succeeded, landing back at Croydon after ten days, twenty-one hours and twenty-two minutes, having established eleven records. He joined the RAFVR in March 1939 as a sergeant pilot. Seven months later he was called up and by February 1940 was commissioned as a pilot officer.

Eighteen-year-old New Zealander Pilot Officer 'Sam' McHardy was another one. With fifteen fellow countrymen, he had sailed to England aboard RMS *Tainui*. Six weeks after leaving New Zealand, with a brief stop in Kingston, Jamaica, *Tainui* berthed at Southampton docks on a bleak wet morning. McHardy wrote: "We had colonial ties, if our home country (Britain) was threatened, New Zealanders would hear the call".

Daniel Wright had followed his father down one of the north Staffordshire coalmines:

> "It was natural progression, except I didn't like the idea and hated it. Schooling was at a mining college where I joined the newly formed Air Defence Cadet Corps. It was my ambition to join the Royal Air Force. When war was declared I went to the local recruiting office but, being only seventeen, needed my parents' signatures. My mother wouldn't go against my father who forbade me to join up. So rebelliously I forged both their signatures! I was in!"

These are some of Churchill's 'few', just as courageous as their counterparts who flew Hurricanes and Spitfires. Remarkably little has been chronicled of these men, their colleagues and the aircraft they flew: the Bristol Blenheim Mark IV Fighter.

I go forward light of heart . . .
One of the few . . .

Remembering those who served,
on the ground and in the air with
235, 236, 248 & 254 RAF Squadrons
between October 1939 through to October 1940.

CHAPTER ONE

God Be With You Till We Meet Again

A startled group of women turned their faces skywards as an open cockpit Miles Magister trainer sped past. In the front sat a figure wearing a thick RAF greatcoat and a forage cap and goggles, in the rear flying suit, helmet and goggles were worn, on this morning in the winter of 1939. Pilot Officer Norman Jackson-Smith lightly touched the stick. Instantly responding R1870 darted below the level of the café roof as the propeller cut through the bitterly cold wind. Pilot Officer Alan Wales then caught a glimpse of a face as the tandem trainer sped, at 90 mph over Royal St George's golf club fairways, now frequently used for low flying training by young aviators. The pitch of the Gypsy Major I changed as Jackson-Smith flicked the agile machine around to head back. Both men were beginning to feel the cold and even the sea gulls had ceased flying! After forty minutes RAF Manston aerodrome came into view. The machine lost height while below the station expanded. Temporary wooden-hutted accommodation was still being erected by local contractors under the watchful gaze of the station works engineering foreman. The little monoplane zipped over the edge of the boundary fence and touched down onto the grass. Taxiing around Wales kept watch for other aircraft while Jackson-Smith used the rudder to steer the Magister towards its resting place. Reaching the dispersal area he switched off, its propeller rotating to a halt, and both men clambered out. Wales had completed his second flight in a Miles Magister.

A day earlier these two nineteen year olds had soloed on Fairey Battle L5017. It is remarkable how quickly the situation could change. Both pilot officers had gone from flying a thoroughbred fighter designed by Sydney Camm – the Hawker Hurricane Mk I L1897 on A Flight 11 Group Fighter Pool – to flying a carthorse; the Fairey Battle with the newly reformed fledgling 235 Squadron.

The once quiet country lanes near the Kent aerodrome were now thronged with military traffic. Freshly minted officers and sergeant aircrew in sharply creased air force blue uniforms and stiff new caps called into The Jolly Farmer in Manston village high street for a cider or shandy before doing battle with the enemy. Straight from training schools or posted in from other Royal Air Force squadrons, men seemed to be joining in the blink of an eye. 235 Squadron's adjutant's office, with its fresh light green and cream paintwork interior was quickly christened 'the knocking shop'.

They knocked, entered and stood smartly to attention in their freshly pressed uniforms and saluted. "No time to stand on ceremony" came the reply from behind the desk. 235 Squadron received sergeant pilots mostly, but the numbers of pilot officers were steadily rising. The worrying thing was that the majority only had between eight and twelve hours experience flying trainers, and at present there were no aircraft on the squadron. The question on everyone's lips was which monoplane would they be engaging the enemy with; the Hawker Hurricane or the Supermarine Spitfire? It was one of the main discussions at Hendon, Manston and Stradishall as the young men of 235, 236, 248 and 254 Squadrons began to bond.

Many of the men that made up squadrons in RAF Fighter Command that winter of 1939 described themselves as just 'ordinary'. These new aircrew had been recruited to fly a new breed of futuristic monoplanes, except the machines were painfully slow in coming from the factories and reaching the designated squadrons. Unfortunately the decision as to what type had already been made for the four new squadrons with one of the swiftest moves of a pen at the Air Ministry in months. To get these squadrons their machines Air Marshal Sir Hugh 'Stuffy' Dowding had approached Sir Cyril Newall. Newall was Chief of the Air Staff, level headed and decisive, a great fisherman and an erstwhile whipper-in to the Quetta and Peshawar Vale Hounds in his youth as a subaltern in the Royal Warwickshire Regiment.

In the end, thanks partly to his own pertinacity and partly to Newall, Dowding got what he required. Supply and Organization had acknowledged that it was possible to form two or four Blenheim squadrons. Dowding had asked the Air Staff to create four fighter squadrons to act as 'trade protection' to be built up to full strength as occasion permitted. The finer details of trade protection for convoy routes were raised by Admiral Sir Dudley Pound prior to his appointment as First Sea Lord. Newall got to his feet in response, his five-foot-nine stature lost in the cigarette and tobacco smoke that filled the room. Placing both his hands firmly on the table Newall asked, "what foundation is there for the statement that 'nothing would paralyse our supply system and sea-borne trade so certainly or immediately as successful attacks by surface raiders'?" Pound's answer was thus: "sufficiently severe as it would necessitate locking all our traders in ports and harbours". Newall stroked his grey moustache, "unfortunately there is not enough jam to go around". Twenty-one British merchantmen had been sunk in the first fourteen days of the war, with nine Hawker Hurricanes being lost whilst deployed on this duty. Newall gave his consent to Dowding's suggestion. Here the matter might have rested for the time being, had it not been for Newall. He wrote: "I had been convinced that the demand for fighters would soon grow still more insistent." From all aspects of logistical possibility no more fighter squadrons could be formed at the moment; for the entire output, not only of single-engine machines but of Blenheims, was already fully earmarked – the latter largely to cover wastage in Bomber Command. These four new trade protection squadrons might have been ready for action – on the right types – precious weeks earlier but their formation was delayed until the production position improved.

With no aircraft forthcoming 235 Squadron's commanding officer, Squadron Leader Ralph McDougall, embarked his men on a strenuous programme of ground instruction whilst all around, the peacetime scenery was changing. The whitewashed aprons and parade grounds of Hendon, Manston, and Stradishall were covered in coal ash in an attempt to disguise the stations from the air. Hangars received a third coat of green and brown camouflage paint from junior aircraftmen wielding one-inch brushes. Alfie Potts remarked:

> "Painting the station took hours, brushes were in short supply, and we ended up mixing paint from the colours available in the station stores when the two colours ran out! It was heart-rending watching the obliteration of the stations under gallons of paint for airmen and especially station warrant officers."

A quarter of the ground staff arriving were not regulars. Mechanics, riggers, armourers, wireless operators and clerks had previously earned their living in every walk of civilian life. They joined the RAF Volunteer Reserve during the great RAF expansion period, which gave the chance to thousands of young men from a variety of backgrounds to learn a trade or, if they were seen to have the right aptitude, train as pilots, observers and wireless operators. Some just wanted to be employable, their families having suffered severe hardship in the recession in the north and Wales, where the British Government enacted a number of policies to stimulate growth. The rise in employment levels occurred mostly in the south, where lower interest rates had encouraged a housing boom, which in turn spurred a recovery in the domestic industry. Although unemployment had fallen in 1937 by 1.5 million it had then risen sharply to 1.8 million by January 1938. Realization that the recovery was short lived saw a remarkable increase of men between 18 and 50 years of age joining as ground trade.

These different trades made their way to Manston with no illusions or pretensions. It was a scene of confusion as the build continued. Officers arrived in the odd car with golf clubs, tennis rackets or their dogs, individuals arrived on the smoke-stained local Kent omnibus or from the railway station. With the influx of so many being 'called-up' it began to put a strain on the manufacturers supplying the Royal Air Force. Manston ran out of flying boots for pilot officers and sergeant aircrew! This situation was overcome by the men wearing all three pairs of socks under thin black leather motorcycle boots to guard against the dangers of frostbite when flying. With mixed ability amongst the aircrew McDougall ordered compulsory flying practice. Flights were limited to around twenty to forty minutes. Luckily the fleece-lined flying boots arrived within four weeks.

The syllabus comprised practical flying, navigation, and blind flying using two primary trainers – the Miles Magister. Instruction was still intense even after completion of training at flying schools. A former aircraftman metal rigger, now a qualified pilot Sergeant Harold Sutton was taken on a thirty-minute flight for instrument flying. Sutton wrote that it was "the wrong time of the year to fly in open cockpits". When the day came that he actually went up without the reassuring presence of the man in the front cockpit, the sergeant found that he liked it, despite having only four hours on the type written in his logbook.

Before going up a second time he met Leading Aircraftman William 'Lelly' Day, a young rigger. Despite having joined the Reserves in 1936, Day found that he was more knowledgeable than Corporals Crouch and Wolford and was frequently called upon and recognized by aircrew. "Bloody Marvellous" commented Sutton, later writing; "I found Day a very likeable fellow, treated more for his ability than his rank".

On his next flight Sutton began practicing landings on the aerodrome. He lost height quite rapidly by 'side-slipping' perilously close to the ground before straightening out. This was achieved by banking the aircraft to, say, the left – giving right rudder so that the thing didn't turn left at the same time. Watching attentively from the perimeter he couldn't recall actually seeing anyone else doing this trick; usually a chap would start gliding in from about a mile away. In all, Sutton spent some eighteen hours flying Magisters, much of the time in R1830. On his last circuit he was warned not to over-fly the station range, as elsewhere on the aerodrome there was gunnery practice for volunteer leading

Leading Aircraftman William Day known as 'Lelly' joined the Royal Air Force during the expansion period in the mid-1930s in which he learnt a trade and it also supplemented his income. By the time he reached 235 Squadron at RAF Manston in October 1939 he was highly skilled. This was recognised on the squadron and although he did do an air gunner's course in 1940 his CO Squadron Leader 'Ronnie' Clarke thought it wise to recall him after two weeks into the gunnery course. (*Lisa Faulkner*)

aircraftmen wishing to become air gunners. With little breeze the red warning flag hung limply on its flagpole, as if already surrendering before the first volley was fired in anger at 11.00 hours. A regular RAF officer gave the instruction, with First World War ribbons pinned above his left breast pocket. He was described as a very forceful character with a walrus appearance due to a large black

235 Squadron Fairey Battle being refuelled with the ground crew muffled against the cold. Due to production delays in the factories, 235 Squadron was given Fairey Battles which represented the RAF's best light bomber at the time. Sadly they were obsolescent and in 1939/40 were woefully inadequate. The squadron began to replace these with Blenheims in February 1940. (*Andrew Bird via Norman Jackson-Smith*)

moustache. He was an expert in the 0.303 Vickers medium machine gun, a spindly weapon. A minimal quantity of live ammunition was fired. Frequent short bursts of machine-gun fire resounded across the aerodrome. Several managed to fire the Vickers without mishap, but there was an occasional stoppage due to the 1918 vintage of rounds being used.

Gunfire was interspersed with the sound of aero engines as another batch of pilots went aloft. They had spent the morning with the squadron intelligence officer having aircraft recognition tests; they were being taught formation flying in Fairey Battles for an hour and forty-five minutes, followed by forty minutes doing circuits and bumps. Pilot Officer Reginald Peacock's machine, Fairey Battle L5383, stalled at a height of thirty feet, causing a marked bump. The instructor referred to it as "not enough circuit; too much bump!" Fully expecting admonishment Peacock was therefore astonished to hear that he was now considered competent. As he walked back from the dispersal area the pilot officer noticed that more men were arriving. He wrote in a letter to his father: "'it was like going to a London derby football match except, instead of carrying rattles and wearing scarfs, they wore uniform and carried suitcases".

Pilot Officer Peter Dawbarn was one of those who Peacock saw. He had flown his first solo on his eighteenth birthday in Perth, Scotland and was then posted to No 2 Flying Training School at Brize Norton, Oxfordshire about a fortnight after the balloon went up and a notice was posted saying the group would be joining fighter squadrons whether trained on fighters or bombers.

"I found I'd been posted to help reform 253 Squadron at Manston, along with ninety percent of the pilots from the same course, having only flown Airspeed Oxfords. On our arrival there were no aircraft, there weren't any to be had apparently! After about a fortnight of playing monopoly, twist, chess, and going to a local public house to drink ale, our commanding officer called Elliott rustled up two primary trainers in the form of Miles Magisters. Our Fairey Battle light bombers turned up to train fighter pilots in January 1940. 253 were told to practice on these until some fighters arrived. Because of the extreme shortage we pilots of 253 occasionally shared ours with another reformed unit at Manston, 235 Squadron. Socially it was very pleasant, everything that you ate or drank was billed at the end of the month, and was very cheap. Dinner at night was a 'must' on four nights a week; two in mess kit, and two in dinner jackets, the other three nights were mufti, [civilian attire] or eat out."

All around the domestic site temporary accommodation was hastily being hammered together by contractors. These wooden-hutted constructions went up rapidly but despite this more beds were to be crammed into existing buildings to accommodate the sudden influx. As further RAF units began to reform on the station the airmen's cookhouse was supplied with two additional Aga stoves. A porter at Ramsgate railway station remarked in a local newspaper: "it was like people flocking to Ramsgate for their summer holidays from the Edwardian period". A utility van pulled up outside the station, nondescript young men piled kitbags into the back then it went sweeping through the countryside. The aircraftman driver applied the brakes sharply as he swung into the RAF station entrance. Kit bags careered headlong towards the cab. A face appeared at the driver's window, removing an identity card from his right breast pocket whilst pulling the sliding window back. The serviceman waved for the barrier to be raised. At its highest point it vibrated like someone using a fishing rod when fly-fishing recalled Leading Aircraftman James McCarthy:

"A burly flight sergeant marched us to our billets. Going through the door I entered a long corridor which had rooms off it, each door had a small cream oval plate with a number painted on. Shown into our rooms, I found to my dismay many had 'biscuits' [mattresses] strewn everywhere. The flight sergeant made us fall in outside and said he would try and get everyone some breakfast. At the cookhouse it was a mess, everyone had left leaving a river of water interspersed with tea down the central aisle with all sorts of rubbish, half eaten breakfast and toast on the tables. I was hungry. We all lined up in single file at the hatch. I held out the plate and a ladle of brown horse manure was put on it, at least that's what it looked like to me. Later, I learned that it was supposed to be liver and onion gravy with potatoes! The rest of the day was spent finding our feet and watching single-engine aeroplanes darting across the skies. Listened to the wireless all evening and lights out was at 10.00 hours sharp otherwise we'd be peeling 'spuds' [potatoes]. Didn't sleep much, it was cold and the bed was hard. There was a washroom backing on to the hut and it was one step out of one door and into the other. There was only one light in the washroom and the time between 05.00 and 05.20 hours drastically disappeared. It was extremely crowded as well, with everyone trying to get washed and shaved. Shaving that early in the morning was a bit of a shock to the system and the face. We marched in the dark to breakfast, which consisted of liver, bread, porridge and strong tea. The 'gen' is that the catering staff put bromide in our tea. Returned to one of the hangars as directed, switched on the wireless and started to walk up and down in order to keep ourselves warm.

"There were large hangars where aeroplanes which had completed a given number of flying hours were stripped down for servicing [Battles and Magisters]; fitters worked on the engines, riggers checked the airframes and electricians, instrument technicians and wireless mechanics overhauled the equipment. We were issued with a set of tools and it was nice to work in the trade for which we had spent so long in training but work at the bench was less interesting than working on the aeroplanes in the weeks prior to me becoming aircrew. We had a rota for night work but we were restricted to work as wireless mechanics. Somebody had had the brilliant notion that as we had to work with our minds we must not get too tired and therefore wireless mechanics were

Members of 248 Squadron air gunners pictured at Hendon, North London. The squadron remained on active service within Fighter Command until mid-1940. Photo dated October 1939. (*Theo Boiten*)

Officers of 248 Squadron pose in front of a Mk IVF at North Coates. Seated left to right are: Flt/Lt J Pennington-Legh (A Flt); Sqn/Ldr J Hutchinson; Flt/Lt R Morewood (B Flt).

exempt from all guard and fire duties. On November 3 in the evening there was a show given by the station concert party entitled 'Call to Arms'; the first part was variety and the second Adolf, which was most amusing, well produced and supported by an orchestra. Sandwiches and beer in the mess afterwards for the performers and others – which meant everyone."

The same pattern of preparation was being repeated throughout Great Britain. Newly reformed 248 Squadron at RAF Hendon in a suburb of north London saw a flux of new arrivals of all nationalities. Eighteen-year-old New Zealander Pilot Officer Sam McHardy was one. On March 17, 1939 McHardy put pen to paper, the first entry in blue ink:

"Air Experience: Effect of controls, taxiing and handling of engine. Seven days later I soloed after six hours of dual instruction. Looking around carefully to assure myself I was alone and in sole command. It was an extremely wonderful feeling and I began to lap it up. By November 2, 1939 I had completed the senior course and received my 'wings'. Once again I got the same 'exceptional' assessment which made a hat trick and brought oneself a great deal of satisfaction. My assumption was that I would go to a single-engine fighter squadron, but that was not to come off. Several of us were to join a twin-engine fighter squadron just forming at Hendon. We left RAF Sealand near the Dee estuary and caught a train to Cardiff, then boarded coaches hauled by a Castle Class steam locomotive which made a brief stop for water at Reading railway station. I alighted for refreshments. We passed quaint villages then at Paddington I travelled with my kit on the underground to Colindale, walking a few hundred yards or should that be half a mile to RAF Hendon's main entrance."

Meeting up with new members of the squadron and their two flight commanders, he found himself posted to A Flight with twenty-five-year-old Flight Lieutenant Alan Pennington-Legh as McHardy's flight commander who had come from 43 Squadron. B Flight's commander was the handle-bar-mustached Flight Lieutenant Roger Morewood posted from 56 Squadron at North Weald where as a pilot officer he had flown over 200 hours on single-engine Hawker Hurricanes. Morewood was busy from the word go:

"I started flying immediately which suited me, I found my fellow officers and SNCOs a very decent bunch but I wept when I left 56. It was a bit like getting out of a Bentley and getting on a number 36B London omnibus. The Avro Oxfords we began training on prior to the arrival of the Bristol Blenheims were ghastly – so slow. I made time to become familiar with the established pilots on the flights. Most of them were very experienced on monoplanes. As Bristol Blenheim Mk IFs began to arrive flying intensified, although a number of days were lost when TR90 radio transmitters were installed."

They stood or sat around a large unlit stove in a brick building waiting. At 09.00 hours their machine N6193 was ready. McHardy wrote in his diary:

"Because of the vast expanse of Hendon aerodrome using the radio transmitters was quite a novelty. We practiced radio transmission (R/T) procedure from our Blenheim, sitting in various locations on the aerodrome until we felt proficient enough to talk to the watch office."

One evening a couple of VR officers invited 'brother officers' to a lecture in Store Street, London. The lecture was on meteorology and engines. After they had bid their farewells they walked towards Russell Square Gardens then on to The Lamb public house, describing it as a 'lively place'.

248 Squadron, RAF Hendon, October 31, 1940. Posing against the backdrop of a Blenheim Mk I fighter and the First World War hangars at RAF Hendon. The line up includes: Squadron Leader Hutchinson, Flight Lieutenant Pennington-Legh (A Flight's commander), Flight Lieutenant Morewood (B Flight's commander), P/O Hopkins Adj. A Flight – Pilot Officers McHardy, Hamilton, Bennett, Bourgeois, Gane, Garrad. B Flight – Holderness, Elger, Atkinson, Fowler, Arthur, Baird, Hill and W/O Chambers. (*David Hamilton*)

Two hundred and forty-five miles north at Stradishall, Suffolk, Leading Aircraftman Tom Wilkinson was reporting to join 236 Squadron, which had recently reformed on October 30, 1939. Seventeen-year-old Wilkinson had joined the RAF Volunteer Reserve during the great RAF expansion period. He arrived at the station camp at 22.30 hours and was shown to his accommodation by an RAF policeman using a dimmed torch.

"It was a double bunk bed so I chose the top bunk and was then left in the dark to sort myself out and climb into bed. This was the farthest I had ever been away from home, I felt quite excited. Ten minutes later the policeman returned with another airman who was directed to the bottom bunk and then left in the dark. After breakfast with much chattering we hastened to the hangars, anxious to get our first look at our new charges. We got there and they were completely empty. There weren't any to be had apparently!"

Stradishall was still under care and maintenance; quite a number of the men had already arrived prior to the formation of 254 Squadron under the command of Squadron Leader Philip A. Hunter. This situation abruptly changed when the next day 236 Squadron was formed at the same station. Pilot Officer Kenneth Illingworth arrived:

"There were twelve officers spread around the ante-room reading or smoking. A mahogany clock ticked. No one spoke. After some time I summoned up sufficient courage to consult a young man in the chair opposite, reading the society page in *The Times*. He was an Australian of 236 Squadron. 254? No, he didn't know it. Was it due to be formed? My heart sank. I replied politely that it should be here."

Then salvation, a pilot officer named Bright introduced himself: "You're one of the first to turn up". Letters were sent to Fighter Command headquarters at Uxbridge to ascertain when the aeroplanes were going to arrive. After about a fortnight spent kicking their heels, playing draughts, chess and wandering the country lanes a single Miles Magister arrived for 236 Squadron, delivered by a maintenance unit. Two Blenheims finally arrived twenty-six days after 254 Squadron had formed.

As the nights drew in, post office telegrams were sent out informing commanding officers of aircrew being posted. Kentish born Flying Officer George 'Wiggs' Manwaring joined the RAF Volunteer Reserve in 1936 having attended Ardingly College. Whilst studying there he had joined the college's officer training corps and by September 1934 he had a confirmed rank as pilot officer. The last chief flying instructor's entry judged that he was "an above average pilot; little above average in ground subjects too. I do consider that he has a genuine interest in flying". Pre-war he had joined 74 Squadron and flew Gauntlets then, in February 1939, he converted to the Supermarine Spitfire Mk I. His flight commander on A Flight was South African Flight Lieutenant Adolf 'Sailor' Malan, and New Zealander Alan 'Al' Deere had become a true friend, later acting as best man at Manwaring's wedding. At the beginning of November 1939 it was with much regret that Malan had to tell his friend that he was posted with immediate effect to 235 Squadron. The pilot officer had an ominous start:

"On a sunny day, whilst flying a Fairey Battle, I took off, intending to drop in on my former colleagues at 74 Squadron. I arrived over Hornchurch and my undercarriage would not lock, the machine had a full load of fuel onboard too. I had no alternative but to fly around for nearly two hours to exhaust the fuel. Then one wheel of the undercarriage jammed. Prior to landing I radioed the watch office to say I was coming in. I landed on one wheel and put the wing onto the grass, the Battle then swung a full 180 degrees. I got out and smiled – not a scratch on me. Our Fairey Battles were disastrously unsuited to the demands of aerial warfare. The squadron passed its days and nights training on these obsolete aeroplanes, carrying out affiliation exercises with Spitfire and Hurricane squadrons and mounting the occasional patrol."

Taken at North Coates, in April 1940, during one of the wettest months on record. Standing: Sergeant Phil Lloyd WOP/AG; Pilot Officer Norman Jackson-Smith and Pilot Officer David 'Dave' Woodger. Kneeling: unknown. Aircraft is possibly Blenheim MkIVF 'LA-E' L9396. (*Phil Lloyd*)

Near the end of November after a fine cold day with brilliant sunshine eight pilots, including the CO McDougall, jumped into his car and drove to London. In spite of the two wonky springs the car coped with its passengers remarkably well. After a few rounds of the most excellent Simmonds beer they sat down to some eggs and gammon. This was to be a definite highlight of the evening according to Sutton. There was a dance next door, which necessitated more drinks and 'rests'. They sought out eight 'Belles' but after one dance 'politely' passed them onto some 'khaki' types. Comparing notes afterwards all their reactions were written down as negatives! Packed into the car once more, they started off on the London Road near Canterbury when MacDougall accidently put the car in reverse, but with his usual presence of mind he saved the situation and the novice pilots and eventually got them back to base. Singing lustily they went to bed.

As December rang in, the British Isles and western Europe was carpeted in deep snow. With the added apprehension and emotions of the Phoney War daylight hours were spent clearing snow, training or on courses. A number of riggers celebrated gaining their 'Ground Engineers' license, category A – which meant more pay! Around these aerodromes, the blanket of snow hid the machines of war as death moved a little closer for all. A few personnel managed to get home but many were absent from their traditional Christmas. During his speech on Christmas day 1939 King George VI tried to reassure his subjects:

"Through the dark times ahead of us, and when we are making the peace for which all men pray. A New Year is at hand we cannot tell what it will bring, if it brings us peace how thankful we shall all be, if it brings us continued struggle we shall remain undaunted . . . as the almighty's hand guides and upholds us."

Despite the festivities and being apart from loved ones, everyone's minds were upon what would happen in the following months and where they would be for Christmas 1940. For those personnel in Coastal Command it would be a new dawn.

CHAPTER TWO

Bitter Springs

On January 12, 1940 Under-Secretary of State for Air, Captain Harold Balfour MC sat hunched over his briefcase rifling through papers in the back of a black Daimler, dressed in a dark pinstriped suit. He was on his way to RAF Manston, where he would officially tell Squadron Leader Ralph McDougall what type of fighter this newly formed squadron could expect to receive. Balfour paused momentarily as the tyres crunched to a halt in the drizzle, he was then driven into the station. He was accompanied by his private secretary Frederick Howard. Their tour began with the aerodrome's units that were still awaiting fighters. Balfour toured throughout January 1940, with Fighter Command's blessing, reassuring squadron commanders. After formal introductions, Balfour told McDougall that the unit would likely be re-equipped with Bristol Blenheim Mk I fighters within a fortnight. A walk around the expanding station followed after which a three-course luncheon was served in the officers' mess. It was still drizzling as Balfour and Howard were driven back through the Kent countryside to his London residency.

Blenheim Mk I fighter pre-war. 235 Squadron started to receive these in February 1940. (*Royal Air Force Museum, London*)

It was not until February that the first machines arrived, and the unit was still receiving them two months later. 254 Squadron had only a few weeks of relatively calm conditions in which to get accustomed to their Bristol Blenheim Mark I fighters. Many had time-expired engines having completed the regulatory 360 hours, so the situation was acute. The transition was still in progress when the first upheaval had taken place; transferring from Stradishall to Sutton Bridge had begun shortly before the beginning of January 1940. The squadron was still far from being operational. Pilot Officer Kenneth Illingworth recorded:

"The first days of January were uneventful, on the 17th in flight a cylinder became loose on K7065. I then had a slight mishap. After landing, I raised the undercarriage selector lever instead of the flap selector lever. The starboard leg collapsed, causing damage to the mainplane, undercarriage, tyre and airscrew. My morale began to droop. Flying Blenheims couldn't possibly be so difficult."

Fellow pilot Thomas Rees' first efforts to do a barrel role were not impressive either. Surrounded by a mass of instruments and new-fangled systems he fiddled with the airscrew pitch, and with a heavy hand banged the throttle through the gate. He reported:

"With too much speed I commenced the half roll at 200 mph and whilst easing out of the inverted position my control stick didn't respond to my command. My machine was then diving vertically and the speed had increased considerably. The engines were howling in agonized protest. I reached down and wound the tail trimming gear back slightly and, after a short pause, the aircraft came out of the dive. With emotion and relief I regained control at 200 feet with my air speed dial reading 320mph. Shaken by this incident I got into further difficulty whilst approaching to land, my speed wouldn't drop below 110 mph. Hurling down towards the grass the port undercarriage inboard axle trunnion bolt sheared, my momentum stopped abruptly and the tip of each airscrew got slightly bent through contact with the ground."

The turn-around time (re-arm and refuel) for the Blenheim fighter pre-war was 26 minutes, while in 1940 on the trade protection squadrons it was 9 minutes, which increased its effectiveness. (*Royal Air Force Museum, London*)

Rees was held to account but was reprieved when the squadron was transferred to Coastal Command and a new station Bircham Newton. In the process 254 absorbed the Blenheim D Flight of 233 Squadron which then became B Flight on the squadron.

Pilot Officer Vincent Broughton was at RAF Leuchars in Scotland with 233 Squadron, D flight, working on 'short nosed' fighter Blenheims where the guns were harmonized in readiness for war. "Our D Flight provided the extra machines required to get at least one of the trade protection up to full strength," continuing, "our composition included Squadron Leader George Fairtlough. He assumed command of 254 Squadron with immediate effect, Hunter becoming vice, poor man" under orders of Leigh-Mallory.

Flying Officer William 'Bill' Bain, pilot on 254 Squadron Fighter Blenheims, in a tub at Aldergrove, 1941. (*Wing Commander Randall*)

At RAF Bircham Newton, Norfolk, 254 Squadron flying training continued with short patrols over the North Sea. Twenty-four-year-old Flying Officer William 'Bill' Bain and his crew were dispatched on yet another uneventful convoy patrol over the North Sea. The A. V. Roe-built Blenheim Mk IF L6641's unnamed observer described in fascinating detail the subsequent events which started before dawn on Saturday, January 6, 1940:

"A knock on the door. A voice bellowed 'time to get up, sir'. Raising my head off the pillow, turning to glance at the brown leather-cased travel clock on the bedside utility table, I focused on the glowing dials 5:30 – duty calls!

"The bedroom door swung open, brightness splayed into the room, my eyes adjusting to the sudden change of light density. A white mug of steaming hot brown liquid was planted on the table, at the same time my mind registered someone talking to me in a cockney voice; 'Morning – plenty of layers today as it's bloody cold outside, even more so at altitude I wouldn't wonder.' The reply that came out of my mouth was just a groan, as the figure in blue disappeared and flicked the switch. A light bulb pulsed from the ceiling, it was as if each pulse gave me energy to extract myself from my pit, the light reminded me of a Sexton Blake detective story, The Devil's Brood.

"Outside loud noises were emitting from fellow members of the squadron one presumes going to or from the ablutions, which were situated at the end of the building. I pushed the sheet and blanket over to the left allowing me to swing my body around. My feet touched a cold floor as I walked over to switch off the light then over to the window. Proceeded to turn the wooden blocks and take down the blackout protection boards. Peering through the window panes I saw the aerodrome coming alive. Wintery conditions from what I could see through the thin film of ice. A frozen pool of water lay on the windowsill from the build up of condensation. Sat down on the edge of the bed; the biscuit sagged. I grabbed hold of the steaming mug by its handle. Carefully taking small sips, I cupped it in both hands, contemplating what lay ahead.

"Grabbed my wash case and towel out of the compact utility wardrobe. The new wash hand basin stood forlornly waiting for the plumbing to be finished. Shutting the door firmly behind me, I turned and briskly walked down the central corridor towards the washroom. On entering smoke filled my nostrils from pipes and cigarette tobacco; it was a real pea souper. The wash hand basin I'd chosen had a layer of grime running around it. Using some Izal toilet paper I tried to wipe it away, but all it did was smear rather than soak it up. I placed the plug in and turned the hot tap, hoping that there would be some 'hot' left in the system (I would wash and shave in cold water as a last resort. If our hot water ran out we had to go to the sergeants' mess, taking our washing kit with us). As the water filled the basin steam curled up covering the mirror, except the bits that had water condensation on it. Turning the tap off I splashed water onto my face. It felt terribly refreshing, except someone had removed the bar of soap. Finding a bar further along, I wiped the mirror ready with my hand then began lathering my face using a shaving brush. Shaving with an almost blunt Gillette safety razor my bristles floated on the surface of the now discoloring water. Wiping my clean-shaven skin with my RAF issued white towel, I replaced the razor in the dark leather travel case, a present from my mother on my going into the Royal Air Force.

"Invigorated I walked back down the corridor, stopping outside my pilot's door. Knocking I pushed Bain's door open, the twenty-four year old was sat in a loom chair bending down, doing his shoelaces up. Bain's head turned to see who it was. His voice was sweet I recall; 'I'll walk over to the mess with you for breakfast once you've got your ruddy shirt on!'

"Wrapped up in our greatcoats we walked to the mess, watching our step as we went as the ice was gradually thawing. The chill bit into my face, my nose was freezing (must ask mother to send a scarf!). Snow had marked out the elaborate cobwebs on the barbwire. I noted that the cloud base was low whilst we both stopped to listen to the mournful cry of an owl – thought they only flew at night?

"An airman went cycling by us and saluted, nearly losing control of his machine in doing so; it was hard to keep a straight face. Luckily he managed to regain stability whilst ringing his bell to clear a path ahead. Laughter, clapping and cheering could be heard from a dozen airmen. One thing I was still getting used to in those early days of the war was saluting airmen and women of all ranks.

"As we approached the pre-war officers' mess flakes of snow began to fall. We darted through the double doors into the warmth and met Flying Officer Shawe on his way out. Exchanged pleasantries and said we'd see him in the bar for a jar that evening. The carpet was a burgundy colour with a well-worn path towards the mess. It was a home from home. The meals were lovely. The chefs operating the cookhouse had boxes of provisions: bacon, eggs, sausages, bread, sugar, butter, strawberry jam and marmalade. The smell was reminiscent of a roadside café.

"We were shown to a table by a young pretty WAAF named Mary. It was ironic that she had joined to escape domestic service at an established London hotel, where she had to wait on others and answer bells, only to start again in the officers' mess. Shortly afterwards she brought plates of piping hot eggs, bacon, sausages, and fried bread.

"We ate between gulps of tea served in thin white porcelain cups with a fading blue RAF crest enameled on. Although, more often than not, more liquid was poured into the saucer, milk being in short supply. Two aircraftmen had put up a poster by the exit declaring 'Avoiding Waste Will Help The Fleet'. Our ante-room or lounge had a bar and leather armchairs and there were portraits of past aviators hanging from the wall.

"Did nothing until after midday except drink tea and re-read the previous day's newspapers. A Flight was called to readiness earlier; our flight has now been called too. Fog is still persisting. Despite this we are to rotate individually on a (leisurely) patrol. Dispersal is damp, coal for the burner nearly gone; ashtrays are overflowing, looks more like a university common room.

Walked to the runway's edge. A Blenheim emerged from the mist, wing tips soaring nearby, then the machine was lost in the fog, its wings and belly pack showering water droplets on the bystanders.

"Ordered off urgently, borrowed some naval binoculars that were lying on a table. Ran outside, clambered aboard L6641 our Blenheim Mk IF, closed the hatch, (just behind the gunners' position) making sure it was firmly shut. Once Bain was strapped in he carried out standard pre-flight checks. We soon got both motors running, the noise was deafening as we moved off to taxi out. Given the all clear, throttles opened and we were off. As L6641 climbed the wheels clunked into place. Visibility was slightly better as we gained height. Flight uneventful; checked position at our destination and began our offensive patrol. Weather deteriorated considerably, our gunner's heat packs were almost exhausted. The wind whistled through our machine, the heater did little to alleviate our problem. Patrolling the area is becoming increasingly difficult. No ships sighted! Encountered snow showers – it became sluggish; captain tried to gain height. Our R/T had to be shut off because of shorting; blue sparks were playing around and there was danger of fire, so good dead reckoning navigation is now vital without radio. My Prestwick and subsequent training would be put to good use! Pray to God I remember . . . Rechecking the charts Bain asked for the heading to the next waypoint and signed to me that he was going to circle.

"Weather foul, snow twenty miles out over North Sea, interlaced when descending to 1,000 feet with heavy fog. I looked intently out through the Perspex nose as we completed our second 360-degree downward spiral. Fuel gauge readings were extremely low. We recalculated our position allowing for drift using the Dalton computer [early mechanical hand-held computer used in air navigation]. Both hands were freezing, holding the pencil in my gloved right hand it was physically shaking as I scribbled the coordinates down. The Blenheim was being buffeted by the wind. Making the full stop, my pencil lead broke off, but that was the least of my worries; I tapped the right shoulder of Bain, pointing to the calculations and distance of Docking, the nearest aerodrome (Bircham Newton would be an outside chance). Bain nodded in acknowledgement, giving a thumbs up sign. He was moving the lever to alter the propellers to positive coarse pitch, the rpm (revolutions per minute) deafening noise from both engines increased. He then worked the de-icing hand pump on the instrument panel. Gazing down at the sea, I could just make out through the nose the white breakers, which reminded me of an artist flicking white paint randomly onto a dark canvas. The fishing village of Brancaster lay somewhere ahead in the murk (if my calculation was correct otherwise we'd be in the drink). Behind Bain I attached a piece of paper with the calculations on to the pulley system linked to our turret (two small meccano-like rotary grooved wheels and copper wire). As I turned the handle the thin strand of wire with the attached metal safety clip holding the paper began to move over the main spar. The gunner would be frozen back there too!

"Abruptly the engines coughed, it occupied our minds with another thought – we were going to ditch. Five hundred feet, signalled the pilot to me just before one engine spluttered and died. And almost in the same breath 'standby for impact' was mouthed to me. The nose tilted forward, Bain clinging to the controls. I opened the top hatch and put my seat into the stow position. Bloody cold! I clipped my mask to my face for protection. I saw the fuselage twitch as we lost height rapidly. There were no other thoughts except what if I broke a leg or arm on impact? Would it hurt much?

"I sat on the floor as we skimmed over the water. It got closer until all of a sudden the Perspex nose hit. I grabbed something to stop my forward momentum. The pressure built up until the Perspex imploded showering me and Bain in salt water and glass. Instinctively raising an arm up to protect my face sent me catapulting forward into the water, the weight of my

Wareing sheepskin flying jacket weighing me down. I was drowning, in icy water!

"Our Blenheim fighter suddenly came unexpectedly to rest and the water levelled off. There was a fevered scramble, me bumping clumsily against Bain inside the marooned fighter. Clambering out using the pilot's seat on top of the fuselage, I sniffed the salt air whilst being pelted by snow flakes. Looking back along the fuselage I saw the shape of the exiting airman from the gunner's escape hatch, then looked across to starboard. The propeller seemed to be missing. I stared again in despair; I'd never wanted to be a sailor for Christ's sake!

"In the stuttering seconds it took to recover from the shock of the ditching the consistently positive Flying Officer Bill Bain restored hope. The captain pulled himself through the canopy above his seat and sat precariously on its edge with his back to us. He turned around and as he pulled his legs clear, grinned broadly and shouted 'Well boys, we made it!' It was a moment of triumph; the look on his face said it all. I knew then that the three of us must get through this one miserable set back. The dinghy was floating nearby. Bain jumped into the icy water, but hampered by his bulky clothing he struggled trying to swim with it to his crew mates. He was a good swimmer but his strength was waning. I think he was afraid that the dinghy would be swept away. He dipped his head underneath the water a dozen times searching unsuccessfully for the green cord. On his seventh attempt Bain found it. As I clambered into the dinghy I reached down to pull him up, then his Mae West got hooked on the ratline around the dinghy. He was pushed back in the water but managed to get untangled before flopping into the drenched dinghy. It seemed to be a sensible idea to move away from the dysfunctional L6641. We began a flurry of paddling, but the effort used was disproportionate to the distance travelled as we only crawled some forty yards. Above us the snow was getting heavier, fog seemed patchy and the sea swell became stronger, tossing the little dinghy about with increasing vigour. We all felt seasick. Bain was holding a soaked bloody handkerchief. I was concerned; 'What have you done, David?' He leant across, lifted one corner of my flying helmet and said into my ear 'it's nothing to worry about'.

In the confusion I had forgotten that I'd stuffed a map inside my flying jacket. I pulled it out and estimated our current position to be less than five miles from land. I realized that our machine must have hit Scolt Head Island!

"We were now covered in snow and our feet were becoming increasingly submersed in water. We had nothing to bail with. We kept paddling towards the shore. A few minutes passed then our gunner said he had seen a light. We all looked through the thinning fog and saw nothing. The gunner again saw a light then, as the dinghy lifted on a swell our captain exclaimed: 'I see it. It's a torch'. We all shouted 'Help! Help! Help!'

"Our dinghy rose again but as we tried to paddle forwards it felt like playing tug-of-war as the icy wind, together with the swell tossed the three of us up and down. There were fears in the back of my mind that we might be washed away into the fog never to be seen again. Eventually we got ashore, totally exhausted. The dinghy floundered on some sand or mud on the north Norfolk coast. We could hear birds chattering somewhere in the murk. Once out, we heaved the dinghy over to get rid of the excess water. Our final effort was pulling our dinghy (made by P. B. Cow & Company) along behind us in sodden flying boots, which the sand and mud stuck to like glue. I could hardly feel my toes. It was hard going for all of us. We could see a light coming towards us, LDV (local defence volunteers) on patrol in the vicinity. Someone shouted 'Halt!' A rusting antique rifle was aimed at us, then the corporal directed questions to confirm who we were. One was, 'who won the first division and who were the runners up?' I replied, 'Everton and Wolverhampton Wanderers'. Satisfied we three fell in. The LDV party retraced their steps along a snow-laden track through a hedge into a ploughed field. At one point we halted and were made to put our left hand on the shoulder of the person in front because of the fog. This was funny whilst being serious. It reminded me of a photograph I had once seen as a boy of gassed soldiers of Kitchener's Army in the First Great War. We slipped, slid and fell over. Our party stopped after a few hundred yards then began walking along a small lane with hedges on both sides. All the while my teeth were chattering and my feet and hands were like blocks of ice. Bain was struggling too. We were led through a copse and down a well-worn pathway or bridleway and came out into a churchyard at Burnham Deepdale. Three extremely wet, tired airmen crashed through the heavy doors and dropped onto a pew exhausted. Breathing very heavily, steam rose off our wet flying gear. Grateful and appreciative of mugs of hot cocoa, cigarettes were lit, and our cuts and bruises were attended to. Given half the chance I would have slept there and then. Bain was sent to the nearest hospital suffering from extreme hypothermia. This was just one of many crashes on our shores."

Around Britain's aerodromes those pilots flying the Bristol Blenheim were discovering that though used to Avros, Mentors, or Fury biplanes, the Bristol although faster and nimble was not quite perfect. As Bain discovered 'it would fall out of the sky quite easily'. His was to be classified as a forced landing. Air Staff and squadron commanders wrote to the Air Ministry, "The Blenheim continues to force land or have engine failure. We need reliable machines." Training continued on a daily basis. The air was full of flying bodies in tight formation. Harold Sutton describes one such occasion:

"Down, down, we went. Kept right in, tucked right in, occasionally the controls went stiff when doing 250 mph in the Mk I. Peacock is the other side, buildings flashed by underneath. We're nice and low, the headphones crackle 'Keep in'. It required strong arms and strong nerves. Good fun this. Pulled up over the aerodrome. Down we would go again, up over the trees, round and back – Bet everyone's enjoying it!"

Sergeant pilot Norman Savill certainly was as a pink-cheeked twenty year old with 235 Squadron.

"After lunch it would be more of the same. Evenings usually started in the 'local' just after six, where we sat over our shandy, cider, or light ale, and ended back in the mess. Then we'd write letters and read the newspapers before turning in to sleep, only to rise at dawn, wash, shave, and breakfast to start the process once more."

Two weeks into February the Mk I Fairey Battles were made ready to be flown out to a maintenance unit from 235, leaving them free to convert to the type with a couple of dual Blenheim Mk Is and re-equip them with the Mark IV Fighter (Mk IV F) versions. Their first new example, P4833, a long-nosed (and longer-range) Blenheim Mk IV F, was delivered from its former unit, 29 Squadron, on the morning of Thursday February 15, 1940. A diarist described the spectacle thus:

"All seemed very peaceful in the surrounding countryside, and then a deafening noise resounded around the station. Blenheims filled the sky like locusts. 29 Squadron had begun the handover."

On hearing the rumble of aero-engines Squadron Leader Ralph McDougall smiled, raised himself up and looked out of the open window. He turned and said "our fighters have arrived". Those still seated in lounge chairs let out a cheer, leapt to their feet and walked outside to see Blenheim fighters descending, landing, bumping and rumbling over the grass, taxiing in, switching off, and applying brakes off.

A few minor injuries not related to flying occurred as tradesmen, working on the expansion

On February 23, 1940, Sergeant John Bessey flew L6792, a 235 Squadron Mk IF Blenheim. At Manston, his undercarriage did not lock down and he crash landed. Bessey was slightly bruised. Aircraft L6792 was repaired. (*Andrew Bird via Norman Jackson-Smith*)

scheme, were blown off their ladders as the twin-engine aircraft arrived. One required four stitches in his forehead. A dozen window panes were also cracked with the vibration. Two Aga deliverymen delayed the fitting of a four-oven heater storage cooker in one of the messes by forty-five minutes to watch these new machines arrive, much to the annoyance of the works engineer. More machines came from 23 Squadron based at Wittering, and 5 Maintenance Unit Kemble Gloucestershire. Most of the Battles were ferried out to 10 Maintenance Unit at Hullavington, Wiltshire.

Squadron Leader McDougall wondered whether his new pilots would be able to cope. He received a telephone call from Bentley Priory from Air Chief Marshal Frederick 'Ginger' Bowhill who was visiting Air Chief Marshal Dowding: "Can your average pilot fly a Blenheim fighter without dual instruction and a period of training?" MacDougall replied "No". He said, "Thank you, that's all I wanted to know". So the tutoring began but with numerous upsets. Flight Lieutenant Richard Cross took off in K7122 to give dual instruction to Pilot Officer William Smith on the afternoon of Saturday February 23. Taxiing out they turned into the wind and lined up for take-off. Accelerating down the grass runway the immediate scenery began to become blurred from inside the cockpit. Cross, unfamiliar with K7122's characteristics, reached for the hydraulic selector control; the valve plunger was fortunately selected to the 'up' position. But before becoming properly airborne both occupants were simultaneously thrown forward without warning. Their Sutton safety harnesses held, as their Blenheim slammed straight into the ground. Propellers buckled and shards of earth were flung into the air as their machine's forward momentum slithered them through the grass, gouging a rut over 500 yards. Pilot Officer 'Wiggs' Manwaring wrote that both pilot and pupil exited after their "successful landing" as "the Bristol's hydraulic system failed".

There were similar rude awakenings onboard L6792. Sergeant John Bessey was making good progress doing circuits and bumps whilst skirting around the Weald of Kent countryside. After nearly an hour he prepared for his final approach. Height was suitably lost, the throttles were closed, the cowling gills almost closed, the hydraulic selector control was pushed downwards and the valve plunger was pressed into the 'down' position. There was a slight shuddering caused by the irregular airflow over the tail surfaces. Bessey lowered the flaps in turn, the glide was quite steep, air speed decreased to 90 mph approaching the aerodrome boundary, then a red light illuminated up on the dash board on the portside of the control cabin – the left undercarriage leg wasn't locked down properly. Acceleration was applied, lifting it over the boundary hedge away from the aerodrome. A wide single circuit was then made whilst using the hand pump to tempt the undercarriage down. The young sergeant brought the Blenheim back in, slowing down. The tail wheel momentarily floated as all the weight lay at the front on the undercarriage assembly, then without warning the left undercarriage leg collapsed and the port wingtip dropped, gouging the ground. Bessey was briefly jolted off balance. Regaining control he stopped the engines by pulling out the carburetor cut-out switches located behind his seat. The agile sergeant scrambled out of the top hatch and no injury was sustained to him except for the odd bruise and to his pride. Sergeant Harold Sutton poured the twenty year old a cup of steaming sweet tea from a large teapot as Bessey sunk into a chair after his ordeal.

The wastage of aircraft was causing the Air Ministry headaches; a violet typed slip inside one of the ministry's daily summaries reads: "These woefully inexperienced flyers continue to crash our valuable 'fighter' aircraft".

This was certainly the case with a volunteer reserve pilot, Pilot Officer Sydney Gane at the north London aerodrome in Hendon who was realizing his ambition; "learning to fly the RAF's only twin-engine fighters". Pilot Officer Gane was getting his flying kit organized when he heard a voice, "Go and get L1291 started and ready to go. I want you to do the odd circuit. Here you are, sign the Form 700 and look lively." Grabbing helmet and parachute, Gane strolled out towards the waiting Blenheim with a lump in his throat. His palms were sweaty; knowing that he only had one hour on the type the over exuberant nineteen year old was finally taking controls for a second solo practice. It was time to leave. As the ground crew retreated, pulling the chocks away, and carrying the magneto starter, their flight sergeant gave a thumbs up signal and one was returned in reply. A beaming smile was just about distinguishable as the portside window slid shut. Gane checked his instruments. Then catastrophe struck. While adjusting his parachute harness with the engines running, he accidently applied left rudder with the brakes locked. L1291 swung violently colliding with the stationary P4847. Gane wrote his entry for Thursday, February 15: "Second solo in a Blenheim – pranged it!"

A publication named *The Trade Protection Times* tried to keep spirits up with humorous entries such as this one which appeared in the February 16 edition:

FOR SALE: Two Aeroplanes. Slightly soiled. Price moderate, or would exchange for a pair of pigeons. Owners desirous of leaving. Apply to RAF Hendon or RAF Manston.

Blenheim IF of 235 Squadron, April 1940, North Coates. (*W.J. Groendjik*)

Meanwhile at Coastal Command's Eastbury Park headquarters, the grandmasters stroked their moustaches, surveyed the deadlock and plotted their next moves. Ever since the war had begun frustrated air chief marshals in Coastal Command had blamed their failures on shortages of the right fighting machine. These complaints had some degree of justification and they waited apprehensively as decisions were made at higher levels. There was no time to settle down for these four squadrons as senior air staff decided their fate during a lengthy meeting in London's Whitehall. A change of command beckoned. Acceptance, resignation and a certain apprehension seem to be the predominant attitudes and emotions in the last days of February 1940. As the second month faded away a transition from Fighter to Coastal Command began taking place. Trade protection squadrons were moved like pieces on a chessboard around the countryside. 235, 236 and 248 Squadrons found themselves at North Coates, Lincolnshire.

Air Chief Marshal Dowding was glad to be rid of his wretched chore of protecting the British coastline even if it meant losing his professional standing. Many officials were happy to see the Blenheims dispensed with, although more than one of these senior figures would find themselves praising the work of these men and machines in the months ahead as they were frequently called upon, officially and unofficially, transposing from Coastal to Fighter Command shoring up Dowding's Air Defence network.

After the briefest of formalities, which lasted just under two hours, the organisational change was complete. Afterwards three senior officers exited the building, a khaki figure snapped to attention in the blackout as they headed off along Parliament Street towards King Charles Street. Once inside Sir Cyril Newall's room, Air Marshal Sir Frederick Bowhill drank a toast to finally having aircraft with a sting in his Coastal Command! The new arrangements were not to everyone's liking though and criticisms mounted between the navy and Coastal Command. Senior officers debated the trade protection squadrons into the early hours.

On February 22 Flight Lieutenant Henry Mitchell, a pre-war flyer with 605 Royal Auxiliary Air Force, surveyed the flooded fields surrounding the aerodrome in Norfolk. With his Blenheim dispersed away from the hangars, he glanced along the far side of the aerodrome towards a cluster of sodden bell tents erected to house the extra ground crews. Eighteen-year-old Leading Aircraftman Reginald Smith from Gainsborough wrote home: "It is a bit like 'Swallows and Amazons'. Tents, corned beef, except the only dinghies we see are fishing boats." As aircrew lay in deep slumber Squadron Leader Philip Hunter introduced a readiness system so that one flight was always dressed and ready to take off at short notice. "What's the idea?" protested Mitchell, "Why do we have to get up at such an ungodly hour?"

Today was going to be a day of aerial combat for the squadron, with armourers finishing 'C for Charlie' while other ground crew nearby played football with two sandbags as goal posts. Pilots, observers and air gunners sipped mugs of strong tea. Pilot Officer George Taylor adjusted his silk scarf which he'd tucked behind his detachable starched collar to prevent neck burn from the constant turning to look for the 'Hun in the sun'. It also staved off the chill that blew through the aircraft. Taylor and his crew were part of A Flight, commanded by their CO, Squadron Leader George Fairtlough. They were scheduled for a fishery patrol again. The telephone in the dispersal rang four times. Outside the ground crew paused their game of football. It was 11.10.

Fairtlough answered the telephone.

"Yes, sir?"

"Scramble."

Fairtlough, Mitchell and Taylor ran for their fighter Blenheims with their observers and air gunners. Their dull green Mae West life preservers bounced limply on their chests. Slightly out of breath they all clambered into their allotted machines. In seconds Mitchell had lowered himself into the cockpit through the pilot's hatch, closed the canopy and strapped himself into his parachute and safety harness. After a quick check of both his radial engines, oil pressure and fuel gauge, and an acknowledgment to the ground crew, their magnetos began helping the Mercury radial engines roar into life, once unhitched with the engines running at 2,400 rpm static. Mitchell released his parking brake, opened up his engines and L4481 taxied out, following Fairtlough's lead, then Taylor crossed the grass. Their pace quickened and all three undercarriages rose into place, with lights flickering on the black instrument panel. The pilots adjusted their position then climbed for a comparatively short duration at full throttle – 150 mph ASI up to 5,000 feet, switching from 100-octane to normal fuel. Their take-off was timed at 11.14 hours.

Between Fighter Command's 12 Group and Coastal Command's 16 Group there was some confusion about reports of unidentified aircraft coming in over the North Sea. Only one plot had been received. As the machines climbed through the haze the pilots caught glimpses of fishing boats as they flew in and out of patches of mist. Mitchell reported, "We had increased our speed to 200 mph, it was turning out to be a beautiful hazy day – not ideal for flying". Fairtlough was well in front. His headphones crackled into life as 254's fighter controller instructed him "Steer 093 degrees, height 2,000, full throttle".

Eighty miles east of Flamborough Head on the Yorkshire coast in position 093 degrees they sighted a twin-engine type (Heinkel III-J) at 12.14 hours. One minute later the enemy aircraft was on course 300 degrees, height 1,500 feet. The three chasing fighters were at 2,000 feet on track 090 degrees altering course to get on its tail. Instinctively they switched their firing button to 'Fire' as fear and exhilaration ran through them. This was their 'going over the top' moment. Alerted, the Luftwaffe pilot pushed his control column forward as one of his gunners called out "Schauen sie heraus kämpfer". The water was fast approaching in front of him as he pulled up within a few feet and began a series of evasive manoeuvres. A second German rear gunner shouted "Kämpfer" and began firing intermittently as the Blenheim fighters came rushing in.

In the lead machine Fairtlough turned his microphone switch: "Attack, attack – Go!" followed by the attack cry, "Tally Ho!" Three against one, the Heinkel filled their fixed gun sight. All three began making beam attacks with wide deflection sightings, the guns shaking the aircraft as bullets sped towards their target. The aircraft then quickly pulled away in order to approach at speed once more: "We then attacked individually, jostling amongst ourselves, firing from 500 to 200 yards, as bullets splayed out from the Heinkel's front and upper rear machine-gun positions." Mitchell heard the rattle of incoming rounds hitting his fuselage close by; yanking the control column to haul his Blenheim round, he began to climb. Fairtlough and Taylor were moving in his direction too as they had experienced a click and a hiss having expended all 2,200 rounds from their four 0.303 machine guns in the belly pack and the single Browning in the port wing. Their combat was not too successful. An intelligence officer at the Air Ministry wrote: "Damage [to the target] apparently nil".

Undeterred the Luftwaffe pilot flying Heinkel III-J of 3/FüFlGr 806, flew steadily back 250 miles to Norway. Thoroughly frustrated, Fairtlough, Mitchell and Taylor swooped down for a final charge. One by one they manoeuvred to within twenty yards as their rear gunners fired the Vickers K, methodically changing magazines and "raking it with fire", one quoted. This tirade continued until practically all ammunition had been expended, the Heinkel gunner replying with accurate return fire, but the enemy machine 'evaporated' into the mist towards the east at 12.35 hours.

Now all alone in the sky with fuel gauges fluctuating they set course for Norfolk. Twenty-five minutes afterwards the section was ordered to land immediately. 254 Squadron's intelligence officer noted in the squadron diary, "The fact the German machine escaped into mist after receiving concentrated fire from twelve machine guns does not necessarily mean it got back safely". All three pilots were awarded a 'probable'. In fact the Heinkel had received only ten to thirty rounds from the thousands fired, and the crew reached their aerodrome safely. However, the first two Blenheim aircraft L8786 and L8841 had been peppered by the Luftwaffe gunners, achieving considerably more hits with their 7.92 rounds. The latter had seventy puncture wounds. An air intelligence officer found that about one in four of the enemy's rounds appeared to be of the incendiary type.

During a spell of apparent inactivity, Fairtlough was mildly concerned as he lingered over tea and jam tarts listening to the sombre news on the wireless and reading of stories of another merchantman sunk. It was all very civilized and friendly. A few apologetic coughs could be heard from Coastal Command Northwood, as Ginger Bowhill heard the navy had gone begging to Fighter Command. The Admiralty demanded that all convoys around the British shores be defended. Dowding received a call to assist with this convoy protection and while he was not sure that this was the best use of his fighters, he did tell all his fighter squadrons to be especially vigilant when convoys sailed through high risk areas. "I soon realized that this active duty gave valuable training to everyone concerned, on the ground as well as in the air," wrote Dowding in correspondence to Bowhill a year later. One of those placed temporarily on a 'jolly' on Saturday March 16, was 19 Squadron who saw two flights rotate with another for convoy duty. Six Supermarine Spitfires made the short journey from Duxford to North Coates. The circuit was cleared for their arrival and by mid-morning the sky was once again filled with the ominous sound of radial engines. Flight Lieutenant Wiggs Manwaring managed unofficially to scrounge a quick trip in a Spitfire – of course he loved her. It was a sheer delight to fly and so sensitive, he'd lost none of his touch. With good flying weather sections of two Spitfires carried out several exhausting convoy patrols before returning to Duxford at 19.00 hours.

Two hours after their departure heavy rain begin to fall. For the remainder of the month the Norfolk aerodrome was under water. The ground was saturated and no flying took place. The vice-chief of the air staff, Sir Richard Peirse was asked to produce figures for Newall's War Cabinet meeting as to when North Coates, Bircham Newton and Thornaby could accurately resume operational flying. A single runway service test was carried out from North Coates in a Miles Magister. The light-trainer aquaplaned along the grass. As Sergeant Harold Sutton corrected its course with the rudder its fixed undercarriage then got bogged down. Sutton switched off the motor. The small windscreen provided little protection against the elements and Aircraftman Terrance Pickering appeared on the port wing with an umbrella – with the compliments of the officers.

Peirse's official answer was "Not until something is done about the drainage". The Ministry of Works was therefore instructed to undertake the work with immediate effect. Fresh drainage channels were dug to a depth of six feet and shingle brought in from a nearby quarry to line them, converging in an eighteen-foot drainage hole. Local contractor's machinery was used to dig and fill in the hole.

At the end of March squadron commanders tried to catch up on correspondence. A request was received from the Air Ministry to make a list of volunteers to go to France to replace the casualties should the need arise. As April began there was another flap which cancelled out anyone being posted to France. The month was soon dominated by events in Scandinavia.

The situation had steadily become more and more tense and on April 5 Coastal Command was hastily requested to move men and machines to Scotland to cover a naval detachment led by the battle-cruiser HMS *Renown* which had mined Norwegian waters in Vestfjord, but within hours the British where on the back-foot.

In a do or die gamble at dawn on Tuesday April 9, 1940, Operation Weserübung finally got underway. Germany would live or die by the – sabre there would be no turning back. With a powerful thrust, all the weight of German mechanization poured into Scandinavia seizing strategic ports and airfields.

On the British mainland orders to move were surrounded in chaos as the army, navy and air force units hastily prepared for fighting in arctic conditions in an ill-organized and amateurish expedition.

The air force was now charged with helping grasp Norway back. The Blenheim fighter was to extend the range of the Royal Air Force's (north) sea fighter patrols to encompass the northern and southern Norwegian coast and fjords.

254 Squadron had been notified to move a detachment to Lossiemouth and be operational within twenty-four hours on April 4. Equipment was hastily assembled at picket posts then moved by trucks. Ground crew crammed into L8840, L8841 and L8785, for a journey to Lossiemouth, on the Moray Firth, in northeast Scotland. On one noted transit flight north two crews arrived in high spirits over Elgin, both flying low over the village in a display of exuberance that impressed the school children and the locals. Nearby at Gordon & MacPhail Grocers & Wine & Spirits Merchants employees sprang outside as a wave of aircraft thundered overhead, ran into the yard then sprinted up the road and saw twin-engine machines, their black and white undersides clearly visible, streaking away across the roof tops of Elgin. In the distance more engines could be heard. The newly arrived airmen, regardless of rank, took the opportunity to make peace with God at church services on Sunday, April 7. A handful of crews were now going to get a taste of what lay ahead, some would not survive.

Five hundred and eighty-two miles away on that same Tuesday, April 9 the War Cabinet met at 08.30 in 10 Downing Street. The mood was gloomy to say the least. In the Cabinet Room Air Chief Marshal Sir Cyril Newall got to his feet to report on the situation to those sat around the highly polished oak carved table. Prime Minister Neville Chamberlain said nothing as Newall spoke about Oslo fjord, Stavanger, Trondheim and Narvik. There was a pause as he picked up a piece of paper and said: "Bergen: Five enemy warships approaching at 3.25 a.m. At 6 a.m. our British Consul reported that the port was occupied by German forces and that he was unable to reach the quayside to investigate." Additional information was then brought into the room by messenger that German aircraft were over Stavanger and German troops had landed at Egersund. Newall responded to this saying that he would order an immediate air reconnaissance to clarify the situation in Norwegian waters, in order to ascertain the positions of the German naval, military and air forces and until this had been done no bombing of German forces in Norway should take place.

With a solid knock on the door, Minister of Information Sir John Reith entered the meeting, apologizing for the interruption. At this point the declaration on the Norwegian invasion, which the German government had put out by wireless, was read out to the War Cabinet. When the meeting broke up Chamberlain walked Newall to the front door, both shaking hands before going outside. Once back in his Whitehall office he asked the operator for Air Chief Marshal Sir Frederick Bowhill. He was put through by the operator but that conversation went unrecorded. Communications were sent to Lossiemouth at 01.45 on the 'tie-line'. The text set out their objective: "Headquarters 18 Group: The following Squadron [254] is to carry out an offensive patrol to the district of Bergen harbour Norway".

Flight Lieutenant Henry Mitchell recalled: "As I waited a little apprehensively, I was treated to a catalogue of helpful hints by a tall, rather disheveled young naval officer, on German naval craft. Finally myself, Kingham and our naval passenger boarded L8786. Our orders to report all warships immediately by wireless transmitter." Hampered by fog Blenheim L8786 hastily flew out with naval officer Lieutenant Commander Geoffrey Hare RN of 800 Fleet Air Arm Squadron accompanying them as an observer. Hare had knowledge of enemy surface ships and they were armed with powerful naval field glasses to help identify friend from foe. Hare settled down for the long journey. Mitchell pushed the control stick forward; the nose descended so they could hug the choppy waves and fly the 300 miles to unfamiliar territory undetected. As they drew ever nearer to Norway Hare pointed the field glasses through the nose of the machine, searching for signs of enemy vessels. Navigation was spot on, the Blenheim making landfall at Fedje, then Mitchell used the leads to good advantage; everything seemed dead easy. Maintaining a distance Hare successfully sighted two cruisers in Bergen;

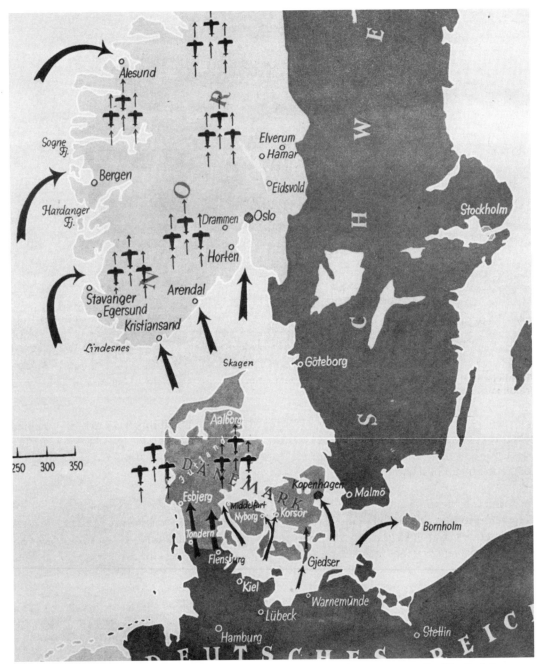

Map featured in the April edition of *Der Adler* showing the invasion of Norway. *Der Adler* (The Eagle) magazine was the official publication of the Luftwaffe from March 1939 to September 1944. (*Iain Duncan*)

Königsberg and *Köln* plus the gunnery training ship *Bremse* and torpedo boats, E-boats and armed trawlers. Hare sent a signal at 13.27 hours. Elated, the crew flew a reciprocal course home, also sighting a dozen grey seals before landing safely. Reports were hastily written down then wired to 18 Group, and Naval Command at Rosyth. The chief of naval operations at Rosyth considered mounting a naval attack on the German ships in Bergen. Admiral of the Fleet Sir Dudley Pound

Blenheim L9313 of 254 Squadron 18 Group Coastal Command, took this photo during an early morning reconnaissance on the second day of the German invasion.

gave an appraisal at a War Cabinet meeting: "In view of the possibility that the Germans had obtained possession of the coastal shore batteries, it was decided that we the Royal Navy would not carry out this operation. It was therefore up to the Royal Air Force. It had to be realized that this operation might be a hazardous one."

As this was being considered, Lieutenant Commander Hare RN got aboard an Airspeed Oxford and flew across to HMS Sparrowhawk the Royal Naval Air Station (RNAS) Hatston on the Orkney Islands – the premier naval air station in the north where 800 and 803 Squadron Fleet Air Arm were based, providing fighter cover for the fleet's anchorage at Scapa Flow. Although the two squadrons had only trained and operated fighters for a few months and their dive-bombing skills were recorded as rusty, it was decided to try for a dawn attack on Bergen harbour. This prime target was just within the limit of the naval Skuas. Lieutenant William 'Bill' Lucy together with Lieutenant Commander Hare approached the station commander, C. L. Howe, and proposed that he take all serviceable Skuas for a dawn attack on Bergen. The naval air operation was hastily approved. A London flying boat of 240 Squadron reported soberly at 23.10 hours: "Köln or Königsberg class cruisers in Bergen" in their rightful place.

This mixed force, armed with semi-armour-piercing bombs, took off thirty minutes late due to prevailing weather conditions at 05.15 on April 10, breaking through the layer of cloud over the target at 07.18 hours at 12,000 feet. It was observed that one cruiser was now anchored at Skoltegrund Mole, the other must have slipped anchor. Approaching from the southeast they circled around, Lucy positioning them up-sun. 803's Blue, Green and Red sections rolled away, instantly behind 800's Yellow and White sections and two spare Skuas, in order to attack out of the sun, which had gradually risen from behind the steep peaks of the Floyen and the Ulriken – two of the seven mountains that

A bomb (seen on the upper left corner of the photograph) dropped from an aircraft of Coastal Command, falls on Junkers Ju 52 transport seaplanes of KGrzbV 108, moored in Bergen harbour.

surrounded Bergen. They dived at an angle of 60 degrees from bow to stern at 07.21 in the dawn's radiant light. Releasing their 500 lb bombs from between 1,500 to 3,000 feet above the target, the ship's crew were caught off guard and there was no anti-aircraft fire as Yellow and White sections completed their dive. *Königsberg* was rocked by explosions which knocked out all the cruiser's electrical power. On the aft deck a gun team scrambled to a 3.7mm anti-aircraft gun, it was hurriedly traversed skywards and shells were pumped out once every five seconds using manual power into the blazing sun. Behind them thick smoke billowed from twisted gaping holes in the cruiser's 40mm deck armour which could not defend against 500 lb bombs. Minutes separated the Skuas during their dives. They were defenceless against the flak from shore and from auxiliary vessels scattered around the harbour. Lieutenant William Church in Green Three failed to release on his first dive "having simply miscalculated". He made a second run in at 200 feet. The darting grey shape made a tempting target and exploding shells buffeted the agile aircraft. In the exposed rear open cockpit Petty Officer Bryan Seymour sprayed out defensive fire, hearing "bomb gone" in his earphones. Their bomb exploded – shrapnel like spears hurtled into the still air towards a neutral bystander, the *Flying Fish* a cargo ship of 8,875 tons of the American Moore-McCormack Line. Impacting on the starboard side they sounded like pebbles gouging into the steel. Fifty-year-old Captain Wollaston laid flat on the floor in darkness on the ship's bridge with its large panes of glass rattling as the next three waves of British aircraft screamed down.

The Skua pilots opened fire. Lead spat out from their two front machine guns. Rounds cascaded like a helter-skelter onto the *Flying Fish* fore deck, ripping into it and several drums of fish oil. One

A fine study of a 254 Squadron Mk IVF L9406 over the Scottish countryside. It took part in offensive operations in the Norwegian campaign. The squadron saw the campaign out and continued operating in the area throughout 1940. (*Royal Air Force Museum, London*)

by one they released their load. Some bombs missed the target only to skim along the mole and hit the side of the cruiser before exploding. Two naval aircraft sustained damage from heavy anti-aircraft fire from *Kriegsmarine* gunners on Kritiansholmen Island adjacent to seaplane tender *Hans Rolshoven*, but they remained airworthy. "It was much too early for a swim", commented Captain Donald McIver flying Blue Two. The pilots opened their throttles and escaped out into the North Sea to fly back to the Orkneys. On the inbound journey one Skua spun into the sea whilst climbing through dense cloud killing the leader of 803 Squadron's third section, Lieutenant Bryan Smeeton, and his crewman, eighteen-year-old Midshipman Fred Watkinson. Despite this sudden loss the remaining fifteen landed, jubilant at their first successful 'strike'. Captain Richard Partridge commented: "It was hair-raising – constantly glancing at the fuel state we all landed on fumes. There was literally nothing in our tanks after a trip of four hours thirty minutes." The de-briefing room was full of chatter and cigarette smoke, as naval combat reports were written up, either in pencil or ink. Then all they could do was wait for the confirmed result from RAF Coastal Command's long-range fighters.

A 254 Blenheim was made ready; its Dunlop tyres sagged even further into the damp grass once the fuel had been loaded into both tanks. The various trades primed the machine for the follow-up reconnaissance. Two further aircraft were scheduled to fly after midday. The pilot indicated with a hand motion for the ground crew to prime engines and switch on starting magnetos. After eight full pumps of the cold Mercury XV engines the pilot set the throttle levers forward at half an inch and with the personnel clear the magneto switched the two starter buttons. His gloved left hand was kept on the throttle lever, which was slightly opened, the rate of tick-over gaining. With the engines warming, the pilot completed his other formalities before taxiing out, using the rudder and throttles to turn his machine into the wind. A 'Green' lamp was flashed, the brakes released and the pace quickened as its 14,500 lb long-range load lifted off the ground then steered over the skerries. Just before 5.30 it turned to starboard, skirting along the Moray Firth coast before passing Fraserburgh, the last distinguishable landmark before the grey sea and sky merge into one. The monotony was broken only momentarily when a shoal of fishing vessels were sighted before arriving near Bergen.

Using a Williamson F24 hand-held camera, the observer began taking reconnaissance photographs showing the position of the sinking *Königsberg* and the hive of activity as her crew tried to save their ship. Two hours and forty-five minutes after the Fleet Air Arm's attack *Königsberg* was to become the first major vessel to be sunk by air attack in this second Great War. The unnamed observer said:

"Just before we set off at midday I was handed a photograph newly developed and taken by another of our crews much earlier in the day. It showed all the shipping clustered in Bergen: the cruiser stood out quite clearly against the jetty, so I knew exactly where to look for it. We flew over the harbour at about 2,000 feet. The only trace left of the cruiser was oil and the stern sticking out. Just to make sure, we had a look in all the neighbouring fjords too."

Captain Wollaston, having been badly shaken by these events, watched a single aeroplane circle from the bridge as a steady rate of shells pumped out from anti-aircraft guns. He later recorded his thoughts in the ship's log:

April 10 – 7:30 a.m. Air raid by allied warplanes. One German cruiser, name unknown, was hit amidships between the two funnels by bombs dropped by an allied warplane. Bombs were also seen dropping on Skoltegrund Mole – seemed to skim on the mole, where the cruiser was lying.
April 10 – 9:00 a.m. Clouds of smoke and flames were seen to rise quite high from the cruiser and an explosion was heard. The cruiser began listing to forward and sinking by the head as flames rose to about 100 to 200 feet. The cruiser's head sank deeper and deeper, making 45 degrees starboard list, her stern projecting into the air, showing her propellers.

The transport ship SS *Barenfels* was very badly damaged during the raid by three Skuas led by Lt William Lucy on April 14, 1940, was refloated and her valuable cargo of anti-aircraft guns salvaged. SS *Barenfels* was sunk four years later by naval divers using limpet mines. (*Norwegian Air Force*)

The *Königsberg* is rocked by explosions which knocked out all the cruiser's electrical power at 07.19/07.20 hours. (*Andrew Bird via the Norwegian Air Force*)

April 10 – 9:40 a.m. One allied warplane flies over the city, anti-aircraft guns returned a steady rate of fire, all firing ceased as plane flew over the hills to the west of Bergen.

April 10 – 9:50 a.m. Cruiser capsized and sank completely out of sight while columns of black smoke rose high into the air. Two German freighters manoeuvred around our anchorage. Their names were the SS *Barenfels* and SS *Marie Leonaheart*.

At Rosyth Naval Command the personnel received confirmation that a German cruiser had been sunk by aircraft. An unnamed RAF Coastal Command liaison officer wrote: "The navy is feeling a loss of confidence. The naval commander brought out very clearly in plain language the fact that the navy has now realized fully that its position on the sea has become seriously undermined with the advent of aircraft. Their supremacy is no longer what it was." Unfortunately, those in Admiralty House, Whitehall, though impressed with the bravery, ignored the technique and military significance of this novel form of attack. Vice-Admiral Thomas 'Tom Thumb' Phillips, responsible for such Admiralty matters, was a convinced battleship man. Phillips disregarded the signal from Rosyth. The sinking of the *Königsberg* did not make the slightest impression on him. However, this error of judgement came back to haunt him a year later when he was sent from his Admiralty desk to take command of the *Prince of Wales* and *Repulse*, whence they were immediately sunk by air attack off Eastern Malaya.

Frustrated, Rosyth naval and air staff issued orders to both RAF Coastal and Bomber Command squadrons based in Scotland: "Engage and strike German-held aerodromes in Norway. Your aim is to attack Stavanger with up to twelve aircraft daily from both commands." Squadron Leader George Fairtlough thought it ill-conceived; "they'd forgotten about the weather in Scotland, our 254 detachment flew patrols whenever the weather let us. Some mornings our wheels were frozen – the controls locked solid. They'd not looked at the weather reports for Norway either, in some places we'd be flying in zero degrees." However, operations continued apace the next day. Shortly after 13.30 two Blenheims set off towards Hardangerfjord, the second longest fjord in Norway. Flying Officer Derek Shawe led in L8785 with Pilot Officer Kenneth Illingworth's L8840 on the portside. Flying at 1,000 feet the crews were unceremoniously tossed from side to side in a most uncomfortable manner. After a few seconds Shawe glanced at the sensitive altimeter. To his astonishment what had started at 1,000 was now 50 feet. With both hands on the stick and with all his strength he started to pull it back into the pit of his stomach and his machine rose up. Shawe could hear Illingworth calling over the R/T enquiring if everything was all right. Nothing else interfered with their pursuit of Hardangerfjord. Nearing the enemy coast the weather closed in, with intermittent snow and rain showers. Shawe had tucked his Blenheim right in close to Illingworth's, some two feet away from his wing tip, in order not to lose contact with him. Bømlo passed on their portside as they swept up the fjord. With nothing sighted they flew up the leads at 500 feet towards Hjeltefjorden.

Alert observer Sergeant Kendrick onboard L8785 spotted the wake of a vessel through the showers. In earphones the words "target dead ahead" were heard. Kendrick hastily noted their position as 305 degrees 13 miles at 16.30 hours. Shawe was pumping de-icing spirit into both carburetors before instantly flicking the gun button to 'Fire'. Intoxicated by the sheer joy of a contact Shawe, followed by Illingworth, dropped down to 500 feet. Using the aft ring sight suspended from the top of the cockpit, he lined up the target. Both Blenheim fighters opened up at the same moment, eight machine guns firing. The sound vibrated off the surrounding mountains as bullets streaked towards the unsuspecting *Dristig*, a Norwegian torpedo boat fitted out as a minesweeper steaming near Radøy island, having journeyed from its station at Håøy near Oslo sixteen hours earlier. 1,500 rounds tore through the structure; Lieutenant Finn Tørjesen died as the first volleys penetrated the bridge. *Dristig* stopped. The gun crew, unable to identify the machines, rapidly returned fire. A Norwegian official commented in a letter sent to the Air Ministry: "This will probably be the first of many accidental friendly fire incidents". Watching their fuel gauges, both Blenheims headed back to refuel and rearm on the same track over dark grey sea.

Suddenly, the calm was broken at 17.40 hours as a call of "enemy aircraft" echoed on the R/T. There was a quickening of pace and a sudden rush as the lone Do.18 K6/AH of 1/406 was caught in the air by both pilots. The two gave chase. Using boost to good effect, their exhaust stubs belched out black smoke. Adjusting their air speed they closed. Illingworth clipped the combined oxygen mask and microphone across his face, pulling his tinted goggles down for protection too. Applying pressure both pilots fired at the Do.18 from astern, although the effect of their attack was limited owing to the fact that on both L8785 and L8840, two single-wing mounted machine guns had malfunctioned and their ammunition was low. Both RAF machines were repeatedly hit by extremely accurate return fire and the pilots were forced to break off, as the petrol tank on L8840 was holed, reportedly leaving their quarry with both engines ablaze, though in reality the Dornier only suffered minimal damage. Landing back at 19.07 everyone had gone to tea. Illingworth would later write about the earlier action: "The destroyer's decks were raked with machine-gun fire".

Forty-five minutes after Shawe and Illingworth had left on this operation a third Blenheim took off for Stavanger. There was little to do except cautious reconnaissance, relaying the information to the troops on the ground as coherently as possible. In the end these deficiencies were academic – the allied armies were operating with only scant resources for air cover and soon found themselves being mercilessly strafed and blasted from above by the Luftwaffe.

Occasional sudden flashes of enemy gunfire were spotted inland by 254 aircrew. In a desperate attempt to help the beleaguered allied troops on the afternoon of April 10, the unfamiliar drone of three Blenheim fighters was heard flying at speed towards Stavanger airfield as the first known attack on Sola airfield near Stavanger began. Independently Mitchell in R3628 and Rose in L8783 commenced strafing Stavanger/Sola airfield at 16.00 hours. Their machine-gun fire ripped up the layers of earth and sped like a steam locomotive towards two Junkers 52s that had recently landed from Aalborg. Rounds punctured the wing and fuselage ripping the metal open. Observer Flight Sergeant Harold Brown peered out of L8783 then saw an explosion which lit up the sky. KGrzbV. 107 Junkers 52 (6892) was now a complete write off. Another caught in the hit and run raid was KGrzbV. 107 Junkers 52 (6314), with startled German soldiers and airmen diving for any available cover. Uffz Walther Gloger was a casualty during the attack and died of his wounds. One Heinkel

59D floatplane of KGrzbV.180 in the adjacent seaplane harbour sank while moored at Stavanger/ Sola having been flown in during the day.

With the element of surprise gone, anti-aircraft fire was put up by 9 Flakregiment 33 together with concentrated small arms fire. Bullets whizzed into the cockpit striking Rose and damaging the port undercarriage. Wincing in pain Rose took evasive action. Pointing the nose for home he met a Heinkel III midway across the North Sea at 58.30N 01.08E and made a stern attack at 18.20 hours. Some of Rose's first shots struck Fw Rainer Wilde, penetrating his right shoulder and taking tiny pieces of flying clothing into the entry wound. A crewman went to his aid, plugging the entry point and large exit holes using field dressings around flesh and protruding bone fragments. It required extensive surgery to reconstruct Wilde's shoulder. Gruppenkommadeur Major Vetter and the rest of the crew were unhurt. Immediately after this brief skirmish Rose pulled up alongside and turned for a beam attack, his turret gunner getting a number of hits on the bomber using three hundred rounds. A returning burst of fire from the Heinkel ripped into the cockpit and a single bullet wounded Rose. Grimacing, he looked at his fuel gauge needle which showed they were running extremely low due to the dogfight. He disengaged and headed for home.

Suddenly the 'Tommy' was gone. Vetter's smoking port engine was badly damaged and ahead of him lay a three-hour flight though bad weather conditions to reach Stavanger. His battered machine reached its destination and was subsequently written off. During this air-battle Blenheim L8783 sustained more damage than Rose was immediately aware of; lowering his undercarriage it seemed to lock into place, a green light flickered but as the tyres touched the grass the port oleo leg collapsed and the propeller buckled. Fighter Blenheim L8783 became unserviceable. Sergeant Rose's flight mechanic counted over thirty bullet holes in his charge. As the day closed Squadron Leader George Fairtlough jotted: "10 April 1940 felt like a week rolled into a single day – I'm sure there will be many more days like this".

The messes at RAF Lossiemouth were full to bursting with coastal and bomber crews. The main topic of conversation; who was going to hit Stavanger next and would bomber crews be able to find the target in the daylight let alone in the darkness? Command rivalry was strong in the RAF and the evening of April 10 was no exception. A raiding party was dispatched into the officers' mess cookhouse. From somewhere a crate of carrots appeared with a note; 'For 115 Squadron – So you're able to see in the dark – Courtesy of 254 Squadron'.

The problem was that only Stavanger/Sola was within range of the Handley Page Hampdens and the Vickers Wellington Mk 1As, a distance of 450 miles from their aerodromes. Bomber Command had only played a minor role until now. Their first bombing raid against a target on Norwegian soil was at last sanctioned.

A single Blenheim flew off into the rising sun just after dawn to act as the eyes for the bombers, which were later to launch their attack on Stavanger. After crossing the North Sea above cloud the pilot put his machine into a shallow dive as he approached the Norwegian coastline. The observer's calculations were spot on; land fall just north of Bergen then flying down Byfjorden, with Bergen on the starboard side then out over Stord Island, turning to port and darting back into the leads, past Haugesund then weaving towards Stavanger. They then flew over the town of Stavanger, skimming the roof tops of the houses and railway station in which the pilot noted three or four passengers and a luggage train. Now only fifty feet above the ground, he flew over the aerodrome, commenting: "We apparently took Jerry completely by surprise". He was able to carry out the reconnaissance uninterrupted, making a second flight at forty feet over the aerodrome to confirm their original observations. The pilot reported: "Stavanger is asleep, nothing moving". With one last sweep the pilot said into the intercom, "Let's go home". As his left hand moved the throttles, departing seaward over Sola airfield 20mm anti-aircraft guns opened up, straining into the sky behind them. Satisfied that the primary duty of taking photographs and gathering information on German activity in the area was complete, they made the 300-mile journey back to their Scottish base. Rolling to a halt, the camera was handed over for the film to be processed. The images captured were then used in the forthcoming briefing. As the crew walked to the de-briefing preparations were beginning in earnest around them. Ground crews worked to get a dozen bombers ready only to find their bomb trolleys were still on a train making the long journey to Scotland. After a search of the whole aerodrome three appeared from somewhere. With six Wellington Mk IAs, 115 Squadron were eventually prepared. Their crews were locked into the briefing. An extract from an unofficial diary reads: "at the end, somebody got up at the back and said, 'You've told us how to evade one fighter, sir. What happens if you meet four?' To which our intelligence officer answered 'most unlikely'. We were still apprehensive at the proposition that we might come face to face with two of the Luftwaffe's most lethal fighters [BF109E and BF110]."

Bf 110 of 3./ZG76, four of which attacked Sergeant Albert Tubbs on July 6, 1940 whilst flying Blenheim L8842. Sergeant Arthur Johnson and Tubbs survived but their observer Sergeant Robert McVeigh died of his wounds onboard HMS *Cossack* and was buried at sea. (*Norwegian Air Force*)

Two Blenheim fighters were ordered up in the early afternoon to act as fighter cover for the Wellingtons which were now under Coastal Command control. Two officers were on the aptly named 'To Fly List' pinned on the notice board at Bircham Newton; Flying Officer William Bain and Sergeant Albert Tubbs, in R3603 and N3627 respectively. The day of their impending success, April 11, was a fine day with high, dark patchy cloud as they departed to meet the bombers off the Norwegian coast and escort them to Stavanger. Somehow the bombers were twenty minutes late getting away, so when the two arrived at the rendezvous a wireless message was sent to them telling them to "Hold position". Bain told his wireless operator to send back "Message not understood".

After a stooge about, the two proceeded to raid the aerodrome; "Found a lot of bombers lined up in Germanic precision – proceeded to strafe the airfield". Simultaneously they positioned themselves wing tip to wing tip at 4,000 feet, skirting the aerodrome. An observer counted fifty Heinkel bombers dispersed. Blenheim N3627 and R3603 came in from the east, maintaining their fixed height. Below a single siren sounded as majestically both swooped down to 3,000 feet at 19.45 hours. Mercury engines throbbed away, with a slight glow from their exhaust stubs. As if performing at a pre-war RAF Hendon air display the pilots swept north to south in close formation dispensing fire from their belly packs, occasionally traversing with the slightest touch on their controls and raking the three lines of Heinkels, Junkers and Messerschmitts. N3627 dispensed 1,600 rounds and R3603 1,500 with its rear gunner getting off 100 rounds. Tubbs pulled the stick back into his stomach to haul his Blenheim over the bluff, which afforded protection from the increasingly intense small arms and anti-aircraft fire being directed at them. Both pushed the aircraft down on the deck to 150 feet and flew a reciprocal course for their Norfolk base, with just the clouds for company. Half way across the North Sea a WAAF's voice crackled in their headphones "'Q-Queenie' and 'R-Robert' land away at Lossiemouth". Suddenly they were over the rugged Moray coast, touching down at 22.30 hours. Behind a blackout their de-briefing notes were written up:

"One would think that ordinary 0.303 machine-gun bullets, including tracer and incendiaries would not do a lot of damage to aeroplanes, but they do set light to fuel tanks and I believe in this instance they set light to a refuelling tanker as well. Anyhow there was quite a good blaze as they scraped over the top of the neighbouring hill to get out of the way of the anti-aircraft guns whose gunners had just woken up. Then, instead of going home, they came around again and split up and shot up the aerodrome a second time; also with good results, because by then, thinking they had gone, the Germans had come out to inspect the damage. So Bain and Tubbs did a bit more just for luck. Again they got away without harm to themselves and by that time they had come to the conclusion that the bombers' raid had been scrubbed. Their ammunition for the gun-pack machine guns was virtually no more; they went home, undamaged except for extensive holes from machine-gun rounds."

In the prologue to the main assault, six Wellingtons roared in from the east at low level, at 21.00 hours, half an hour after the first strike. Fierce defensive fire was put up by 9 Flakregiment 33. In the wake of the barrage the Wellingtons roared over at low level dropping 500 lb bombs. The RAF machines replied to the increasingly intense heavy and small arms fire with machine guns. They were led in for a second time by young New Zealander, Pilot Officer D. Rankin flying P9284. They machine-gunned enemy aircraft, hangars and stores. Vickers Wellington P9271 was hit three times. The pilot, Flight Sergeant Powell, and one other member of the crew brought the bomber back and crash-landed. Powell was later awarded the DFM. A second Wellington, P9235 flown by Flying Officer Scott was also hit, with the navigator sustaining injuries. Wellington P9284 failed to return, crashing into a school in Stavanger and killing the crew, three civilians and wounding many others. Several houses were set on fire.

Neither was the ordeal over for Bain and Tubbs. A terse phone call was put through to their dispersal hut. During the operational debrief it was duly noted that the two Coastal Command fighters had not waited for the Wellingtons. Both 254 pilots were summoned to 115 Squadron's flight office, where they were asked to wait outside like errant schoolboys. They were reprimanded by 115 Squadron's commanding officer Wing Commander George Mills saying they were naughty boys and were not to leave his aircraft and crews on their own again. Fortunately a red rubber stamp marked with the word 'Reprimand' did not appear in their logbooks due to the intervention of a senior officer, who argued that both should be congratulated on using their initiative and perseverance. A pre-dawn reconnaissance flight at 03.57 revealed limited damage to the airfield runway, but later the bomber squadron was credited with damaging Do. 17P of 1(F)/120.

There was media frenzy in newsprint and on the wireless as the Air Ministry released information about the first raid on Norwegian soil. The BBC demonstrated the RAF 'gung ho' spirit in two transmissions in mid-April 1940 during their Air Log broadcast on the Forces Programme. Tubbs and Bain spoke into the microphone about the April 11 attack on Stavanger: Tubbs:

"Two crews of three were on standby for an attack on Stavanger, acting as escort for our bombers. We took off while it was light from our aerodrome in Norfolk. I had been doubtful if we could make it across in the weather conditions, as flying over the North Sea takes a lot of concentration as darkness falls. When we were just off the enemy coast we decided to go in. We simply streaked across that enemy aerodrome at a great rate of knots with our guns firing, and then turned to come in again, hitting a number of aircraft. The Germans put up a barrage, with different coloured tracer rounds coming up, and some flaming onions. We flew across the aerodrome again raking enemy installations and aircraft before flying over a bluff out of harm's way."

During the next week the Blenheim squadrons' operations were 'ramped up' with ground staff and aircrews working at full stretch. Tubbs and Bains' colleagues completed several more operations over the rolling snow-capped hills and quaint brightly coloured villages and harbours of Norway. Fighter protection followed for the senior service's Fleet Air Arm on April 14, led by Pilot Officer Phillip Beal. Together with two other machines they flew out of Hatston in two waves between 05.00 and 05.50 hours to attack the reported anti-aircraft transport due to arrive at noon. This information came courtesy of the deciphering done inside Hut 4 of Ultra at Bletchley Park, Buckinghamshire. At 0700, six Blackburn Stukas and their escort made landfall near to Marstein Light at the entrance to Korsfjord, its light assisting vessels sailing to Bergen. Commander Charles Leo Glandore Evans RN led the first formation, skirting between the leads and towards their target. Pilots from 800 Squadron instantly strafed *schnellbootes* S.23 and S.25 causing casualties amongst the crews inbound from Wilhelmshaven. The weather then drastically deteriorated as the second formation led by Lieutenant William Lucy arrived, their grey paint scheme merging with the backdrop over Bergen. One of Lucy's sections found themselves in an almost 'white out' situation. Piloted by Harris, Torin, Church, Filmer, Riddler and Spurway they were unable to locate the target despite their persistency. Lucy's flight found the target and made a low altitude glide-bombing attack through the snow below fifty feet. As snowflakes camouflaged the Stukas' arrival, anti-aircraft shells flashed into the surrounding sky, hitting one aircraft which nosed into the water. Lucy's single 500 lb bomb exploded alongside SS *Barenfels* (7,569 BRT), between her and the jetty. It caused severe damage that ultimately caused the vessel to sink stern first, carrying her valuable cargo of anti-aircraft guns and ammunition with her.

Shortly after this operation a signal came from Coastal Command Northwood that the squadron was being sent to the Orkneys as fighters were the order of the day. Fighters, fighters and more fighters! The naval commanders were thankful for any fighters they could get. Hatston's resident naval squadrons boarded *Ark Royal*. With this 254 Squadron moved its fighter Blenheims as a whole from Bircham Newton and the detachment from Lossiemouth. New aircrew travelled the length of mainland Britain to join their new 'fighter' squadron. Pilot Officer Hal Randall was one: "The journey to Scotland was pleasant enough, usual over-crowding in railway carriages, lots of naval ratings. Our accommodation is in bell tents. It was up to us to provide long-range support to our embattled troops in Norway by hopefully engaging the enemy bombers." Patrols resumed shortly after arriving, covering allied troop landings which were being made in Romsdalsfjord.

Two aircraft took off at regular intervals to patrol overhead. One pair spotted a twin-engine aircraft at 16.16 hours, forty-eight miles from the entrance of the fjord. An astute observer identified it wrongly as Heinkel III. Its pilot, Ofw Friedrich Katzmair, increased speed, pulled his stick back and climbed for cloud base. The pursuers, Flight Lieutenant Henry Mitchell in R3682 and Pilot Officer Kenneth Illingworth in L9406 opened fire from 600 yards out and sped towards their intended target. Katzmair instinctively executed a stall turn, enabling Mitchell to get off some good deflection shots from close range at between 200 to 300 yards. A steady rate of return fire splayed out from the upper turret, but ceased as the weapon malfunctioned. Fw Heinrich Cordes struggled to clear the weapon.

After two more bursts of fire, smoke could be seen beginning to drift from the machine's port engine. With his adrenaline flowing Mitchell accelerated R3682 within 180 yards but as he pressed the firing button all guns jammed and he was obliged to break off, cursing the inadequacies of the gun oil lubricant after only firing 1,250 rounds. Illingworth came in at 7,000 feet and opened the throttles to get nearer. His machine started to vibrate. L9406's engines strained but he kept within distance. Now down to 5,000 feet the pilot officer sent out bursts intermittently from astern. Suddenly without warning three white Verey lights were fired out in quick succession from the upper turret of the enemy's machine. Three trails of white smoke arched lazily over the aircraft's tail before each one burst. Illingworth and Mitchell took this signal to mean Katzmair was about to ditch. L9406 broke hard right and was joined by Mitchell, flying straight and level at 5,000 feet. They watched the machine reduce height and both Blenheims wheeled over and followed. At 2,000 feet Katzmair opened his throttles and set a course inland over the mountains. Illingworth immediately engaged his nine plus boost and attacked from astern, with the enemy now skimming over the water at an estimated height of 10 feet. Two more bursts of 0.303 rounds set the starboard engine alight. Flames and smoke trailed behind. Katzmair stopped the engine, making an emergency forced landing on the plateau of Hanekamben near Stadlandet. With the snow having melted it was a sea of water and the aircraft sank nose first. One occupant was seen paddling, but no dinghy was put out. Katzmair, together with crewmen Gef Gerhard Betzin, Fw Heinrich Cordes and Gef Willi Holthausen, exited the crippled machine and set it alight. Shortly afterwards the whole crew were captured by the Norwegians and were later shipped to Great Britain. Illingworth claimed a 'kill'. Their victim was later identified through an intercept at RAF Intelligence as a Junkers 88A-1 of 7./IIILG1, from Sola airfield Stavanger, reported shot down by Blenheim fighters.

After numerous encounters the Fleet Air Arm crews aboard *Ark Royal* were exhausted and on April 28 the aircraft carrier retired out to sea for two days to rest her tired aircrews and to allow maintenance on the depleted number of naval aircraft. With the carrier unable to continue giving this vital air umbrella on April 29, it was fighter Blenheims of 254 Squadron that filled the void. Over the coming hours, until 16.00 two 'Battle Flights' consisting of three machines encountered the enemy at close quarters. They set off early at 07.00 for Andalsnes with Squadron Leader Philip Hunter in the lead. They made landfall south of Romsdalsfjord at 09.00 hours. Fifteen minutes later they were over Andalsnes as dense smoke bellowed into the still air.

Patrolling in a tight vic formation at 09.25 a lone Junkers 88 was sighted. The three turned to attack, commencing a chase at speed but at 6,000 feet the Junkers opened the throttle, outdistancing itself from the Blenheims at an estimated speed of 300 mph. "No contest – our boys just couldn't catch the Junkers", the intelligence officer wrote hours later. Regrouping, the three began sweeping back and forth, encompassing Rauma River and two small villages to the east and west. Heading low back in over Andalsnes the observers in the Perspex nose could see first hand the extensive damage along the waterfront with the quayside ablaze. Suddenly shouts of "Bomber!" were heard over the R/T, as two He 111s lined up to begin bombing troops below in Andalsnes.

Royal Marines from HMS *Hood*'s HQ Company turned their heads skywards watching the encounter ensue from their forward position. Even though the air temperature was eight degrees outside, as the pressure mounted sweat seeped through Hunter's off-white RAF-issued roll neck sweater. As he engaged the boost the engines of R3628 picked up and he was able to stay within 400 yards, willing the machine ever closer. When he was in range of 350 yards down to 150 yards a long stream of 1,000 rounds shot out from the belly pack, which seemed effective. The Heinkel returned fire – hitting R3628 with well-aimed rounds during the duel. Hunter noticed the revolutions on his port engine dropping and his oil pressure falling. With his right hand he moved the throttle off the port engine so it was closed. As Hunter broke away a Messerschmitt 110 was spotted climbing from below. The two RAF pilots executed a tight turn to come around, making shallow dives astern and abeam; "The 'Hun' pulled up at about fifty degrees with one astern in 'T-Tommy' still firing long bursts savagely into him". During this three-minute dogfight the belly pack and wing-mounted machine gun continued the steady rate of fire until their ammunition ran out. On leaving the scene what was left of the Messerschmitt was observed spiraling down, as if in distress.

All three machines were never more than a mile apart, as Hunter sidestepped the duel. His observer gave him a course to clear the Norwegian coast. At 10.35 hours this course was readjusted for landfall in the Shetlands. Flying at 9,000 feet with nothing but the sea below, there was a deafening noise as the port Mercury engine seized up. Within seconds the airscrew sheared away from its mount and fell away, clearing the turret and fuselage. Power was reduced and the remaining fuel switched to feed the starboard engine. "Although there were a number of sizeable bullet holes, and with no propeller, the aeroplane seemed quite happy to fly manually straight-and-level." With an extraordinary display of airmanship Hunter nursed his machine along until at 12.05 the grey green outline of the Shetlands was sighted. Less than twenty gallons of fuel registered on the gauge. All on board 'Y-Yorker' R3628 began preparations for a forced landing. Hunter was heard on the intercom: "Throw out anything not required", his comments were also picked up by a local wireless station. To lighten the load the remaining 1,000 rounds were fired off. With the weight now reduced Scatsta was chosen as the proposed landing ground. On approach the cockpit escape hatch was dispensed with as the machine crossed the boundary flint wall. Hunter then skillfully held off with the good engine until the last possible moment. R3628 landed at 1250 hours, its starboard propeller buckling and the belly pack digging into the rough soft ground and getting torn away from its mounts. The wreck came to a halt in a shower of aggregate and sand while the three scrambled clear and construction workers looked on in bemusement at their new arrival. The works engineer reported that this unwelcome intrusion had delayed the laying of the main runway, which now had to be levelled and cleared a second time. Hunter remarked, "I thought the aircraft was a complete write off". Upon investigation the inspecting officer found that one bullet had punctured the oil system to the port engine. 254 Squadron's Blenheim was smashed beyond repair and was signed off for disposal.

As the remaining two landed at 13.45 hours, the second patrol was already making contact with the enemy. The three Blenheim fighters made landfall at the entrance to Romsdalsfjord at a thousand feet, moving into line astern at 11.55 hours. The observer of the lead aircraft spotted a Heinkel flying at speed dead across and slightly ahead. All turned to starboard in order to bring them in from behind to within 600 yards. A pursuit took place but the enemy bomber could not be caught. Again the inadequacies of the Blenheim came to the forefront, one pilot writing "We're not fast enough to close for attack". Twenty minutes later the shape of a Junkers was seen silhouetted against the sky at 8,000 feet. Climbing to commence an attack, thick black smoke was observed coming from an adjacent island 62.39N/16.79E. As they gained the unnamed pair split up, one flying in from the starboard quarter and the second from astern. The Luftwaffe gunner returned fire, with reflex reaction the first banked to avoid the 7.92 rounds, which passed under the port wing. Closing to within 150 yards astern the second lined his fixed sight up, but its nose flew into a considerable amount of

1./Kü.Fl.Gr. 506 and 2./Kü.Fl.Gr. 506 were based in Trondheim from April 9, 1940. The 1./Kü.Fl.Gr. 506 He 115s flew several operations primarily attacking convoys on the coast of Scotland and England but these lightly armed Heinkels proved to be too slow and vulnerable to attacks by RAF fighters. (*Norwegian Air Force*)

exhaust smoke emitted from the two Junkers Jumo 211 engines, and it subsequently lost height. After following for three minutes a second Junkers was observed and a chase ensued but it disappeared. The leader radioed to check their fuel state and, having been airborne since 09.30, the aircraft set course for Hatston, with one Blenheim hit in the wings and cowling. They passed Molde just after the town had been bombed, transformed into a sea of flames on the starboard side. The return trip was uneventful; flying back in an orderly but fairly loose formation, they pulled themselves together approaching the aerodrome and came straight in to land on the grass. They reported ten minutes after landing at 16.00 hours that "it appears to be practically written off, several fires were burning fiercely", the brief report ends "5,800 rounds were fired".

In Andalsnes intermittent bombing continued to such a degree that reports from the line noted that commander Brigadier Douglas Hogg was forced to contemplate a withdrawal. An arduous night of bombing ensued, the fires illuminating the ruined dwellings and stiff corpses which the stretcher-bearers had been unable to collect. Hogg was unexpectedly wounded by shrapnel and was made ready to be evacuated at the earliest opportunity. In his absence Captain John McCahon of the Royal Marines assumed control having received a signal from Great Britain stating that a Blenheim 'Battle Flight' was leaving Scotland and would arrive at about 06.59 hours. The pair of Blenheims flew out in the darkness at 03.40 hours on May 1. McCahon was a former serving flight lieutenant who relinquished his air force temporary command in December 1937 to rejoin the Royal Marines. He commented, "The aeroplanes sent were not noticeably dissimilar from those used by the enemy when they arrived in the sky above". Enemy air activity was in full swing again when at 07.05 hours the message "Much activity near Andalsnes – very many 'Huns' near Andalsnes" came over the R/T.

They closed in and swung away. Immediately making a sighting, Pilot Officer Hal Randall gave chase, his observer Sergeant Joseph Foster's keen eye having spotted a twin-engine machine a distance away. The penny dropped, it was a Heinkel III. The hound was off its leash and after the quarry. To close the distance extra boost was required. Randall reported, "Our Mercury XV engines needed 100-octane fuel to run with this boost. At this time we were short of 100-octane, so the squadron had been flying on the larger inner tanks, leaving the 100-octane fuel stored in the smaller 140 gallon fuel tanks." To get this extra 2,750 rpm Randall reached across the cockpit and rotated two large spoke wheels (renowned for their ability to catch fingers) configured one behind the other (port/starboard) at about shoulder height behind the pilot's seat. Once he had switched the fuel he had a chance to catch up with the enemy.

Watching his tail, the German gunner noticed the aircraft moving behind him but was unsure whether it was friend or foe – waiting to see if any opened fire. When two did his pilot stall-turned left and dived steeply in a long graceful dive into a nearby fjord, the precipitous and narrow valley presenting difficulties in focusing on a moving target. "Nothing prepared us for contour flying; our judgement had to be correct otherwise we'd have flown into the mountainside." Randall and Hunter kept on his tail. Eventually, Randall was 400 yards behind him and Hunter started to gain to 600 yards. Both fired alternately. Randall explained, "My gun button moved with ease as I followed his evasive action, excitedly using all my front gun ammunition, as did Hunter. Despite our best efforts we had no effect. Worse still, the German rear gunner was able to get some accurate fire in at my machine before sliding away over the mountains at low level." The action lasted thirty-seven minutes. Rounds had shredded both wing areas and one port cowling. Disengaging and making good speed they got there at about 09.00 hours.

McCahon recalled: "There was a lot of droning in the sky and the inhabitants took cover. An escort vessel near the jetty began pumping out defensive fire towards a Junkers when two friendly fighters attacked." The first indication was when 'J-Johnnie' and 'L-London' of 254 Squadron opened fire at right angles. Flight Lieutenant Henry Mitchell in 'J-Johnnie' opened with full deflection, ending with a quarter attack. Fw Ernst Schade opened the Junkers' throttles and drew away. Mitchell's report

A 206 Squadron Hudson. With these the unit roamed along the continental coast attacking shipping, together with anti-invasion patrols and with offensive strikes against the ports. (*Royal Air Force Museum, London*)

reads: "No fire returned by enemy aircraft, enemy believed to have been hit but there was no external sign of damage. 1,160 rounds used." Back at Hatston, Mitchell dozed. He awoke to the sound of engines and saw the boys were peering up. He jumped up and looked too. The sky was almost clear with occasional fluffy white clouds. "Over there! Turning, look!" Clarke exclaimed. Yes, there they were. About a dozen Lockheed Hudsons wing tip to wing tip.

It was raining steadily as tea finished. A group of officers sat chatting around the mess stove, an RAF tradition. It was a friendly atmosphere after a memorable week, talk was of individual battles. But, as the prime minister was all too aware, individual successes counted for little in the face of such disproportionate losses. Given the weight of German numbers and the strains imposed on the allied forces it was inevitable – Norway was a hopeless situation. It was a terrible waste of men and equipment. The demoralized force began to withdraw at the beginning of May. Maps in the newspapers showed huge shaded areas captured by the Germans in Norway. On closer inspection the scale revealed that the gains were measured in dozens of miles rather than in hundreds of yards.

Coastal Command's token trade protection squadron deployment would be reinforced. The RAF committed to providing attacks on shipping and mainland targets in Norway as the war escalated. But it was all coming a little late and Air Chief Marshal Bowhill spoke of the regrettable delays of the army chiefs of staff. There was a whiff of sour grapes. Both air and ground crews sat tight. Sergeant Albert Tubbs wrote: "Asked the chief engineering officer to get some more heating in the kite if we're off to Norway again soon. Those of us left dined and drank some beer in the mess." The following day they got rid of their hangovers with a low level flight to the mainland then an impromptu cross-country flight skirting Elgin, Banff, and MacDuff as new faces took the place of lost aircrew. As exhausted veterans nodded off into a doze, some relived aerial combat in their sleep with knees, feet, and arms twitching. Illingworth sat bolt upright; the telephone was ringing: "Reconnaissance to the Norwegian coast between Utvar Light and Marstein Light. Single Blenheim required – take off at 06.15 hours." With no delay the pilots flicked the rudder to correct the Blenheim fighter's movement and raced away into the distance. The wheels rotated into their slots immediately and the start of the long journey began. Sergeant Joseph Foster used his binoculars to count thirty assorted merchant vessels at anchor in Bergen harbour. A strike was on.

The Royal Navy reacquainted itself with RNAS Hatston as newly formed 806 Fleet Air Arm Squadron were equipped with the versatile Blackburn Skuas, ready for coordinated operations with 18 Group. However, these operations were delayed because of the atrocious weather. A very heavy gale and intermittent snowstorms kept them grounded for three days. Eventually a meteorological reconnaissance found the weather front had cleared sufficiently to mount a sortie. An RAF observer wrote: "Visibility ten miles increasing to the north, with temperatures at 8,000 feet zero degrees centigrade with ice secretion in cloud. Wind 10 mph at ground level, sea state calm." Planning got under way, but as Pilot Officer Phillip Gaylard discovered, "the naval aircrew had been issued with different charts to the RAF which didn't help matters". Inside the briefing room a stove crackled away, its extractor pipe glowing red with the heat as it tried to radiate some warmth to the aircrew hunched over wooden tables. Observers were plotting their course while an intelligence officer handed out illustrations of lighthouses and silhouettes of merchantmen. On the blackboard a diagram of the harbour was unveiled, showing where the main target was positioned.

Muffled from the chill Lieutenant Colin Campbell-Horsfall RN led eight Skuas off the concrete runway at 16.10 with five minutes separation. Meanwhile Flight Lieutenant George Fairtlough in the leading arrowhead of six Blenheims swept over the cliff face towards the circling monoplanes. The 350-mile journey began. There was a rude awakening for the Bergen population that Thursday afternoon. Arriving over the target area the airmen found it covered by 3/10ths cloud. The Fleet Air Arm force streaked down from 1,800 feet, targeting merchantmen. In the sights of Petty Officer Anthony Jopling flying L3014 was the minesweeper M134 which increased in size as the sea rushed up towards him. Pressing the release button the 500 lb semi-armoured piercing bomb fell away passing through the hull of M134 and detonating on the bottom of the harbour. The vessel sank in ten to fifteen minutes – three dead and seven mortally wounded. A couple of 500 lb bombs demolished two nearby houses injuring seventeen and killing one civilian. As they cleared the target area, the Blenheim crews came in, with Fairtlough calmly ordering "Attack, attack, attack". Each dropped eight 20 lb bombs, clusters hitting the six fuel storage tanks on Askøy Island.

In the mêlée advancing vessels waiting to enter the town's harbour were struck with machine-gun fire. An Elbe merchant vessel with a team from a construction company on board was decimated. In reply there was spasmodic anti-aircraft fire. A multiple burst hit machine L9482 shredding the instrument panel and control cables. Flight Lieutenant Alick Heath was in a dazed and bleeding state as L9482 went into a left hand spin over Bergen, finally crashing into the harbour and disintegrating when it hit the sea bed. The twenty-five-year-old South African pilot was unable to escape and died of asphyxiation. On the surface oil stains marked his resting place. Ashore a loud cheer went up from members of 6.Batterie/Flakregiment 33. Later troops watched as a boat dredged up two bodies, that of Sergeant Stanley Nicholls and Lieutenant Robin Nuthall (RN). They were laid out on the wooden deck. "Both looked as if they'd fallen into a deep sleep in a pool of water" commented a Norwegian fisherman to an American diplomat.

Somewhere in the murk their colleagues flew back over the sea, constantly checking their fuel state as the Scottish Islands drew ever nearer. Desperately short of fuel six Skuas landed at Sumburgh on fumes, refuelling before departing for Hatston. One machine crashed. One pilot logged a four-hour thirty-minute flight in an aircraft that had an official endurance of four hours and twenty minutes! At their de-briefing 254 Squadron's intelligence officer wrote: "A considerable amount of damage has been caused, at least three vessels sunk".

As more British troops continued to arrive off a sloop at Narvik, thick black smoke pitched hundreds of feet into the cobalt blue sky. Flames spewed from a wooden warehouse and buildings. Above, the drone of aircraft thundered over. Bombs whistled earthwards and explosions erupted as they hit the ground and men let off small arms skywards. "Where was the ruddy air force?" was a cry that would be heard again all too soon. The proposed air cover of three Blenheim fighters on escort duty sighted a Dornier 18 at 0630 hours. The enemy machine dived for the sea. As it reached water level its pilot began zigzagging at speed across the empty expanse of water. A quarter attack was made by a 254 aircraft and at 100 yards rounds struck the aircraft. It dropped another ten feet, bullets ripping a path in front of him and sending water spurts over the forward fuselage and wings. As the third machine attacked the enemy gunner was seen hanging out of his position. More avoiding action was taken and the enemy aircraft was last seen disappearing into low cloud at about 100 feet. They then returned and landed having fired 5,050 rounds from their front guns and 1,900 from the single turret guns.

Fitters and riggers prepared for the next likely sortie while administration wheels were turning. There was some concern on Friday May 10 when the equipment officer for 254 was notified by Coastal Command's Northwood supply officer that stocks of new tyres for their Blenheim Mk IV Fs were to be delayed. Six hundred workers at the Fort Dunlop factory in Birmingham had ceased work following a refusal to accept a 'war bonus' offer. By May 11 both day and night shift production staff were involved. Four thousand out of 4,500 employees had stopped production. With no respite and certainly no war bonus the unit went back into action against shipping and enemy fighters at first light. There was worse news. With success no longer possible in Norway across the English Channel there were increasingly worrying reports of large troop movements along France's frontiers. From now on 254 Squadron's men and women would be fighting on two fronts.

CHAPTER THREE

Norfolk Rhapsody

As fighting continued over Norway, aircraft were being dispatched from North Coates and Bircham Newton whilst others continued to train. Two petrol bowsers, even with their load slightly lightened, were still heavy enough to leave impressions in the grass like railway tracks snaking off towards the fuel dump. P4836 was one of those fuelled and sitting heavily with its extra burden. Aviation fuel vapour hung like a cloud in the air as Flying Officer John 'Bodsie' Laughlin clutched his leather-flying helmet and approached the fighter. The aircraft's rigger and fitter were busy giving 'their girl' last-minute checks in preparation for flying. Jock led Laughlin around the Blenheim for the external checks, carefully tapping the belly pack. With both hands Laughlin placed his helmet on his head, pulling it firmly down then making slight adjustments before climbing onto the port wing. Placing his left hand in the grip hold and left foot on the step he hoisted himself then walked towards the cockpit. Again he hoisted himself up and dropped down into the cockpit. As his aircraft rumbled into the sky heading for The Wash the weather clamped down without notice. Flying Officer Laughlin was entirely on his own, clawing his way back along the coast whilst night flying to North Coates. He had been up for what he thought was a long time and approached the aerodrome to land. Unfortunately he managed to over shoot in P4836 and did a spot of hedging and ditching – to the detriment of the machine. The watch office heard the wail over the radio-telephone. It was not unlike that heard at morning prayer somewhere in Palestine! The noise and commotion disturbed the chief engineering officer who was busy looking at the men's exercise books and their answers on the refinements of the Mercury XV engine, marking off their week's work and making comments in the margins. After this little episode Laughlin had an inferiority complex and felt like the worst pilot in the squadron.

With the month of April closing 235 Squadron received orders from 16 Group to be at Bircham Newton within twenty-four hours without fail. It was frantic, those in the advance party literally grabbed possessions and threw them into their kit bags, scrambling out in less than an hour, kit bags hastily stowed in the fuselage. Jackson-Smith left with an advance party but the weather intervened before the air party could take off. Pilot Officer Hugh Pardoe-Williams, a twenty-two year old with 235, was having a brew while waiting for lorries to take him and 166 non-commissioned officers and men to their new aerodrome. Their reveille was at 06.00 hours, breakfast 07.00 – 07.30 hours, between which time the officers who required their kits to be conveyed in the service motor transport had to ensure it was packed and ready for collection by 08.00 from the officers' mess steps, clearly marked '235 Squadron' to facilitate collection. Pardoe-Williams recalled:

"Amid a balmy silence I could hear the song of a single blackbird which was then drowned out as the trucks pulled up – three tonners – the usual transport. Everyone had his or her respirators, tin hat and kit bag, together with a brown paper bag, hastily prepared by the cookhouse, which contained a pork pie, jam sandwich and fruitcake. Hurling the kit into the trucks, we then got ourselves onboard, leaving at 11.00 hours for Bircham Newton."

Officer aircrew in the anteroom, officers' mess 235 Squadron Bircham Newton. Left to right: Robby Foster; Pilot Officer Reginald Peacock (died after the Battle of Britain); Dudley Relton; Pilot Officer Mick Ryan (killed in action May 24, 1940). (*W.J. Groendjik*)

Without their full complement of Bristol Blenheims a private car party was hastily organized. In an assortment of motor vehicles Squadron Leader McDougall, Flight Lieutenants Richard Cross and Wiggs Manwaring, Flying Officer John Laughlin, Pilot Officers Michael Ryan, Pinnock, Keat, Algeo, Saunders and Sergeants Allison, and Sutton snaked passed North Coates' guardroom and with a hoot of their horns disappeared. Wiper blades frantically motioned back and forth as the rain lashed down. Drivers peered out into the darkness, whilst two unfortunate souls in a water-logged MG TC sports car stopped at North Thoresby to put the canvas roof up. As the column sped through the blacked out villages and countryside, the weather closed in considerably. The main air party was still unable to leave, except Pilot Officers David Woodger and Norman Shorrocks in the 'all weather' Miles Magister. The weather got severely worse and the Magister was buffeted in flight. Woodger had no alternative but to put down at Sutton Bridge. The wheel base slithered to a halt and the two bedraggled pilot officers made their way to the watch office, leaving pools of water on the floor whilst one filled in the visiting aircraft form. The senior officer in the watch office lamented that the water would leave stains on his carpet.

235's main air party finally departed North Coates at 10.30 hours on April 25. Seventeen officers and men from A and B Flights crammed into eight Bristol Blenheim fighters, headed by Pilot Officer

Reginald Peacock. Unfortunately, the Southern Rhodesian Pilot Officer Anthony Booth's mixture control on his machine failed, forcing an about return to North Coates where he landed without mishap. Booth was able to continue his journey later that day.

The war felt closer at their new location of Bircham Newton, thirty-six miles northeast of Norwich. The squadron diarist noted: "we feel very pleased about it all". However, after five days the crews were fed up with the lack of flying caused by a protracted period of fog and low cloud base. An aircraft recognition lecture was laid on from 13.00 to 15.00 hours for 235 and a visiting squadron. Finally, on the last day of April, the fog lifted and in the afternoon permission was obtained for live firing over The Wash at air and ground targets. By day aeroplanes towed targets over Hilly Piece, Fox Covert and the Hang High; wheeling over the meadows and The Wash. Thud, thud, thud, thud, thud, thud; six splashes along the edge of the blue sea. Round again the machines droned, their two-engine noise amplified. "The tractor seemed to have two or three engines at any one time", recalled farmer Williamson of Stiffkey, Norfolk.

On May 1 conditions improved and the stalemate broke. "Shortly after, I was seated in my office when the station commander telephoned and said five new Blenheim Mk IVs were allocated to 235 Squadron for collection from Kemble. I duly organized Flight Lieutenant Richard Cross to lead a party to 5 Maintenance Unit at Kemble, Gloucester to collect them," recalled MacDonald. Amongst the pilots was Pilot Officer Reginald Peacock, "I remember being elated when we received them". P9256, 9395, 9261, 9401 and 9404 were flown into their new home and dispersed around the aerodrome. That evening the normal throng invariably around the bar in the messes were absent as every able-bodied male worked on fitting out their new charges and harmonizing the belly-pack machine guns. Leading Aircraftman 'Taff' Morgan, back from leave, applied himself with particular dedication.

"It was similar to the Mark I gun-pack. We had no manuals to work from, just a rough drawing. The fitting was done by torch light and flares at night and a very tough job it was too. We lacked the right tools for the job. We had just moved from North Coates and not all the equipment had reached us. We draped dark sheets over the aircraft, so we didn't show any visible light. Everyone worked in shifts, even our officers helped. It was a good bonding process. The highlight was when we had mugs of steaming hot tea brought out by the airmen's cookhouse with a fried egg sandwich."

16 Group reported the unit operational the next day. A heightened state of alert was declared, despite there being so much still to do. The calibration of wireless transmitters (W/T) was somewhat troublesome. The wireless electricians worked into the small hours and shortly before breakfast at 06.00 both A and B Flights' machines had functioning wireless communication. The stillness of the late afternoon was broken by dispersal's telephone ringing. B Flight was called to readiness at 17.35 hours, with take-off at 18.00/18.10 hours. Emerging from a poorly insulated dispersal hut Cross, Manwaring and Booth were detailed on a reconnaissance off the Dutch coast. The Royal Navy and Air Force needed information on the composition of enemy forces.

Surface water still lay on the aerodrome's runway despite airmen piercing it repeatedly with forked spikes to aid the drainage. Flight Lieutenant Richard Cross flew out in P9262, shortly followed by Flight Lieutenant Manwaring in P9261 and Pilot Officer Anthony Booth in L9401. They were under orders to investigate Borkum Island, Germany. A small crowd watched attentively as the first operational sortie commenced. As Bircham Newton disappeared from Cross's view, with butterflies in his stomach he commenced what would soon become a routine activity: "Patrols over an expanse of sea looking for the enemy but very seldom seeing them". It was now just a question of binoculars and eyeballs. Crossing the North Sea to the island of Borkum some 250 miles away they approached through a slight rain shower, but emerging through the clouds there was nothing. All the while controllers directed them. To the WAAF plotters' amusement 'Dick' Cross caused great hilarity by sending a report back in plain language that "there was nothing to be bloody seen near the Dutch coast". He was ordered to turn about and land back at Bircham Newton. Flying over the expansive Norfolk countryside, glancing at the odd flint and brick cottage outlined in the dark, P9262 joined the circuit and touched down, watched by the Australian station signals officer Acting Squadron Leader 'Russ' Darby Welland. He would be delighted when the other two put down, as he couldn't wait to see his charming wife Helena.

In the failing light of late evening Manwaring and Booth were flying low at 100 feet when they took an enemy convoy of three by surprise, ten miles from Borkum at 20.02 hours. Anti-aircraft fire rained from a single flak ship whose gunners managed to get off twelve to fifteen rounds before a stoppage occurred. The firing was very wide, bursting astern. "We didn't think a great deal of the Jerry's aim," wrote Booth. Onboard the middle transport vessel a five-star cartridge was fired, as outgoing trace rounds emanated from their stern and bridge and lit up the sky like the annual Cowes Regatta firework display on the Isle of Wight. The grey shape of P9261 made a wide sweep, before turning back in for another run. It was then subjected to a concentrated barrage. Booth called a warning over the R/T as Manwaring raced in at 255 mph at a height of under 100 feet. He could see men diving for cover as 0.303 rounds punctured the structure. Within a split second P9261 and L6790 were briefly out of danger before two more enemy transports opened up, firing between 12 and 15 rounds. Their speed carried them clear and back towards England. For 200 miles of the journey they were covered in darkness, except for the glow of the instrument panel. On their way home the wind transported them swiftly and they contacted the watch office controllers to talk them down. Swinging off the grass runway to a dispersal area, they both switched off their engines. Their propellers milled to a standstill. Grey figures ran underneath placing chocks in front of the tyres as pilots, observers and air gunners extracted themselves from their machines. An expectant and jubilant crowd awaited them. 235 Squadron had completed their first combat operation of the Second World War. De-briefing took place in the operations room. "A few glorious moments of low strafing" was the description given.

That night there was a celebration, first in the officers' then in the sergeants' mess and later the airmen's. Toasts were drunk in the officers' mess from a special bottle of navy rum and a 'first op' card was signed before everyone got too 'tanked up'. During the evening's proceedings Pilot Officer Reginald Peacock was christened 'Pissy' Peacock. Whilst laying underneath a barrel he began drinking Cameron's bitter ale straight from the tap before filling up his handled pint glass. With forthcoming operations the padre, priest and reverend from the different church denominations gathered their flock and got them safely to their accommodation. One flying officer decided to fall asleep in the fetal position in a trench!

The following morning they blew away their hangovers with reconnaissance off the Norwegian coast. After preflight checks startled crows fled skyward, their shrills masked as six Mercury radial engines roared into the air. Cross led in N6193 with Robinson portside in P4844 and Peacock on the starboard side in L9401. They set out towards the foreboding southern Norwegian coast. Their destination: Lista lighthouse. A sudden improvement in the local weather had brought a resurgence of E-boat activity in central Norway.

Twenty-five-year-old Pilot Officer Norman A. L. Smith from Cambridge did the navigation. Fifty miles from Norway they were practically flying blind in a snowstorm "snow was making a carpet on the gunner's Vickers K mountings". After a further five minutes the aircraft came out of the storm and their enthusiasm increased when Smith's precision navigation was found to be on track and Lista's lighthouse came into view. No resistance was met and the three were able to return. As N6193, P4844 and L9401 approached the aerodrome from two miles away a wisp of smoke rose skywards. Passing over the aerodrome they saw below the remnants of Hudson N7319 which had been mauled by two Bf109s of II (J) TrGR 186 over Norderney. Its captain, New Zealander Pilot Officer Raymond

Kean and his navigator Sergeant Deverill, had somehow managed to keep their machine in the air when the sieved aircraft should by rule have crashed into the sea. As the undercarriage collapsed Kean, although severely weakened by loss of blood, was able to land with the help of Deverill. The turret gunner, twenty-eight-year-old Leading Aircraftman Ernest Townsend's body was wedged in the turret, having first shot down one of their attackers from 50 yards. He was killed in the ensuing mêlée. Kean wrote: "Owing to the violent manoeuvres of our own aircraft, it was found impossible to remove him from the gun turret." Townsend was carefully extracted, his limp body laid out on the aircraft's floor where two large blankets lay. He was wrapped in them and then brought out on a stretcher to the waiting blood wagon. His mutilated body was placed in the station morgue. Kean had his wounded left hand bandaged and Deverill received attention to the open wound on his left leg. The New Zealander commented, "Both MEs flew in formation with us and then waved goodbye."

The ground crew counted 242 bullet and twelve cannon shell holes in N7319. Group Captain John Grey, officer commanding the RAF station, was awe-struck by the sight before him and declared that he had "never seen anything like it" and "how the two survived is beyond comprehension". Jackson-Smith said, "To see this brought the stark realities of war closer. Everyone got drunk until about two in the morning, having a wonderful time with 206 Squadron types. Some 'light weights' gave up and turned in early, this was seen as bad form and raiding parties were sent out debagging the culprits."

After a hectic night's drinking, it was a tranquil scene at 235's dispersal hut on May 5. Some played games of bridge or Monopoly whilst a number had gone to local Sunday church services. Flying Officer 'Bodsie' Laughlin and Pilot Officers Patterson, Savill and Ryan were out between 08.45 and 12.50 investigating the activities of a Royal Navy minesweeper. "Nothing else was seen and we returned home," recorded Pilot Officer Norman Savill. Shortly after lunchtime Flight Lieutenant Manwaring and Pilot Officer Alan Wales were tasked with supplying the Royal Navy with intelligence, accompanied by Lieutenant 'Pinky' Haworth RN of 815 Fleet Air Arm Squadron: "Directed along the German coast near Wilhelmshaven, our real work had now begun, though the weather was steadily deteriorating, the wind was breezy, there were such terrific bumps that the gunner frequently banged his head when flung upwards out of his seat." L9261 and P4844 observers took photographs of Borkum.

Manwaring led Wales back to circle Borkum before returning, having reported three destroyers and ten to twenty small vessels. Unseen because of their camouflage a trio of Bf109Es from of a force of seven from II/JG 186 hit the unsuspecting pair fifteen miles north of Norderney, "they came out of goodness knows where". Manwaring was first aware of shots being fired at 15.50 hours when one of the Bf109s did a beam attack on L9261 from the portside. His gunner was unsighted at the time, having lowered his seat instantly their port engine cut. Wiggs in the confines of his 'office' knew speed was of the essence in a combat situation. Automatically readjusting, the dead propeller went to coarse pitch and the live starboard propeller into fine pitch. He closed the gills of the dead engine then mechanically moved the high boost control to the down position. One hand pushed the throttle levers fully forward and with 2,750 rpm and plus nine boost L9261 broke into a canter. Wales in P4844 was attacked by a single Bf109 which did a quarter attack then carried on past him. The dogfight was broken off at 17.30. Ofw Reinhold Schmetzer and Uffz Herbert Kaiser reported intercepting two Blenheim fighters and claimed both shot down.

Manwaring found himself completely alone in the sky, flying over the North Sea. Wales caught up and eventually the monotonous flight ended. L9261 turned towards the aerodrome and Wiggs' undercarriage locked into place. When nearly within gliding distance he lowered the flaps fully, closed the throttle and landed. Wales came in feeling the wheels bumping along and stopped by the dispersal. He crawled out, wet with sweat. Continually the questions kept coming from 'Spy' during the debriefing. A WAAF passed them cups of tea. After a three-hour and thirty-five minute flight they were all shattered and after storing their flying kit they slumped down into armchairs. Within half an hour they were asleep.

Two days later RAF Coastal Command made a concentrated effort to bomb a cruiser of the *Nuremberg* class, which had been reported between the islands of Norderney and Juist. Flight Lieutenant Richard Cross in N6193, Flying Officers Laughlin in L9404 and Peacock in L9295 assembled at 02.30. All the crews were briefed together in the operations room. They were to act as fighter escort. Twenty minutes later the three were airborne. The weather ahead was not ideal as they formated at 3,000 feet and circled, watching Beauforts and Swordfish of 22 and 815 Squadrons take off, form up, and prepare to head in the direction of the East Frisian islands for the first sortie of the day. Their performance was weakened once again by low cloud and sea mist, which caused a considerable amount of confusion within such a compact formation. Another stark realisation was that radio communication between the three types of machines was non-existent. Every change of course was done by Aldis lamp, consequently when aborting the operation one 815 Swordfish continued on the proposed route while the remainder returned to Bircham Newton. Attempts by Laughlin and Peacock to contact Dick Cross got negative responses. L9404 groped along, landing after dawn when the weather improved. Peacock was directed to land away at North Coates in time for breakfast. Cross was still flying over the North Sea; "As my eyes scanned ahead I couldn't see anything, I reduced height. My observer said by his calculations and allowing for drift we should be near Terschelling." Conscious of wasting fuel and the state of the weather he flicked the machine around and returned.

Bristol Beaufort Mk Is L4449, L9891 and L4461 of 22 Squadron RAF at North Coates in Lincolnshire, July 19, 1940. (*Harry Mellor*)

B Flight gathered and were on standby all morning to provide fighter escort to 22 Squadron, "but it didn't come" reflected Jackson-Smith. The Admiralty had been given intelligence through a Bletchley Park interception that the cruiser had been seen still anchored off Nordeney. In the belief that a strike could be mounted, Air Chief Marshal Bowhill brought 22 Squadron to instant readiness. Operations began shortly after 14.45 hours. There was competition amongst the six squadron pilots at North Coates to take off first. The first to get away left at 14.52, while the last was clocked at 15.07 hours.

Having formed up over the airfield, they set course for the Dutch-German border. They climbed to 5,000 feet and as they were crossing the North Sea "there was a hum in the earphones as a voice said over the wireless, 'returning to base'" and one Beaufort left the formation with technical trouble.

The formation regrouped, keeping up the squadron motto 'Valiant & Brave' but unbeknown to the remaining five they had been picked up by Freya radar. Both light and heavy anti-aircraft fire streamed up from the island and mainland. Beaufort L4464 was rocked by a smack in the floor from a shell while a burst showered L4472 with shrapnel. The first bomb was launched from one of the machines towards the German cruiser anchored off Nordeney, but missed. As the bombing finished six Bf109Es intercepted in response to the intrusion, and as the Beauforts flew out into open water a voice came on the R/T shouting: "Messerschmitts – Break!" The five instantly split in all directions. L4472, flown by pre-war pilot twenty-seven-year-old Flying Officer Stuart Woollatt, was sent crashing into the sea off the Frisians with the loss of all life. Meanwhile L4464, flown by Wing Commander Harry Mellor, was badly damaged by Lt Hans-Wilhelm Schopper. His well-aimed machine-gun rounds pierced the machine's painted skin and debris was flung into the pilot's confined space. The air gunner, Aircraftman Traynor, was wounded as shards of Perspex splinters embedded themselves as his turret canopy shattered. Badly shot up L4518 eventually reached English shores. "It's been one hell of a struggle", remarked Mellor after crash landing at North Coates at 19.20 hours.

Training flights continued all day at Bircham Newton, only stopping when 206's Hudsons returned from operations as dusk fell to shortly after midnight. In the latter half of the day it became depressingly clear that more training was needed. Night flying was a skill which had thus far received insufficient attention. Twenty-three-year-old Sergeant Victor Allison from Boyndie in Banffshire had remarked six days earlier: "It is automatically assumed that the flight commanders would just send you off into the darkness to get experience and there would be no problem." At 23.55 hours on May 8, Allison found himself in extreme difficulty over The Wash whilst piloting Blenheim P4844. Sergeants Allison, Eric Schmid and Leading Aircraftman Victor Neirynk were muffled against the cold. A 'Green' Aldis lamp flashed and Allison released the parking brake and opened both throttles. The aircraft's tendency to swing to the right during take-off was corrected by use of the rudder and P4844 lifted off the ground with a 'clunk' as the undercarriage locked into place. Flying a single circuit of the airfield they gradually gained height, levelling out at 5,000 feet. The young pilot encountered changeable wind speeds with scattered rain showers and dense mist. With the air turbulence Allison required all his experience to keep the Blenheim airborne, terribly aware that he'd only completed one hour of night flying in this type of machine. As midnight approached Allison made brief contact with those directing him from the ground, whilst reducing height. The darkness and the bad weather made it hard to see the aerodrome because of sensory deprivation, and all three strained their eyes for familiar landmarks. Down below locals heard the sound of two Bristol Mercury XV engines as they scythed through the rain. Just for a moment they caught sight of the aerodrome as the flare path was lit for a few brief seconds before being extinguished. Allison made adjustments but his approach was slightly off. He pushed the throttles forward to increase power and both radial engines gave an agonizing scream. P4844 dropped rapidly and before being able to react, the machine nosed into the ground at Bircham Common two miles from the airfield at 00.10 hours. Just as suddenly, there came an awesome silence. A tangle of twisted metal and hissing engines greeted those first on the scene, and nothing could be done for the occupants. Later a flying accident card AM1180 was filled out in black ink. The senior investigating officer wrote, "Pilot inexperience at night flying and adverse weather conditions did not justify the flight". Nursing Sister Beth Cadman reported in her diary, "three boys died tonight, there was little left of them".

Good weather and excellent visibility up to about 8,000 feet followed. Jackson-Smith watched as pilots whizzed around the sky. The first loss had hardly registered with the majority of the unit when

The Reverend John Waddington officiates at a pilot's funeral in 1941 at St Mary the Virgin, Great Bircham, Norfolk. The steady losses mounted and the local churchyards became littered with rows of fresh graves of aircrew whose average age was twenty years old. In the foreground can be seen white crosses from those who died in 1940/1941.

a second occurred. In total darkness Pilot Officer Walter Smith boarded K7136, a Blenheim Mark IF, on a solo night flying exercise. Having completed the preliminary checks, the ground crew primed the engines and switched on the starting magnetos. Smith started each engine with his gloved left hand on the throttle lever, warming the Mercury engines to the right temperature and making doubly sure the oil was at five degrees. He then gestured through the open side Perspex window to the figures in overalls to switch off the starting magnetos. K7136's brakes were released to travel forward. The twenty year old's movements were fluid inside the cockpit. There was a faint glow from the instruments as his feet worked the rudder pedals, correcting the aircraft's direction. Smith completed the final checks, all 'tickety-boo'. Off to port a signal flashed and the silence was broken. With both throttles opened K7136 gathered pace. The tail lifted up almost to a flying position, the short nose held at a constant attitude and the machine lifted off the ground. As the undercarriage was retracting the aircraft swung to the right without warning, turning the Blenheim like a spinning top. K7136 continued turning 500 degrees. Losing height, Smith tried to correct, bringing the control column back to regain height but the starboard wing and nose went down instantly causing it to stall. In less than a minute K7136 plummeted into the ground, 200 yards from Bircham Newton. On impact 280 gallons of fuel ignited and burst into flames. It was 23.10 hours. People staying in The King's Head public house in Great Bircham reported hearing a loud 'crump'. Minutes later residents reported seeing a red glow reflected in the sky as the fuel burned. Crash crews responded quickly but the intense heat forced them back. The extent of the crash was revealed the next day. The land was badly scarred and littered with the twisted wreckage and a body beside the aeroplane wrapped in a parachute. A local policeman spent twenty-four hours guarding the wreckage. Senior officers found that Pilot Officer Walter Smith only had one hour of experience flying this type of machine at night and this was over two months previously, which is somewhat lax together with no dual flying either. Again the investigators found that in view of the changeable weather conditions and Smith's total inexperience of night flying on the Blenheim, the flying exercise was not fully justified.

As men flew and died, earlier during the day the country's leadership changed. Neville Chamberlain resigned and Winston Churchill replaced him as British prime minister. This was the day the Germans opened their offensive *Blitzkrieg* which began at dawn on Friday May 10, 1940 with coordinated assaults across the borders of Holland, Belgium and Luxembourg and synchronized relentless air attacks along the Western Front. Headquarters staff had been requested by the Royal Navy to mount patrols in the vicinity of the Dutch coast. At Bircham Newton it was stifling hot even before midday, as crews waited for the next sortie. 'Pissy' Peacock took off in L9404, leading Norman Smith in P4845 and Norman Savill in L9256. They flew an uneventful morning patrol off Borkum, Dutch Texel, and the Frisian islands. The crews of 235 were then active almost constantly until dusk. Laughlin (L9404), Ryan (L9259) and Woodger (L9256) moved hurriedly in the afternoon from Bircham Newton to Manston to provide air cover for No 1 Ground Reconnaissance Unit being deployed to Holland. Sergeant Norman Savill wrote:

"It was an extraordinary day; arriving at Manston as 600 Squadron was just being debriefed. Outside, Pilot Officer Richard 'Dickie' Haines was levied. Unfortunately someone high up who had no conception of modern warfare or what was happening in Rotterdam expected them to be able to do circuits of Waalhaven aerodrome, which was in German hands, strafing and shooting everything up and returning unscathed. Jimmy Wells, Hugh Rowe, and Mike Anderson had all been shot down. It was a great loss. Our squadron had recently done some training with them."

The last reconnaissance flight from Bircham Newton for the day took off at 19.30 as the light began to fade. It was described as 'an uneventful flight' to Holland until N6193 was targeted by anti-aircraft fire. Pilot Officer Robert Patterson in the confines of the Blenheim cockpit was having major difficulties reaching the fuel cocks to switch over to the main fuel tanks, his bulky Mae West encumbering his movement resulting in premature engine failure. Believing that there was insufficient fuel in the tank of the remaining engine to remain aloft he manually pumped down the undercarriage and flaps. Having informed the watch office at 10.15 hours of his situation, Patterson was relieved when the wheels touched the ground at 10.30 hours. However relief turned to horror within a split second upon realization that the undercarriage had not locked into place. The legs folded, sending N6193 slamming into the grass runway. The propellers buckled as it careered along, sparks flew into the air and N6193 caught fire. It finally came to rest and the three crew scrambled clear. Patterson and naval observer Lieutenant David Ogilvie RN suffered slight injuries and were rushed to the station medical centre. Both recovered fully and returned to active duty. Sadly, in two months Patterson would die, and Ogilvie was killed on HMS *Glorious* in June. Despite the sketchy information from the Low Countries the Air Ministry requested Bowhill to draw on Coastal Command squadrons in the north, using a minimum number of crews and twin-engine fighter aircraft to help reinforce those squadrons who were to be embroiled in the forthcoming operations.

Like many others New Zealander Alfie Fowler, a Neon sign erector, with 248 Squadron recoiled at the idea of killing or being killed yet he had volunteered for the RAF in 1938 knowing that he would be putting himself in exceptional danger. According to fellow New Zealander Sam McHardy their conversations centred on waiting to be called upon to start operations against the enemy and fighting for their ultimate goal of freedom. Fowler didn't have to wait long. In the late afternoon of May 10, Blenheim fighters of 248 were ordered to fly to Bircham Newton to bolster 235 Squadron. The crews detailed were a typical mix of class and nationality. "Myself, Morewood, and Fowler were dispatched to fly to RAF Bircham Newton in Norfolk with three machines to reinforce and make our presence known to the Dutch," recalled McHardy. As the aircraft sped over the countryside, sat inside the cramped fuselage were two aircraft mechanics and a 'bag of tools' in each machine. Overalls done up to the neck, they tried to stay warm as the wind blew through the mid-upper turret. "It was like sitting on Brighton pier in a force ten gale." On arrival they were wild with excitement but at the same time apprehensive. All would be in action at first light the next day, thrust into the forefront over the Netherlands.

CHAPTER FOUR

Prelude and Fugue

Further re-enforcements landed at Bircham Newton in the shape of N3529, R3623 and L9409 from 254 Squadron. "We all got on well together and I think that applied throughout the trade protection squadrons. We were thrown together so much. You just had to get on with people, you could not afford to be indifferent as our activities increased and became more intense," recalled Pilot Officer 'Hal' Randall. 235 Squadron's A Flight and 254's detachment were called upon early and had their first encounter with the enemy over European soil. It would be a memorable day, both for 235 Squadron and one of its flight commanders, Flight Lieutenant Manwaring. It marked the day when he shot down his first enemy aircraft, the first for the unit in this war. For those from 254 exchanging the bleak surrounds of Lossiemouth it was like being on a pilgrimage. Woken at 02.30 the prospect of breakfast cheered them. After a lengthy coordination talk all eighteen men left the dispersal hut, the dew making elaborate patterns on their flying boots as they walked. Armed and fuelled, ground crew waited patiently by their charge, making small talk and adjusting their kit before they heaved themselves up on the portside.

Flying Officer Bain was in R3623, Pilot Officer Hal Randall in L9409 and Sergeant Albert Tubbs flew N3529. They climbed into their cockpits, setting off at 04.30 hours. After a quick circuit of the aerodrome in a few minutes all were formed up. Manwaring in L9324 led the section. Leaving the comfort of the English coastline they climbed through 4/10s of cumulus cloud. The remainder of the sky was completely empty and the grey sea stretched out below. Everyone kept a sharp look out, it was difficult to imagine there was a war on. Finally, after a monotonous flight Manwaring's observer found the escort vessel and convoy amongst the waves off Texel. They began flying in circles over the ships, gradually increasing circumference and in time covering the area south of The Hague. Whilst patrolling the convoy a black shape was sighted – the outline of a Heinkel III.

The Luftwaffe crew was on an unescorted reconnaissance sortie inland over Oostvoorne. Manwaring immediately pulled out giving the instruction "stay with the convoy but watch my back". He increased speed and closed, intercepting it near Middelburg. His observer glanced quickly down at the seventeenth and eighteenth century large merchant houses standing near the canals, as his pilot let go a burst from astern at long range. This unsuspecting crew saw nothing "until the bullets ripped into their bomber". With no return fire a second later the Heinkel exploded into a ball of flames and plummeted earthwards. Unbeknownst to the Blenheim crew a high explosive shell from a nearby Dutch anti-aircraft unit had hit the Heinkel at the same moment Manwaring's rounds impacted. Out of the twisted wreckage, a single parachute fluttered open. Obergefr S. Klug, seeing the ground rushing up towards him, bent his legs slightly at the knee and tucked his elbows in at the side trying to prevent injury. As he touched the ground he hauled in his parachute and was

Royal Marines – Hook of Holland May 12, 1940 – pose for a photograph, whilst overhead 235 Squadron Blenheims keep guard. (*Andrew Bird*)

captured. At 06.30 hours the Heinkel crashed onto the beach at Renesse, north of Haamstede. The Dutch sifted through the wreckage and recovered and later buried the bodies of Uffz E. Steussloff, Uffz R. Wunderlich (FF) and Uffz H. von Hoff. Wiggs, satisfied at a job well done and pleased that months of training at 54 Squadron and with his new colleagues at 235 hadn't been wasted, started to have a little more faith in his Bristol Blenheim fighter. After continuing their escort they headed home, landing at 08.30 hours. They switched off their motors and began clambering down, in unison the ground trades swarming in to turn the machines around quickly for the next sortie. Manwaring's ground crew were jubilant, elated that their boy had got a Hun.

With unlimited visibility along the Dutch coast the Admiralty requested further reconnaissance patrols. Bain in R3623, Randall in L9409 and Tubbs in N3529 were pitched in at the deep end again, sweeping along the Dutch coast from Texel to Amsterdam before landing back at 19.15 hours.

The first scramble on May 12 saw one section become airborne, taking off into the dark grey skies at 05.10 hours. These Blenheim pilots and their crews would come face to face with the Luftwaffe's most lethal weapon; the Messerschmitt Bf109E. They had been briefed to cover Royal Navy destroyers that would be putting ashore 200 Royal Marines to secure the embarkation point ready to evacuate Queen Wilhelmina and the Dutch government. Savill recalled: "I had a peculiar empty feeling about this. Peacock said 'how many aircraft? Three!' We were talked to about the operation, there was no arguing: Protect the Navy, Marines and the Dutch Royal family." With little enthusiasm they moved towards the door with these words still ringing in their ears: "Remain until the destroyers have cleared Whistle Light Buoy and attempt to stop ANY interference by enemy machines." With Pilot Officer Reginald Peacock leading in 'L-Leather' L9401, Norman Smith in 'P-Pip' L9324 and Norman Savill in 'O-Orange' L9189, they flew out. The three fighters formated at 4,000 feet above the Norfolk countryside, setting course for Manston whilst, at 05.15, the Royal Navy destroyers with their

This aircraft, Blenheim Mk IVF L9449 was later lost on operations August 27, shot down by enemy fighters. The pilot, Welshman Pilot Officer Charles Arthur and the observer, Sergeant Eric Ringwood, were reported missing after they failed to return from a reconnaissance flight to the south Norwegian coast. The body of the air gunner, Sergeant Ralph Cox, was washed up on the Swedish coast. Arthur and Ringwood were never found. (*Royal Air Force Museum, London*)

consignment of Royal Marines entered the mouth of the Nieuwe Waterweg, near the Hook of Holland escorted by HMS *Wild Swan*. Peacock recorded: "Being up-front I was all right, but I had to think of the poor blighters Savill and Smith on either side and occasionally check my speed." Flying at 4,500 feet they left the southern coast of England behind and were instructed to rendezvous with three Hawker Hurricanes of Blue Section, 151 Squadron. The Blenheims flew a holding pattern until the two sections became one at 06.00 hours. Under a brilliantly clear sky Flight Lieutenant Freddie Ives, Flying Officer Ward and Sergeant Atkinson joined the patrol over Whistle Light Buoy. Ives reported:

"We left Martlesham at 05.00 hours and proceeded to 4,500 feet to the Whistle Light Buoy, just outside the Hook of Holland canal. Here we met three long-nosed Blenheims and patrolled with them. Our objective turned out to be one cruiser, one patrol vessel, four destroyers, two minesweepers and a small vessel painted orange. We noticed that approximately fifty parachutes were lying on the ground about three miles north of the Hook. On a small aerodrome at the same place there were about fifteen enemy aircraft burnt out, or wrecked. Our patrol was over, alerted by our low fuel gauges."

At 06.25 Blue Section, after exactly one and a half hours in the air, peeled away, waggled their wings and broke off into a canter for Suffolk. As they became specks in the distance Peacock barked into the R/T for Smith and Savill to tighten up. Peacock was clearly nervous. The machines circled at 4,500 feet. The view was magnificent but the scars of war could be seen. Peacock's observer Pilot Officer Hugh 'Ollie' Wakefield using an HB pencil noted down, "two thought to be transports, standing off near destroyers which are moored at the jetty. Four aircraft burnt out at The Hague and six to eight at Rotterdam aerodrome."

Three destroyers stood guard off The Hook, whilst a fourth disgorged lightly armed Royal Marines who were awaiting the arrival of the Dutch queen at The Hague. They took up defensive positions as commanded by Major Bertram G.B. Mitchell. Mitchell wrote: "Landed when three Blenheim fighters were circling around. Ten minutes after landing we had our first excitement; a flight of German Messerschmitt aircraft appeared and an air-battle took place."

Unseen and with tremendous speed Messerschmitt 110s immediately bounced the circling RAF aircraft. Momentarily distracted as glowing yellow tracer flashed past L9401's starboard wing, Peacock realized the danger and banked hard over. Oh God! Masses of them! In the cramped cockpit of L9189 observer Sergeant Henry Sunderland had come forward and just handed Savill a cup of hot tea from their thermos flask. Savill was bringing the cup up to his mouth to take a sip when bullets thumped through their aircraft, sending the hot cup and contents flying. The tea smeared the inside of the Perspex window as he moved his right hand instantly down to the control stick to steady it. At the same time his feet worked the rudder pedals and his Blenheim yawed to the right; this instinctive reaction saved his crew. Sunderland frantically screwed the flask lid on, placing it in the bicycle clips attached on the starboard side, and then took up his position to look out of the port window behind his pilot. Lifting the catch it slid back, Sunderland then squeezed his head through the gap, inches aft from a rotating propeller. Looking rearward he could see outgoing bursts of machine-gun fire from the power-operated turret and began signaling with his left arm extended, using his thumb to indicate to Savill exactly in which direction to turn. In three vital seconds the enemy had lost their advantage. All three RAF machines fought back and were bravely holding their own, in a series of individual swirling dogfights.

L9324 was being thrown around the sky with a 110 seemingly glued to its tail. Air gunner LAC Thomas Lowry steered his turret around, then with the butt firmly in his shoulder and the target in sight, the seventeen year old pulled the trigger giving their pursuer a couple of steady long bursts from 200 yards. His tracer thudded home. Smith reduced speed, as had his enemy, and both began trying to turn inside one another. At some point he commenced a stall turn and temporarily lost height and sight of the Messerschmitt, flying through dense smoke before rejoining the aerial duel. Smith called for help "to get the blighter off his tail". Savill opened fire with the belly pack at 300 yards, hitting an engine and dispatching the 110 into the sea, (claim unconfirmed). The odds worsened dramatically when two sections of four single-engine Messerschmitts of II/.JG 27 on a freelance patrol between Waalhaven-Rotterdam joined them at 07.55/08.00 hours. They commenced line astern attacks but broke formation when the Blenheims turned to meet them. A spiralling dogfight ensued for ten minutes. Peacock disengaged from a duel, evaluated the situation then latched onto a Bf109E flying off to starboard. Heaving L9401 around he fired a short burst for five seconds sending bullets ripping into the enemy fighter; the 109 belched forth clouds of black smoke and was seen spiralling down between The Hague and The Hook [unconfirmed]. But the pendulum now swung in the enemy's favour. They were overwhelmed and outgunned.

The observer on Peacock's crew, Sergeant Clifford Thorley, watched helplessly as 'P-Pip' L9324 piloted by twenty-five-year-old Norman Smith swerved off losing height. His starboard engine was ablaze, the engine cowling glowing red like a furnace. Seconds earlier at 08.14 two Bf109Es simultaneously attacked from the port and starboard quarters. Lowry yelled out the range to Smith whilst returning fire towards the starboard 109 at a range of 250 yards. Flashes erupted from his wings, rounds zipping over Lowry's head like wasps. He replied using three magazines. As he lowered his seat to pick another he felt a couple of slaps on his legs as holes rapidly appeared in the fuselage around his turret. The second 109 broke off its attack from the opposite beam but bullets from both enemy fighters had already punctured the thin metal construction leaving a series of holes stretching from the cockpit, starboard wing and upper fuselage. Bullets had thumped into Lowry's back taking his breath away, the small tractor-type seat offering little protection. His turret no longer responded to pressure on the hand bar – the hydraulics had evidently been severed. Thick black smoke and flames belched from the starboard radial engine. Shouts of "Lowry!" over the intercom went unheeded. Midway down the battle-scarred fuselage rays of light glinted through the holes as the body of the youngest air combatant to die over the Netherlands hung limply in the turret, punctured by over a dozen 7.92 rounds. In front, in a smouldering cockpit Smith was alone. His observer Sergeant John Robertson was killed in the same burst of fire, a gruesome sight. Smith believed a round had hit him too. His right side began to ache and his own movements became sluggish as he struggled desperately with the unresponsive controls.

Losing height he singled out a place in which to bring the crippled Blenheim to rest. On a lovely quiet spring day 'P-Pip' crashed at 08.15 in a small field in Nieuwlander Polder, near The Hook of Holland. L9324 slithered along on its underside, brushing past two Junkers 52 transports that had lain undisturbed since May 10. Its twisted fuselage halted near a dyke and the wreckage spread over a wide area. Smith was somewhat dazed having smacked his forehead on the shattered instrument panel. He unclipped his Sutton harness; the locking pin dropped out freeing all straps simultaneously and in some considerable pain he gradually hauled himself out into the sunlight, momentarily shielding his eyes from the glare. He then slumped into a heap beside the forward fuselage. Not long afterwards a joint German and Dutch salvage and medical party arrived at the scene. Miraculously, twenty-five-year-old Norman Smith was found alive. He was sat in the mud beside the wreck, badly injured with his open white silk parachute billowing in the breeze, as if flying a flag of surrender.

Smith was given medical treatment by Dutch medical staff wearing white surgical coats for a head wound and entry hole from a 7.92 round in his side. A shot of morphine did little to dull the pain. Placed onto a stretcher the 'British flyer' was then transported to a hospital in The Hague. In one of the hospital theatres Dutch surgeons tried valiantly for one and a half hours to save the young man but failed. Unable to re-inflate his lung, he relapsed and suffocated because of a hemorrhage. Twenty-nine minutes away at the crash site two bodies were extracted from L9324 and eventually placed in field grey ponchos. German soldiers dug shallow graves beside L9324 and the two ponchos were placed within. Earth was shovelled over them and two simple wooden crosses fashioned to mark their former combatants' field graves. On May 28 Robinson and Lowry were excavated and transported to the Hook of Holland general cemetery where they were reburied in coffins draped with a Dutch flag by the German garrison with full military honours.

As friends died Savill was fighting to stay alive, embroiled in a dogfight with a single Bf109E latched onto the tail of L9189. Savill pushed violently on the control column trying to shake the fighter off, flinging his Blenheim into a sudden dive and losing 2,000 feet. As he pulled out he was pounced upon again by an enemy fighter making a head-on

Norman Alfred Savill was born in Sussex in 1919. He joined the RAF on a short service commission in April 1939. He was posted to 6 Flying Training School, Netheravon receiving the rank of pilot officer on November 6, 1939. Savill joined 235 Squadron and on May 12, 1940, was shot down flying a Mk IVF L9189 during a dogfight over the Hook of Holland. He bailed out injured and was badly burned, becoming a POW. His observer Sergeant Henry Sunderland and air gunner LAC Roy Tyler were killed during the mêlée and buried at Oostvoorne.

attack. Instinctively Savill pressed the firing button, the salvo caught the 109 slap on its nose and engine and it spiralled earthwards (unconfirmed). 'O-Orange' had been transformed into a sieve and both observer Sergeant Henry Sunderland and air gunner LAC Roy Tyler aged nineteen succumbed during this last mêlée. L9189 was alight, and in the now dysfunctional cockpit flames licked all around Savill, scorching through his flying overalls. Undeterred by the increasing intensity of the heat and fumes swirling around he finally decided to exit. The Blenheim was dropping like a stone at an extremely low altitude and flames just missed him as he tumbled out. As he accelerated through the sky he fumbled for the ripcord and was brought the right way up with a violent jerk that nearly knocked the breath from his body as the canopy blossomed. He looked up – it was not fully deployed! With the ground rushing up towards him his body crumpled as he impacted heavily at high speed into flat farmland along the Kloosterweg, between Brielle and Oostvoorne. But his ordeal did not end there; he looked up to find Dutch soldiers approaching. Slightly concussed the young pilot heard shouting; "U bent onze gevangene" (You are our prisoner). Savill said: "The Dutch soldiers who ran to the scene thought I was a German pilot. They were pointing rifles at me with large bayonets, whilst others manhandled me to stand up." The soldiers made preparations to shoot, cocking their weapons and taking aim. Despite being severely wounded and burnt the young pilot officer managed with difficulty to convince them that he was a Royal Air Force officer by prizing open his overalls and showing them the RAF wings on his uniform. Savill recalled: "I was in a bloody mess, in great pain and my wounds hurt like hell. I had a severely broken leg with skin hanging off, like a butcher slices ham. Now some buggers were going to shoot me!"

The Dutch soldiers quickly became very friendly and after collecting Savill's parachute transported him to Vlaardingen hospital, with two soldiers either side helping him. Nurse Kea Bonwman was the first person he saw. Fortunately the Dutch doctors were not busy despite the intense ground fighting. As Bonwman began preparing him for surgery his breathing rate was very shallow. The young officer was whisked into an operating room where the Dutch surgeon was able to save his left leg. Heavily sedated Savill came round; he then spent the next nine months recovering from his burns, receiving saline baths. Kea Bonwman looked after him for the whole period he was in hospital. While he was there Savill entertained the Dutch children on the ward. Ton v.d. Hoeven recalled, "I was aged fourteen, on the ward at the same time. He was a great guy who amused the young children, made up songs for them too." The young pilot officer was often 'exhibited' by German Luftwaffe and army officers during visiting times on the ward particularly when senior officials arrived to visit German wounded until he left in January 1941. Pilot Officer Norman Savill was destined to spend four years in Stalag Luft III Sagan, and later helped with the preparation for the 'Great Escape' in March 1944.

Savill survived his ordeal and was taken to Vlaardingen hospital. There he was placed under the care of Nurse Kea Bonwman until January 1941.

Scarcely had the air battle begun than the sky emptied. Peacock, who had been at the heart of the battle, survived two dogfights and returned to base to re-arm. They had been flying for nearly four hours and his aircraft was damaged, he prayed it would stay in one piece for the return journey. As he flew over Cromer, walkers looked up to see a tatty twin-engine plane's black and white underside stained with the scars of battle. The Blenheim skirted the roof tops on its way to the aerodrome. Bircham Newton waited; their estimated time of arrival of 08.40 had now passed, and another twenty-five tense minutes went by before the watch office was contacted. "Pancake" came the instructions. The solitary machine limped in over the boundary landing at 09.10, the sole survivor of this skirmish. The tatty Blenheim 'L-Leather' L9401 came to a halt. An assortment of men and women rushed to help. Something of the hectic confusion was conveyed through Peacock's quote in an early squadron periodical; "One does not know what happened to my companions. Attacked by four or eight Messerschmitts, I gave two a squirt and may have shot one down before being forced to make a run for it."

The squadron 'Spy' interviewed the surviving crew: Cliff Thorley wrote "being debriefed after this operation myself and the crew were extremely peckish and felt some lunch wouldn't be out of place. I was rather startled to find it was only just after 9 o'clock. We'd been up since 03.30 of course, but already it seemed as though we had done a full morning's work."

Situation reports were typed on a portable Imperial Good Companion Model T with the fading emblem of 'By Appointment to King George V'. Peacock's report is dated May 13, 1940: "One Messerschmitt was seen to be going down in flames and another aircraft believed to be a Messerschmitt was seen burning on the ground five miles south-west of The Hook. One Blenheim was seen with its starboard engine on fire." The young WAAF doing the typing was "short in stature, full of life and energy – it's a pleasure to have her on the squadron", wrote the adjutant. That evening after holding a defensive line the Royal Marines wrote an entry into their diary: "After this air-battle the remaining Blenheim departed in a hurry, leaving the Germans in complete command of the air."

With their first major dogfight came the first casualties. "My God, how ghastly for the parents or guardians". Thomas Lowry was noted in the squadron diary as a "promising youngster from Belfast, Ireland receiving training to become a qualified wireless operator/air gunner (Wop/Ag) and with it promotion and pilot Norman Smith Phd is noted as a seasoned university fellow".

There was no lessening of pressure as the Luftwaffe now concentrated on causing havoc by smashing Dutch sea, road and rail links to prevent the forward movement of men and supplies and wrecking the fragile communications with their Heinkels, Dorniers and Junkers savaging the allies' supply lines. Coastal Command Blenheim fighters were required to give protective cover for the Royal Navy over the port of Flushing as a merchant ship unloaded its cargo of ammunition. Arriving over the port at the specified time R3623, L9409 and N3529 finally located the naval vessels. Whilst circling the town and port Pilot Officer Hal Randall in L9409 noticed bomb bursts exploding below in the town square, close to the ammunition ship and jetty. Scanning the surrounding blue sky Randall located and counted seventeen enemy bombers, a mixture of Junkers and Heinkels in very close formation. Unleashing their deadly payloads, the allied pilots felt no concern that the odds were stacked against them. There was frantic activity as they switched their fuel tanks over to the outer tanks to 100-octane fuel, levers were turned and emergency full boost applied. With a sudden surge of power, the chase was on. With safety catches off and a faint cry of "Tally Ho" Flying Officer Bill Bain in R3623, and Sergeant Albert Tubbs in N3529 followed Randall's lead and engaged this superior force over Vlissingen in a head-on attack.

There was a pitched battle spaced out between 5,000 feet and 300 feet over the Dutch countryside, assisted by anti-aircraft fire from the destroyers. One bomb was seen to explode fifty yards from the ammunition ship as Randall darted in quickly firing short two-second bursts catching four of the bombers on the outer edge of the formation. Seeing this sudden threat three broke away, escaping into a nearby cloud layer. The fourth, a Junkers 88, was slow to react and took no avoiding action and passed underneath the Blenheim. Randall gave chase and as the enemy aircraft loomed in the ring sight he automatically pressed the firing button for a second. His Blenheim rose slightly as 300 rounds spat out, arcing off but falling short. Not wanting to give up Randall suddenly found that L9409 was gaining; so much so that the Blenheim fighter was quickly on the Junkers' starboard side. Drawing level and formating on the enemy aircraft, its drab olive colour upper surfaces and markings were clearly distinguishable. The young Leading Aircraftman Clark in the upper turret unleashed the full contents of three magazines, interchanging until all his magazines for the Vickers K gun were spent. N3529 joined the mêlée, Tubbs attacking from the rear and exhausting all his front gun ammunition whilst receiving return fire. The German pilot regained his composure and began evasive manoeuvres, opening up his throttles and leaving both crews frustrated in his wake.

German invasion map of the Netherlands. The battle lasted from May 10, 1940 until the main Dutch forces surrendered on the 14th.

The Junkers 88 of 7./LG1 returned damaged to its aerodrome. Fw W. Flick was lifted out badly injured and transported to Lingen field hospital, Lower Saxony, Germany where he died of his wounds that night.

After forty minutes of dogfighting the Coastal Command boys made for base somewhat dejected. Their fuel gauge needles read almost empty; they had been so consumed in battle that they would touch down with less than 15 gallons remaining. Below the ammunition ship was able to unload in relative safety once the aerial fight had ceased. Passing over Flushing, it was noted that an aerodrome was littered with abandoned cars, lorries, hackney cabs and horse-drawn carts and other miscellaneous obstructions with only one clear runway on the north side running east-west. Out into open water they streaked over a badly mauled merchantman sinking three miles southeast of Flushing, and another to the east, its Dutch flag fluttering in defiance. Back in Norfolk, Randall and his crew clambered down exhausted onto freshly cut grass. Looking over their aircraft they found two bullet holes in one of the propeller blades and a dozen or more were found in one wing of L9409. "It will have to be repaired", said Chief Cox who had arrived on the scene. Unfortunately repair material was in short supply on the Norfolk aerodrome and for RAF Coastal Command as a whole. The following day Blenheim L9409 was on the unserviceable status sheet. Two more sorties laboured up, Flight Lieutenant Dick Cross in P9256 with Pilot Officer David Woodger but they were recalled. Cross was back in the air within twenty minutes in P9256 and Pilot Officer Michael Ryan in P9259 making an offensive patrol over Flushing and returning at dusk; Cross reporting "no signs of enemy in air or on the land or sea".

After their hectic day of operations the young RAF airmen retreated to either The Norfolk Hero or The King's Head Inn public houses. At The Norfolk Hero the improved trade proved too much for the elderly couple who owned it so they just sat in their chairs and told the men of 235, 248 and 254 to help themselves and put the money in the drawer. Sergeant Aubrey Lancaster noted "I don't believe that anyone missed paying for any of their drinks that night". Airmen and women left to the sounds of 'Roll out the Barrel' being sung while overhead the rumble of radial engines could be heard as Fairey Swordfish of 815 Squadron Fleet Air Arm were coming back from bombing Waalhaven aerodrome after the Dutch had requested RAF ground support. As they returned from their night out they walked along the roads skirting the aerodrome and saw an assortment of machines around the edge; Avro Ansons, Fairey Swordfish, Army Co-operation Lysanders and an odd Spitfire or two picketed down. Three complete crews slept over at the dispersal in order to be ready at dawn, when they awoke to the smell of baked beans, bacon and eggs being sent over from the mess.

Pilot Officer McHardy remembered, "we swallowed the hot tea and dipped bread into our fried eggs gratefully, and then streamed off as a message came through from Group that cover was required for the navy. Five minutes later we were off, in single file, to help our colleagues."

These Blenheim fighters were soon in formation and clambering south, their brief "to protect ships in Helder". Rain ran down the Perspex as a combined section of 248 and 254 Squadrons covered the Royal Navy destroyer *Valentine* together with a Dutch naval warship which were bombarding the coast near the Zuider Zee. Within seconds of crossing into Dutch airspace, five Messerschmitt 110s attacked from out of the sun breaking up the formation into a series of aerial duels. Flight Lieutenant Roger Morewood in L9457, Pilot Officer McHardy in L9450, Pilot Officer Derek Shawe in L9397 and Sergeant Albert Tubbs in N3529 broke apart and went straight in, each picking out an adversary. Something of the hectic confusion was conveyed in the narrative by Flight Lieutenant Morewood: "'S-Sugar' was immediately engaged by three different head-on attacks at close range of 150 to 100 yards all at once, several long and short bursts from my front machine guns and single rear gun

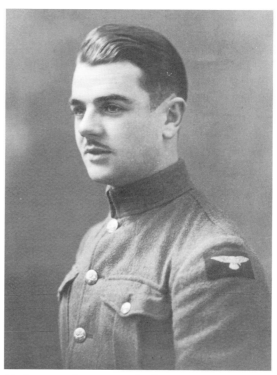

Air Gunner Robert Kenworthy flew with 248 Squadron during the Phoney War. He was crewed with Flight Lieutenant Roger Morewood in July 1940, flying L9456, and Pilot Officer Victor Ricketts in R3625. Unfortunately his operational flights were limited to before the 10th; therefore Robert did not qualify for the Battle of Britain clasp. (*Sue Kenworthy*)

were fired." With perspiration on his forehead Morewood let go a three-second burst at two different 110s, which seemed quite oblivious to his presence, before they entered cloud. No rear gunfire from the 110s was noticed. 'S-Sugar' ultimately ran out of ammunition and left the battle:

"I dived down to sea level, levelling out at fifty feet to head for home, followed by a single Messerschmitt. At this point the intercom was invaluable between the rear gunner and myself. He was shouting as the Messerschmitt was 400 yards away. Opening fire, I was able to make a sudden climb of fifty feet to port and watched the enemy tracer pass underneath. I pushed my machine to 250 mph, aiming towards the grey shape in the water, praying that they didn't shoot me out of the sky. I streaked by the naval destroyer *Valentine* and their anti-aircraft guns pursued the Messerschmitt and ultimately it was shaken off."

In the same mêlée, Pilot Officer McHardy found that his adrenalin was flowing fast, this being his first taste of operational flying. He wrote:

"We levelled off at 3,000 feet and had not been circling long before German aircraft were sighted heading straight at our Blenheim fighters at the same altitude in line-astern. Morewood shouted 'Break, break!' As they came level at 500 yards we turned to port, trying to get an effective short burst in before they passed us. Before I could react a 110 had pulled out of the line and made a head-on attack, with others following behind. I returned fire but one had also managed to get on my tail. Fortunately the cloud base was not too far above and I pulled the stick back frantically, desperately trying to get into its inviting cover. Our rear gunner put in some accurate bursts of 100 rounds, which forced the enemy to break off pursuit. I poked the nose out of the cloud and pounced on a Messerschmitt off to starboard. We brought 'L-Leather' around for a head-on attack, firing 1,000 rounds, and then passed over it off to starboard. With our control surfaces still working we headed back to the scene of the first action, no friendly or hostile aircraft were seen so we returned to station."

Shawe, Tubbs and McHardy landed with no sign of their leader Morewood, the other pilots anticipating the worst. Then a sad crippled 'S-Sugar' L9457 appeared; flying in low from the east with the port engine misfiring it landed gingerly. The motors stopped at the end of the runway. The fighter looked like a cheese grater with considerable damage. There were bullet holes through the Perspex by the pilot and the observer seat was shredded, a portion of Perspex was also pierced severely in the gunner's turret. Pipes to the port engine had been shot through but this only affected the port engine gauge. Morewood recalled, "what I did not realize was that fuel was leaking out". Subsequently this motor had begun misfiring two miles from the aerodrome. Grim faced, twenty-one-year-old Flight Lieutenant Roger Morewood emerged from the cockpit with his big blond handlebar moustache glistening in the sunlight. A fitter counted seventy-two bullet holes in the machine. L9457 was patched up and put back into the air, only to be lost three months later.

235 Squadron was ordered up mid-afternoon to carry out two offensive patrols over The Hague. Flight Lieutenant Richard Cross led Pilot Officers Booth in P4845, Ryan in L9450 and Woodger in L9395 through the smoke which shrouded the coast. Looking down he saw that "The Hague as a whole was ablaze with dense smoke in places". On the ground a German mechanized column was rapidly advancing from Rotterdam. The evacuation of the Dutch royal party and government began at 12.00 hours. Queen of the Netherlands Wilhelmina and Crown Princess Juliana boarded HMS *Hereward*, a Royal Navy destroyer under the stewardship of Lieutenant Commander C.W. Greening, RN, who recalled "I have never seen a woman so calm and reassuring in all my life". The destroyer was to take her south, however, after her party was aboard Zeeland came under heavy attack from the Luftwaffe and "with attacks being made on all sides of your country" Greening politely told the Dutch royal party that it was considered too dangerous to return. Wilhelmina was left with no option but to accept His Majesty George VI's offer of refuge. Meanwhile, as the four Coastal Command fighters kept watch overhead they were subjected to spasmodic anti-aircraft fire. Forming into line

astern Cross led Booth, Ryan, and Woodger abeam shadowing as the destroyer got into open water. A relay of assorted RAF machines covered its crossing and that of HMS *Windsor* until 20.00 hours. Thirty minutes after the final naval party left a heavy raid was staged, during which the jetty was bombed and machine-gunned.

16 Group rang up asking if everyone had got back. Woodger came into the officers' mess still looking rather white after having been shot at, however after a few drinks he decided to stay. Ginger Bowhill knew how badly his own men were suffering. Organizational changes saw Flight Lieutenant Alan 'Penny' Pennington-Legh landed with a new batch of reinforcements, who all joined the party and "everyone had a grand time". This party later moved to the WAAF mess after permission was granted, ending in the early hours with plates of ham and eggs.

Coastal Command pilots and machines were immediately thrown into a futile attempt to stem the German *Blitzkrieg* advance that was cascading freely westwards at an unprecedented speed that a number of British senior officers working to 1914 – 1918 rules did not foresee. This was the new age of mechanized warfare which produced an increased need for aerial activity. Take-off was scheduled for 11.10 hours on May 14, with an estimated flying time of three hours thirty minutes.

Four fighters stood waiting: L9395, P9259, L9396, and L9450. Around them the countryside was blossoming into a wealth of greenness. In the adjacent fields blackbirds were busy among

Pilot Officer Anthony Booth was born in Natal, South Africa and was the son of Alan Foster Booth and Maude Ida Booth, of Selukwe, Southern Rhodesia. He was brought up in Johannesburg. Booth served for six years with the British South Africa Police [BSAP] in Southern Rhodesia, and was in charge of a station. Mention was made of him in *South Africa* magazine shortly before his death on May 29, 1940. It reads: "Pilot Officer 'Tony' Booth, Royal Air Force, passed through London last Saturday with no leisure for anything but a visit to Rhodesia House and a glance at the home newspapers." (*Theo Boiten*)

the new potatoes, eager for slugs and snails. Flight Lieutenant Manwaring learnt his flight would be assigned to protect British troops on the ground leaving Dutch soil. At 11.15 four Blenheim fighters were off the ground within three minutes and arrived over The Hague at midday. They stood watch in tight formation as troops embarked on two naval destroyers.

As the drone of aircraft engines became louder, soldiers on the ground peered upwards. From their defensive positions one of the Bren gun crew turned his gun on its tripod mount towards the approaching twin-engine machines. Suddenly from a vantage point there were shouts of "they're ours, hold your fire!" The Royal Marines report noted: "At 12:00 hours four British Blenheim aircraft appeared for the protection of the embarkation. The feeling of relief on seeing them is great."

The relay continued with a further six machines covering the withdrawal along the Hook of Holland, 235 being just one of the RAF units assigned. Taking a glance at his altimeter Manwaring in the lead Blenheim had taken his vic below 500 feet. He wrote: "Saw the Netherlands on fire. Refugees, horse-drawn carts, a few cars at the port. Bodies were strewn over the roads; all had been torn to pieces by bullets or bombs from German aircraft." Another observed: "Five smashed Ju 52s

A Ju 52 lies near a dyke amongst the cows. Ju 52s were lost in Holland, due to varying circumstances. This was often due to the pilots mistakenly using soggy landing grounds, which were not able to support the heavy craft. Almost an entire year's production was lost in the invasion of the Netherlands. (*Bob van Wye*)

wrecked in the fields behind the harbour, together with one completely wrecked Blenheim, one 109 crashed on the beach. Some mechanized activity on land near the harbour." Speeding away from the scene, heavy thick black smoke was seen twelve miles away down the canal. It was carnage on a grand scale.

It was hard for those drawing breath, whilst writing to loved ones about the scenes of devastation they had witnessed. It was similar to H. G. Wells' *The Shape of Things To Come*. There was a break in Dutch operations when an urgent request for fighter escort to a southbound convoy was telephoned through to their Bircham Newton dispersal hut. This was seen as a brief respite, as three patrols were flown 100 degrees off Lowestoft within a radius of forty-eight miles, between 09.53 and 17.25 hours.

In the evening pressed against the officers' mess bar Pilot Officer McHardy was cornered by green pilots asking "what was it like being under fire?" The young New Zealander obliged, he said with restraint, "This is no 'line-shoot'…" Also listening were pilots from B Flight 213 and 229 Squadrons before their early departure on what one described as the 'Daily Cooks Tour Excursion' by Fighter Command 11 and 12 Group. They did little to disturb the Luftwaffe's flow or freedom to attack unmolested, such as when a Heinkel III was observed twenty-five miles off Ostend bombing a naval unit, one of which fell away exploding thirty yards from its port beam. Flying Officer John Laughlin (L9404) was leading with Pilot Officers Michael Ryan (L9256) and David Woodger (R9396) in line astern, all three pulled out the throttles and begin to climb after the Heinkel which at first escaped by flying into the sun. The three chased it unsuccessfully and it then disappeared into the clouds. That is the only opportunity that presented itself to 235 Squadron on May 17 and all were back by 07.30 hours.

Weather flights were also encompassed into the trade protection units' routines. Sergeant Aubrey Lancaster with Pilot Officers John Cronan and air gunner Phillip Lloyd were to be sent up to investigate the weather. They got to bed early and at 03.00 hours an orderly woke Lancaster, "I made my way to the kitchen where the duty cook always seemed to have a lovely metal pot of nice strong tea ready. Whilst sipping that he asked how I liked my bacon and eggs and in an instant a sizzling plate of bacon, eggs and fried bread appeared in front of me. The kitchen was always lovely and warm." And so they left. The crew saw nothing; good weather prevailed with exceptionally good visibility as far as the Belgian coast, but the allocated crews on readiness had to wait until after lunch for their next encounter.

Having consumed oxtail soup, shepherds pie, carrots, roast potatoes with gravy followed by treacle pudding and custard, three Blenheims of 248 Squadron were scrambled to cover the converted trawler *Arctic Hunter* carrying refugees from Ostend. A Flight detachment, commanded by Alan Pennington-Legh in L9456 was leading Pilot Officers McHardy (L9392) and Alfred Fowler (L9452) from the flax-town Foxton. McHardy's undercarriage lever was a bit sticky but everything locked in place, "at 13.40 we circled twice" sweeping low over the aerodrome then onto Zeebrugge, midway across climbing to 5,000 feet, the visibility was good in the area. Making landfall over Zeebrugge at 14.40: "We duly found the convoy amongst what seemed like thousands of vessels ranging in size, all fleeing the continent." Pennington-Legh banked hard over to starboard, Fowler and McHardy followed, and began circling. Another convoy in the distance proceeded along the coast southwest of Nieuport, then at 16.23 Pilot Officer Morris observed through his field glasses a merchant ship being bombed three miles off Blankenberge by Luftwaffe Junkers 87 bombers. McHardy yelled into the R/T to Pennington-Legh and all three were poised to attack when a strange aircraft was noticed. The leader's machine L9456 advanced, the radial engines picking up as the boost was applied. In this adrenaline-charged atmosphere, chaos then catastrophe swiftly ensued.

McHardy and Fowler lagged behind unable to use plus nine boost, "there was a shortage, the single-engine fighters boys required 100-octane fuel more than us on Coastal, after all in theory we just ambled around the British coastline". The aircraft they'd seen swoop down released its load on an unsuspecting vessel which rocked like a pendulum as bombs burst missing it by 400 yards. Climbing away it then began to dive again, unseen by the enemy's gunners. The fighter Blenheims followed the aircraft down. With the increased acceleration McHardy found himself drawing level, the black and white crosses on the fuselage clearly visible. The German machine was virtually at a standstill, its gunner in the upper turret got a glimpse of the RAF pilot and nodded in acknowledgement. Then machine-gun fire was heard as McHardy's air gunner Leading Aircraftman Heavyside got off seventy-two rounds, "with the close proximities it was like being on a firing range". He watched through his sight as they penetrated the bomber inches away.

Immediately McHardy reacted by decreasing his speed to reposition L9392 to attack from the rear. The aircraft was initially thought to be an early version Heinkel III, but the young officer realized it was a Junkers 88A. The German instantly split right, diving for the deck. McHardy gave him a short deflection burst as he followed him vertically down. Streams of black exhaust smoke temporarily obscured Pennington-Legh's vision as pilot Obergefr T. König opened his throttles. L9456, L9392 and L9452 followed at a distance. Pennington-Legh used full throttle to catch the enemy aircraft that was "manoeuvring like a slippery snake". He continued to chase after it down the coast for six minutes. Skirting the tops of vessels it dropped down to ten feet causing a flock of sea gulls to take flight, narrowly missing the three in pursuit. McHardy was beginning to gain, "at a speed that I felt would pull the wings off the Blenheim, firing whenever I got sight of him". Pennington-Legh had an indicated air speed of 290 mph but was unable to close the 500 yards separating the Junkers from L9456. Now positioned dead astern he pressed the firing button; a fair amount of rounds hit the Junkers 88A, with McHardy's final bursts hitting too.

Within seconds bullets were stitching the water inches from both machines. As Heavyside reacted to the threat and pumped out defensive fire, his pilot broke to starboard violently and began climbing steeply at ninety degrees. Pennington-Legh appeared to have been taken by surprise. As he focused on the Junkers his observer yelled a warning: "Messerschmitt! 2,000 feet above at 2 o'clock". McHardy called a warning over the R/T as he watched two pale-blue bellies of twin-engine fighters fly overhead whilst a third broke away before the action began. Pennington-Legh jammed L9456 into a sharp right hand turn as another came in from the northeast. McHardy then observed it make a diving attack on his leader's machine. Losing sight of his companion, he threw his machine about the sky to get into an advantageous position. McHardy:

"I climbed up underneath the fuselage and gave the enemy aircraft a three-second burst of fire at 300 feet from my five Brownings. L9392 stood up on its tail. Morris observed tracer and incendiary rounds pierce the fuselage and port wing. I wheeled away from the steep climb as the enemy aircraft rolled over and glided vertically down, smoke billowing from its port wing tip. I immediately passed L9392 drawing away from me rapidly, so I opened the throttles and closed, my altimeter showing fifty feet. The Messerschmitt's rear gunner got some rounds off, hitting my starboard motor but there was no loss of revolutions on the gauge. A few seconds later its pilot put his flaps down and attempted to force land alongside a naval vessel. Upon touching the water a great cloud of spray rose up and the machine flicked over and sank, clouds of black and white smoke rose above the spot."

Morris then spotted a second on his starboard side, coloured light brown/green on the top sides and fuselage. "I brought the Blenheim into position astern when the machine broke off and climbed to about 10,000 feet and I saw nothing more of the aircraft." Pennington-Legh attacked another enemy aircraft:

"It flashed passed me on the portside, I turned to port to get on its tail, zooming ahead, climbing. I then gave my machine full throttle. My engines were racing and I caught the machine up at 8,000 feet. At 300 yards, when directly behind, I began firing intermittently. He went over on his back and spun down as if hit and out of control."

He pulled out of the dive at what seemed mere inches above the sea, then went straight into a climb, closely followed by L9456 at full throttle. At 5,000 feet the enemy aircraft began weaving and its pilot attempted a stall turn to port, its rear gunner returning fire. Pennington-Legh put a four-second burst into the upper port wing surface where it joins the fuselage. Tracer and incendiary rounds punctured fuel and wiring cables which ignited, fanning flames inside the glazed cabin. "Immediately sheets of flame were seen swirling around, it reminded me of a blacksmiths, the heat must have been extremely intense," Pennington-Legh wrote. With the enemy aircraft almost at stalling speed, the rear gunner opened his cupola and climbed half out. Flames licked past him and something snagged as he struggled to break free. He reached back into the cockpit and after a few seconds he fell over the side of his machine from 2,000 feet. As L9456 banked away Pennington-Legh watched a parachute open. By now the stricken aircraft was an inferno and plumes of smoke streamed out of the opening.

Those onboard the Blenheim then saw its young pilot struggling with both hands raised above his head attempting to force back his cockpit hood unsuccessfully – the intensity of the heat had fused the metal together. He was last seen banging the Perspex with both fists. His machine flipped over on its back and went into an angled dive of sixty degrees, smashing into the sea near De Panne about three miles off Blankenberge at 16.30 hours.

Out of ammunition L9456 and L9392 joined up together with Fowler in L9452, and flew back in tight formation. Upon landing Pennington-Legh related how he had exhausted all his ammunition from his gun pack, claiming to have downed three enemy aeroplanes off the coast. All three had expended 5,600 rounds. The squadron diarist continued to write in longhand: "They attacked a He. III which was bombing the convoy and drove it away, having registered some hits. They were then attacked by three Me 110s. Pennington-Legh and McHardy each shot down an Me 110 and the remainder headed for home." The three RAF crews involved in this dogfight were convinced that Messerschmitt 110s had bounced them – unfortunately a tragic case of mistaken identity had occurred. In fact two Potez 631s of AC 2 had been shot down, one by Pennington-Legh (R-Robert L9456) and the second by McHardy (G-George L9392), while the returning French aviators were convinced that they attacked three Junkers 88s.

The sole survivor of Potez 631 (serial 169) in this skirmish was Frenchman SM Jean Bot, but for him the ordeal was not yet over:

"In the dogfight, returned fire against the Junkers 88 [Blenheim L9456] but it seemed my rounds rebounded off the Perspex, I also endeavoured to shoot between the fuselage and the engine. At the time the enemy drew nearer with his machine guns and several rounds smacked into our Potez. I contacted my pilot Mtr Dupont – there was silence. I tried once more but he did not answer. More incendiaries struck the Potez, starting a fire. Flames licked my legs and I pulled my hand across my face pulling my goggles down to protect my eyes, flames ran the length of the fuselage. My own blood was everywhere too. My movements seemed sluggish and took immense effort. I was unable to release myself from the aircraft and struggled because of the air pressure, the metal was prickly with heat. The Potez was in a vertical dive at an estimated 345 mph, I guess the air speed indicator needle was going 'off the clock'. . . I had but one thought now – get out and jump. With supreme effort I wrenched myself clear of the aeroplane. I succeeded and still had enough sense, despite the immense pain that ran through me, not to pull the rip-cord too soon. Once out of the slip stream I opened my parachute."

As he floated down there was a great silence, his parachute gliding towards La Panne, Belgium. The town was a mass of civilians and Dutch, French, Belgian and English soldiers. Below faces turned skywards, soldiers unslung their rifles took aim and fired. A cracking noise was heard as rifle bullets whizzed by, "they sounded like French honey bees from Aix-en-Provence" as Bot dangled helplessly from his parachute. Thankfully their aim was off. Unaware as to where the bullets were coming from, he looked around. There were no aircraft to be seen, the sky was empty. Bot suddenly realized that the shooting was coming from the ground. They thought he was a German flyer, and still dangerous – if only that had been the case. The shooting continued throughout his descent, the parachute becoming tattered as volley after volley rang out. He dared not look up, thinking the worst. His rate of descent accelerated, as more air escaped through the bullet holes in the canopy.

Bot managed to change direction so that he didn't land in the sea. Sand cushioned his fall then, getting to his knees, he began shouting *Aviateur français, Aviateur français* his parachute still trailing behind him. "The men and women who ran to the scene had rifles and pitchforks and they were literally coming for me." A rifle butt smacked into his face. Staggering backwards, another was landed above his right eye, the skin ripping open above the temple. Blood flowed from the open wound and there was a cheer of "Kill the Bosch, Kill the Bosch!" as women tore at his flying overalls. "The mob wanted blood and they were going to lynch me." A single shot rang out and the crowd froze as a young Belgian army lieutenant with six soldiers forced their way through to the Frenchman, fixing bayonets for protection. Disentangling Bot from his parachute the officer led him away along the promenade, to the battle-scarred Hôtel de l'Océan, a field dressing station and command post crowded with casualties, "in all forms of decay like the building", Bot recalled. As he was treated the doctors told him of his burns and that the whole of his body was lacerated and bruised. As they moved *l'aviateur français vaillant* into a corridor, he passed out. Later German troops overran the area and captured the field hospital. They also discovered the burnt-out Potez 631 two days later whilst doing a sweep of the area.

Shortly after this incident the repaired Blenheim L9404 with Flying Officer John Laughlin at the helm led Canadian Pilot Officer Curran Robinson (L9395) and Sergeant John Bessey (L9396), taking off at 17.49/17.51 and climbing away towards the coast, skirting the edge of Great Yarmouth which was littered with vessels. In line astern the three proceeded north in a sky that was relatively clear, until nearing the continent when the clouds became more prominent. Coming out of cloud a dozen fighters crossed their path as the sun disappeared behind clouds. The Blenheims were silhouetted against the sky and the dark blue-green sea below. It was an adrenaline-fuelled day, everyone was on edge and suddenly the pilots of the lower section of single-engine monoplanes saw what they thought were He 111s protruding from a cloud. With a swift move of the stick and pedals the three peeled off, picking up speed. Touching 300 mph they swept round to make a line-astern attack on their quarry, and within minutes the rear machine filled their sights. They instinctively opened up with machine-gun fire until in their headphones a shrill voice screamed "Break! Break! Friendly fighter – long-nosed Blenheim!" Each one heaved his stick and broke to starboard.

This incursion happened within the space of less than two minutes, during which Laughlin reacted quickly, firing the colours of the day twice. Nerves were somewhat frayed. After this incident Blenheim L9395 suffered a catastrophic malfunction. With no indication Robinson, his observer Sergeant Donald Mosley and air gunner LAC Albert Waddington disappeared less than one mile off Nieuport. Unaware, Laughlin and Bessey pressed onto their rendezvous eight miles away with the trawler near Ostend however, after a short time Laughlin realized L9395 had disappeared without trace. The pair found the trawler and began circling at 5,000 feet. Onboard L9369 twenty-two-year-old observer Sergeant Walter Westcott looked through his binoculars towards the Belgian port. Thick black smoke was swirling over Ostend, the town itself obscured. Troopships, ferries, fishing boats and pleasure craft could be seen evacuating the refugees, a prelude to Dunkirk. Upon their return the squadron diarist wrote, "It is feared the aircraft L9395 with crew is lost, although we live in hope". At first Robinson, Mosley, and Waddington were posted as missing on the operational board, but when there was no news they anticipated the worst. However, in true air force style they celebrated their losses and the victories with a party, entertaining McHardy and Pennington-Legh in The Eagle Hotel, Norfolk Street, King's Lynn. Three taxis transported them back to base, giving the journey free of charge as one elderly driver said they were only too pleased seeing as they had 'killed the Bosch'. Pennington-Legh looked somewhat bedraggled as he retired to bed.

In the morning there was a high state of excitement as all of 235 Squadron were ordered into the air. Five high value targets had presented themselves to the Luftwaffe: destroyers *Impulsive, Intrepid, Esk, Espress,* and *Ivanhoe* and the trawler *Princess Victoria*. As a precaution continuous RAF long-range fighter escort was provided to the 20th Flotilla and one ancillary vessel.

It was a first for the squadron and Flight Lieutenant Manwaring led. Unfortunately this impressive sight aloft was marred by an accident. Blenheim L9256's engines cut as Sergeant John Bessey took off. Automatically closing his throttles to land on the boundary of the airfield L9256 swung violently. Unable to rectify, the machine collided with a static Avro Anson N9897 being refuelled. Twenty-year-old Leading Aircraftman Leslie Curry was killed instantly as a propeller blade spliced through his skull. His torso toppled while a spark ignited the fuel. Flames projected out from the nozzle as if from the Wyvern on the 235 Squadron coat of arms. Its intense heat consumed the paint and metalwork. The three crewmen onboard L9256 miraculously escaped uninjured. Sergeant Walter Westcott was one: "I just jumped out of my seat which was at the very front of the aeroplane and tore to the middle as it was coming down, my adrenalin got me over the central spar." His pilot, Sergeant John Bessey, managed to extract himself as L9256 struck. Flames immediately flooded into the cockpit as they scrambled to get the escape hatch open. "I was very ungentlemanly," Westcott confessed. "I was scrambling over Bessey and Smith to get out. As far as I was concerned it was not a time for politeness, 'After you, my dear John…'" A gruesome sight greeted the fire crew and medical orderlies as they arrived on scene.

As the devastation and carnage unfolded below, the remainder flew out over the British coastline between Aldeburgh and Felixstowe. After a trouble-free flight they began skirting around the naval destroyers. "As soon as we went anywhere near the Royal Navy tried to blast us out of the skies. Firing off the correct cartridge of the hour just seemed to incense them still further," penciled one. Anti-aircraft and machine-gun fire was experienced with several shells exploding within twenty yards of the 'friendly fighters'. Manwaring then replied with the correct cartridges again, but the fire continued until they got out of range. They headed home. After debriefing and a drink Manwaring fell asleep in the mess anteroom. Peacock draped a tablecloth over him for warmth. Wiggs was woken at 04.00 hours to lead an early sortie. Half asleep and mildly hung-over, the flights slouched into the briefing room. Wiggs sat down with his crew, Sergeant Ian McPhail and Leading Aircraftman David Murphy. Pilot Officer Alan Wales pulled out his cigarettes from his striped pyjama pocket, offering each crew a smoke. Pilot Officer Algeo and Murphy accepted. The order of the day was fighter escort for three Lockheed Hudsons of 206 Squadron. The 'met' report said good weather over the continent. Their steeds waited silently. The crews began to board, Manwaring in L9401, Wales in L9397 and Algeo in L9260 but just before starting their motors word reached them from the watch office; the sortie had been scrubbed due to a lack of usable bomb trolleys apparently. Lumbering laboriously out of their Blenheim fighters McPhail lit a cigarette but realized he'd forgotten his Thermos flask. Having retrieved it, he clambered out as six Spitfires screamed overhead and peeled off to land. B Flight of 266 (Rhodesia) Squadron was on an overnight stay.

This short pause from operations for a few hours at Bircham Newton saw McDougall leave 235, transferring to RAF Detling, Kent. The new man to lead the squadron in the forthcoming battles was Squadron Leader 'Ronnie' Clarke. Clarke had spent his formative years combining flying with small bore shooting at Bisley, Surrey for the Royal Air Force. On the station he walked into the tall glazed entrance hall, to be met by a mess servant who took his luggage and led him to a room on the first floor. It was large and airy with white painted walls, a bed, wash-basin, carpet and a single chair, all spotlessly clean. The light brown lino was polished to mirror brightness. After an elderly batman dispensed with his bags he entered the officers' mess where he found a group of 235 officers, gathered around the radiogram in the anteroom as tea was served at 16.00 hours. Flight Lieutenants Manwaring and Cross introduced themselves as his flight commanders. Life was comfortably lazy and the enemy still seemed remote. There was no comprehension of the importance of events unfolding in France, just a few hundred miles away, "in fact until now our entire war sometimes seemed to be nothing but a series of trench raids – hysterical mêlées" said Jackson-Smith, "essentially the fate which unrolled that morning on Friday May 24, saw our ghastly war truly beginning!"

Sitting in silence, it was like waiting for confession. Finally Ronnie told them, "Reconnaissance from Bircham to position 350 degrees Terschelling 72 miles, thence to the mouth of the River Jade then return coastwise along the islands to Texel Island, back to base escorting one Hudson aircraft. Take-off 04.10

Sergeant William 'Bill' Martin pictured on his wedding day, November 11, 1939, to Doris Pittman in St Alban's Parish Church, Streatham. The couple would have five months together before he was lost on operations on May 24, 1940. (*Nigel Pittman via Ruth Pittman*)

hours." As there were no other 'dawn' operations scheduled this lonely group presented the sole target on offer to the entire Luftwaffe that morning.

Dick Cross led in P6909 with Pilot Officer Michael Ryan flying L9259. Ryan was slightly apprehensive, not having flown on operations for two weeks but nevertheless followed Cross off at 04.15 hours, flying out between Sheringham and Cromer protecting the Hudson by flying 2,000 feet above it. Nearing the Dutch coast four miles from Borkum, the Hudson bombed the *Hertha Engeline Fritzen* from 2,000 feet, a merchantman sailing at 9 knots, recording: "Bombs exploded within 10 yards, stern rolled heavily". Thirty-one-year-old Sergeant Alan Slocombe scribbled a note "Believe bombs grazed the ship". LAC John McMahon "shouted unidentified aircraft". The danger became all too clear as one pair of Bf109Es were sighted. Cross immediately flicked the microphone switch on his face mask, "Increase speed". They both shepherded their lamb out of harm's way but suddenly L9259 began to lag behind his leader. Onboard the outer flywheel for the fuel switch had caught Michael Ryan's fingers. The former telegraph boy 'Bill' Martin tried to assist. It was an invitation that two Luftwaffe pilots could not resist. At 07.18 the pair of Bf109Es attacked Ryan from the rear. Twenty-year-old Smith rattled off rounds in a desperate attempt to keep all three alive. Ten minutes later at 07.28 hours Uffz Otto Rückert of 4.(T)/186 'hissing steel' finally felled twenty-year-old Pilot Officer Michael Ryan and his crew, observer Sergeant William Martin and air gunner Leading Aircraftman Albert Smith. The navigator onboard the Hudson saw "a splash in the water, evidently made by the machine" when it was shot down, plotting its position as 270 degrees Borkum ten miles, near to Schiermonnikoog Island.

Inside the Rootes-built Blenheim L9259 Ryan could feel the straps biting into his flesh as the Blenheim entered the vertical with airspeed building up alarmingly. There was nothing more he could do. With fear mounting, the control stick was useless, and Martin sat on the floor next to him having tried desperately to help. They now prepared to ditch. The Blenheim suffered a violent impact. Then, sudden deceleration pressed Ryan against his Sutton harness with tremendous force and the nose and windscreen Perspex disintegrated. As Bill raised his arm up to protect his face he slid forward through the nose after the initial impact. Water poured in and Ryan swallowed a large amount. He had great difficulty in pulling the pin on his Sutton harness because it had been bent in the deceleration process. Struggling, he felt the pressure of water getting greater and greater as the machine went down. Finally he was released from his impending tomb.

Unseen from the sky in the water ten miles off Schiermonnikoog Island, gasping for air Ryan reached the surface. His lungs hurt as they expanded and contracted with every breath. Christ! That was a lucky escape. Looking around he could not see any sign of Martin. His partially inflated Mae West kept his head just above the water level. With his mouth open he reached for the rubber tube on the left while with his right hand, trying to inflate his Mae West. During this time he was repeatedly submerged by breaking local swells. He inhaled and swallowed mouthfuls of water. In these turbulent conditions the twenty year old gasped for air before being submerged.

Despite being a confident swimmer this continued for one hour after which Pilot Officer Michael Ryan, the eldest son of Sir Gerald Ellis Ryan, 2nd Baronet became unconscious and drowned quietly. His lifeless body was washed ashore in the tidal current onto the Engelsmanplaat, a small sandbank between the Dutch islands of Ameland and Schiermonnikoog on May 30. On June 5 Sergeant Martin's body was marooned on a mudflat. He was unable to swim and had suffered a similar fate and was laid to rest with full military honours near his pilot in Schiermonnikoog cemetery.

Dick Cross appreciated the unpredictable nature of death in wartime, "My Blenheim undamaged with not even a scratch on the paint" he penned in blue ink. Outside, the bustle of life on the station continued. Six Bristol Beauforts of 22 Squadron took to the skies from their sister station North Coates. After traumatic encounters with a fighter and flak the listening watch picked up a message at 01.58 hours; it began: "Cannot fly much longer – position 082 degrees North Coates 152 miles". Beaufort

235 Squadron Pilot Officer Michael Ryan's burial. P/O Michael Ryan was set to succeed his father to the baronetcy but was killed in combat on May 24, together with his crew by Uffz Otto Ruckert of 4.(T)/186. With no union flag available the local Dutch civilians draped one of their flags over his coffin. Local Luftwaffe troops provided the guard of honour. (*Derek Ryan*)

L4450 was in extreme difficulty, forcing Wing Commander Harry Mellor to put the aircraft down. Another Beaufort fired Verey lights over the position but got no answer. Searches began with Fairey Swordfish sweeping the waters at 100 feet between 03.45 and 08.00 and continued with Blenheims searching between 10.00 and 12.00 hours. The diarist recorded: "Searched for over two hours for the missing Beaufort, but saw no sign of it". The loss of Ryan on 235 a day earlier was still fresh on that Sunday May 26 when the Beaufort's disappearance was confirmed by the doleful letters FTR – failed to return – chalked up on the crew blackboard. Officers and non commissioned officers stood pensively, smoking cigarettes and poring over large unfurled maps that flapped and crinkled in the brisk morning breeze as Coastal Command operations were curtailed, with the exception of the Ostend, Dunkirk, Calais areas. "Men, desperate moments are upon us," Squadron Leader Ronnie Clarke told them, "Our main effort is now concentrated on covering the eastern half of the English Channel."

Pilot Officer Michael Ryan.

825 Squadron Swordfish near Detling. They were active in covering the Dunkirk evacuation, during which they lost eight of their twelve aircraft; five were lost in a single bombing raid on May 29, 1940 over Calais, including its commander Jimmy Buckley who was captured. He was awarded the DSC for his actions during this period. The citation sums up the gallant work done by these aviators: "Daring, endurance and resource in the conduct of hazardous and successful operations by the Fleet Air Arm working with the Coastal Command in France and over the Channel." (*Fleet Air Arm Museum*)

From 06.00 the air force pooled its resourses till dusk. Six Hawker Hectors of 613 Squadron dive-bombed an enemy battery southwest of Calais, "aeroplanes whizzed like black hornets, strafing the enemy". Naval gunner 'Shorty' Little wrote home of his observations during the day whilst the cruisers *Arethusa* and *Galatea* shelled the German positions. Two shore-based Fairey Swordfish from 825 (FAA) Squadron, Detling, were 'spotting' for *Galatea* off Calais, from 07.15 to approximately 09.15 hours. Their target was the same battery of four field artillery guns. The observers, spotting the fall of shot, radioed gunnery corrections back to the ships and shortly afterwards two 4.7 field artillery guns were believed destroyed. However, at 8,000 feet both Swordfish were attacked by two Bf109Es northwest of Sangatte in position 270 degrees Calais 6 miles. In Swordfish '5H' Sub Lieutenant John Kiddle began violent evading action by diving. His observer Lieutenant Geoffrey Beaumont immediately behind him was knocked completely off balance and thrown out of the aircraft at the beginning of the dive. He was killed instantly, leaving a shocked Naval Airman 1st Class Victor Moore in the rear, as the machine continued turning down to sea level at 132 mph at forty-five degrees. For less than half a second Kiddle got the upper hand, engaging the 109 because of the slowness of speed, whereby the Messerschmitt's superior speed carried it through into the line of fire. Retaliating, Kiddle pressed the gun button for all it was worth but a stoppage occurred after only fifteen rounds had left the front gun's chamber. '5H' was then instantly torn to shreds by a torrent of bullets which punctured the petrol tank, oil tank and air brake system, fraying the control wires. After the brawl, the second Swordfish was back on station at 09.15, receiving a signal from the naval unit to carry on spotting as communication from Swordfish '5H' had ceased. The cruisers used an Aldis lamp to indicate 'fresh targets' and this, coupled with a changing weather front, made sighting difficult for the crew. With less than twelve gallons left they made for the Kent coast; both got back safely. Kiddle recalled: "It was a very tight squeeze in the back of '5H' as additional auxiliary fuel tanks were mounted in the rear to increase range and endurance for these sorties. A modification that was hardly ideal for Geoffrey, which may have had something to do with his demise."

After this incident the Admiralty demanded that their aircraft be given fighter protection. 235's Flight Lieutenant Richard Cross (L9404) and Pilot Officer David Woodger (P9658) were one such pair, commenting "black rolls of smoke, the like of which rise from factory chimneys swirled skywards, spreading majestically like a protective layer out of which our Swordfish spotted and strafed into the late evening till 21.00 hours". From so far above these aviators were unaware of the weight of enemy numbers and firepower that was overwhelming the few troops left defending Calais. The very thought of the British Army being in retreat to the extent that they had to abandon everything was unbelievable, so began the trek to the French coastal town Dunkirk, east of Calais. Morale among the British troops had dropped drastically. Men were on half rations if they were lucky. Trooper John Davis:

:

> "I'd just had my twentieth birthday, we'd been to the Belgian border and had done nothing but retreat, dig in and retreat ever since. My section and I made our way back as best as we could. Word reached us that a National Day of Prayer had been proclaimed by all faiths for us at home – that made me even more determined to get back."

But for some it did little to lift their spirits, RAF aircrews reported "very large fires in Dunkirk town and dock under a pall of thick black smoke". In the thoughts in London among the honourable members of the War Cabinet and chiefs of staff there was a dreadful foreboding. In the late afternoon the cogs of the hastily organized evacuation plan Operation Dynamo gained momentum. At 19.00 hours Admiral Ramsay at Dover received a signal from the Admiralty in London: Operation Dynamo was to commence, with the message, "Implement with the greatest of vigour". The chief of air staff was told "The Royal Air Force should dominate the air above the area involved". Instructions were relayed to Lord Gort that a provision of a fleet of ships and small boats would evacuate the British Expeditionary Force, not only from the ports but from the beaches as well. Air Marshal Hugh Dowding, over a late supper at Bentley Priory with his counterpart in Coastal Command Frederick Bowhill, pointed out that "a good deal of the re-embarkation would be carried out by day, which would afford a real test of our air superiority, since the Germans would attempt to bomb the ships and boats".

The RAF rose to the challenge, with Coastal Command trying to glean intelligence for the British Army and Royal Navy whilst shielding the Dunkirk evacuation which began in earnest. RAF Bircham Newton was thronged with machines ready for the business of war. All waited for the signal to scramble. As May 26 dawned aircrews were awakened by a shrilling telephone. Manwaring peered at his wristwatch, 05.07, as the duty orderly shouted "Three machines scramble – reconnaissance of Zeebrugge". Nine men sprinted for their machines and took off methodically within three minutes, whilst overhead forked lighting streaked the sky, accompanied by the mutter of thunder. As brilliant flashes lit the sky three silhouetted Blenheim fighters could be seen, climbing away in vic formation. 16 Group had paid surprisingly little attention to the ominous development of the deteriorating weather with "a zest to help the Royal Navy at every whim" wrote a correspondent, unaware of the plight of British and French ground troops.

Manwaring in L9401, Wales in L9260 and Pilot Officer Dudley Warde flying P6956 hauled their steel monsters into dense cloud. The Blenheims spread out to avoid collision. At 5,000 feet Warde was deep within the impenetrable mass and becoming totally disorientated. Unable to see any external visual references he struggled to maintain controlled level flight as turbulence, lightning flashes and thunder claps added more pressure. Totally confused, one junior officer suffered a case of 'shell-shock', abandoning P6956 through the top hatch and tumbling into total darkness, narrowly missing the tail plane by inches. His sudden exit did not attract his observer Pilot Officer

Alfred Murphy's attention until the aircraft's nose dramatically pivoted forward. Cupping his mouthpiece he screamed a warning over the R/T which went unanswered. The air gunner aft was an ex-Halton apprentice, eighteen-year-old Leading Aircraftman Ernest Armstrong. He tugged the communication cord, aware something was amiss and heard muffled shouting from Murphy. On the aircraft's instrument panel its onboard altimeter ticked over persistently until the Bristol Blenheim went screaming into the ground at Court Farm, Docking, out of dense cloud and rain at 17.45 hours. The entombed Murphy and Armstrong were unable to escape. Farm labourers and some Home Guard reached the scene first – a sight both pitiful and incongruous. By 22.00 hours the bodies had been recovered, the diarist entering "machine – complete wreck".

Its pilot had made his way back to the aerodrome and was in a total state of shock. An old combatant from the 1914-1918 war, Flying Officer Robert Jamison diagnosed Dudley Warde as having a reaction similar to a neuropathic disorder resulting from an experience beyond his capacity to assimilate. "Outwardly he is quiet normal. If you asked him his name he knew it." In the early hours a senior officer gave him a hell of a dressing down. "It appears Warde is quite useless to this squadron and Coastal Command in general. People rely on each other in a coastal fighter squadron; how can he be relied upon to do anything as he had let his crew die?"

The subsequent board of enquiry criticized the pilot for "losing his head in the heavy rain". Warde became confused under more pointed questioning, "the Air Officer Commanding 16 Group, Air Commodore R. G. Parry, DSO applied for Pilot Officer Dudley Cecil Warde's services with the Royal Air Force to be dispensed with forthwith". It is unclear what became of him after he resigned his commission in January 1941.

With aircraft P6956 unaccounted for the other Blenheims continued heading for Zeebrugge. Grey clouds perceptibly thickened and became a solid mass beneath which L9401 and L9397 spluttered trying to glean some information through the relentless downpour to bring back. A wireless transmission interrupted Manwaring's concentration as he and Wales crossed the wide expanse of the North Sea. "Land away, nearest aerodrome – Detling". Altering course eventually both Blenheim fighters touched down at 19.00 hours. An utterly black evening crept on as Manwaring telephoned Bircham and Jamison relayed what had happened to L6956.

The six 235 men found RAF Detling at bursting point. Tempers were short and accommodation sparse as RAF, FAA, and Army Co-operation crews regardless of rank competed for space. Both crews spent the night sleeping on a mess floor until a sofa became available shortly after 03.00 hours as three personnel left to board Harrow K6998 bound for Bircham Newton, Kinloss, Wick and Sumburgh. K6998 carried out a continual anti-submarine patrol between destinations until reaching Sumburgh. Blenheim fighters L9401 and L9397 resumed patrols over Zeebrugge between 15.00 and 18.15. The surrounding sky was grey and overcast as a second pair were tasked with searching the waters between Nieuport and Zeebrugge. Out of sight Cross in L9404 and Woodger P6909 saw a gaggle of fifteen Messerschmitts at 1,000 feet on the same reciprocal course. They did not engage but diverted inland, with further sighting of three Heinkels west of Nieuport, which were being subjected to a cascade of anti-aircraft fire. As the last shell burst the two fighters pounced. They clashed between Ostend and Diksmuide in a swirling dogfight between 1,000 and 9,000 feet. Woodger got within 300 yards, firing 500 rounds then cursing as a stoppage occurred. Peeling off to starboard Cross brought his guns to bear, firing 2,400 rounds from the belly pack, the last bursts injuring a gunner. As he broke away heavy smoke was giving a measure of protection from the Luftwaffe as soldiers were lifted from Dunkirk, reporting "smoke extends to Calais, Gravelines, Nieuport and Ostend". This was the unit's last encounter with the Luftwaffe as the month drew to a close.

The days blurred into one with constant patrols. As the scale of operations carried out by the Luftwaffe increased the whole of 235 Squadron were moved to RAF Detling, Kent. "There was a suppressed commotion, packing our razors, toothbrushes, soap, shaving brush into our gas mask canvas bag and off we went in our Blenheim fighters in the afternoon." Sergeant Aubrey Lancaster, a twenty-year-old observer from Hartlepool who had become a sales engineer at Expanding Metal Company, but had applied for the Volunteer Reserve, watched what happened next:

> "Our machines landed on the soft grass, there we found the place in pandemonium; there was literally no accommodation. We were shown to bell tents with damp straw strewn on the grass, no blankets, or biscuits [mattresses]. A local farm offered accommodation in an oak barn sleeping on bales of hay. After consideration we decided that we would rather sleep in the armchairs or Lloyd Loom chairs in the sergeants' mess."

Sergeant Aubrey Lancaster photographed wearing a great coat, smoking, whilst at Stalag Luft III, (Sagan). Aubrey helped do the main wiring for the tunnels prior to the 'Great Escape'. He became good friends with the actor Peter Butterworth and the writer Talbot Rothwell who later went on to write many of the Carry On films which featured Butterworth. (*Simon Woddy*)

Other fliers were given the remaining floor space in the barn and at a seventeenth century public house The Cock Horse Inn in Detling, near the famous pilgrims way. There they were privileged to eat locally produced bacon, eggs, sausages, and drink local cider and ale whilst sharing the kitchen after hours with their host. Their sleep was disturbed by the constant rumble from across the channel. In the blackout a man coughed, a bird twittered, a muffled voice spoke up; "Cross, Jackson-Smith, Booth – you're on!"

As the skies lightened on Wednesday May 29, men filtered into the briefing room yawning, stretching and cursing in the way of early risers. The burden of the fighting was to be borne by squadrons based around London and the southeast of England, which would be fully engaged for the first time. The fitters, riggers and armourers were no longer betting that the war would be over by the following year. They had begun to whisper that it might last a lifetime, lamenting that "they say the first year is the worst". When orders came to start patrolling, coloured tapes marked the route on a map pinned to a blackboard: Dover – Calais – Ostend. Dunkirk was now less than fifty miles away. These routine operations began with Pilot Officer Peacock leading the 'Dawn Patrol' reporting "plenty of ground activity on the French coast and sea, with thousands of troops lining the beaches awaiting embarkation".

The second shift sat attentively waiting for the weather to lift. Smoke rose where some men were frying bacon. Cross, Jackson-Smith and Booth were stopped briefly as they walked towards the smell by a senior officer saying "the situation as it now stands is at the least disconcerting. You should all be in the air supporting our army, if those are your machines take off immediately!" Jackson-Smith described the take-off:

> "The weather was foul, raining heavily. Nine of us ran, or rather waddled like ducks, to our machines, did the preliminary checks and warmed the engines up. The gunners made sure the turret rotation operated and did not jam. Within three minutes after bumping over the grass at Detling, Booth and I climbed away, Cross followed in P6909 shortly afterwards."

As events unfolded the weather became a physical obstacle and barrier that couldn't have been apparent to the glance of the senior officer on the ground.

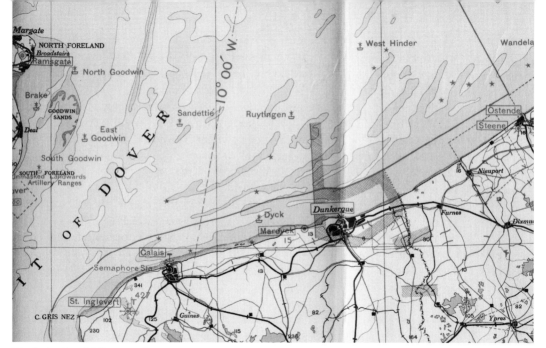

The "miracle of deliverance".

Dick's machine was drenched in the rain, the liquid running off the Perspex as the single wiper blade battled to keep the pilot's vision clear. The noise of its operating motor was lost above the two Mercury engines. He tried to climb above the abysmal weather, levelling out at 10,000 feet but there was no way through. The A Flight commander wheeled his Blenheim around to fly back to the aerodrome. Reducing height at a steady rate he spiralled down. Cross levelled out at 100 feet but was a nightmare path as the landscape merged with the sky. Within a split second and allowing no time to respond, the Blenheim's front glazing hit the top canopy of a tree and ploughed into a copse two miles from RAF Detling. The highest tree in the area was reported at 158 feet in 1940.

Fields of hops climbed strings ready to blossom on both sides as the fuselage and wings crumpled and buckled on impact. Cross and his observer Sergeant Alan Slocombe died instantly and their air gunner Leading Aircraftman James North was mortally injured. Soaked, bloody and in pain he stared out into the gloom waiting for signs of the approaching rescuers or death. The copse was covered in aviation fuel but fortunately there was no large blaze recorded.

Personnel at Detling station heard the impact and described it as "a rumble like thunder". 235 Squadron's Sergeant Steve Hebron "heard a terrible explosion followed by dead silence, it was pitch black, with torrential rain at the time and the aircraft probably hit a tree. I was orderly sergeant that night, and went with others to search, for the wreckage and bodies."

As the rain continued the rescue party reached the farm track but were forced to leave their vehicles as the conditions became 'Somme like'. They walked and slid on foot into the copse where they were met by a scene of devastation. The rescue party worked into the night, with the local police hanging 'No Smoking or Matches' signage. They shrouded the dead, gave a moment's pause, then three of them carefully reached the smashed central Bristol type BI gun turret and the bleeding body of the still shallow-breathing twenty year old.

They carefully extracted North from the wreckage, and while he could not speak he squeezed one of the rescuer's hands as they gave him a dose of morphine. He was quickly stretchered to an awaiting vehicle which transported him to Chatham Naval Hospital. Upon arrival his condition was described as 'not good'. The nurses revealed the full extent of his multiple injuries whilst removing his flying clothing. Naval surgeon Lieutenant Clarke worked feverishly to save him, together with a number of their Red Cross Voluntary Aid Detachment. North survived the surgery "because of his age and fitness" and was stabilized. Unfortunately the promising air gunner died three days later on an unnamed ward at the hospital.

The two remaining Blenheim fighters continued their flight. The sea was choppy, the monotonous ripples broken only at one spot by the ugly hull of a small merchant vessel that reared almost vertically out of the water, presumably the victims of an enemy bomb or mine. The clouds cleared sufficiently to allow Jackson-Smith a glimpse of the scene below: "You didn't need a map, you flew to where the oily black smoke was rising from the burning sea front buildings and harbour of Dunkirk, it rose an estimated five miles high into the still air."

Away from operations Flight Lieutenant Wiggs Manwaring was lucky enough to spend some time with his wife Zena in the evening at Horsmonden, prior to leading his first operation from Detling. He described the build up: "As midday neared, the skies emptied and I became tense, like experiencing the build up to a rugby match at my former school Ardingly College." His section was the next to take off in the relentless relay. Sergeant Aubrey Lancaster was with B Flight:

"We pulled ourselves together about 05.00 hours and had some bacon sandwiches, which 235's fitters cooked. Upon learning that a flight had already gone we were told our task would be to go off in threes and we would be the second flight taking off, taking over from Cross, Jackson-Smith and Booth on their return. They got back minus Dick just before 11.00 hours. Booth reported 'it was a piece of cake, no aerial activity or Junkers 87s'. Our 'Spy' told us to watch out for our own fighters and particularly the Boulton Paul Defiant, which none of us had seen before – a page with a photograph from *Flight* periodical was waved under our noses. Our patrol instructions were to fly for the full duration of our fuel."

South African 'Tony' Booth was tasked to fly a second sortie; Manwaring led Booth and Cronan, taking off at 11.30 hours. Buildings flashed by underneath as Cronan kept L9260 tucked right in, flying to North Foreland near Ramsgate. Wiggs on the R/T instructed "Form vic – Go!" and they were off, over the sea towards Calais with Manwaring at the arrowhead, Cronan to port and Booth to starboard. The three Blenheims closed up a bit and soon saw Calais, reached without mishap. As they cut the corner for Dunkirk at 5,000 feet Manwaring commanded "Come on section, reform. Keep in, Cronan".

Even from Calais columns of dense black smoke could quite clearly be seen coming from the oil refineries at St Pol, together with lots of boats like ants heading backwards and forwards between England and Dunkirk. Before long they approached Dunkirk, Aubrey continued:

"From our vantage point five miles out you could see the troops more clearly through the naval binoculars. On the beach were orderly lines with or without rifles held above their heads, others without battledress at the water's edge then as their turn came they waded in up to their waists or neck towards a waiting small boat. The blazing oil refinery burned feverishly nearby, the smoke rising quite high. I noticed single-engine monoplane silhouettes against the black smoke. Advising Edinburgh-born 'Will' Peebles our gunner on the R/T he immediately came back 'they're coming round high on our tail fast'. Our New Zealand pilot Cronan was looking for them in his mirror but could not see them!"

At precisely this time large numbers of Bf109Es were reported off Dunkirk/Calais between 10.20 and 12.00 hours. Visibility and weather conditions were very poor indeed. It was then that the sheer terror began as the inexperienced had an induction into the art of aerial warfare northwest of Calais against JG27.

A Bf109E swept round the bows of L9260 at thirty yards, whilst the lead Blenheim's air gunner Murphy shouted "Look out behind!" Manwaring banked hard into a high climbing turn to starboard, whilst Murphy watched his tail, to turn in towards his attackers. Cronan, on seeing this instinctively broke right to come up behind into line astern to protect Booth's tail. Before he was able to complete this manoeuvre two Messerschmitts slightly above came down. Booth pushed the stick forward, hastily engaged plus nine boost and pushed on towards the sea with the 109s on his tail. For a second Cronan got behind one and fired a two-second burst, whilst Peebles was heard returning fire as another pair attacked L9260 from astern.

Manwaring's Blenheim presented a steady target, much to I./JG27 Lt Igor Zirkenbach's frustration. Solid flashes erupted from his Bf109E's nose and wings whilst he in turn received returning fire from Murphy. L9401 survived for ten minutes as glowing white tracer pulsed into its starboard air-cooled radial engine and orange flames erupted from its two fuel tanks. The wing was a burnished red colour as its pilot struggled. Losing control his machine twisted 180 degrees down underneath the Bf109E's nose and the Blenheim was seen going into a watery grave northwest of Calais. Zirkenbach finally had his third victory.

Burning oil depot at Dunkirk. (*Andrew Bird via Basil Quelch*)

At this moment Booth heard someone shout "Fighters! Still behind you!" He immediately pulled his Blenheim into another turn then craned his neck to look into the rear mirror he'd had his fitters install. The sea-green water flashed by, but even with full boost the two 109s were still much faster than L9397. One was so close Scott opened fire. Sergeant Elliott, Booth's observer, calmly gave him instructions as Booth pushed the stick forward to get lower still at about 1,000 feet off the water. With a solid 'bang' Booth's starboard engine disintegrated and with rounds slicing through the main fuel line which then ignited, he suddenly slowed down.

Lancaster watched from L9260, "I looked to starboard and there was a solid sheet of flame erupting from the nose of the enemy fighter and bits started flying off into the air from Booth's machine. I remember saying 'How ghastly!'" His attacker, Stab/JG27's Hptm Adolf Galland, turned in again to fire a good burst allowing for deflection into the fuselage then pulled away to his right and saw L9397 dropping its nose simultaneously to the vertical. It went straight into a vertical spin. Inside Booth was dead or terminally injured and L9397 went straight into the English Channel, nine miles north of Gravelines, no survivors being seen.

The third Blenheim had no hope of escaping two single-engine fighters in a cloudless sky. Evasive manoeuvres were carried out which saw L9260 twirling and weaving through the sky. Two enemy aircraft shot across the bow, their light blue undersides clearly visible for a mere second or less. Opening up his throttle Galland turned 180 degrees and chased down the Englander. Air Gunner Alan Peebles was constantly rotating his turret, searching the sky. "Two 109s astern, six o'clock, high", he shouted.

Immediately Adolf Galland's Bf109E was onto Cronan, firing a burst. 7.92 mm rounds cut cleanly through the nose, one grazing Lancaster's temple as he strained to look out through the port Perspex glazing. "I stared out blindly", recalled Lancaster:

> "To try and shake our attacker off, Cronan switched fuel tanks, over to the outer tanks with 100-octane fuel. Levers were turned and the emergency fuel nine plus boost kicked in. He put the Blenheim into a dive but the 109 followed us down, with bullets shredding everything in their path disabling the port engine, port outer tank and oil chamber, peppering the fuselage and instruments. The port engine shuddered to a stop, we were still making for the wave tops at 240 mph."

Galland was being kept at bay by Peebles' resolute firing, whilst Peebles shouted to Cronan, indicating the position of their enemy during this encounter and all the while they received bursts of return fire from their pursuer. The Blenheim was upon the wave tops as Cronan pulled the stick back into his stomach without any effect. He put both feet on the instrument panel, which began to break up under his weight and the damage already caused by 7.92 mm rounds, but he finally managed to yank the stick back to its furthest point. "Inside the cockpit I had the extraordinary sensation of my eyes wanting to leave my head and my head being isolated from the rest of my body. I was perfectly conscious." L9260 levelled out less than twenty feet above the waves. Suddenly a flash of tracer ate into the water ahead of their aircraft's nose – their pursuer was still with them. Peebles got off a couple of bursts while Lancaster calmly gave Cronan a course to steer for the nearest aerodrome (Manston) but his pilot realized that with one engine out and extensive battle damage the machine was unable to maintain level flight. Added to this he could not fly a straight course as the trimming tabs were unresponsive. In the cockpit to overcome this problem Cronan put both his feet on the pedal operating the port rudder and Lancaster sat on the floor amongst the accumulated debris and pulled the starboard pedal with both hands to try and force L9260 onto some sort of course. There was a sudden realization that the fuel gauges were rapidly reaching zero, as petrol leaked out of puncture wounds from both port fuel tanks. Loss of fuel was causing the remaining starboard engine to peter out. A landing on the water looked inevitable.

Leading Aircraftman William Peebles climbed down from his turret to make preparations for such a landing by moving the dinghy from the valise to nearer the hatch behind his position

Adolf 'Dolfo' Joseph Ferdinand Galland. On May 29, Galland (the Geschwader adjudant of JG27) shot down Bristol Blenheim Mk IVF L9260 of 235 Squadron over the sea. L9260 was flown by Cronan, Lancaster and Peebles. Fortunately the crew were rescued from their dinghy by a passing paddle steamer.

ready for ditching. Hptm Galland realized there was no hope for his stricken victim and did not try to follow. In his memoirs he described his encounter with Blenheim L9260. "The second one escaped me for some time by extremely skillful evasive action, until low over the water my bullets ripped open her oil tanks, and then she hit the water at a shallow angle and sank immediately. When I landed at St. Pol I found my Bf109E (W.Nr. 2764) was covered with oil."

In the Blenheim cockpit Cronan forced back the top hatch, as Lancaster moved his observer seat into the stow position.

"I sat in the same position on the floor where I had been pulling the rudder and watched the water rush by while at the same time getting closer. Soon the glazed nose was brushing the surface, like a sailing dinghy ploughing through the water. Then it was as if we'd hit a brick wall and we came to a standstill. Water rose against the glazing until the pressure was too great and the two panes shattered, showering me with Perspex. With the initial impact I shot forward into the nose and was immediately submerged. My most urgent problem – I could not swim and had not been shown a technique to hold my breath."

The observer tried to make his way back to his former position but was unable to retrace his steps. Taking a last gulp of air he squeezed through the nose. Muffled but clearly audible, he heard himself saying "God! I want to live". Lancaster kicked out in the murk, unable to orientate himself until he reached out and gripped hold of the muzzles of the belly-pack machine guns. He started swimming doggy-paddle style and found himself lodged underneath the wing; he edged along until he saw daylight. Desperately kicking, propelling through the water Lancaster broke the surface twenty feet from the Blenheim, gasping for air. He was safe!

Pilot Officer John Cronan had tightened his harness before the impact, and while he watched his observer propel forward, Cronan calmly banged the harness to release himself. As the water rose at an alarming rate he climbed over the main spar to the dinghy and got it out of the hatch. Eighteen-year-old air gunner Peebles had been knocked about during the ditching and was beginning to feel some pain so he rested a second then doubled his efforts and clambered out of the hatch. Hauling himself out onto the starboard wing he joined his pilot and both stood half submerged. Five minutes later Lancaster came up near the starboard wing and all got aboard the dinghy. Cutting the cord, Cronan began to paddle away from the sinking machine.

Lancaster and Peebles began looking around for shipping while their pilot paddled. After thirty minutes a paddle steamer *Royal Daffodil* was sighted heading for their dinghy whilst on its way to the Dunkirk beaches. It halted and lowered a small rowing boat and within minutes they were hauled aboard. The two sailors rowed back to the paddle steamer with the three disheveled airmen. "All three airmen were in good spirits" the sailors remarked, while also ribbing them that they were only five miles out from Margate and could have paddled in! Lancaster reported:

"We were feeling very sorry for ourselves when someone gave us a hipflask of brandy, which soon went down, and warmed our insides. An even bigger bottle was handed to Peebles who promptly took a swig, it was then passed round to myself and Cronan, and this too quickly disappeared. What we did not know was that the *Royal Daffodil* skipper Captain Johnson had radioed Margate harbour, which had organized a naval launch to take us off. It arrived and a strong sailor picked us up individually and took us onboard the launch. The three of us were ushered below into a small cabin and asked by the sailor to lie down on the three bunks inside. Cronan, Peebles and myself found that it made our heads spin, coupled with the fact we had 'got plastered'. We started to wander up onto the deck, so naval ratings strapped us down. For the remainder of the journey we just laughed and giggled. When the naval launch arrived in

Margate there was a crowd three or four deep lining the walls. Seeing the uniform (still wearing our Mae West, and parachute harness) a big cheer went up. The three of us wanted to leave of our own accord but were told 'Not bloody likely mate' – the ambulance men and women were not going to be cheated out of doing their work! We were strapped onto stretchers with brown woollen blankets draped over us and then carried up to the waiting ambulance. We were then driven at speed through the lanes to RAF Manston and placed in the station sick quarters. Two doctors examined us, gave us an injection and said we'd sleep for twenty-four hours!"

John Cronan, Aubrey Lancaster and William Peebles slept indeed for many hours.

Sitting nearby in a folding chair was Pilot Officer Anthony Algeo, who had flown in to Manston from Bircham Newton, on 'Spy's' instructions to get details of the aerial duel and losses. On the ward he watched a haggard man in blue battle dress leaning over one of his wounded companions. There was a fetid smell of unwashed bodies and disinfectant. Blackout blinds were taken down and rays of light streamed in. A nurse brought a tea for Algeo and eyeing his pilot wings she made polite and friendly conversation in a hushed voice. He diligently watched over his comrades, with a second nurse described as "blond, beautiful and curvaceous" supplying tea in the afternoon as the hours ticked by. The ward was busy, with new cases constantly arriving. In the commotion the young New Zealander woke, somewhere there was a hysterical scream, a Red Cross volunteer put a cup of steaming hot sweet tea on his bedside table and rushed off.

Algeo recorded Cronan's recollection of the dogfight: "I was flying No. 3 in the section of three Blenheim Fs who were attacked by 109s. The Blenheim leader [Manwaring] broke away and was not seen again." The squadron diary records: "So in one day we lost most of those who have been the back bone of our squadron, round whom we had hoped to build a useful fighting unit". A reminder of Tony Booth lay in the *South Africa* magazine in the anteroom (see page 71).

Despite the dramatic developments in the evening a group walked to The Cock Horse Inn. The losses prompted a debate among the few remaining aircrews about whether they could continue to fly and fight or if the squadron would be absorbed into another Coastal Command unit. Squadron Leader Clarke convinced them replacement Blenheim fighters and a new batch of reinforcements would arrive the following evening.

All newcomers would be thrown in at the deep end as routine patrols off the Dover Straits continued. In Dunkirk aid stations were overflowing with casualties and outside the dead lay piled in heaps. The latter were no problem any longer, but what of the living? The evacuation was in full swing. The RAF watched the many thousands of troops returning to the English shores, laden on various craft as they tried to protect the troops from the Luftwaffe in the skies over Dunkirk as tired soldiers milled on the beach. Eventually they were able to board a boat after being in the inevitable queue to get away. Pilot Officer Peacock was patrolling over the vessels in the late afternoon on May 30. Ollie Wakefield communicated with a naval destroyer by flashlight: "Survived five hours of dodging bombs!" Soon the white cliffs of Dover came into view. Here they berthed and clambered ashore. The month of May proved a very hectic one for those at Detling too. As an unidentified diary page describes:

"We practically lived in our flying clothing, and always seemed to be at readiness. I hadn't been to my billet for days, I found the old couple of the cottage at home. Both were glad to see me, having feared the worst. In my room I had a cold sponge down with a flannel and it was good to get the dust and oil and the sweat off my body. It was almost peaceful with the hens clucking outside, then I lay down, closed my eyes and slept. I woke up with a jerk that nearly threw me out of bed at 1.15 a.m. It was if a shell had exploded."

Anson R3389, still only an invisible noise, appeared from out of the darkness at 01.14 hours.

Corporal Joan Pearson heard an engine spluttering as it headed for the aerodrome. Jumping up she looked out of the window and saw something terrifying and ominous. Quickly pulling on her RAF off-white roll neck jumper and gumboots, she grabbed her tin hat and ran out of the building in to the blackout, towards the aircraft as it crashed through the trees at 01.15. Then it disappeared from view. The light identified its resting place as she ran over the grass and onto a cement road towards a picket post. In the distance bells could be heard that meant the blood wagon was on its way. An airman shouted as she ran by, his voice lost after the noise from the crash site. As Pearson kept running towards the glow a figure emerged in the light given off by the blaze. It was an RAF policeman, his shadow enormous, almost frightening. "You can't go over there it's out of bounds" he yelled, trying to stop her scrambling over a fence. But she did. Men's voices could be heard beyond a hawthorn hedge. She fell down an incline and was stung by stinging nettles in the ditch. She scrambled over a slippery bank until finally she reached the field with the burning wreckage. There against the backdrop of the blaze she saw men in a dazed condition. "Our pilot's still in there, he's knocked out," shouted Leading Aircraftman Petts as they walked towards the bell of an ambulance, too shaken to get their pilot out themselves. Others appeared and someone yelled "leave the pilot to me – go and get the fence down for the ambulance".

Faces and ranks were indistinguishable and unimportant at this time. They barely focused on the slim form of the twenty-nine-year-old medical corporal as she worked her way into the wreckage, releasing the machine's navigator Bond from his seat harness. Amid the scalding heat she unclipped his parachute harness, and moving his Mae West she found that his neck was injured and feared his back might be broken too. Bond then mumbled that there was a full load of 120 lb bombs! Dragging him away from the blazing wreck with all her strength she reached the other side of the ridge that she had just fallen over, minutes before the petrol tanks blew up. Laying him on the ground she threw herself on top of the pilot to protect him from the blast and shards of metal splinters, placing her tin helmet over his head. As they lay there still, he murmured about his face. There was a lot of blood, with a tooth protruding from his top lip. She was in the process of reassuring Bond when a bomb went off, holding his head gently in her hands to prevent any further dislocation. A young soldier then crawled forward and lent her his handkerchief so that she could clean his face. Pearson was about to examine his ankle when R3389 exploded, lighting up the sky. The huge explosion caused the air to be sucked out of their lungs and they were then showered with hot debris. Other helpers from the three services rushing to the scene were blown flat on the grass. Fearing another explosion, Pearson reassured Bond and then ran to the fence to help the medical officer over with the stretcher. To prevent any more injury to his neck he was carefully moved to the stretcher and slowly removed across the ditch to the waiting ambulance. As it drove off there was another fiercer explosion. Undaunted Pearson put her helmet on and went calmly back to the wreck to search for the fourth member of the crew, the pilot. Flying Officer Richard Chambers was found dead. Pearson went straight on duty to see to the crew's wounds herself, finishing at 03.00 hours. At 08.00 she was back on duty as usual for the station's sick parade. Seven weeks later Corporal Joan Pearson was awarded the Empire Gallantry Medal and one year later this was changed to a George Cross.

As a cheerless dawn arrived, a scorch mark was all that remained as Blenheims, Hudsons and Swordfish took to the skies. Life went on in the farmlands surrounding the aerodrome as death held sway on the Continent, where on the Flanders' front the all-powerful German army and air force turned to the business of decimating the remaining British and French forces. In Great Britain the religious prayed, the rich in the city of London drank harder, flirting and lovemaking, dancing and living as usual, but with more urgency.

CHAPTER FIVE

Sea Pictures

In a sense, Operation Dynamo cleared the air. "The majority thought it had gained us time, though it had achieved nothing but a few devastating miles at enormous cost to men, machines and self-esteem. Our tight knit squadron as a consequence has been decimated," wrote Sergeant Harold Sutton.

A most testing time for all three services began. A crossroads had been reached and Fighter Command was stretched. Air Chief Marshal Bowhill authorized the use of his trade protection Blenheims and in a reshuffle 248 Squadron appeared on the 'Organization Change' sheet, transferred to Fighter Command with A Flight to Dyce and B Flight to Montrose to beef up defences in Scotland and start patrolling off Norway. As a detachment of 254 Squadron flew south, Air Vice-Marshal Keith Park contemplated his available Spitfires and Hurricanes which were limited to forty minutes over Dunkirk. Coastal Command was requested to keep up a perpetual patrol over these Dunkirk waters, to frustrate the enemy, although there were not enough of them. The incessant patrols which these aircraft flew were called 'Sands Patrols'. They started before dawn each day and flew till dark.

Pilot Officer George Spiers noted in his logbook:

"I'd just completed a five-hour forty-five minute patrol to Voss and Stadtlandet, Norway, in my capacity as observer with Pilot Officer Beal. I lay down on a camp bed to get some sleep only to be awoken and told 'You're off to Detling, with Flying Officer John Baird in L9481'. Leaving Sumburgh at 15.16 the visibility for take-off was down to thirty yards with bad storms over Norfolk."

After four hours they landed at Detling, Kent. On arrival the RAF airfield was beginning to resemble a modern Saxon hill fort, the battlements being replaced by mono and twin-engine fighter aircraft. With machines arriving and taking off the grass aerodrome became cut up and personnel moved warily around the now extremely muddy and slippery dispersal areas. Conditions were hazardous; jams were chronic as men and women worked on an assortment of aircraft, naval and RAF. Heads turned skywards as four Blenheim fighters joined the circuit and landed one by one. As their motors stopped the different trades approached and enveloped the machines. With these reinforcements was Corporal Maurice Taylor.

"Four Blenheim fighters of our unit, 254 Squadron, were detached to RAF Detling, together with the appropriate ground staff with a responsible non commissioned officer in charge – me! No sooner had our machine halted, the hatch was opened from outside and a face appeared shouting 'Need a hand mate?' The aerodrome resembled a hackney carriage rank, this was probably the hardest four days of our lives, we all slept when and where we could and hot meals were brought to us at dispersal by a junior mess orderly. Washing facilities were confined to three filthy enamel bowels and a single shower an inch deep in mud and cloudy water. Our kits were refuelled and armed immediately."

In rotation L9481 took off on an offensive patrol at 09.05, Spiers writing, "Foreland, Calais, Dunkirk, Ostend. Attacked two E-boats, shot down one Ju 87 in flames. Four circuits. Flying Time 3.05." The remaining two 254 aircraft were in the air from 10.12 until 13.12 on May 29 and reported "Visibility nearly zero. Wreck near Calais of about 4,000 tons sighted at 10.40, screws and stern showing. Considerable flak, starboard engine rendered unserviceable."

An afternoon sweep of the Dunkirk beaches the next day saw Flying Officer John Baird tangle with a Heinkel. He noted "Port engine on fire, believed destroyed" and "BEF on the beach waved at us". He landed back at 17.00 hours. As the light faded at dusk a hangar door rattled shut. Hesitantly they slept. Four hours passed quickly and they were awoken at 02.30 hours by a batman with tea. Pilot Officer George Spiers recalled:

"I opened my eyes to see the beaming face of our temporary batman, Capel of 235. He left and put the light on, another day began. Washed, shaved and dressed I walked to the mess. I recognized a couple of faces who turned to greet me, and I ate my way through the locally sourced breakfast. Little did I know it was going to be my last meal for some considerable time on June 1, 1940."

One by one they all assembled. Squadron Leader Clarke got up and walked to a blackboard. The briefing was somewhat rushed as things were getting rougher for the troops at Dunkirk and Clarke was anxious for them to get on the scene without delay. "Reconnaissance over the continental north coast between Gravelines and Ostend" was to begin at 05.00 and end by 23.15 hours. These sorties then alternated between Detling and Bircham Newton. Overburdened with navigation charts, parachutes, helmets, gloves and steel helmets they hurried out to their charges and were soon in their positions onboard, most in shirtsleeves or roll neck sweaters. At 06.45 hours, there were cries of "Get them off". Twenty-six-year-old Flight Lieutenant Alan Pennington-Legh led the first off, a foursome, two pairs from 248 and 254 Squadrons. Pilot Officer George Spiers illustrates the severity of a Sands Patrol:

"Over the intercom, from my pilot, [Baird] came: 'Come on, we're off,' and we taxied past twenty-year-old Sergeant Richard Bate in 'Q-Queenie' R3630 and Pennington-Legh in 'B-Bertie' L9456. With a deep roar, slowly at first then gathering speed we bounced over the grass. Flying Officer John Baird [L9481] had the stick between his knees, hauling the machine into the air. The wheels came up with a thud. Climbing away, soon we were passing over Tenterden."

One 248 Blenheim fighter turned back due to technical difficulties, "its pilot waved" reported Leading Aircraftman Richard Roskrow. Soon they were flying over the sea and past the South Goodwin Light. Pennington-Legh flicked his R/T, "Section astern, section astern – Go!" Bates backed off a bit, levelling off at 3,000 feet. Below hundreds of 'little ships' could be seen. Pennington-Legh, Baird and Bates turned right towards Calais, Gravelines and Dunkirk and began their circuits, with an average time of fifteen to twenty-five minutes over each area. Whilst over Dunkirk the R/T crackled into life, Spiers shouted "Enemy aircraft – Junkers!" L9481 gave chase. The Junkers was a mile away and to the right, slightly lower, on a parallel course with their own easterly direction. Chasing it over the troop-laden beach a short burst was fired from the belly pack but the Ju 88 jettisoned its bombs and escaped into cloud.

In approximately the same position Baird spotted Junkers 87s at 07.45. The Blenheims opened up to full throttle, black smoke pouring from their exhausts and engaged briefly from close range to about 250 yards. After one sharp burst L9456's belly pack malfunctioned owing to a leak in the system. Breaking away to the left Pennington-Legh headed home as Bates and Baird got onto the Stuka, now only 1,000 feet above the ground. The warm air was condensing on the cold Perspex windscreen and forming ice on the inside, so observer Sergeant James Love began scrubbing at the ice with his clenched fist. Bates pressed the firing button, but things were made tricky by the ice and by now the 87 was right down on the deck unleashing its deadly cargo on to the troops below.

One mile west of Dunkirk the black smoke spread wider and denser as eleven Bf109Es raced in from the south, flying parallel with the beach. Spiers realized the danger. "I was sitting next to Baird, looking to my right at the endless black lines that snaked from the sand dunes into the water to embark onto rowing boats and other manor of pleasure craft. Glancing upwards I saw the recognizable outline of 109s. I managed to count eleven whilst shouting into the R/T 'Fighters, fighters.'"

Baird flicked the stick to port, his feet working the pedals while with his right arm he reached across and began to turn the fuel cock control hand wheels for the switching of port and starboard fuel tanks to the remaining 100-octane fuel. The nine plus boost kicked in slowly as L9481 swung towards North Foreland. The two radial engines picked up and Baird pushed the stick forward. The nose dropped towards the deck and Roskrow called out their range as 109s rapidly gained. At 250 yards he let fly with the Vickers machine gun, "it was like using a spear against a musket". Spiers shouted to Baird to take evasive action, then before their eyes the instrument panel broke into fragments, dials shattered, sending shards flying in the confines of the enclosed cockpit. The fuel gauges disintegrated on the starboard side and the air was filled with acrid smoke and flashes. Suddenly it was quiet. The smoke dispersed and as Spiers looked down the fuselage over the mainplane he could see the bullet-riddled fuselage down to the turret, accentuated by the sunbeams which shone through the smoke and sparking wiring. There was "nineteen-year-old Roskrow, his body limp and slumped against the turret controls, his right hand twitching as blood dripped onto the floor below as his life ebbed away". The young LAC had volunteered to join 254 Squadron from 48 Squadron because of the trade protection squadrons' increased shortage of air gunners and the chance for quicker elevation through the ranks. Staffelkapitän of 2./JG27 Oberlt Gert Framm watched his victim head for the sea. His distinctive Bf109E named 'Samao' peeled away with his wingman tight at his side.

LAC George W. Spiers November 1939, later Sergeant Spiers. After completing an air gunnery course, Spiers rejoined 254 Squadron, flying 31 hours and 30 minutes in May. At the start of June he found himself with P/O John Baird and LAC Roscoe operating out of Detling. They completed 3 hours and 20 minutes flying in L9481 before it was shot out of the sky one mile west of Dunkirk. George was the sole survivor. (*Malcolm Spiers*)

In the cockpit the observer turned to let his pilot know about Roskrow when he realized that Baird had been hit too, although his hands still grasped the stick. His head was slumped forward onto his chest as blood fell down his right cheek from a wound in the temple that showed through the side of his flying helmet. Another round on his left side had made a large exit wound out of his internal carotid artery and had covered him with blood. It had gushed all over Spiers' left shoulder and down his sleeve without his realization. Baird looked very peaceful with his eyes shut and Spiers was sure that his friend had passed away. Miraculously Spiers had survived an intense volley of machine-gun fire entering the cockpit. The Perspex panels had many holes, the bullets had passed him and gone into Baird, the cockpit instrument panel and the forward observer's position. He was now in the unenviable position of flying on his own and more importantly saving himself.

"My immediate reaction was to bail out, so I calmly walked into the forward compartment and attempted to lift the navigator's seat which was on top of the bail-out hatch. The seat would not fold back and was locked solid in the down position. After struggling to raise it for what seemed minutes, I realized the momentum of the Blenheim fighter was beginning to make it roll to port. I then clambered back to the pilot's cabin and viciously hit Baird's arms and his clenched hands off the stick. With my pilot's grip broken I leaned over and attempted to reach the throttles and pulled them back as the engines were still at full power and vibrating excessively. Yellow flames from the port engine were beating against the front and side windows or what remained of them and standing at the side of Baird I was about to level the machine to prevent the vicious sideslip that was causing the flames to play on the cockpit, when suddenly the windscreen imploded inwards. I felt a hot searing wind on my face, I felt my cheeks, nose, throat and mouth shrivelling under the immense heat, but I have no recollection of any pain. As soon as L9481

Sergeant Richard Roskrow who died June 1, 1940, aged twenty-one. His parents were officially told of his death on February 6, 1941. (*Paul Emery*)

righted the cockpit cleared of fire and smoke and a noticeable peace descended as the cut back engines purred and the wind gently whined through the shattered Perspex. Some miles off to port I saw a cluster of ships, an armed trawler was the nearest. As the aircraft was now at an estimated 5,000 feet I thought I could glide to it without having to open up the engines, one of which was misfiring badly, the other on fire. As I lost height, the speed of the sea passing beneath magnified alarmingly, and although the thought of using the flaps and lowering the undercarriage to reduce speed, occurred to me, I realized that I could not take my eyes off the sea for the impending ditching.

"The wind speed had decreased to about ten knots and the machine had dropped to 1,000 feet. The trawler was now only a quarter of a mile off and closing fast, and I was only slightly higher than masthead height. The Blenheim was not easy to control from my awkward position leaning over my pilot. I concentrated on trying to keep the wings parallel to the water, aware of the danger of dipping a wing tip. The ripples on the calm sea closed nearer and nearer, I estimated the air speed indicator (ASI) to be roughly 85 mph. The tail was now slightly down,

I pulled the stick and the tail slid into the water first, slowing the machine down to an estimated 40 mph and acting as an anchor. The nose smacked into the water, raising the tail unit horizontally. As it came back down into the sea, it broke off with the turret attached, because of the damage inflicted by several cannon shells and numerous machine-gun rounds. The nose then went under the waves. Water flooded in through all the imploded Perspex, principally entering through the nose. The aircraft sunk to twelve feet, then rose to the surface. I can still visualize the water bounding in through the nose like a dam which had burst; with the water also came debris, from a bombed or sunken vessel, wooden planks, rope and other material. I remember turning my back to the barrage and gently cushioning on it. This probably saved my face from severe lacerations. The silent cockpit was now full of dark blood-coloured water and I struggled to reach the normal entry-sliding hatch above the pilot's head. My feet kept slipping on the floor and I could make no progress in trying to climb up on to the seat's armrest despite numerous attempts. I sank back down.

"My mind began wandering, as I held my breath, to many of those happier occasions from my past as I realized I would not escape. I had never prayed to God with such agony or earnestness. I tried to suck water into my lungs to hasten the end but I was unsuccessful and only swallowed it. My lungs were bursting and my pulse pounded in my ear drums, brilliant flashes and yellow spots appearing in front of my eyes. I thought of the sea bed and its creatures and plant life. I had relaxed my efforts and I had started to sink downwards. I had sufficient consciousness to realize my right leg was straight and not in contact with what I thought to be the floor of the aircraft. I had actually sunk into the observer's/navigator's forward compartment. Thinking this may be a way out I drew my left leg up to it and fell out through the smashed nose. Pushing myself away from the nose I swam up to the surface and broke water about five yards away from the starboard side of the aircraft. I blew up my Mae West then released my parachute harness as the parachute was floating in front of me.

"To my surprise our machine was not lying horizontal below the surface of the water but the stub end of the fuselage was pointing upwards at 80 degrees with a jagged scar from which the turret and tail had been torn off. I think that I had been trapped inside the fuselage for over three minutes. My face now started to sting and I carefully abandoned my flying helmet and goggles as I bobbed up and down in the water. During this time I could see a trawler steaming up towards me and they were starting to lower a boat. Using front crawl I swam away from the ditched aircraft, heading towards the trawler. The seamen stretched out a pole on the end of which was a fishing net and this they passed down to me. I thrust my right fingers through the mesh and they started to pull me up, but my grip failed when I was just clear of the water and I fell back into the sea. My second attempt was successful as I interlocked my fingers on either side of the mesh. I was hauled up over the side and stood on the deck with the seamen supporting me. One pointed to my blood-stained shoulder and asked if I had been wounded, I said I didn't think so and added that if they took my wet clothes off they would soon find out. They helped me to walk along the deck towards the galley but as I stepped forward my injured ankle hurt, but it was not very painful when I walked on the toes of that foot. In the warm galley they sat me in front of a hot stove but the cheery warmth of the fire was agony to my face so they moved me away nearer the door where it was cooler. They cut open the left sleeve of my tunic with a knife but soon found I had not been wounded. After dressing my face with ointment and goose fat they took off my wet clothes. My legs had several small lacerations and they found there were small particles of shrapnel and other fragments in my skin. These they quickly removed and bound up the small wounds. After dressing me in seaman's clothing they took me below to the skipper's bunk and he came down and introduced himself, clutching a half pint glass filled with rum. I remember downing the rum in virtually one gulp and asked him for a cigarette – he soon returned with a tin of Woodbines and put them in a net that was above the bunk that I lay on. The slow drags of the cigarette and rum soon put me into a dreamless sleep.

"I woke up at about ten o'clock to the sound of heavy gunfire and a crashing of feet running on the deck above then suddenly there was an ear-splitting explosion that shook the ship; I was thrown out of the bunk with the blanket I had placed over my sore face. A sailor came down to the bunk via the vertical iron steps and took me on his shoulder to the upper deck where he told me there had been a bombing and strafing attack by a large number of German aircraft on the shipping lane they were using. The skipper came over and said he had notified the Admiralty of my rescue and added he hoped the trawler would be ordered to Ramsgate to put me off. He said his crew were exhausted after a continuous week of tireless work at Dunkirk and I might have been an excuse to get them back for a brief respite, however the Admiralty had refused this request so the skipper said he had called over a tug which was heading to Ramsgate. I noticed we were just off-shore in about five feet of water when the tug came towards us. The skipper offered me back my Mae West for the voyage remarking it was better than the navy issue. I told him he could keep it as a present and he was delighted adding that he could soon patch the bullet hole in the neck rest, which he demonstrated by inserting his finger. The tug, which I later found out hailed from Portsmouth, came alongside. One of the seamen scooped me up into his arms, took me across and helped me clamber aboard. I waved goodbye to the trawler crew on whose decks squatted forty or fifty exhausted Moroccan troops.

"I think the tug's skipper was delighted to see me as he had no other crew and wanted to have a chat with someone in English. He soon let me know he didn't think we would reach Ramsgate, he cursed the fog and he cursed the dive bombers but what really seemed to disturb him was a horrible knocking noise coming from the engine and he was sure this would soon pack up. We set off in the direction of England and after an hour or so ran into very thick fog and the sound of ships that were accompanying us soon disappeared and we found ourselves very much alone. The skipper had no chart aboard and the fog closed in to only fifty yards visibility. After a time we could hear surf breaking but he consoled me by saying it was the Goodwin Sands and asked me to go forward and point in the direction of any deep channels that I could see on the sand bottom. I seemed to spend several hours doing this apart from one or two breaks when the fog lifted. We saw no ships neither did we hear anything but the breaking of the surf. Suddenly, at about six o'clock in the evening the fog lifted and we were not too far off Ramsgate. He sailed up to the pier and I was taken off at 19.00 hours and sat on the ground. Some of the injured from other vessels made a terrible sight, particularly one Frenchman who had a large chunk of shrapnel protruding from his forehead. I seemed to be the only airman but there were many, many troops of various nationalities who looked unkempt, filthy and completely exhausted."

Military morale was tolerable as the volunteer Red Cross workers weaved amongst them making the boys and men in khaki comfortable. During the lulls the wounded called or groaned, whilst above them sounded the joyous songs of seagulls. More wounded arrived, begging their friends to stay with them as they moved slowly and vulnerably past the solitary airmen. Spiers was attended to by an extremely attractive young auxiliary nurse who looked at his face and asked him to turn his head to the left and right. She immediately burst into tears saying how terrible it was that the sailors had put goose fat on his face. She then started to gently wipe it clear with wadding which was a painful cleansing process as layers of his skin also peeled off, leaving the young Coastal Command observer with red raw bleeding patches of flesh. She then put a cooling salve on his face and he felt more contented. The nurse briefly disappeared, returning with a clipboard and asking where he would

Dunkirk: Men of various British Army units stare into the camera whilst around them their colleagues sleep. Although seen as the salvation of British forces, Dunkirk was in fact a defeat. The evacuated Allied troops had to leave all their heavy equipment and transport behind. (*Andrew Bird via Air Historical Branch*)

like to go, Ramsgate Hospital or the nearby RAF Station at Manston. Spiers decided he would rather be with his colleagues. An RAF Hillman utility van arrived and he was lifted into the passenger seat, the young auxiliary nurse waving goodbye. After his particulars were recorded by an orderly Spiers peered into one of the wards at the station, seeing a few familiar faces from Detling. After X-raying his foot and ankle the doctors found a small broken bone and treatment began on his burns.

The fate of those on board Blenheim R3630 hung in the balance too. Sergeant Richard Bates heard Leading Aircraftman William Harrison's voice through his headphones: "Fighters on our tail", then the recognizable sound of the Vickers K being fired. Harrison shouted "Break star . . ." the sentence went unfinished and Bates' headphones fell silent. A red mist spread across the turret as projectiles were thrown into the cockpit at terrific speed. With little armour plate protection Bates, Love and Harrison became casualties of the aerial duels fought in the skies off the Dunkirk beaches, where enemy fighters lurked in broken cloud. Shot down by Fw Otto Sawallisch R3630 crashed into the English Channel at 08.08 hours. 'Overdue' was originally chalked up but with no sign of the two Blenheim fighters and having calculated that all their fuel would be exhausted the orderly replaced this with the word 'Missing'. That was all that they knew at this stage. The aircraft and crews might be safe or they might not. Later a message came through: "The navigator of one was picked up at sea … brought the Blenheim which was in flames onto the sea. No further details available yet".

The relay continued. Australian Flight Lieutenant Frederick Flood, flight commander of A Flight was off at 08.00 on the third sortie of the day. Flood was flying P6957 with Pilot Officer David

Woodger in L9404, Anthony Algeo in N3523 and Sergeant Harold Sutton in N3531. The sun was out with just the odd cloud as they began their patrol. At 10.15 hours they glimpsed a Heinkel 111 way ahead, about to attack two naval units. Pushing their throttle wide open they advanced while ahead the enemy bomber was already under heavy anti-aircraft fire. Flood could only watch as the Heinkel's bombs quite plainly tumbled down, exploding. The destroyer HMS *Ivanhoe* was damaged and the rescue tug *Persia*, which had the destroyer in tow, was lifted bodily out of the water; it crashed down the right way up, toppling the men like pins.

Flood eventually got astern of his juicy target, attacking in direct line astern at 250 yards. Unfortunately the gun button on the control column was sticking in and L9494's ammunition was almost wasted. Tracer rounds disappeared as thick heavy smoke from the beaches obscured his prey. The Heinkel from KG54 escaped into cloud and headed inland, and with at least one injured crewman it staggered to get home.

Flood and 235 Squadron had yet to fly their last sortie over Dunkirk this day, when their squadron commander received notification from Coastal Command headquarters in Chatham in bold underlined type: 'Your pilots and crews must provide as adequate cover as feasible'. His men continued to cover the regiments, although they could not prevent the heavy toll of naval ships sunk. By the afternoon out of forty-one precious destroyers only nine remained, the rest either sunk or damaged. Jackson-Smith recalled:

"Like our single-engine counterparts flying from Biggin Hill, Kenley, Hawkinge and Manston it's a round trip of 100 miles. The machines devour so much fuel in the process that if the pilot was involved in a dogfight they would be limited to twenty to twenty-five minutes over Dunkirk before heading back to their airfield. The emphasis was on us and the Hudson crews to put the long hours in."

Pilot Officer Pissy Peacock was at the controls of P6957, one of fourteen 235 Blenheim fighters taking part in a Goodwin Sands – Calais – Dunkirk routine sands patrol. The unit notched up another forty hours of operational flying on the first day of June, 1940. Filton-built L9261 flown by Pilot Officer Robert Patterson was the last to land in fading light. Exhausted aircrews relaxed in chairs or lounged in deck chairs brought in from Whitstable beach. Others caught a lift into Maidstone where they met a cluster of soldiers who had been evacuated. Sergeants Owen and Copland were shocked to find that instead of gratitude they were met with open hostility. "'Where the bloody hell have you fly boys been?' was the question we were often asked in an aggressive manner of contempt", noted Owen. "We were often obscured by the smoke and cloud. We were suffering too."

Shortly after midnight having made efforts to locate the missing members of 254 Squadron, their surnames were unceremoniously wiped away with a duster. Five more casualties were entered into the log at 16 Group and their CO was notified. It was a steady toll of bodies that Bowhill and Dowding could ill afford to lose.

With the situation in Dunkirk becoming critical, training in ground defence 'for all ranks' began between operations at Detling. Trenches were dug in front of the hangars and dispersal areas. "The ground was hard, pickaxes then shovels were used and the dug-out soil was placed into sandbags. It resembled something from the 1914-1918 War." Fifty airmen were given a single 0.303 rifle for firing practice whilst officers had a solitary pistol to fire. Ammunition for the two was scarce. During a flight near Dunkirk Pilot Officer Hugh Pardoe-Williams at 11.31 hours on June 2 reported seeing a single-engine machine shot down by a similar type. His observer Sergeant Clifford Thorley thought it looked like a Hurricane. The pilot bailed out but his parachute caught fire and was instantly consumed by the flames and he fell into the sea. On a similar flight an Anson of 500 Squadron confirmed that a Blenheim bomber was apparently submerged near the edge of the Goodwin Sands with the escape hatches open. Journeying back it was warm in the sun as Pardoe-Williams passed over the English coast, near Southend-on-Sea. He and Thorley were astonished to see below long lines of children snaking towards Southend central railway station from the tree-lined avenue of Nelson Street as the Southend Educational Department began the evacuation of 9,300 adults and children. Blenheim P6958 was put into a 360-degree turn, Thorley noting down in pencil, 'There were just lines and lines of them'. With P6958 skirting Chatham the Blenheim soon neared the airfield circuit. Pardoe-Williams throttled back, closing the cowling gills, pulling the throttle right back with his left hand, whilst pulling the stick back to raise the nose to reduce the air speed further. He began to carry out the drill for landing S-Selector, U-Undercarriage, P-Pitch. In his turret Pilot Officer Edward Saunders turned his head to watch a farmer going along a hedge with a plough attachment, leaving the soil broken up behind. In his headphones crackled the voices of Pardoe-Williams saying "OK port" and Thorley "OK starboard" confirming the undercarriage was fully down. Nearing the end of the circuit P6958 turned towards the grass runway at about 1,000 feet. Its pilot reached down on the right for the flap handle and lowered the flaps fully at 100 mph ASI and approached at level flight across wind, easing the stick back and eventually holding the aeroplane just clear. With full concentration they came in just a little bit lower and the Blenheim fighter made smooth contact with the ground, wheels and tail wheel. "Not bad that one", Saunders remarked on the intercom.

Talk at the dispersal hut was of the RAF losses and replacements, the names Dunkirk and Operation Dynamo beginning to convey a special significance to all by the third day. Owing to the sudden collapse of France and the vulnerability of Britain the Air Ministry ordered a trio to transfer to fighter squadrons. The names were not drawn out of a hat but predetermined by their superiors. Flying Officers Joseph Carr and William Goddard from Boscombe Down and Sergeant John Farthing were informed that three vacancies with 235 (Fighter) Squadron were to be filled by them. The rest groaned, held out their hands and said "goodbye and good luck". Arriving in the early evening Carr, Goddard and Farthing were all in high spirits. Squadron Leader Ronnie Clarke informed them that they would probably be put on readiness straight away then shepherded the three through the blackout to their billet, a farmhouse. Shaking hands with the farmer and his wife, they retired to bed.

Pilot Officer David Woodger's batman had made his bed in one of the bell tents while most of the boys lay in soft straw under the stars, sleeping through the air raid warning. They knew there was an early start for them in the morning. "We were up again at three, groping for our tunics in the dark," Pilot Officer Norman Jackson-Smith recalled, "we all must be crawling by now, I had only taken my sweaty tunic off once in ten days, and we had lain ourselves down to rest or sleep in some queer places around Detling." On Tuesday June 4, amid the noise of chickens, eighteen crewmen awaited dawn for an order to take off. They waited but the order did not come, even by the time the sun had appeared on the horizon. The day dragged on and still the bloody telephone did not ring. "This waiting is very bad for everyone, especially those poor souls on the Dunkirk beach," wrote Sergeant Harold Sutton. At last, after seven and a half hours, the order came.

Everyone ran and clambered into their respective machines. As the light faded A Flight was ready for take-off. They powered away from the hill, climbed and levelled out. Pilot Officers Alan Wales (P6958), Peter Weil (P6957), David Woodger (N3542), Pardoe-Williams (N3531), Norman Jackson-Smith (N3523) and Flight Lieutenant Frederick Flood (L9256) and their observers and air gunners all had excellent visibility with the onset of dusk and the green hamlets of Kent transcended into the green-blue waters of the English Channel. They reported hordes of men in all kinds of craft from battleships to a small wooden rowing boat, three miles off Dunkirk containing two soldiers and a Lewis Gun, pulling hard for England. Jackson-Smith skimmed low, his air gunner, New Zealander Sergeant Colin Crystal, briefly waved. The two soldiers looked up as the machine waggled its wings saying "goodbye". Crystal stared out from his turret, within minutes they were just specks on the water. After a further three hours, the six machines were guided towards a fine white line – the cliffs of Dover. In a short time they approached the airfield, the distant mound of Detling Hill but at the last minute they were diverted by the controller to Norfolk due to overcrowding as an assortment of Fleet Air Arm machines had landed for the final push. In the lead aircraft L9256's observer leaned over his small wooden table working out a new course. Within forty minutes Bircham Newton came into view. Circling patiently, there was emptiness in their stomachs as they landed at their home base. Back in familiar territory the quietness was deafening. The men walked away from their battle-weary machines, at least all of them could get a hot bath before dining, if there was any water. Everyone turned in at 10.30, having heard a repeat of Churchill's pledge to "fight on the beaches…on the landing grounds…in the fields and in the streets".

Rising before 05.00 hours the next day, four crews assembled. Flood spoke softly, "We'll make the forty-minute trip to Detling then patrol Calais to Dunkirk, keep a good lookout for friendly and enemy fighters". They climbed through the 4/10 of cumulus cloud and headed out over Margate in tight formation and were continually fired upon over 'friendly' naval destroyers. Reaching their patrol line they spent a little time getting extra height to 10,000 feet. Now and again they caught sight of formations in the distance, but saw none near enough to engage. Skirting the beach three miles either side

An assortment of French soldiers cling to a rope from the vessel guided to pick them up having been sheltering on board a bombed French cruise liner. Fortunately they were spotted by Jackson-Smith and were rescued to fight for the freedom of their mother country. Three months later a bottle of French brandy arrived at RAF Bircham Newton for him from the French Embassy, courtesy of one of the Frenchmen. (*Operation Dynamo War Museum, Dunkerque*)

"it was deserted, littered with debris of a mechanized war, with abandoned kit, we could not fully convey what had happened there". Flood in L9256 turned them for home. Reducing height further, Jackson-Smith in N3523 located twenty-eight French soldiers five miles off Gravelines taking refuge on the hull of a bombed French cruise liner. He immediately set off for help. A fishing vessel was sighted and directed towards their location. He circled to give protection until all the occupants were safely boarded, then rechecked the situation before doing his last 360-degree turn and heading for home, only to be diverted to Manston as Detling was fog bound. Entering the dispersal hut one of the first people Jackson-Smith saw was Alan Wales quoting Shakespeare's Henry IV, "Talk not of France, sith thou hast lost it all". Flight Lieutenant Flood was speaking to the controller. "OK everybody that looks like it for today. We're at thirty minutes readiness, anyone for the mess?"

Fine weather spread over England during the day and continued into the night making conditions ideal for night bombing. Within forty-eight hours of the end of the Dunkirk rescue, on the night of

P/O Norman Jackson-Smith survived the Battle of Britain on 235 Squadron after service in the Middle East. He rejoined the unit in late 1944 when part of the Mosquito strike wing at Banff in Scotland. He became commanding officer of 248 Squadron in March 1945 which he held until October 1945. (*Norman Jackson-Smith*)

June 5-6, the Luftwaffe started air activity over British shores, targeting east coast aerodromes and ports in 12 Group Fighter Command and 16 Group Coastal Command areas. These opportunist raiders crossed the Norfolk coast and ambled around the darkened skies until they saw an aerodrome lit up as night flying training took place. At 23.55 hours a pair of unidentified aircraft flew in at speed dropping incendiary and high explosive bombs on Bircham Newton. One unexploded bomb was disarmed, damage was light and no casualties were sustained.

In the southeast the battle was now entering a new phase, relocating and increasing intensity of operations. 16 Group posted two flights to RAF Thorney Island, Hampshire to commence sorties. Squadron Leader Clarke recollected that he "received instructions to proceed to Thorney Island, after refuelling crews and machines with the necessary substance". Clarke got his gear and crew then headed straight for his new station. 235 thus severed a pleasant connection with Detling for now.

Within two hours a convoy of ground staff was heading down the narrow twisting countryside roads away from Detling Hill, on the way to Thorney Island, encountering changeable weather. At Chichester the roads were awash with motor transport. It took considerable time to locate the airfield because of its isolation and the blackout. When 235 Squadron's air-party arrived a number of 59 Squadron's advance party were still in the process of growing moustaches. It was a trend that started because nearly all of them came from Army Co-operation after France. Wing Commander John Stratton mentions in an album "my men simply decided to grow moustaches in order to make themselves look older. They were conscious of how much younger they looked without them. Everyone tried to grow moustaches but for some there was simply not enough growing on their top lip."

Blenheim fighter operations commenced immediately, but poor visibility and haze over France seriously hampered Coastal Command as they maintained a vigil over convoys bound for St Valeryen-Caux and Le Harve, 235's new operational zone. Ships approaching the harbour at St Valery were attacked by Stukas and came under sustained fire from artillery installed in cliff top positions, operating off the coast in support of the 51st Division. With reconnaissance photographs showing the quayside within range of enemy mortar fire, air cover began early for remnants of the two countries' armies to ease their evacuation. They provided seven hours cover per day over a period of four days but this was not enough for the beleaguered British and French troops on the ground. Three Blenheim fighters awaited their crews at Thorney Island, as Sergeant Aubrey Lancaster was cleared 'fit for flying':

> "The flight board said our crew was available to fly. The situation of our army was dire. 235 had been tasked by Group to harass the enemy to our limits, so we had to fly up the valley which we hoped would give us a lead on the German mechanized infantry and tanks. We got to our machine 'R-Robert' and found that I was still unable to lift my foot high enough to place it in the first foot hold, and had to be lifted onto the wing. My stomach is the colours of a rainbow and in all my rugby playing days I had never seen a bruise to compare. Our three Blenheims arrived, unfortunately 'Spy's' intelligence was forty-eight hours behind. The German heavy artillery troops with small arms and Panzers were concealed and dug in along the valley's ridge. We three naively flew up the centre of a cone of fire. 'R-Robert' was hit, my immediate thoughts were 'Here we go again!'"

Cronan's machine kept going through the hail of ground fire. His cockpit filled with smoke, there was a smell of burnt rubber, and sliding the portside window open a blast of air was washed in by the rotating propeller and the smoke began to disperse. 'R-Robert' could not be used as a fighting machine as the enemy had knocked out the compressed air pressure reservoir. The crew were defenceless; no machine guns, no operational turret, together with no brakes or flaps. Cronan swung his aircraft round and headed out into open water for home.

Forty-five minutes before landing Lancaster wound the undercarriage down by hand, praying that it was locked and would hold. With their flying speed drastically reduced to almost stalling speed the klaxon horn blared out inside the cockpit – it was deafening. The aircraft skimmed over the labyrinth of inlets and mud flats whilst approaching the boundary fence, through which is the long runway then water. Cronan struggled with the stick to keep the nose up, pushing hard with both feet on the rudder pedal and using the throttles to try desperately to control the descent and avoid disaster. With a great deal of skill Cronan put the aircraft down on the runway and eventually the Blenheim fighter halted at the northern end with literally inches to spare. Lancaster was lifted down as their two flight mechanics Hadfield and Ponaford jumped out of an approaching Humber inquiring "Are you all right, sir?"

"Close shave, why?"

"You three should see your kite."

It was full of holes. Cronan paused, "Mice". He and Lloyd climbed into the back of the Humber and pulled Lancaster aboard. It then sped off round to the dispersal hut at 12.10 hours.

As they were not required for evening operations, their commanding officer offered them a pint at the Crown Inn, with transport leaving the mess at 19.30 hours, after the briefing. For five minutes the crews listened to Ronnie hammer home the inevitable; increase the rate of operations. Individual Blenheim crews found themselves flying four operations lasting three to four hours per day. Pilots watched the fuel gauge as much as they scanned the sky. During their second patrol on June 12 a dozen Blenheim fighters patrolled near St Valery, not realizing that it had fallen in the morning and that fighting in the area had ceased. Flying Officer William Goddard (L9447), together with Pilot Officers Norman Jackson-Smith (N3524), David Woodger (N3530), John Coggins DFM (N3523) and

Sergeant John Farthing (N3542) sighted Junkers 87s near Le Harve with no protection. Unfortunately as they plunged into their dive it was impossible to keep up with them. When cruising they had a speed of 238 mph and although the Blenheim fighters had 255 mph there were few chances of getting them because of friendly anti-aircraft fire. The 51st Highland Division was unable to get clear and the evacuation was cruelly thwarted: "The bulk of the RAF's effort was completely wasted from the point of view of the land forces, it was like trying to hold the tide back with a sand wall".

Six days of perfect weather meant their focus switched from the Le Havre evacuation to the Channel Islands. Late afternoon sun streamed in through the open dispersal door. Aircrews of 235 found themselves in unfamiliar territory with the arrival of Vickers Wellingtons L4212, L4221, L4342, L4352, L4354 and L4356 which were fitted with the cylindrical directional wireless installation (DWI). Squadron Leader Clarke entered with Flight Lieutenant Ian Gallaway and naval Lieutenant David Luard. Both introduced themselves and as an airman brought a tray of tea, Peacock switched off the radiogram. Jackson-Smith said of the arrival, "We sipped our tea whilst Gallaway explained they were to be attached to our squadron for a month for operations around the English Channel and Channel Islands". Regular convoy patrols were kept up whilst keeping a close eye on the Channel Islands. Alderney harbour was straining under the weight of men as the main body of troops left around midday on 17th, sailing along the windward side of Sark to Jersey on SS *Joy Bell*. Five miles out a pair of fighter Blenheims kept watch as the *Courier* began taking families of soldiers to Guernsey.

On Tuesday June 18, Winston Churchill made his stirring speech to the British people: "Never in the field of human conflict was so much owed by so many to so few"; it was repeated on a broadcast by the BBC in the evening. 235 Squadron crews, split between RAF Hendon and Thorney Island, listened intently to it in the messes.

Jackson-Smith commented: "We joined other airmen in painting a country which we looked likely to die for – most remarkably red". Wales, Woodger and Flood, with the restraints of youth and caste no longer upon them, had no time to make formal advances to members of the opposite sex, so they raided the Chichester shops and offices in search of youth and beauty, and took them out. Other aircrew left the aerodrome walking down the lane that was teeming with wildlife. Sergeant Aubrey Lancaster remembered, "We enjoyed beautiful weather. A popular song in June was 'Indian Summer' by Sidney Bechet. We had found a beautiful old sixteenth century pub called The Crown Inn at Emsworth, the local dark ale and cider was smashing and what's more it was in walking distance." The war seemed a million miles away. Could this be the same world in which they had all battled days ago?

It was frustrating for Clarke and 235 Squadron until June 27 when, shortly before midday, three B Flight Blenheim fighters investigated a bomber which had come down in the North Sea. Flying Officer Carr in N3541, Sergeant Hall in N3540 and Sergeant Basil Quelch in P4845 set off to do a square search in the vicinity where a Waddington-based Handley Page Hampden P1239 of 50 Squadron had ditched whilst returning from night operations. The last two wireless messages received read: '03.00 hours. Flying on one engine. 03.59 hours. Going down 15 miles from Dutch coast'. Carr led the three on a two-hour and thirty-five minute search for survivors, in a twenty by twenty miles square at 52.40N, 04.20E. A further three aircraft continued looking for two hours and forty minutes but likewise found no sign of wreckage or crew. Wing Commander Norman Crockart, the thirty-one-year-old commanding officer of 50 Squadron piloting P1239 had been in his post for two weeks. A charismatic sportsman and leader was lost, a bitter blow to his squadron and family.

As June 27 broached its eleventh hour members of A Flight 235 lounged at dispersal in an assortment of chairs and deckchairs. Lancaster and Pardoe-Williams played draughts, as the outside temperature rose and permission was granted to be on standby without tunics. At about midday they walked to lunch. In the mess hall the smell of stale tobacco hung in the air. Whilst waiting for their meal in the sergeants' mess there was muted conversation. Lancaster borrowed a fountain pen from

Sergeant Sidney Bartlett to write a note to his girlfriend Dorothy Hodgson and posted it outside. Just as the remainder of the squadron sat down for lunch in their respective messes they were interrupted by a call from an orderly: "All 235 A Flight aircrew report to operations room immediately". Everyone dropped their irons [cutlery] and dashed out, arriving breathless. A 16 Group controller was asking for Squadron Leader Clarke. Clarke picked up the receiver and the clipped voice spoke: "Clarke, the British Army request a reconnaissance in the Zuider Zee area. Six aircraft are to take off immediately, this operation is of the utmost importance." In reply Clarke recommended sending a single Blenheim as he believed that it would not create a large response from the enemy. He was either ignored or overruled.

Flying Officer Peacock cast an apprehensive look around the room at the nonplussed airmen pulling up a chair. Except for the occasional scrape or clink of a cup, all was quiet. Clarke revealed that the trip would be to Amsterdam then to the southern coast of the Zuider Zee, looking for invasion barges and troop move-

JUNE 1940.

THURSDAY

27

STAY BUT TILL TO-MORROW, AND YOUR PRESENT SORROW WILL BE WEARY, AND WILL LIE DOWN TO REST.

Jeremy Taylor.

Sergeant Phil Lloyd's parents, James and Laura Lloyd, of Conway, Caernarvonshire, Wales kept this desk diary date page with a fitting verse from June 27, 1940 when their nineteen-year-old son died. (*Phil Lloyd*)

ments. "I began to have immediate misgivings," reported Lancaster, "we had flown a reconnaissance the previous day over the Maas and Scheldt estuaries and it was a rather dicey trip. There was a substantial collection of barges protected by heavy anti-aircraft fire." Intelligence told the assembled crews, "if you encounter trouble you should turn south rather than go north where the Luftwaffe has the main concentration of fighters". Observers unfurled and pored over maps, marking their route in pencil. "Our track would take us right over Schipol aerodrome where 'Jerry' fighters were based", Pilot Officer Hugh Wakefield takes up the tale: "fitters and riggers had got our charges in tiptop condition. Peacock, my pilot, did his preliminary checks and N3542's engines roared into life and thus calmed our anxieties." Clarke boarded N3541, with Pilot Officers Hugh Pardoe-Williams in P6958, Alan Wales in N3543, Peter Weil in P6956, and John Cronan in L9447 consecutively starting up. The Blenheims were weighed down by their long-range fuel loads of 14,500 lbs. They set the fuel cock control wheels as required with the 100-octane fuel supply from the outer tanks turned on and the others turned off. During the warm up, pilots checked each engine in turn, together with the oil pressure, the magnetos and sparking plugs. If none of their individual radial engines sounded rough they held the throttle at a constant 100 rpm and next the air cylinder pressure was checked for the brakes. With a shout from the duty corporal of "chocks away" airmen scurried under the rear wing tips, grabbed the chock ropes and returned out of the way. Parking brakes were released and they rolled out on to the runway. With a quick check on the crosswind the six machines pulled off at exactly 13.00 hours, heading away from the airfield in total silence. LAC William 'Lelly' Day shielded his eyes from the glare of the sun and watched until they were specks in the distance. It would be a long and memorable day for Clarke and 235 Squadron.

Joining up they gained altitude to 5,000 feet as they followed the River Yare which was brimming with an assortment of vessels. They passed over Great Yarmouth's Dutch pier out into clear water, in

The graves of Pilot Officer John Cronan and Sergeant Phil Lloyd. (*Phil Lloyd*)

line astern. There was not a cloud in the sky, scarcely a breath of wind on the sea and the heat in the cockpits was almost unbearable. They wore all their uniform; silk scarf, one piece flying suit or Irvin jacket, flying boots or shoes and the obligatory yellow Mae West. An occasional ship was seen on the way across. Lancaster aboard L9447 checked his coordinates for landfall between Noorwijk and Ijmuiden, "so far it had been uneventful". Five miles from the Dutch coast there was still no cloud cover to hide their approach. Wakefield noted "there was cumulus over land, which appeared to be nine-tenths. This was however changeable. My pilot steered N3542 into a vic pattern, with Clarke leading." Maintaining their height at 5,000 feet the six crossed the Dutch coast.

On the beach at Zandvoort bathers paused, heads glancing upwards as the six English bomber planes turned northeast towards Amsterdam. The clouds were slight and patchy, the anti-aircraft fire spasmodic and the Blenheims spread out to avoid the shell bursts as they sped over countryside, canals and Schiphol aerodrome. Wakefield observed: "it is cluttered with German machines, bombers and fighters, some of which appeared to be taking off. Suddenly the ack-ack stopped." The crews knew what that meant!

Sergeant Phil Lloyd by the port wing of 'P-Pip' at Bircham Newton. (*Phil Lloyd*)

Wreckage of Blenheim N3543 after the air battle of June 27, 1940; the remains would be melted down for scrap one month later. (*Hans Nauta*)

Contrary to intelligence it was not from Schiphol but from Rotterdam that the trouble came. Bf109Es of II./JG54 had moved twenty-four hours earlier and completed two familiarization flights over the local area. The warning sounded at 15.02 local time, "Intercept formation of Blenheim bombers reported near Amsterdam". Within seconds Austrian born Lt Jochen Schypeck was airborne with his wingman, soon linking up with the Gruppen-kommadeur of I./JG54 Hubertus Von Bonn, who had taken off from Schiphol. Through the light cloud they quickly spotted the green/brown upper surfaces of the Blenheims despite losing them on occasion as they blended into the countryside. At full throttle they rolled away and dived. Lancaster watched as the fighters came in like a swarm of bees, while fellow observer Ollie Wakefield reported:

"The most stunning and frightening moment of my young life when the Bf109Es shot out of the glorious sparse cloud in a head-on attack. It was a stupendous sight and lasted for two or three minutes as we found ourselves breaking formation and milling around

Pilot Officer John Cronan was born in Simla, India before his family moved to Birkenhead, New Zealand. He stands in front of a Mark I Blenheim K7122. (*Theo Boiten*)

the sky with 109s as our dancing partners! We knew the Blenheim fighter could turn inside the 109E if we knew precisely when to do it. To this end, we had devised a system for when we were under attack. I moved up from the observer's position, opened the portside window behind the pilot, stuck my head out, looking back along the fuselage, and signalled to Peacock with my thumb exactly when and in which direction to turn."

N3542, having survived a frontal attack, was almost hit a second time from the upper rear port side just south of Schiphol. The 109 closed in to around 400 yards, Wakefield signalled his pilot hard to starboard and the 109 overshot. Peacock automatically turned hard right and got a short burst in as the enemy fighter went away. Peacock made for the nearest cloud. On N3542's starboard side twenty-year-old Pilot Officer Peter Weil found a number of Messerschmitts in front of him and he promptly directed his belly-pack guns on them. Pressing the gun button, he saw streams of incoming tracer rushing past him. Whipping out of formation he found himself amongst the enemy. At once he went into a tight turn inside a 109, his observer Bartlett screaming into the intercom "Break right" as a second 109 joined in the pursuit of 'hounds versus hares' watching for an opportunity to pounce. Weil milled around with the 109s whilst making steady progress towards the coast, as he had no chance of beating them to cloud cover. In his headphones there was a lot of chatter as fellow crews fought over a scattered area. N6957 survived for thirteen minutes then Oberlt Roloff Von Aspern and Franz Eckerle and Ofw Max Stotz shot the Blenheim out of the sky just off Egmond with no escape for its occupants.

The three Messerschmitts moved onto their second victim south of Amsterdam catching Pilot Officer Hugh Pardoe-Williams over the suburb of Ouderkerk on Amstel. The air around Pardoe-Williams was vibrant having evaded the foe but suddenly it was as if P6958 had received a punch in the abdomen, taking direct hits amidships near the gunner's turret. He talked calmly into the intercom but there was no reply. The control column went slack in his hands and there was a smell of burning. His Blenheim lost height as more rounds streamed into P6958. The Exeter-born pilot remained calm and watching the starboard engine cough and splutter he shut it down. Not only had his aircraft been hit, Pardoe-Williams himself had also been shot. His breathing was becoming laboured but he was unable to see the extent of his injury because of his Irvin jacket. In the nose Sergeant Clifford Thorley lay on the floor as if sleeping, a dark red pool moving in motion with the aircraft. Pardoe-Williams struggled to keep the Blenheim level and decided to make a forced landing despite barely being able to see through the shattered and cracked windscreen.

In Ouderkerk on Amstel, Jan Van Dijk was acting chief of air raid precautions. At 15.22 hours a message was received that a plane had been shot down in a polder. Dijk travelled quickly to the site, "it appeared the pilot of the plane had tried to land on reclaimed land". The machine had disintegrated as it slithered along the ground before coming to rest in a water channel, debris lying all around. Blenheim P6958 was completely burnt out, only the tail unit survived. A rescue team of Dutch and German soldiers sifted through the wreckage and discovered the charred remains of Thorley and Saunders. They also found the pilot. Checking for vital signs they discovered a pulse – he was alive! Pardoe-Williams was badly injured with burns, a bullet wound and a head injury. He received first aid and was laid out on a stretcher. Within seconds the British flyer was surrounded by German soldiers. Dijk recalled, "I have never seen a man who behaved so bravely. He was only anxious about his crew and did not give any reply when interrogated by the German officers about his operation as he lay there." The twenty-three year old was transferred to a hospital in Ouderkerk on Amstel where two doctors worked tirelessly, one to prevent his lung from collapsing while the other treated his burns. He was monitored throughout the night. He recovered enough to eat a meal and sip some water and shortly after this was transferred to a German military hospital in central Amsterdam, by order of the German occupiers. Pilot Officer Hugh Pardoe-Williams died a couple of days later as a result of his lung injury.

Lt Jochen Schypeck watched Hptm Von Bonin open fire on a single Blenheim at 3,000 feet. His shots disabled the mid-upper gunner's accurate return fire, Bonin broke away and Schypeck was in the killing zone, pressing the firing button and sending streams of tracer into the forward fuselage. In the process an engine caught fire. Inside the Blenheim the pilot had lowered the seat in an attempt to escape the piercing rounds that thumped at the back of the armour plating. Pilot Officer Alan Wales was desperately trying to evade the 109 and pushed the control column forward, the nose dropping. Below, people near the town of Haarlem saw a Blenheim approaching from a northerly direction, flying at extremely low level and twisting and turning to get out of the 109's line of fire which was flying above and behind the British fighter. The Blenheim was so low that it even had to pull up to fly over a railway line embankment. Wales then desperately pulled up a second time to gain height, allowing his crew Pilot Officer John Needham and Sergeant Tom Jordan to bail out through the front escape hatch. Needham had watched his pilot's forefinger indicate the escape hatch at his side and he had smiled as if there was something funny about it all. The sergeant released the catch, the hatch was jettisoned away and he peered out. People watching from the ground saw the escape hatch open and fall away, however it was too late. The Blenheim stalled and plummeted earthwards, briefly regaining control before N3543 force landed, ploughing through a meadow and coming to rest on an embankment at the edge of a potato field along the Valkenburgerweg in the outskirts of Oegstgeest. The Blenheim broke up due to the bumpy ride, throwing mechanical parts over 170 yards. The starboard engine and fuel tank was ripped from the machine as it hurtled along, ending up some distance away from the main wreckage. Jordan was flung out and found lying in the meadow by local farm workers, dying in their arms shortly afterwards. A second party of farm workers found Needham's body on the other side of the meadow in a lifeless state. Unfortunately the body of N3543's captain, Pilot Officer Alan Wales was only found when the German occupiers salvaged the machine's mangled carcass weeks later.

The final Blenheim was flown by New Zealander Pilot Officer John Cronan, his observer Sergeant Aubrey Lancaster recording: "Everyone began rushing around the sky like madmen, our leader Clarke disappeared to our stern. Then an unstoppable weight of fire came through the fuselage. One nicked my ankle, it felt like a bee sting. There was turmoil inside the cockpit, Cronan was hit in the back of his right shoulder, the impact knocking him forward over the control column." L9447 immediately dropped its nose; regaining his balance Lancaster then grabbed hold of Cronan's Irvin jacket with both hands and tried to pull his pilot into an upright position. "I thought we could then level off, once I'd got hold of the stick, then the idea was to manhandle him out of his bucket seat so I could try and get us back to England." Trying to move him brought the dazed New Zealander around and Cronan immediately lunged for the stick only to find the essential wiring and cables that made it function had melted away. Their eyes met as another volley of fire ripped like razor wire into the aircraft skin. The starboard engine caught fire. The observer looked back down the dark fuselage, sunlight shining through the gaping holes.

"It reminded me of stories a gunner had told us of the Welsh coal mines seeing daylight as you came up in the cage from the coal face. There was no movement from our gunner. Sergeant Phillip Lloyd was slumped forward over his Vickers machine gun, rounds had penetrated his back. Cronan screamed at me to get out. One of the first things that was drilled into us was that you NEVER got out of the top hatch because the tail would hit you. You ALWAYS got out of the forward lower hatch and always went head first so that you didn't get your head chopped off by the propellers, only your feet! He screamed a second time to get out. I went forward to the escape hatch situated on the starboard side in the floor of the nose section."

The handle was set into the escape hatch; lifting it up Lancaster then tugged the handle, it was supposed to drop away immediately, that was the theory, but it refused to do so.

"Nothing happened. I jumped up and down on it, and then stamped on it in desperation but to no avail. Whilst battling with the emergency exit I looked ahead through the nose and saw that we were diving at speed, rapidly approaching a herd of grazing cows. Deciding there was no future in staying where I was I turned to go out of the top. My pilot and friend had disappeared; out of the top hatch since I'd have to use his seat as a stepping stone."

Tentatively climbing into a position where Lancaster was half out of the cockpit his upper body was buffeted by the strong wind. He was holding on to the hatch's central hand-grip and wondering if he could possibly manage to get on the wing and slide off in an effort to miss the tail when suddenly there was a bang. Something hit his head and he briefly lost consciousness. When Lancaster came to he was falling head over heels. He instinctively placed his hand to where the ripcord should have been located but to his dismay there was no parachute!

"I knew I'd put it on when we went into action and on looking around me I saw it floating above my head some five or six feet away, unopened. Reaching up I pulled it towards me by the straps put my arms through and pulled the ripcord, it blossomed. Thinking what a big canopy it was I glanced down and smacked into the ground. My parachute opened thirty feet off the deck! I hit the ground with a hell of a thump which knocked me senseless for two or three minutes."

He came to and found that his billowing parachute was dragging him towards a water irrigation ditch. Battling with his quick release button, hitting it with his clenched fist until it finally released, he wriggled around until he extricated himself from his 'chute. He looked for some cover and found he was less than fifty yards away from a farmhouse. Lancaster noticed a couple peeping at him from round a doorway.

"I walked across to the couple looking at me and tried to talk to them in English and German but they stared blankly back, then gestured me into the house and sat me down. Within a few minutes a Dutch doctor and nurse came to see if I was all right. I had a nasty tear in my left arm and a nick in my ankle. They cleaned the wounds and bandaged them up. They had just finished when a Dutch policeman knocked at the open front door. He entered full of apologies and tried to take me into custody saying otherwise he would be for the high jump by the Germans. He indicated that we should all get into the doctor's car – a Renault Primaquatre Sport in which we sped through the lanes. After a five or seven-minute journey we got out and there was quite a crowd of Dutch people who gave a little cheer. There was my pilot, John Cronan, lying under his parachute. The policeman and doctor pulled back the parachute. One side of his face was smashed like a piece of rare steak. He had gone out of the top hatch and the tail had hit him. His parachute had opened just before impact. I fell to my knees and I went to pieces for a while and shed a few tears – we had been great pals for what seemed ages, all our operational life, we three never changed crews. I felt alone when a hand patted my back and a gentleman in fluent English asked if I was all right. He explained that he was a former KLM pilot. At this point a German motorbike and sidecar combination roared up with a German officer in the sidecar. He gave me a smart salute and told me in English that I was his prisoner. Since I had no head gear I told him that we didn't salute without a hat on and he said it was the same in the Luftwaffe. He offered pillion or sidecar, I opted for the sidecar and off we went. Thus began my five years behind barbed wire, finishing up in Stalag Luft III."

The Van Wyk brothers watched the air battle unfold. It was a pleasant summer's day in Waverveen village. The temperature had risen to twenty degrees and the sky was dotted with white puffy clouds.

Ted, aged sixteen with his two brothers Cor (twenty-one) and Egbert (eighteen) found themselves cutting hay by hand in a section of a field just west of their dairy farm buildings. "We heard engine noises in the distance coming from the south, British engines. Next there was a sound 'tick-tick-tick-tick' of machine guns as the German fighters mercilessly attacked the scattering twin-engine Blenheim fighters. We watched transfixed as the six scattered, two made for the clouds and most went out of sight."

There were two aircraft on fire, one was Cronan's. It made a wide descending turn towards them. Cor recalled:

"We were sure that it would land on top of us in the field that we were working in. Dropping our tools we began running towards our house to escape, as fast as our young legs would carry us. We were barely there when the machine hit just west of our farm track on the neighbour's side on a raised dyke that formed the Poeldijk Road in front of the farm. We ran up and watched it burn. It was at this point that we noticed a second machine trailing smoke in the distance and going down far to the northwest of us, near Ouderkerk ann de Amstel at 15.30. As our plane burned it drew a crowd of onlookers who gathered around L9447. There was a man still inside the turret as it burned, he looked dead already. The pilot of the plane had landed somewhere south of us towards the town of Wilnis."

Peacock had managed to evade the Germans. Observer Wakefield reported:

"After the attack we decided it would be unwise to return the way we had entered, so we flew south to Amsterdam, photographed the harbour with no sign of German naval units, flew along the inner coast of the Zuider Zee and passed Hoorn to Texel where at 14.30 to the southwest we encountered a Heinkel 115 seaplane flying at 400 feet. Peacock attacked and only broke off the engagement when all remaining 1,000 rounds were expended. During the first mêlée and evasive manoeuvres we lost our Perspex canopy and the side and front windows, and so we returned in a somewhat draughty condition to Bircham Newton."

Peacock was credited with one Bf109E destroyed and another one damaged, the latter shared with another pilot. The second machine to make it back to Bircham Newton was the squadron commanding officer Ronnie Clarke, in 'L-London' N3541. Pilot Officer Norman Jackson-Smith recalled what Ronnie said: "He was leading the five machines. He twisted down underneath Cronan's machine, two came down on his port quarter, taking violent evasive action. Gave one a short burst, then fought his way out and escaped."

The operation was both a failure and a terrible shock to the closely-knit squadron, as is recorded in the unofficial diary:

"These four pilots and 'Gunner' Saunders, all old members of this squadron, are a great loss as they represent practically all that is left of the original 235 Squadron. 'Johnnie' Cronan, a New Zealander, with Sergeant Aubrey Lancaster put up a splendid show a month ago when shot down into the sea. Weil, Wales and Williams have just recently developed into useful, resourceful fighter pilots and 'Gunner' Saunders, a friendly and amiable fellow will be universally missed as will plucky 'Phil' Lloyd. As this action took place over the Zuider Zee it is hoped that some of them escaped."

Waiting patiently for news of her boyfriend Sergeant Thomas 'Tom' Jordan was Miss Dobson. News of his death whilst on operations eventually reached the eighteen year old:

"I received word from the War Office after making several enquires. Both of us were head over heels in love and had planned to marry once he had sought permission from both families. Tom's family lived in Belfast, Northern Ireland. It was deeply upsetting losing Tom. I have never got over it, and cherish those few days, weeks and hours we both had together."

The young lady never married. Jackson-Smith commented:

"I recall going over to the village church opposite the aerodrome to say a prayer for those lost with 'Dave' Woodger, before we got too boozy. The door was locked, so we knelt on the brick steps and prayed for 'Johnnie' and the boys and those who loved them."

Unaware, across the English Channel in Berlin an evening broadcast announced the particulars of the daylight operations: "Yesterday six British planes crossed the Dutch coast. They were immediately engaged by German fighters and all shot down."

A mere forty-eight hours after this 'black day', Peacock was flying again with Flight Lieutenant Andrew Fletcher and Flying Officer William Goddard. Not many watched them go as they left to conduct a reconnaissance for the Royal Navy of Texel and Terschelling in Holland. Wheels touched down, Ollie Wakefield described their return:

"Pissy turned crosswind to look around before taxiing to dispersal. Fletcher was landing behind us and to one side. He rolled to a halt thirty yards away. We opened our side windows and let the cool air from our slipstream blow in. That felt good. We were debriefed by Spy and two WAAFs named Betty and Mary who handed us sweet tea and packets of cigarettes – as many as you could smoke."

Later a dozen went for a pint, then nodded off into an uneasy doze.

Six crews were wanted for reconnaissance patrols off the Channel Islands for two consecutive days, which provided a welcome respite. Time passed as they droned back and forth, totally unaware that two days earlier the Luftwaffe had bombed St Helier and St Peter Port, which by then was empty of troops, causing quite unnecessary casualties to civilians. Forty-four killed, including four disembarking at White Rock after rescuing distressed animals from evacuated Alderney. One Blenheim returned after four and a half hours with less than ten gallons of fuel, with his engines throttled back. As the squadron packed up for the day, four days leave was granted for several crews. Their time was mostly spent sleeping, bathing, writing letters and catching up with loved ones. The dispersal seemed more settled. Leading Aircraftman William Day was surrounded by engine cowlings as he helped a new LAC patch bullet holes. Soon the ground crew had done their work and the fighter Blenheims sat waiting.

As the month of June closed and July came in Sergeant Harold Sutton noted, "At least we were not afraid to fight, or if necessary die, and were in a confident mood that we should give a good account of ourselves".

CHAPTER SIX

A Pastoral Symphony

Air force personnel living off base walked or cycled the two miles towards their aerodrome. Foxgloves, daisies and swathes of poppies flourished in nearby hedgerows, as local gardens were given over to vegetables. Drawing level with The King's Head Inn the proprietor was taking the wooden blackout boards down, it was 04.02 hours. Sergeants Basil Quelch and Harold Sutton stood outside the pub as an MG TA accelerated past with two indistinguishable figures inside, the roar of its S4 engine lost as it travelled north towards Church Lane. Both sergeants walked north too, passing a pair of brick and flint cottages, their front gardens brimming with vegetation as the wooden picket fence tried to stem the tide. In the meantime the Luftwaffe started to make probing attacks on shipping in the English Channel. As July 1 dawned on the European side of the Channel the principal bomber within the Luftwaffe's II Fliegerkorps, KG 2 Dornier 17Z, was unleashed.

Just after 05.30 hours the pilots, observers and air gunners were settling down for forty winks before breakfast. A light breeze ruffled the pinned foolscap sheet of typed initials and surnames of the twenty-one crews required for 'special convoy duty'. It had been a reasonable morning; two crews had already flown operationally. Flying Officer Joseph Carr on his first sortie since being promoted was in L9393 with a scratch crew. He flew on the second trip accompanied by Sergeants Quelch in N3540 and Coggins in N3541. All were now heading back after completing a rather nervy four-hour patrol which saw them report that Guernsey and Jersey aerodromes were fully serviceable.

Flood in B-Bertie along with Carr in T-Tommy, climbed away from Thorney Island, ten miles clear of Ventnor on the Isle of Wight. A controller told them of two unidentified contacts. Below the unmolested convoy steamed onward unaware of the potential danger, as the warm breeze announced the onset of summer. In an inconclusive combat with a pair of Dornier 17s off the east coast of Guernsey, the two RAF machines closed to within fifty yards of the stern. Two hundred and fifty rounds struck the rear gunner's position, its machine gun hung limply, the gunner either wounded or dead after three heavy bursts. "Our two Blenheim aircraft were unable to press home their attack owing to the superior speed of the enemy aircraft. The engagement was broken off when all our aircrafts' front gun ammunition had been expended," wrote the Air Ministry intelligence officer in a later report.

It had been a reasonable day with anti-invasion patrols; "we realized the severity of the situation when we heard twelve Swordfish had taken off at 23.00 hours from Detling and none had returned!" These naval crews had gone to bomb barges holed up in the River Maas, east of Rotterdam. They were torn to shreds by anti-aircraft fire which lit up the sky brilliantly, claiming two victims. On their inward journey, the Swordfish were battered by the weather. Crews put down at Manston, Sandwich, and Harwich, with forced landings at Harrocks Island and Birchington. "Of course I said

235 and 236 Squadron acted as fighter escorts to 53 and 59 Squadron aircraft during the bombing of invasion barges in the continental ports by day and night. (*Andrew Bird*)

to myself it was an unfortunate case, as we walked to our aircraft," Sergeant Basil Quelch recalled. He spent about an hour pottering around his machine, checking and re-checking, then with Flight Lieutenant Andrew Fletcher and Pilot Officer David Woodger, Quelch cruised around the skies at 6,000 feet before signing the RAF Form 700. For want of something better to do Flight Lieutenant Frederick Flood deposited a gramophone and a collection of 78 rpm records at the squadron dispersal, then accompanied Fletcher and Woodger for an early meal. The mess was crowded with a throng of nationalities in varying shades of blue, with WAAF women serving. The air was filled with smoke. After eating Fletcher, Woodger and Quelch immersed themselves on a photographic reconnaissance operation covering Germany's Lower Saxony; Hamburg to Bremen encompassing Cuxhaven and Bremerhaven with particular attention being requested to check the estuaries leading to Hamburg and Bremen.

They taxied to the far side of the aerodrome, turned into the wind, checked the instruments and opened the throttles. Flying out at 12.15/12.25 they were soon at 5,000 feet and penetrating big dirty grey clouds. Quelch in P4845 kept in close to Woodger in L9252, with Fletcher in L9446 leading. Isolated and alone, the air gunner onboard P4845 started to suffer from cramp. Weather conditions worsened and Woodger's machine was buffeted about. He was unable to maintain his station, the air turbulence making his eighteen-year-old air gunner sick over the turret controls. He turned back, landing at 13.15 hours. Accompanying Fletcher became increasingly difficult and Quelch struggled to progress. With some reluctance the Oxfordshire man turned 180 degrees and headed in the direction of base saying "it's not worth putting our lives at risk". Entering a landing time of 16.20 in his flying logbook, he said: "As far as I could see in three directions the cumulonimbus cloud lay like a great heavy grey wall which we flew through, losing contact."

The remaining single Blenheim fighter flew on toward Lower Saxony. Onboard observer Pilot Officer George Hebron checked their course, allowing for the changeable wind speeds, whilst eighteen-year-old Sergeant William Peebles tightened his Irvin collar. Even though it was summertime in the exposed turret the air was howling through. With Hebron's guidance they found all the locations despite the low cloud base over the target areas. Spasmodic and intense anti-aircraft fire greeted Fletcher as Hebron took several photographs, visiting Cuxhaven, Bremerhaven, Bremen near the River Weser and Hamburg. As well as the normal long flight fuel load of 468 gallons his pilot made use of the 100-octane fuel, turning the inner and outer wheel to engage the boost to evade the ack-ack. With a rollercoaster of a ride across the Channel L9446 joined the circuit at 17.30, landing at 17.50 with only ten gallons remaining "and the contents of two petrol lighters", the squadron diarist added.

Later Flying Officer William Goddard led Bodsie Laughlin and Pilot Officer Robert Patterson, escorting and shadowing five Lockheed Hudsons of 206 Squadron. Departure was at 16.45 on an offensive sortie against shipping at Schulpan Gat near Texel on the Frisian islands. After a monotonous flight with no sightings in Willemsoord they all flew to the mouth of the River Mass where a gaggle of Dutch fishing trawlers were retrieving their nets. Seven miles north of The Hook of Holland merchantmen were sighted. The five Hudsons dive-bombed from 5,000 feet. Going vertically straight down they saw the last reflections of sunlight on the charcoal-coloured sea. One vessel received a direct hit though concentrated return fire made it hell as 'flaming onions' battered them, their remaining bombs dropping wide. The starboard wing of a Hudson was heavily damaged. Limping home they successfully landed at 19.30 hours. A diary entry from 235 reads: "sighted and bombed without any hitting the targets".

Three members of the squadron's B Flight went to escort a convoy going into the mouth of the English Channel. A twin-engine biplane was sighted with floats, a red rudder with white disc and a black swastika in the middle. It displayed the lettering 'Da' with red crosses. Ronnie Clarke "believed it may have been a Heinkel 59". He was also taken aback when information was received from Northwood that Fighter Command had been casting their net around for volunteers from other branches of the service and had already requisitioned fifty-two pilots from the Fleet Air Arm. Despite the fact that the really serious fighting had barely got underway, some fighter squadrons were already considerably depleted. As Clarke knew all too well!

As paperwork was being completed in the day-to-day running of the squadron a senior officer from 16 Group Headquarters telephoned. In the conversation it was caustically suggested

He 59 on the water shot down by 217 Squadron. Despite a broken port float, in a position 146 degrees from Start Point, its three crew are seen taking to the dinghy. The sea swell was described as moderate. (*Andrew Bird via P/O Len Murphy*)

to the 235 acting adjutant, Flying Officer Robert Jamison, that a detachment be seconded to RAF Detling to act as fighter escort for Swordfish of 825 Squadron Fleet Air Arm, after a number had failed to return during night-time operations two days previously. He sat dumb-founded. Fortunately as the evening dragged on the talking dwindled and the military plan was rescinded. But things were getting pretty rough; as the Luftwaffe tried to close the English Channel to allied shipping and clear the air of RAF fighters, adrenaline was running high on both sides. In preparation for a possible invasion on the southern English coast barges were moved to Belgian and Dutch ports, with 800 hemmed in at Rotterdam. A number of raids were plotted off the east coast during the day as the wheels of organizational change turned. South African Air Vice-Marshal Sir Quintin Brand motioned 236 Squadron with immediate effect from Fighter to Coastal Command as its commander-in-chief Air Marshal Bowhill was fearful of weakening his own frontline fleet by transferring any of his forces or materials elsewhere. At a sprawling conference of RAF military leaders in Whitehall he kicked off the meeting by encroaching into other commands, confirming that 53 and 59 Squadrons from Army Co-operation were seconded to Coastal Command, 53 going to Detling and 59 to Thorney Island. There was no disagreement and the deputy chief of air staff Air

Commander-in-Chief of Coastal Command Frederick 'Ginger' Bowhill was elated to have 'some teeth' when the trade protection squadrons were passed to his command. However the four squadrons were frequently called upon by Fighter Command to plug the gaps during the Battle of Britain. (*Royal Air Force Museum, London*)

Vice-Marshal Sholto Douglas emphasized the requirement to intercept German naval craft in the continental ports. These two squadrons would play a greater part within the command. Without prior arrangement Sholto Douglas stood up, his portly frame silhouetted against the panelled wall, taking on the appearance of a Fougasse character. He spoke at length of the work being done by Bowhill's fighter Blenheim squadrons operating from Scotland.

Enemy attacks were becoming more frequent in northeast Scotland and interceptions made by 254 Squadron had helped the Scottish fishing fleet, furthermore their incursions into enemy airspace over the fjords and coastal waters of Norway hampered the German movement of supplies by sea when combined with the Royal Navy, as they were to do on the first Saturday in July.

Pausing at the dispersal tent flap there was a dull glow from the stove in the middle whilst outside a continuous waterfall of rain bounced off the canvas. Sergeant Albert Tubbs put his Mae West on. The telephone orderly lifted the Bakelite receiver "254 now at readiness". The waiting started. When the phone rang two aircraft were instructed to stand by. Tubbs and Pilot Officer Victor Patterson's observers and air gunners lifted themselves up out of their chairs. Sergeant Robert McVeigh dropped his reading material *Murder in The Submarine Zone* face down on the chair's arm. They left at once, hurrying to their Blenheim fighters. The light outside was stronger, the sky a cobalt blue. A small gathering muffled against the chill watched them take off.

Saturday July 6 was just getting started. Sergeant Alan Tubbs flew L8842 with Pilot Officer Victor Patterson in P6950. Their brief: "to protect a Naval Fleet Air Arm Stuka raid on Bergen and act as escort to HMS *Southampton* and *Coventry* and four destroyers." Fifty miles from Stavanger they rendezvoused with the naval force, Tubbs's observer Sergeant Robert McVeigh keeping in communication via the Aldis lamp with a cruiser. It was their ill fortune four miles further north at 10.00 hours to be 'bounced' by four Bf 110s of 3./ZG76.

They attacked alternately and continually from astern out of the sun. Tubbs and Patterson tried to evade the cascade of tracer but their machines had no chance. Sergeant Arthur Johnson briefly returned fire as Uffz Erich Zickler's tracer systematically hit the port petrol tank. In the cockpit Tubbs reached to feather the engine but then found within minutes that the starboard oil tank was shattered, 'M – Mother' L8842 was coaxed steadily down. McVeigh had been hit, his yellow Mae West punctured by 7.92 rounds. The twenty-one year old was clinging on. Tubbs ditched the Blenheim fighter yards from HMS *Cossack*. Johnson had already got the dinghy to hand, and as the machine began to fill slowly with ice-cold water "it was as if someone had turned a tap on, water started to pour in through the punctured aircraft's skin". Two clambered out, then leaned in and hauled their injured sergeant out. McVeigh was gasping for air, encouraged by the sight of the destroyer's sea boat, all were soon aboard. HMS *Cossack*'s naval surgeon, Lieutenant Kenneth Scott worked swiftly. McVeigh lost a lot of blood through his perforations and ultimately succumbed to his wounds, dying prior to midday. Leading Seaman 'Dusty' Rhodes described the events:

"HMS *Cossack* was searching for the damaged submarine HMS *Shark*. Unfortunately, this small task force could not find the *Shark*, but the enemy found us. In an air battle that lasted minutes a long-range Blenheim fighter was shot down. Fortunately we were able to rescue the aircrew. I was one of the burial party, we buried the fallen airman in the Royal Naval tradition and ceremony. His body was shrouded in hammocks, placed on wooden forms (planks), then the burial service was read over the fallen by Captain Philip Vian of the *Cossack* and his mortal remains were committed to the deep in southern Norway."

The second machine was hit simultaneously off Stavanger by a pair of Bf109Es. Blenheim 'N-Nuts' P6950 flown by Pilot Officer Victor Patterson went down, its starboard engine ablaze. The hydraulics were shot away and dangerously exposed at the stern. Without an operational powered turret Sergeant Alan Savage watched and prayed. The forward cockpit instrument panel, navigation table and Perspex disintegrated after a head-on attack, showering Sergeant Richard McLaren with fragments. Patterson was slumped forward over the stick, either dead or injured. With severed wiring and fuel pipes, flames spread into the cockpit, enveloping and devouring everything in its wake. McLaren was in agony as his shirtsleeves evaporated, exposing the bare skin. His hands became like burnt parchment and their machine crashed vertically into the sea in flames at 10.50 hours, a victim to Oblt Wilhelm Moritz of 7./JG77. Miraculously Sergeants McLaren and Savage escaped the stricken P6950 and both emerged into the cold, fresh air which was frighteningly damp against their faces after the petrol-doused burning interior. HMS *Fortune* picked them up. McLaren had extensive burns to his hands and arms but Savage was uninjured. Savage was made welcome and handed a coffee which was promptly topped up with brandy by a naval rating. As soon as he had taken a drink, they insisted on filling the cup again with cognac. An unnamed naval lieutenant bathed McLaren's injuries. Onboard HMS *Cossack* Tubbs, McVeigh and Johnson were provided with a meal of soup, bread and cheese. Never was a meal more welcome. Surviving members of both aircraft were put ashore at Rosyth. From there the 254 Squadron adjutant received a call from Tubbs saying who had survived and who was missing. He entered in the diary: "Two Blenheim fighters on escort were shot down by Me 110s and Bf109Es. Five out of the six crew were rescued."

A Royal Air Force car raced along the road, as it drew level Tubbs waved his arms and it stopped abruptly. Some officers appeared. As they all shook hands, they sped north towards RAF Dyce. 248 Squadron's Sam McHardy reported:

"It was here that Patterson took their two drivers in for a drink. Inside he met some of us 248 boys having a late tea in the mess. We laughed when he said: 'Shot down, sod it!' We swapped stories, hearing that 235 Squadron at Bircham Newton had all but been decimated. We'd arrived at Dyce to pick up more bully beef and spam, which we seemed to have lots of whilst at our new outpost of Sumburgh. There were no trees, just the odd crofter's stone cottage with a thatched roof. Our accommodation was in tents pitched on a sandy dune, being July it was no great hardship except sand got in literally everything. It seemed funny we'd not heard from any of the chaps from our Sealand course, who had gone into 236 Squadron."

In an uneasy doze, six days passed with standing convoy patrols covering the breadth of Britain. A single enemy 'weather reconnaissance' flew over the southwestern region. A fighter section was scrambled but didn't get near it. There was more sitting around waiting as crews were dispatched at three-hourly intervals to Cherbourg. Some slept, like 'Freddie' Ripley, although that could have been thanks to the navy rum he put away the previous night. The squadron seemed to enjoy the naval Wrens and partied a lot at The Seven Stars in Falmouth which served a good pint too. The following morning, July 7, six sergeants were out trying to find suitable lodgings for their wives. One promising property was in Lister Street, being close to All Saints Church. As it was a lovely day they strolled past Castle Beach too before returning to base for tea. At 16.19, as the vehicle moved off, a raid warning sounded. A minute later, "eight black shapes fell out of an enemy aircraft and hit the ground with a great cloud of dust and black smoke". Geoffrey Maynard was at the centre of the explosion seen by the sergeants from 236 Squadron:

"Our family was hit at 31 Lister Street. The air raid siren had sounded and the whole family took refuge underneath the stairs. There were seven of us, four from our family and three relatives evacuated from London. Within a few minutes the bombs fell and the house came down around us, all buried and choking with dust. The bombs also broke the main gas pipe – the gas being poisonous – and the main water pipe. The water was rising quickly, we could have drowned, and we realized there was a large crater that was filling up. After some time, it seemed like hours, we heard the rescuers shouting 'Is there anyone alive in there?' Eventually we were rescued and taken to the FAP (First Aid Post) where we were treated for cuts and lacerations to our heads and bodies and for loss of hearing and concussion. Our house was completely demolished. I then spent thirty-six hours in Falmouth Hospital."

The initial reports came in that three houses were demolished, five civilians killed, a number injured. Falmouth docks were closed for two days for repairs as buildings were made safe. People were shocked at the raid's devastation but it was a portent of events to come.

First light on July 10 exposed a characteristic charcoal grey English summer's day, with sporadic lashings of rain flowing in from the southwest. Shipping was the target, with a particularly heavy bombardment of three ships alongside the Northern Arm at Falmouth, killing over a dozen dock workers at 14.37 hours; the steamer *Marie Chandris*, the British tanker *Chancellor* and the Greek tanker *Tuscalusa* were all set alight. The *Chancellor* was not badly damaged, but three crewmembers died; the *Marie Chandris* carried a highly inflammable cargo of cotton and was towed burning to a small bay near St Mawes and sunk by gunfire. Similarly, the *Tuscalusa* was taken under tow to St Just Pool and sunk.

The enemy took advantage of cloud cover, firing bursts at extreme range before entering cloud as a single Blenheim 'T-Tommy' climbed to engage. "We were all amateurs" recalled Australian Flying Officer Richard Power. The next day fellow Australian Bryan McDonough would complete his baptism. On the second patrol of the day, three machines of 236 Squadron ran into Luftflotte 3 armed raiders on reconnaissance sorties to southwest England. On this dull morning, B Flight had just relieved A Flight of 236 so they could get some breakfast. But after an Avro Anson of 217 Squadron shot down a Heinkel 59 floatplane they were scrambled. The Luftwaffe pilot of DAG-10 made a successful landing, despite a broken port float. In a position 146 degrees from Start Point, its three crew were seen taking to the dinghy, the sea swell being described as 'moderate'. There was then a rush to extract the Luftwaffe crew, with two naval destroyers being deployed for the purpose.

10 Group fighter controllers relayed new co-ordinates as Blenheim pilots adjusted their course and height, their orders to "protect two naval destroyers sailing from Plymouth to retrieve the He 59 airmen". HMS *Wolverine* and HMS *Witherington* arrived in the area with their 'air umbrella' at 11.55 hours. Beginning a second sweep an alert observer sighted a black shape at 170 degrees darting along 1,500 feet above the wave tops near Start Point. A second was then spotted bearing 175 degrees. Pilot Officers Frederick Ripley in L6797, Bryan McDonough in L6816 and Charles Peachment in L6776 banked to bring themselves astern of the first aircraft, a single Junkers 88A-1. Ripley's observer noted the time as 11.58 when their leader's voice was heard on the R/T: "Red Section astern, Red Section astern – Go! Don't waffle Ripley, or Peachment will be eating up your tail."

Ahead the Junkers pilot opened up his throttles and dived low, hugging the wave tops as Ripley gained. He tried to keep the aircraft steady and, lining up his ring sight at 450 yards, his gloved right thumb pressed the gun button. Five quick bursts of 0.303 spirited away from the belly pack, the third burst penetrating the Junkers' starboard engine. L6816 broke hard right allowing Red 2 (L6797) to bring his guns to bear. Red 2 and Red 3 (L6776) were unable to get an effective burst in as the Junkers performed aerial manoeuvres inches from the waves, his rotor blades leaving a wake as the skillful Luftwaffe crew out-flew them, even with nine plus boost engaged to the astonishment of the twenty-eight-year-old Mancunian Ripley. A naval unit spotted the Junkers making its way from the encounter with its starboard engine badly damaged. "With our adrenalin pumping we restrained from chasing the enemy aircraft for fear of leaving the destroyers unprotected", McDonough reported. As the Junkers 88 snaked towards the French coast the aircraft suffered mechanical failure and was reported by its unit, 1./KG51 as "lost on operations, circumstances unknown", together with four non-commissioned officers.

McDonough's air gunner Sergeant Frederick Head shouted "unidentified aircraft on our tail". Red 1 flicked his microphone switch; "Reform, reform! Come on Red 2 and 3". Suddenly the unidentified aircraft drew level with the lead Blenheim Red 1 on the left hand side. Shouts of "Junkers" bellowed into the intercom, "'it was like being at a Punch and Judy show on the beach, with Punch battering Judy". Head frantically traversed the turret to port then repositioned himself and squeezed the trigger, getting a steady rate of outgoing fire from the Vickers K and using five of his magazines. He claimed hits as the enemy aircraft accelerated away. The Australian throttled back and led Ripley and Peachment in a steep turn to starboard. With Ripley's starboard engine running unsatisfactorily he brought the section into line astern. Having expended all 2,000 rounds in the first mêlée Ripley was unable to resume the fight and withdrew. McDonough and Peachment pulled their nine plus boost out just in time, and as the German machine went down to sea level they followed. Ripley delivered a burst from 350 yards but the Junkers turned away, the Luftwaffe pilot Oblt Adolf Vitense taking avoiding action. 0.303 rounds missed his port wing and snaking from side to side Vitense got the upper hand. One of his gunners fired a burst through the fuselage of Ripley's aircraft during the low level dogfight. At 1,000 feet the German gunners put rounds into the starboard wing and as the aerial duel continued one of L6797's cylinders of the starboard radial engine received hits. Ripley throttled it back and continued until he had expended 1,000 rounds. He reported smoke from both engines. Meanwhile, Peachment in Red 3 shot off 500 rounds from 400/350 yards. Return fire shattered a panel of Perspex and a single 7.92mm travelled past Peachment at high velocity and exited through the turret, narrowly missing his nineteen-year-old air gunner. HMS *Witherington*'s Lieutenant Commander Jack Palmer saw the whole thing unfold: "We had the best seats in the house, splendid show by one's coastal brethren." Owing to the proximity of the French coast, shortage of fuel and ammunition the three machines made for St Eval to refuel and rearm. At 12.35 hours Oblt Adolf Vitense and crew were shot down into the sea twenty-two miles south-southeast of Start Point, a naval officer logging their position at 282 degrees. The young men of 6./LG1 were shocked to lose Vitense, their Staffelführer. That evening they had little appetite at dinner, consuming a lot of readily available French liquor instead.

As LG1 crews nursed hangovers, 236 woke at their base at 04.30 hours to see two Avro Ansons departing across the rough terrain. The rest of the morning was spent waiting whilst outside airmen and women toiled. At 16.45 their peace was interrupted as a red air raid warning wailed into the surrounding countryside. It came too late; nine high explosive bombs detonated across the aerodrome. Fortunately they caused minor damage, with three failing to explode. A dozen personnel suffered minimal bruising from when they hit the dirt and deafness from the blast, one being the county controller who was visiting the station, his car covered with mud from one of the craters. The intruder opened his throttles and was harried all the way by fighters from 243 Squadron, "we intercepted and chased out to sea, being damaged". By the evening the rain had started to fall again. Just over a week later on July 17, on the French side of the English Channel II./JG2 Gruppen-kommandeur Wolfgang Schellmann and Willi Melchett each shot down a 236 Blenheim at 13.15 hours on a reconnaissance off Le Havre.

The following day saw offensive convoy patrols around the English shores continue. Pilot Officer Norman Jackson-Smith led his first patrol, accompanying him was Pilot Officer Robert Patterson flying N3541 with Sergeants Lawrence Reece and Ronald Tucker as crew. It was a short briefing for Jackson-Smith: "collect your maps, weather forecast and off you go". Swathed in layers, they struggled into Mae Wests, then picked up their parachutes and a thermos flask of tea or coffee which was handed to them by the duty clerk. Lowering his newspaper, Flight Lieutenant Frederick Flood bade them farewell, having been part of the first convoy patrol at 0345-0645 hours. Jackson-Smith and Patterson departed. There was a pause for a last-minute cigarette, whilst L9393 and N3541 stood with their backs against a hawthorn hedge in which birds could be heard rustling to get out of the rain, most definitely not part of the long hot summer.

It was a relief to climb into the dry. Upon starting up the propeller blades made jerky revolutions which disappeared as the engines warmed. One by one the pilots edged their Blenheims forward. Jackson-Smith and Patterson were side by side as they rolled down the grass strip, labouring into the air fully loaded to capacity. At 09.45 hours, sweeping by the patchwork countryside, they flew over Brancaster out into the North Sea. A sea of grey cloud above them shed hail stones, "they sounded like marbles hitting the fuselage and cockpit". The air gunners in the turret tried to stay dry as the hail streamed in through the seventeen-inch gap which their single Vickers K traversed. Pilot Officer Alexander Green onboard L9393 peered out through the Perspex, water modules partly obscuring his view as he searched for the convoy that had departed Methil Roads bound for Gravesend. After an estimated forty-five minutes somewhere off the northeast coast of England the convoy was found, "grey objects moving at a snail's pace". L9393 and N3541 began to keep watch. Reducing height Green flashed a response to the deciphered "glad to have you along for the ride" from one of the naval vessels. Outside conditions were deteriorating. Both crews expected to face another two hours of uneventful flying over the featureless sea. At an altitude of only 1,500 to 2,000 feet Jackson-Smith's gunner Pilot Officer Raymond Kent shouted "Fighters coming down 2 o'clock".

Three unidentified Hawker Hurricanes challenged them over the convoy, swooping down in line astern out of the clouds, as recognition flares were quickly fired off from L9393.

After this close shave the crews continued with their task of keeping watch. In the deteriorating conditions N3541 disappeared unnoticed. Jackson-Smith landed back at 12.45 hours. The next pair had already departed at 12.15. Patterson and his crew failed to return. The diary entry revealed "it is feared that he has gone down in the sea". Sergeant Ronald Tucker was dead, nineteen years old and a newcomer of two weeks to the squadron. Jackson-Smith recalled, "Ron also had the distinction of being shot down by Spitfires whilst flying with his last unit 219 Squadron". All three were posted as 'Missing in Action' circumstances unknown.

The daily forays continued and in spite of the bad weather very few patrols and reconnaissance flights were cancelled. 236 Squadron dispatched three aircraft from Thorney Island led by Pilot Officer Charles Powers who had joined the RAF on a short service commission in June 1937. The aerodrome was awash with water, the top soil could neither absorb nor the drainage cope with the torrential rain. As their tyres lifted off the grass runway and rotated into place at 11.20 hours shards of water droplets darted earthwards.

Heading towards Le Havre and Cherbourg on a reconnaissance they snaked along past the Channel Islands. Unsuspectingly on the island of Alderney information of 'three hostile aircraft' approaching was passed to the battery near Auderville village, close to the lighthouse Cap de la Hague, Normandy. The aircraft flew towards the northwesterly Cap de la Hague, when torrents of rain and heavy anti-aircraft fire swamped L6779, L6639 and L1278. All scattered, losing contact with each other. Pilot Officer Charles Thomas together with his air gunner Sergeant Harry Elsdon checked L6779 for damage while twenty-four-year-old Pilot Officer Robert Rigby carried out a similar procedure. Desperately scanning the skies they'd been lucky for nine minutes when suddenly two Messerschmitts came swooping down like hawks out of the grey clouds. A minute later, at 13.15, one Blenheim with its altimeter racing hurtled earthwards. The victor was JG2 Major Wolfgang Schellman. The second was shot down by Uffz Willie Melchert of II./JG2 at 13.25 hours. Powers in L1278 emerged from cloud and scanned all around, searching for signs of the other two machines.

A fine study of a 206 Squadron Hudson at Bircham Newton. (*Royal Air Force Museum, London*)

A RAF operational control room showing a map of Norfolk and the Dutch Frisian islands 1940. (*Royal Air Force Museum, London*)

The sky was empty. "I came to the conclusion both may have been hit by anti-aircraft fire." The word 'missing' was chalked up. It was a year and one month before they were 'presumed killed', their sweet hearts and families notified of this change of circumstance by the Air Ministry.

The pace quickened as sorties continued into the night. Flying Officers Peacock, Hugh Wakefield and Pilot Officer Steve Hebron boarded N3542 for their second sortie together with Flight Sergeant Nelson in N3533 and their flight commander Flight Lieutenant Andrew Fletcher in his usual steed, L9446. He would be leading an escort sortie with six Lockheed Hudson aircraft of 206 Squadron to attack Emden. Pilot Officer Wakefield recalled:

"It was the first time 235 had taken part in a night operation. Having returned from a three-hour trip at 14.30 'Pissy', 'Steve' [Hebron] and myself were in the mess sitting down for our evening meal, when some clown produced a plate of chopped carrots and blacked out flying goggles to help us see in the dark. It was hard enough to find a target in daylight!"

"Let's hope they've left the lights on with your dead reckoning", remarked Fletcher to Wakefield. Taking off at seven-minute intervals N3524 headed out at 22.07 hours behind L9446, with 'Dick' Nelson last to leave. There was little cloud and a partial moon. They each carried four 25 lb bombs in racks under the fuselage, increasing the drag which in turn reduced speed to 248 mph. They flew at an altitude of 10,000 feet, with the Hudsons below and slightly ahead at 8,000 feet. They were clearly visible over the North Sea but disappeared nearing the Frisian islands. Neither group had been able to make radio contact because of radio silence but "worryingly both groups used different frequencies". As prearranged during the joint briefing, they skirted skillfully between the outlying Texel islands then split into three sections, using the islands and mainland as camouflage as both types proceeded towards Emden. On the ground lights were extinguished and sirens sounded. Fletcher led them into the inlet. At 23.30 they dived towards Emden railway station dropping twenty-four incendiaries as 206's Hudsons attacked through flak and searchlights, hitting the docks housing barges which had recently arrived from the Netherlands with high explosive bombs. As they left at 23.45 several fires raged.

Wakefield described the attack:

"It was interesting over Germany, the scale of thunder and lightning storm, until I realized that we were being subjected to heavy, wildly inaccurate anti-aircraft fire. Dropping our bomb load on Emden station or near enough, Pissy set course to head back over the Channel. Navigation was done on dead reckoning and at night after 300 miles or so N3542 was either over the River Thames, Ipswich or The Wash. Fletcher was on the R/T requesting a fuel check, Peacock and Nelson both had limited supplies. Fletcher had conserved his fuel more wisely and had the most, he came back suggesting we land away at Fakenham, the dummy aerodrome eleven miles from Bircham. Pissy had throttled right back to almost stalling speed; we eventually landed at Docking with less than nine gallons in the tanks."

All landed safely between 01.15 and 01.20 after an unusually long sortie. Flight Sergeant Dick Nelson wrote home: "We were feeling pretty hungry after our long trip but had to make do with bread and strawberry jam scrounged from the mess."

However accurate these operations were there is no denying that the crews put the effort in. Convoy patrols started at 03.45 hours on July 19. Later that afternoon Fletcher in N3525 and Peacock in N3542 followed on after Squadron Leader Clarke watching convoys clinging to the Norfolk and Kent coastal waters. Operating Defiants, 141 Squadron from West Malling moved to Hawkinge, bringing them forty miles closer to the 'frontline' for convoy protection

Flying Officer Hugh Wakefield was Flying Officer Reginald Peacock's regular observer on 235 Squadron. He joined the RAFVR in July 1939 and was called to full-time service at the outbreak of the war. After further training at Perth and West Freugh, he joined 235 at North Coates on April 1, 1940. He was awarded the DFC on October 22, 1940. (*John Wakefield*) duty. In a one-sided air battle five were shot down, four landed at Hawkinge. This disaster made it Fighter Command's worst day. Pilot Officer Norman Jackson-Smith: "We had been briefed at midday to watch out for friendly fighters, particularly the Defiants on our patrol. It wasn't until I landed after my four-hour stint that I learnt from Peacock that they'd got a serious mauling at the hands of Jerry."

That evening A Flight's Flying Officer John Laughlin led Jackson-Smith and Pilot Officer David Woodger out at 21.30 escorting six Hudsons of 206 in a repeat operation, striking shipping and barges in Emden. As the drone of their engines died away into the distance they flew into heavy rain showers which became increasingly unfavourable. Visibility through the spray was blurred and down to less than one mile. Laughlin returned after twenty minutes with an unserviceable turret, his sergeant air gunner trapping his fingers in the electrically powered turret swivel mechanism. All the others landed as the flare path was extinguished without warning. Shortly after 01.30 hours two Hudsons returned having been unable to locate the target. Q-206 dropped six 250 lb bombs on Willemsood and N-206 bombed Harlingen waterfront.

Sergeants Basil Quelch and Peter Hall played chess whilst waiting for the morning to come and someone could be heard sucking on their pipe behind the previous day's newspaper. Everything stopped as the 'ops' telephone rang, the duty clerk answered, relaying the message: "Dawn convoy patrol – take off 03.45 hours". Hall sunk lower into the recesses of the brown leather armchair recently acquired from Fortnum & Mason, a present from the missing Pilot Officer Michael Ryan's father. Putting a cigarette between his lips with his left hand he lit it with his right using a small alloy lighter. He inhaled, steadying his nerves, then resumed playing chess. Their third game remained unfinished when at 03.00 hours both prepared for their flight, picking up a map, thermos flask and three pork pies for the journey. These ordinary fellows stepped outside and walked towards their machines. Their fitters wished them luck. Upon completing preliminary checks Quelch eased N3531 out, giving a thumbs up to Hall in charge of L9393. Both trundled down the grass runway and managed to take off, heading towards Cromer, passing Westcliff, then out into the grey/green North Sea. This monotonous convoy patrol lasted three hours and thirty minutes. After a brief interlude Flight Lieutenant Andrew Fletcher and Flying Officer Reginald Peacock repeated their patrol, making it eight hours each for the pair. Hours later they would be drinking with the locals in their pubs.

On Saturday evening, July 21 the local 'watering holes' were crammed full with young men holding straight or handle pint tankards of beer or cider. Nelson, Woodger, Sutton and Peacock set off in a borrowed Ford 8 for drinks at one of the popular RAF pubs in the area, where they ran into some of B Flight with two WAAF controllers and got stuck into the local ale. Some of these young men had been on readiness since before first light and dozed in a corner, exhausted. Squadron Leader Clarke drunk a tankard of warm sudsy local beer, Steward & Patteson, served from an aged wooden cask by the proprietor.

As these airmen drank, out over the English Channel four Blenheim fighters were on a collision course with Messerschmitts of Stab./JG27. 16 Group headquarters at Plymouth had tasked three 236 Squadron machines (A, D and L) to provide fighter escort to a Blenheim of 59 Squadron on a vital reconnaissance between Le Havre and Cherbourg. They reached their necessary height of 13,000 feet, occasionally cloud partially obscured vision but they came out into clear skies over Le Havre sighting one cruiser and one destroyer.

Near Cherbourg airfield, Bf109Es of Stab./JG27 were scrambled to intercept. The RAF machines continued towards Cherbourg in fading sunshine, its glare glinting off their Perspex. At 18.00 hours three Bf 109Es pounced. Two of the three Blenheim fighter pilots reacted instantly by diving away at a 45-degree angle in line astern. It took eighteen seconds for Sergeant Eric Lockton to lose 3,000 feet, his air speed indicator reading 280 mph. With both engines screaming he levelled off at 6,000 feet, his new air gunner Sergeant Henry Corcoran calmly calling out the distance and position of the two Messerschmitt fighters. One of their prey, Blenheim L1300, was momentarily static as

Lockton reacted again, reaching across with his right hand to turn both fuel cock hand wheels to switch to the 100-octane fuel in the outer port and starboard tanks as a hail of cannon and machine-gun fire flashed past inches from his starboard window. Lockton heard in his headphones "stoppage". Corcoran had fired only fifty rounds. Seizing this opportunity Hptm Neumann opened up at extremely close range, machine-gun rounds cascading into the Blenheim. Pieces were seen hurtling off the aircraft's port wing as cannon rounds disintegrated the framework. Smoke and flames poured from L1300 as it entered a steep uncontrollable spin and crashed into the sea. Hptm Eduard Neumann had scored his first victory of World War II days into the Battle of Britain. The following day he was appointed Gruppenkommandeur of I./JG27, replacing Major Helmut Riegel.

As the month ebbed away 236 moved to Detling in relays, continuing "convoy protection as usual", interspersed with covering Royal Navy minesweepers which were clearing magnetic mines dropped into the Humber. On July 22 they were patrolling over convoy Pilot. With the threat of thunder in the air, that afternoon Flight Lieutenant Andrew Fletcher led a reconnaissance to Texel to assess whether enemy troops had been moved in strength into the immediate area, including the strength of shipping and number of barges. Nothing was sighted. Frustrated, the four machines headed home. The sky was patterned with dark rain clouds. At 20.30 hours, thirty-three miles off Cromer, Blenheim 'H-Harold' on the portside of the vic received a volley of rounds from a Hawker Hurricane. The culprit disappeared into the gloom.

This weather front enveloped Norfolk, halting operations until 04.00 hours. On July 25 it was sunny with clear skies and 21 degrees and the Luftwaffe took advantage of this improving weather. German reconnaissance pilots of Luftflotte 2 noted down the substantial westbound convoy tacking towards the Dover Straits with a heavy escort hoping to get through unnoticed. Enemy fighter and bomber attacks ran throughout the day at fifteen-minute intervals from 12.07 hours to 18.30 hours. The sorely pressed men of the convoy realized and came to terms with the fact they were the Luftwaffe's principal target. This encounter united all three of the enemy forces: army, navy and air. As the army bombarded the convoy from positions near Cap Gris Nez, nine German naval E-boats combined with Junkers 87 Stuka dive-bombers caused the ships to scatter as they left Dover. Out of the original twenty-one ships, eleven were sunk or seriously floundering. It was the sinking of HMS *Boreas* and *Brilliant* which had charged out of Dover at full steam to rescue the convoy that was even more alarming. The Admiralty and the Royal Air Force belatedly agreed that future convoys should use the shipping lanes in the English Channel after dark, and that convoys should sail the east coast route, by going around the top of northeast Scotland and head out into the Atlantic from there. Fighter Command's 'Stuffy' Dowding had suggested it earlier in the month. Coastal Command was requested to move another of their trade protection squadrons to patrol the English Channel. Air Marshal Bowhill agreed in principle, stating, "depending on our operational commitments it will happen as soon as it can be arranged. All four Coastal Blenheim fighter squadrons are highly mobile, with detachments around our shoreline." Senior air force officers started thinking of which squadrons to move, like pieces on a chessboard. At Bircham Newton men not on active duty dozed, cleaned their pipes, wrote letters and made tea, as they relaxed under the sound of pre-flight checks. Aircrews watched as a dozen airmen formed a chain bailing water out from an air raid slit trench after the recent deluge. The water was recycled over a potato patch. One-penny bets were placed to see which airman would drop a full bucket first.

The two flight commanders, Flight Lieutenants Fletcher and Flood, walked into the crew room on July 28. A crackly 78 record played on the gramophone, aptly named 'Summertime' the lyrics 'and the living is easy' striking a chord. 235's A and B Flights had been stood down from further patrolling duties and given two days respite before the next offensive patrol. Newly arrived Pilot Officers Douglas Wordsworth and Phillip Stickney were being spoken to by their CO who was pointing out the importance of the fitters, riggers, the maintenance section, armament section, and the Flights themselves. There was a great spirit of teamwork and comradeship on and off the aerodrome within the squadron. On Tuesday July 30, Wordsworth and Stickney found themselves ordered off on a patrol which lasted three hours and thirty minutes over the North Sea protecting minelayers. In the evening 236 Squadron's Flight Lieutenant Richard Powers, flying R2777, took off from Bircham Newton, only to touch down then crash in bad weather on take-off at Carew Cheriton near Tenby at 19.00 hours. The pilot's visibility was obscured by heavy rain and his undercarriage clipped the sturdy cement bags forcing the legs to buckle as he tried to get back to Thorney Island. The Blenheim was a write off. Powers was unhurt apart from a cut and some minor bruising. A local doctor cleaned his bloody face and deemed him okay. In twenty hours he would be fighting for his life over enemy soil.

With the break of day 235, 236, 248 and 254 Squadrons shook themselves and went back to work. Air Marshal Bowhill and his group commanders were concerned about whether their four trade protection squadrons could sustain any more losses in their forthcoming battle. The answer to this question was as obscure as the early morning fog that drifted over the River Thames and locked in its grey arms the towers of the Houses of Parliament where Winston Churchill waited patiently – for victory against the odds.

CHAPTER SEVEN

The Wind at Dawn

August opened with mist enveloping the coastal waters and inlets around Britain. The low cloud was slow to disperse over England as four convoys cast off from east coast ports. The loaded steamers sailed freely and were not inconvenienced by the recent enemy minelaying spree. At 12.00 hours the convoys were spread around the coastlines of four counties: Yorkshire, Lincolnshire, Suffolk and Kent. Fourteen squadrons made up from Coastal and Fighter Command flew relays "shepherding their flock like border collies", from above. The ships, all types and sizes, rose and fell on the swells. As the daylight faded they dwindled to little specks against the sunset. Naval movements then ceased. An unnamed naval lieutenant wrote:

"Our lecturer said we may find ourselves in command of a dirty little ship dropping anchor for the night in a lonely bay or port. I found myself in one such place; Southend-on-Sea. The town was a handsome conception, but past its prime. I strolled along the seafront and caught a fish dinner in the Royal Restaurant. It was full of military, with a sprinkling of locals."

These men like many others waited patiently in British ports for the convoy system to resume through the English Channel. A few days previously CW8 (convoy westbound) convoy had been devastated by Stukas as had naval destroyers. Meanwhile Coastal Command had been sent out to reconnoitre the continental coast.

In the recesses of Coastal Command Headquarters, Northwood military analysts pored over aerial photographic evidence. "The first piece of the jigsaw had been placed" enabling them to identify with unusual accuracy the objects seen. A single photographic reconnaissance Spitfire took off in the early morning of August 1, 1940. Having flown out from St Eval the skies became relatively clear over the Cherbourg peninsular. They found a high concentration of enemy fighters and transport aircraft located at Querqueville aerodrome, four miles northwest of Cherbourg in northern France. Pilot Officer Gordon Green:

"Our unit was still in its infancy. The technique of high altitude photography on this operation using a single-seat Spitfire was largely dependent on being able to judge where the cameras were pointing. One flew alone to the general area of the target and then tipped the aircraft on its side to check one was properly lined up."

With vital military information gained, RAF Fighter Command Headquarters, Stanmore, Middlesex was notified of this enemy concentration at Querqueville. Senior Air Staff Officer Douglas Evill

Blenheim IV TR-J of A Flight 59 Squadron at Thorney Island. (*Alec McCurdy*)

prepared a briefing note prior to a meeting at the Air Ministry. It was the express wishes of Dowding and 11 Group controllers that the airfield should be bombed before the Luftwaffe had a chance of drawing them into the battle. Despite the extremely unfavourable weather Bomber Command had been in the thick of the action as usual the previous night, carrying out strikes against various targets. The command had experienced often enough the effectiveness of light anti-aircraft fire between Calais and Boulogne, and over this area the burden fell on Coastal Command.

A signal came through to Thorney Island just before midday on the 'tie-line' each individual character forming on the fading white paper spelling out their objective; Querqueville aerodrome. Wing Commander Reginald Morgan-Weld-Smith was concerned by the signal, but nevertheless the commanding officer of 59 Squadron notified the necessary people by telephone. Thirteen aircraft were made ready by the ground crew. Squadron Leader Peter Drew, commanding officer of 236 Squadron, was told he would lead the fighter support. Ten Blenheim fighters were armed and placed at readiness. "Everyone was togged up in their yellow Mae Wests. We played cards, darts, draughts or talked to each other and read newspapers, waiting to be called." Apprehension grew as the operation was pushed back until 15.00 hours, as more intelligence was gained from a Blenheim over flying Querqueville between 12.30 and 12.39. Although Morgan-Weld-Smith had emphasized to this young crew "to avoid contact with the enemy", in their youthful exhilaration the observer dropped two 250 lb general-purpose bombs and six 40 lb bombs on the forty-two enemy machines below with little effect. Unfortunately it would result in repercussions later that afternoon. 3./Flakregiment 9, Reserve Flakabteilung 321 and 8./JG27 on the aerodrome were now placed on high alert. When the RAF machine landed both the pilot and the observer confirmed their find to their intelligence officer; "sighting thirty enemy aircraft of which twelve fighters are near the hangars whilst others are dispersed".

For those waiting to 'go' the hours ticked by laboriously. One of those at the dispersal hut was Pilot Officer David Davis from Smarden, Kent. Described as having a stocky build with a tanned complexion built up from many years serving in the pre-war North-West Frontier in India, Davis looked younger than his age of twenty-seven and always seemed to be smiling.

Suddenly the telephone chirped. Newspapers were lowered, conversations paused, chess pieces clutched between thumb and forefinger. Worry lines on their foreheads were pronounced, then they subsided with relief as the orderly spoke: "Lunch is being served in the messes". Davis led one of the groups off to eat. With full stomachs they were like young children with the promise of a trip to the circus. WAAF Marian Wordsworth: "In the officers' mess at Thorney, we were eating together – the WAAF officers with the pilots, observers and the occasional pilot officer air gunner. They finished the pudding of jam roly-poly and off they would go . . ." A lot of them would not come back.

Morgan-Weld-Smith briefed his squadron for the last time, summarizing the situation thus: "Our job is to stop them, or at any rate make things so hot for them that they couldn't function as a fighting unit." He described the nature of the target – Bf109Es near the hangars and Junkers 52 transports with more fighters dispersed on the aerodrome – and how they would go about their business, emphasizing the absolute necessity of keeping close formation, and to follow him completely in any and every progress. The weather over the Cherbourg peninsular was "fine with clear visibility for two/three miles". At 15.08 hours twelve aircraft took off forming into two vic formations with L8792 leading one arrowhead. Each carried four 250 lb GP (general-purpose) bombs and clusters of 40 lb GP and 25 lb incendiary bombs. All were routed round the Isle of Wight over the English Channel taking up a holding pattern a few miles off the French coast. Five minutes later Drew led 236's Blenheim Mk IV fighters off on the first of three flights, at intervals of six minutes. The last off was led by an Australian whose orders were to cover both squadrons' withdrawal route as 'top cover' at 8,000 feet.

Drew and his party were to rendezvous with 59 just prior to the French coast but ahead, over the gradually approaching enemy coast, all was not going according to plan. Luck was not with the RAF meteorologist's forecast. It was overcast, with heavy low cloud covering the entire peninsular. Flight Lieutenant Richard 'Dick' Powers leading the first vic of 236 fighters entered cloud which was so dense that the three were consumed within the mass. Powers completely missed the peninsular and flew within one mile of the Blenheim bombers, unaware they were flying deeper into enemy territory before turning for home. Pilot Officer Short, of 59 Squadron: "You're just left in suspense waiting for the fighter escort. It was much the same as waiting for a date, would or wouldn't she turn up?"

Living up to their squadron motto, 'From One We Learn', the thirteen bombers crept forward under their leader's guidance. Very soon the area pinpointed should have drawn near. Morgan-Weld-Smith called to Davis on the intercom: "How are we doing Davis?" "Getting nearer" came the reply at 15.40. A chance break in the clouds and Davis called him back, "We're coming up on the area now". Sergeant Peter Pryde "kept his eyes skinned" searching for the enemy. Their target was nearly visible. Reducing height in a controlled dive to 1,000 feet, they began their run in. Morgan-Weld-Smith called through to the squadron racing in hot on his heels, "Stand by for bombing". In the nose of L8792 Davis was lining up the drift-lines of the bombsight. The air around them was vibrant. A thumping sensation buffeted the machine whilst ahead six plumes of smoke curled upwards into the sky. Against hardening resistance the bombers furnished a vulnerable target for the heavy and light German guns. The side cockpit window of 'A-Apple' was blown in, a blast of wind whipping into Morgan-Weld-Smith's face and shards of Perspex cutting into his leather flying helmet causing lacerations to the left side of his face. Dazed, he regained control and righted the aircraft, its artificial horizon straightened.

Davis was on the intercom, "Steady . . . hold it . . ." then a second long-drawn-out shout, "Bombs gone". He felt the aircraft kick as its load fell away. Morgan-Weld-Smith swung the control column to port. Then events began to unfold in a grim pattern. As the bomb doors were nearing closure, L8792 bucked like a bronco. In sudden anguish and helplessness Morgan-Weld-Smith knew immediately that they had received a direct hit somewhere aft.

His gunner Sergeant Peter Pryde was caught in the blast, his seat and turret offering little protection. Pryde's seat was decompressed as the elevation and decompression cylinder was shattered by shrapnel or a piece from his own machine. The gunner's perch and the Vickers K were connected by a parallelogram arrangement and left a lifeless nineteen year old see-sawing in motion to his aircraft's movement. Shouts to the Nottinghamshire lad received no answer. Forward in the cockpit the smell of burning filled Morgan-Weld-Smith's nostrils. He pushed the stick forward but his control column was completely useless, there was no response, its control wires had been severed. With another sudden thump and a thud L8792 was drifting over in a slow spiral. Ablaze it smacked into the sea just outside Cherbourg. There were no survivors, their bodies were gradually given up by the sea, washed ashore in the coming weeks and buried.

Crews behind the stricken craft were already commencing their run in. Some machines were hit by accurate ground fire or the German gunners rattled the RAF crews so much that they pulled out of their bombing run altogether. Contrary to official reports 59 Squadron's bombs did little damage. A total of twenty to thirty were dropped on their objective, causing limited damage to the runway and destroying a large field kitchen tent of the 3./Flakregiment 9. Two soldiers of 4./Flakregiment 32 were slightly injured by bomb splinters.

Streaking in behind the bombers at 15.55 hours was their escort. Squadron Leader Peter Drew in N3601 led Australian Pilot Officer Bryan McDonough in N2774 on the port and Sergeant Reginald Smith in N3603 to the right. These three followed the contours of the land, hedge hopping and startling a horse that instantly unseated its rider and galloped off, frightened by the noise. It was last seen jumping a fence by 'M-Mother', commenting: "You should have seen it my dear boy, it was as if it were at Ascot". Flying with their throttles wide open at 250 mph between fifty and seventy-five feet all three streaked in over the airfield strafing. "It is an exhilarating experience," recalled Smith, "my machine was at a height of seventy-five feet when we were peppered by anti-aircraft fire causing severe damage to our tail unit." The trio continued firing upon machine-gun and coastal-gun positions west to east of Cherbourg along to Querqueville.

Jagdeschwader 53 – or as it was better known the 'Pik As' (Ace of Spades) – pilots discuss the downing of a British fighter.

Messerschmitt fighters of 8./JG27 were on the prowl above the shielding clouds. Rumanian, Oblt Walter Adolph thought it an unbelievable sight. "Everywhere was danger," he noted, "from the British fighters, and our own flak." Unseen the Bf109Es half rolled to come down, bouncing the Blenheim fighters as they finished another strafing run. McDonough pushed his stick to starboard, moved the rudder pedal and turned to come around, momentarily observing the figures below hit the dirt instead of watching his own back, a cardinal sin. Realizing this, McDonough began to climb. Swooping in like a red kite on its prey Oblt Ernst Düllberg of 8/JG27 fired a long burst at short range from the port quarter. The twenty-three-year-old Australian took evasive action, opening the throttles as simultaneously these opening shots pierced N2774's structure. He began to zig-zag, arching for the coast and its expanse of water. But Düllberg managed to get on his tail. Defensive bursts were hosed out from the gunner's position by Sergeant Frederick Head, as incoming rounds hit home. The machine was ripped apart, crashing into the sea off the peninsular at 16.45 hours.

The starboard machine's air gunner Sergeant Arthur Piper watched in horror. Calling out a warning of "Fighter!", his pilot struggled to maintain height. Oblt Hans Richter of 8/JG27 saw strikes hit. Although Piper and Smith were unhurt N3603's exhausts emitted dark black smoke and the engines screamed, the control column rattling in Smith's hands as he attempted to get away. Succeeding he headed back across the Channel towards the Isle of Wight. Also in the thick of it was Oblt Walter Adolph of 8/JG27 in the front of his yellow-nosed Messerschmitt. At 16.45 hours a Blenheim sprang up, growing until it filled his sights. Squadron Leader Peter Drew and his recently appointed thirty-two-year-old signals officer, acting Flying Officer Benjamin Nokes-Cooper, were flying it. Drew wrenched his machine into a tight turn, and English voices filled his headphones as the negative gravity began to take hold.

A voice then shouted, "Watch out, Messerschmitt!" and at the same moment, the fourth section led by Flying Officer William 'Bill' Moore dived in, driving off the German fighter. His Jamaican observer Pilot Officer Herbert Capstick watched this brief inconclusive encounter. As Moore motored right down on the deck, below the taller trees, his three Blenheim fighters darted at speed across the landscape. Light small-arms fire arched towards them but the speed built up during their dive carried them through unscathed and they headed north over the splaying branches of a copse of oak trees on the edge of the airfield. This was the last recorded sighting of their CO and signals officer; it is probable that N3601 was either shot down by light anti-aircraft fire or Oblt Walter Adolph 8./JG27 who claimed one Blenheim. In total three Blenheim fighters were claimed by 8./JG27, although only two were later confirmed. They proceeded to land back at Querqueville, the pilots excitedly discussing and reflecting on the operation. Some of their machines had the odd bullet hole – but all had safely returned.

Meanwhile, the remaining three fighters left, gaining height to take a good look around but they saw nothing in the sky. Switching from outer to inner fuel tanks they brought the boost off and reduced engine revs. Melbourne-born Moore caught his breath. He and his crew were alive, it was time to head home. Standing beside Moore the former Sedbergh School pupil Capstick handed his pilot a note informing him "twenty minutes to coast". After endless clear water soon Moore was just one of three black specks circling to land at Thorney Island. All clambered down wearily from their machines and began tramping back across the squelching field, and when Moore and Capstick walked through the dispersal door, the Australian and Jamaican learned that the squadron had taken a hammering. Bryan McDonough, Benjamin Nokes-Cooper, Peter Drew and Frederick Head were all missing or killed. Reginald Smith had limped home in his damaged but repairable machine, together with the missing boys from 59; Morgan-Weld-Smith, Dave Davis and Peter Pryde. A further two machines were damaged by anti-aircraft fire. But for both squadrons to lose their commanding officers in one afternoon was wretched. 236's Barbados-born Pilot Officer Aubrey Inniss noted that "the dispersal hut and messes seemed mighty empty that night".

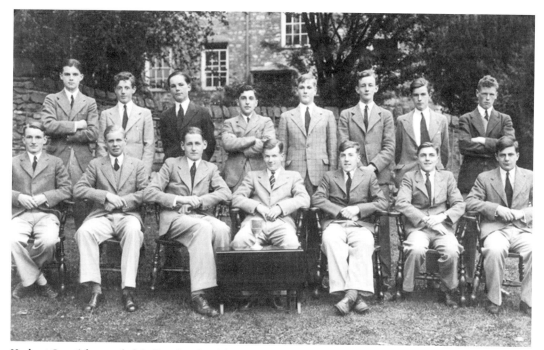

Herbert Capstick attended Sedbergh School from September 1934 to December 1938. In the photograph of the Evans House rugby team circa 1938 Herbert, back row, third from left, is wearing a dark suit. A review in the house magazine describes him as: "H. Capstick (9st. 8 ½ lbs); Second row player. An honest worker at the tight scrums and useful at the line-outs." (*Andrew Bird via Sedbergh School*)

Later that evening it was detailed in the squadron diary, 'Flight Lieutenant Dick Powers assumes temporary command of 236 Squadron until a replacement can be found'. An analysis of the raid was conducted by crews of both squadrons; timing, communication and weather found to be the three key elements. As these discussions concluded Wing Commander Reginald Morgan-Weld-Smith's wet and bedraggled pigeon Percy arrived at its RAF loft. It was estimated to have flown from 16.00 to 18.35 over a distance of eighty-seven miles and gave a glimmer of hope. Perhaps 'A-Apple's crew had made it into the aircraft's dinghy after all?

At teatime, Pilot Officer Jack Beelaerts van Blokland checked up on the weather prospects as there was a lot of cloud, with visibility no more than three miles. In the deteriorating weather two aircraft took off at 19.45 hours but there just seemed no way through as the rain rattled against the aircraft's metal skin. Both returned within minutes. These conditions persisted through to the early hours of Friday August 2, when the sky filled with RAF roundels around the shores of Britain. At the Hampshire aerodrome, inside 59 Squadron's dispersal hut it was decided to get clearance for a single aircraft search of Cherbourg for Morgan-Weld-Smith, Davis and Pryde whilst flying a reconnaissance to Le Havre. This was approved and the met officer told them that the weather may pick up a little over France. Pilot Officer Deryck A. Drew, with his observer and air gunner left to the echoes of Glen Miller's 'Fools Rush In' (Where Angels Fear To Tread). It was an apt lyric for their forthcoming sortie as they clambered aboard N3587, loaded with four 250 lb GP bombs. Drew carried out his pre-flight checks and slowly the machine gathered pace over the water-logged field. Within three minutes they were off the ground.

Drew guided his machine lightly to port, his course dissecting the hamlets of West and East Wittering. Smoke billowed from a white-washed cottage near the beach, then they were over the wide expanse of water heading for Le Havre 102 miles away. The wind was blowing northwesterly and

Vulnerable to enemy Bf109Es and Bf110 fighters, the Blenheim fighter was scythed from the European skies. (*Andrew Bird*)

German-owned invasion barges sailing towards Le Havre port. (*Andrew Bird*)

Sergeant Arthur Herbert was bent over the navigation table in the glazed nose, whilst in the turret Sergeant James Close kept a sharp lookout. A largish town and port was directly in Drew's path, Le Havre. Herbert made ready the F24 on its nose mount, and with the lens protruding forward began taking photographs. At 10.59 hours three Red Cross white-painted E-boats were at anchor within the harbour. Local anti-aircraft batteries opened up tracer darts past the Blenheim, Drew swung the aircraft away into cloud and twenty-year-old Close scanned the visible aircraft surfaces from his turret for damage. Suddenly out of the sky terror latched onto N3587 as it was raked by machine-gun and cannon fire. Their attacker, Oblt Paul Temme Gruppenadjutant of Stab I./JG2, continues the story:

"I was flying the third machine in a Kette of three machines over Le Havre when I saw a Blenheim suddenly appear out of the 650 feet cloud base. It immediately tried to envelop itself back into cover. I gave chase, wondering for an instant whether it was perhaps a Junkers 88. It vanished into the cloud but I kept after it. The rear gunner opened up, it was quite accurate and I returned his fire. Again it disappeared. I remained on its tail pressing my gun button all the while. Damn! Cannon stoppage! But at the very same moment the Englander's right engine burst into flames. Once more it sought cloud cover. This time I let it go thinking it would not get very far. Then I saw it spinning down on fire. I was quite close as it crashed into the main street of Le Havre, exploded and blazed ferociously. I could see the burning fuel running along the gutters and tramlines. A few minutes later explosions occurred causing severe damage to the surrounding buildings."

Htpm Siegfried Bethke witnessed this skirmish. "That was the first kill I saw from the ground," he noted. Upon landing Temme drove to the crash site. All that remained were the two engines. The tramlines were engulfed in blazing aviation fuel and had melted and fused together. As he had feared there had been deaths to the civilian population – three had been killed in the explosion, with two-dozen injured by falling debris and glass. Temme went out to dinner that night with Gruppenkommandeur Wolfgang Schellmann. Afterwards they walked along the seafront before motoring back, making the journey in two hours because of military traffic.

After this extraordinary day of action organizational changes were made at Thorney Island. Flight Lieutenant Dick Powers received notification that 236 Squadron was to move with immediate effect to St Eval, Cornwall, from where the fighting was the hardest. There was frantic movement. Pilot Officer Aubrey Inniss recorded, "One minute we were at readiness, next I'm told to help get the squadron ready to move by next morning. So we moved."

Powers led B Flight immediately towards the west, almost losing a Blenheim to over-enthusiastic Gloster Gladiator pilots from 247 Squadron who initially recognized the outline as a Junkers 88A, forcing its pilot to pull the throttles out and flee! "Thank you for your esteemed welcome", noted the squadron diarist.

Meanwhile in the northeast, the 235 Squadron adjutant jotted down in black ink: "Four patrols of three machines which together with those carried out by A Flight 235 makes a total of sixty-one hours and the petrol consummation of 3,667 gallons for the squadron."

Crews were awoken at 03.00 hours on Saturday August 3 by some silly sod turning the light on and off. There were raised, irritated voices. Who the hell was buggering about with the lights again? All were due at the dispersal hut at 04.30 hours. It was another fine day for convoy patrols, but it was not until 11.00 hours that Laughlin got to his feet and looked at Quelch and Hall. Orders were for three of the six Blenheim fighters to scramble and cover a convoy off Cromer. Having taken off, Laughlin, Hall and Quelch formed up and maintained a tight echelon over the shipping, but eventually the monotony was broken when an observer sighted two floating mines. Responding to the visual reports by Aldis lamp, naval sharp shooters dealt with the threat.

Those remaining all sat waiting attentively, there was muted conversation on Basil Quelch's forthcoming nuptials, Peacock and Westlake flicked through newspapers and flight commander Flight Lieutenant Andrew Fletcher sipped a steaming cup of tea as he was handed a thin slip of paper by an orderly. Above the typed orders in heavy blue pencil was written B Flight.

With the threat of invasion coming from Norway and Denmark reconnaissance was vitally important, and this would be one of two dozen flown around Scandinavia until dusk by an assortment of Coastal Command machines. Order of flight maps were drawn and pored over, as the best route to conserve petrol was worked out. Provisions of pork pies and flasks of tea arrived at their dispersal hut. Collecting their parachutes and synchronizing watches, the nine airmen walked to their waiting Blenheim machines parked near two of the main hangars. At 13.28 a breeze gently blew through the recently planted row of silver birches.

They climbed aboard, Fletcher in his usual steed L9446, Flying Officer Peacock in N3542 and Pilot Officer Richard Westlake in N3524. Ahead of them lay a flight of 425 miles to Denmark. Taking off at 13.30/13.35, Fletcher led Peacock and Westlake around the Danish coast. The workload was divided, one observer scrawled notes down on F500 sheets of paper, whilst two took photographs with a hand-held F24 camera. The sea flashed beneath them. On the return flight there was a slight vibration felt through the stick on N3542 and the R/T crackled, "Bandit", followed by "In we go". The three encountered a Heinkel 115 Seaplane of 3./Küstenfliegergruppe 506 flying at 1,000 feet, seventy-seven miles off Terschelling. In line astern they attacked this unsuspecting giant. Contact with the enemy began at 16.20 hours. Voices over the R/T called out, "A good fine burst, away and come around again!", pursuing it down to 500 feet. Fountains of water rippled forth as rounds edged into the stern of the seaplane. Its aft enemy gunner fired one burst, then ceased. Westlake kept Peacock's Blenheim fifty-five feet away and looked ahead at the target as they began a second run. Tracer hit the target but the outcome was uncertain. Low on ammunition the trio broke off at 16.35, returning to base having expended 5,300 rounds. Fletcher questioned his intelligence officer about whether the He 115 had improved armour as his bullets had hit the enemy machine repeatedly but its pilot had managed to take evasive action.

As 235 Squadron had been tussling with the Luftwaffe, in the north of France Oblt Werner Mölders' JG.51 tigers tore into Coastal Command fighters twenty-one miles north of Le Havre and intercepted a single Blenheim on an anti-invasion patrol. Escorted by three fighters of 236 Squadron they in turn engaged the Bf109Es like prize-fighters standing their ground with no quarters given. The first Pilot Officer Charles Peachment saw of the enemy as he craned his neck was the Blenheim bomber speeding past him in the opposite direction towards England, clearly in a panic. He could see why when four 109s appeared, their black and white crosses and tail swastikas standing out on their light mottled camouflage. From the lead Messerschmitt came flashes of orange as its pilot opened fire. Section leader Flight Lieutenant Dick Powers was wheeling away in a climbing turn. Peachment followed, heaving the stick while in the sudden confusion garbled voices resounded in his headphones. Orange flashes of tracer arched steadily towards 'D-Dog' L8684 then accelerated as they flashed past like fireworks over the starboard engine nacelle and wing.

Ahead of him he saw a mass of twisting, turning machines. "It was as if I was watching an ornate scene of ballet from *Swan Lake*". Powers flung his machine into another tight turn, the blood draining from his head as the force of negative gravity hit. As he momentarily straightened out his head cleared and he reached on impulse for the fuel cock hand wheels, switching over to 100-octane fuel and opening the throttles fully. The control rattled as his right thumb pressed hard against the firing button, within seconds his 2,000 rounds of ammunition was spent. The engines screamed, smoke wafted from the exhausts then he noticed somewhat alarmingly that his machine's starboard oil pressure gauge was dropping. With an eye on the gauge he pulled the stick over and down they went.

A Bf109 E of Jagdgeschwader 51 (JG 51) commanded by Luftwaffe ace Werner 'Vati' Mölders. (*Bundesarchiv, Germany*)

Sweat ran over his forehead underneath the fastened leather flying helmet and oxygen mask. With a feeling of elation at having survived he now headed for base. One by one the squadron staggered back. Peachment and Sergeant Joseph Lowe came through despite severe damage to the oil system, nursing L8684 back across the expanse of water with everything throttled back to the minimum needed to maintain height, 1,950 rpm at 120 mph. Lowe calculated that due to the severity of the damage they would not reach Thorney Island and made straight for Ford airfield instead. Skimming over Ford Road, Peachment lifted the machine over the perimeter and made a forced landing, remarking, "one of its support systems had literally been drained away" adding, "it would be rather improper to go swimming without one's bathing costume – think of all the commotion it would cause". Fortunately 'D-Dog' L8684 was repairable.

The daily irritation of 'hit and run raids' continued by Coastal Command as they enveloped Norway to the borders of Spain but barely a sortie went by along the continental coastline without an aircraft sustaining battle damage. One Blenheim pilot wrote home: "My mood swings constantly. I'd feel daring and excited at the thought of being able to hit back, the next minute overcome by the steady erosion of odds – as colleagues failed to return from nerve-wracking sorties."

Commander-in-chief Air Chief Marshal Bowhill acknowledged that his command had acquitted itself well so far, although like Dowding he worried about the suitable numbers of aircrew to which Coastal Command only had limited access. Training was cut to two weeks which was in reality not enough time to prepare raw inexperienced pilots and observers. However, there were experienced foreign nationals waiting. Out of ten Belgian pilots, five were sent to 236 Squadron and four to 235 Squadron, replenishing and expanding the squadrons. 235 Squadron also saw the arrival of new flying personnel; Pilot Officers Peter Wickings-Smith, Joseph Chamberlain, John Fenton and Sergeant Harold Naughtin together with the first group of Belgian pilots; Pilot Officers James

Kirkpatrick and Henri 'Moustique' Gonay, Sergeants O. Le Jeune and Rene DeMoulin. After the capitulation of France most had escaped to England in June 1940 and been through operational training units.

One retold his story in an early dog-eared edition of 235's September 1940 periodical. No name was given in case of recriminations against his Belgian family.

"And so we sailed towards England on June 18 and I looked out on the blue calm sea, far away from anywhere. On the morning of Friday, June 20, we entered the bay of Falmouth. The country looked so green and peaceful and the little flint and brick houses almost snug, the public house most inviting. I had never been to Cornwall before, I did not think it would look this green, for nearly a whole day our boat lay at anchor in the bay of Falmouth. There were many vessels and no doubt every man had some grim stories to tell. And still, the country looked so calm and peaceful, a different world from the Belgium and France we had left behind. It gave one a strange thrill to see England – England the last free country in Europe. Quotations ran through my head – Richard II, Blake and Tennyson. After being passed by a lady, the medical officer of health, came the passport formalities. We were ushered into a garden then into a large building where we were treated by the local ladies to tea and fresh lemonade, cold meats, cheese and lots of other good things. And after a night in a comfortable boarding house bed, on to the railway station. The porter stuck 'Paddington' labels on cases. Now to fight with the Royal Air Force! Belgium seemed very far away."

This would mean an increase in the number of required Blenheims from sixteen to twenty-four on 235 and 236 Squadron. The Belgians' arrival saw the formation of C Flight on 235 and foraging parties were sent out to obtain extra lockers, mugs and cutlery for the dispersal hut. Operations were curtailed due to the aerodrome being fog bound, which made the foraging easier!

A shipping strike off the Danish coast followed on Wednesday August 7. Jackson-Smith, replenished after leave in Liverpool, was in the lead position. "We waddled like ducks to our fighters, dressed in full fur-lined flying suit, gauntlets and boots like Captain Robert Scott." Three aircraft flew out at 15.00 hours, attacking two armed merchantmen at 16.50, "We had plenty of return fire from the ships, but did little damage". Hits were registered, 4,500 rounds were used, and with the ammo almost out they continued with their search for enemy vessels. Glancing around Jackson-Smith realized at 18.00 it was time to head back.

Back inside the warmth of the dispersal hut Sergeant Harold Sutton wrote a letter after this trip, and also had the personal satisfaction of hearing from Squadron Leader Ronnie Clarke that his diligent rigger Leading Aircraftman William Day was to obtain the temporary rank of corporal prior to going on a gunnery course at RAF Manby, Lincolnshire after being recommended by Flying Officer Robert Jamison. Lelly Day had recently come top in a marksmanship course held for potential air gunners using the 0.303 rifle and Vickers machine gun, and achieved a 85% pass on his written papers.

That same morning 678 miles north off Trondheim, Norway, Pilot Officer Richard Haviland of 248 Squadron was on an anti-invasion patrol in 'R-Robert' L9456 and was in difficulty. Having taken off at 09.30 the weather was absolutely atrocious, with less than twenty yards visibility. In places Haviland could not see the nose of the machine. His observer Pilot Officer Malcolm Wells guided Haviland expertly south along the Norwegian coast for a position fix at Hellisøy lighthouse with its brightly painted red and white cone shape looming out of the fog to greet them. Wells crouched over his small table in the nose plotting a course, whilst in the aft section gunner Sergeant Archibald Kay rotated the turret using the handles in order to keep the circulation in his hands. Suddenly his headphones crackled into life. He heard the faint words "Prepare to DITCH!" due to lack of fuel. After eight hours twenty-five minutes of powered flight everything fell silent aboard L9456, all that could be heard was the wind whistling. High above fighters of RAF Fighter Command watched their plight. The section leader gave coordinates to the WAAF controller. She wrote with fluidity in blue fountain pen, 'Position 97 degrees St. Abbs Head 30 miles'.

Inside 'R-Robert' Kay was reaching for the emergency dinghy, ready for a swift exit from the escape hatch. "Brace yourselves" Haviland calmly shouted into the darkness. Suddenly L9456 hit a solid wall of water near Farne Island off St Abbs Head. They followed emergency procedure that had been drilled into them a thousand times; Haviland and Wells out of the pilot's top hatch, Kay out the rear. As Wells lifted himself out he caught his leg on the metal rim, which tore through his battledress trousers into the flesh. Kay held the dinghy whilst Haviland and Wells boarded, pushing off with the wooden paddle. The three were tossed about like a sack of potatoes and Wells was sick over the side. They hung on whilst praying to God that they would be saved.

Trawler *Ben Screel* picked the three soaked RAF boys out of the water at a recorded time of 15.55 hours. The shivering Haviland, Mills and Kay were shuffled into the captain's galley, a sailor handing a bottle of Scottish whisky labelled 'Old Elgin' to Haviland. Mills' teeth momentarily stopped chattering when he took a mouthful of whisky before passing it to Kay. Above on deck, Skipper David McRuvie of North Shields, Northumberland and his crew managed to fix a line to tow the floating Blenheim fighter L9456 into the Tyne to be salvaged. The airmen were none the worse for their experiences apart from headaches and minor injuries.

During the night in the English Channel's choppy seas enemy activity was rife, E-boat flotillas dropped between six and eight mines each. The Luftwaffe had also been carrying out minelaying operations, the largest number by 9 Fliegerdivision, of which KG4 was a part. The kommandeur of 7 Staffel, Hajo Herrmann, was involved in a number of such operations during the first ten days of August. "Our task was to block up the mouths of the bays, harbours and ports by dropping a variety of mines from our bomb bays. Most were 1,000 kg magnetic or acoustic mines." Herrmann begrudged these operations, "Minelaying and the positioning of mines was a very dangerous thing, at times we were flying at 180 mph or so, easy prey for British fighters".

That night at 01.47/02.00 hours mines were laid in the Thames estuary, near Southend-on-Sea. Royal Navy converted trawlers began sweeping for enemy mines by day and patrolled by night – orders had been communicated that they now had to carry out convoy protection too; improvisation of 'make do and mend' meant galvanizing whatever resources were available. It was indeed difficult to know what lay ahead. "We were more interested in the history of the Hope Hotel bar, and whether or not our drinks were watered down", wrote one mariner. Time forced them to do the bar quickly. Dashing out, back to their vessels ready for the next sailing in convoy CW9. This convoy, bound for the long wharfs of Portsmouth and Southampton, was designated CW9 (convoy westbound), however in the annuals of Coastal Command it was recorded as No 9.

As the lanyards clinked in the blackout and ensigns flapped in the squall, large cloud formations and occasional showers persisted into the early hours. Droplets of rain evaporated on the warm funnels as the vessel's coal-fired boilers 'got up steam'. Those working below in the confined engine room were sweltering in the dry heat, whilst their captains on the bridge heard the order to weigh anchor at 07.00 hours from the convoy commodore. Twenty-four vessels got underway, sailing with the morning tide down river in a semi-orderly fashion for their final position through numerous reaches and channels, their wakes gathering pace onward to North Foreland. As they moved silently along morning changed to night. With no lights showing the convoy proceeded down the English Channel. Lookouts changed shortly before midnight. Their eyes became accustomed to the blackness as the wind bit into their exposed faces. They watched attentively for anything out of the ordinary, as the new day Thursday August 8 commenced. There was nothing visible in the unending wilderness of cold, except the horizon in a variety of lampblack colours.

Convoy CW9 codenamed Peewit scattered after an attack on August 8, 1940.

Suddenly torpedoes struck as a vessel was moving at 8 knots. There was one slamming explosion that was deafening and the ship lifted slightly out of the water with a noise of ripping and tearing metal. Those below deck stood little chance of survival. The drenched lookout hung on steadying himself. "I was alive – just – but still in a silent dream. Barely nineteen I felt like a corpse rising from a watery grave and being forced immediately into some horrendous medieval duel."

Parachute flares illuminated silhouettes of merchantmen as German E-boats from the 1.S-Flottille started to harry CW9 from 01.30/02.00 hours for thirty-seven miles into the half-light of dawn. "For the first thirty seconds there was nothing, we were anxious and a little perplexed, what on earth had gone wrong *this* time?" Captain J. H. Potts recalled; "They ravaged the convoy like wolves from Beachy Head/Newhaven to Nab Tower. It was chaos. In the blackness occasional spasmodic tracer rounds illuminated friend and foe." On one small vessel, in the blackness and confusion no one on board knew if they had struck another merchantman or been hit by a torpedo, all that could be heard from the voice-pipe were shouts and crazy hammering for help. But there was no help for them. The noise was finally shut out when the vessel sank. By 04.30 the violence stopped. Three small vessels of 2,587 tons lay sunk, as the fast E-boats dispersed and victoriously sped towards Cherbourg, where their breakfast awaited. While eating the Kriegsmarine crews excitedly swapped experiences and began tallying up the Englander's losses.

As the skies lightened around Britain in the northwest of London deep in the underground operations room at RAF Uxbridge, the naval and Coastal Command liaison officers watched a WAAF plotter receiving information through her headphones. They placed a new Bakelite plaque with the words CONVOY STOPPED on the map just near Beachy Head/Newhaven. Instantly the RAF Coastal Command liaison officer forwarded the relevant information to the command's Chatham headquarters. With great urgency, a telephone rang at the nearest forward aerodrome, RAF Thorney Island.

Pilot Officer Henry Davis, Sergeants Beaumont and Coulton sprinted towards 59 Squadron's machine 'N-Nuts', and climbed the footholds. Davis jumped on to the wing and hurriedly clambered up, then lowered himself into the tight cockpit. Plugging his leads in, he gave thumbs up to the ground crew and moved across the grass, speeding off. Davis heard their controller repeat the search area and headed out to sea, giving his Blenheim maximum plus nine boost. One hour and two minutes after the E-boats had left the CW9 convoy in tatters 'N-Nuts' unsuccessfully scoured the Channel to within eighteen miles of Cherbourg for the enemy craft until 05.50 hours. Finally turning back at 06.25 Davis reported to his controller: "Contacting convoy CHANNEL westward bound No 9, five merchant vessels and one escort located following about eight miles behind convoy, one balloon ship five miles behind convoy".

Davis' fate would be sealed in the afternoon. Royal Navy ships tried to rally the steamers to shepherd them into two columns. By 10.30 hours, they precariously built up steam and proceeded in a calm sea. A better weather front had dispersed the low cloud and the waters of the Channel were bathed in brilliant sunshine, while above RAF fighters flew overhead as escort. By 12.15 the whole convoy was near St Catherine's Point when Bf109Es appeared streaming out of the sun with Junkers 87s. The Luftwaffe hit the zigzagging convoy whilst individual aerial duels unfolded over the Isle of Wight. Blenheims C, E, and W from 59 Squadron sent an urgent signal, "Westward No 9 convoy attacked by enemy aircraft. Photographs taken".

Both sides were losing considerable numbers as the air battle enunciated single-engine fighters. Air Chief Marshal Sir Hugh Dowding with Air Vice-Marshal Keith Park looked down from the low balcony overlooking the large plotting table before them at Uxbridge. Dowding briefly reflected on the previous day's visit by Colonel Raymond Lee, before requesting the Coastal Command liaison officer to "bring some long-nosed Blenheims to readiness". He then picked up the telephone and requested re-enforcements from No 16 Group. As a result eight machines from 235 Squadron B Flight at Bircham Newton made the short flight to Thorney Island ready to enter the fray, under the guidance of Fighter Command's 11 Group fighter controllers.

With these increasingly intense enemy attacks near the home coastal waters there was only ever the briefest of interludes between air raid warnings, there wasn't even time to take the Mae West off. At 15.35 these crew were scrambled into the air, flying out over the scattered burnt lacquered remains of vessels from CW9 from their two earlier encounters. Fewer than six squadrons were scrambled to intercept. There would be one more attempt as the convoy struggled on. A seventh would also become involved: the 11 Group WAAF controller interjected, "Large formation of snappers" (enemy fighters) to Fletcher in L9446. There was no shipping spotted in Le Havre when they reported back at 16.15 hours. Their machines turned to starboard and thundered rhythmically over the silent sea the short distance to the mouth of the River Seine. When they were eleven miles away Fletcher, Wordsworth, 'M-Mother' T1805 and Hobbs, 'K-King' N3526 went into a holding pattern for twenty minutes waiting to shepherd Davis home. Camouflaged by light cloud a mass of fifteen German twin-engine Messerschmitt Bf110s of II/ZG2 appeared. They were returning from escorting Stukas which had taken part in the final engagement of the day against CW9. Six Bf110s swarmed down. Observer Sergeant Owen Burns jotted down, 'Position 239 degrees, Le Havre 11 miles'. The sphere of battle would soon be spread out over one mile of sky.

Sergeant Sydney Hobbs heard the battle cry, "Tally ho!" and then the vic turned towards the enemy, three Blenheim fighters against an evenly matched German side. He was instantly in the swirling mass in "an everyone for themselves situation". There was great confusion and he only fired his belly pack once in this twisting and turning duel. His air gunner Sergeant Thomas Maslen was frantically reversing his turret; bringing the single Vickers to bear he squeezed the trigger, there was a slight kick then through his fixed ring and bead sight he watched tracer arc towards a Messerschmitt. Instantaneously hits appeared to register on it and with a new magazine he re-engaged. Flying Officer Douglas Wordsworth in T1805 had got the enemy within range too. From the opposite quarter in the rear of his Blenheim Sergeant Alfred 'Duke' Maconochie changed magazine drums, mechanically giving it a gentle tap with his left hand to check it was secure, then pulled the trigger. One hundred rounds were expressed out of the chamber in less than a second at

Coastal Command Blenheim fighters found themselves in a familiar situation as this photograph illustrates showing a Blenheim of 110 Squadron over a vast expanse of water and wreckage. (*Royal Air Force Museum, London*)

the same Bf110. The Luftwaffe machine dived away at a steep angle in flames (unconfirmed). Fletcher managed to hit a Bf110 but was then peppered himself. He turned his machine hard over onto its back, dust from the floor falling around him like confetti, then righted the aircraft before pulling hard on the stick until it was in the pit of his stomach. L9446 began climbing away, "nothing about doing a barrel roll in the flight manual – totally illegal!" Glancing to his right he saw Blenheim N3590 in an uncontrollable spin.

59 Squadron had a Blenheim out on a reconnaissance too. Pilot Officer Henry Davis came into the maelstrom having exited Trouville in 'F-Freddie' N3590. Suddenly a Messerschmitt Bf110 opened fire as N3590 was moving at full speed. There was a slamming of metal into the cowling and smoke burst immediately from one of Davis' engines then he turned and stalled, the blast of heat rising as it spiralled down, smoke engulfing the aircraft. Oblt Hartmann Grasser had claimed another victim. An airman's decomposed body was eventually washed ashore on the French coast and was identified as N3590's observer Sergeant Barrington Beaumont aged twenty-nine from Leigh-on-Sea, Essex. It was then communicated to the Air Ministry that his body was later buried at Hautot-sur-Mer near Dieppe.

Blenheim fighters N, K, and M, dived down and headed back to Thorney Island. Meanwhile, smoke from CW9 wrecks curled into the heavens providing a landmark. Their six engines roared endlessly in an otherwise silent world. Letting down yet again over the village of West Wittering, the tapering waterway curving away toward Bosham and Chichester. Finally, they were brought down and immediately pounced on by ground crew. No sooner was Fletcher out of the cockpit, than Lelly Day enquired, "Are you OK, sir?"

"Just about, got peppered by a 110."

"We'll soon have her repaired, good as new."

The young Canadian flight lieutenant from Cardston, Alberta wrote: "I don't understand why Lelly Day hasn't been promoted, his work ethic is second to none and he puts some of the established senior NCOs on both flights to shame." Lelly had been taken off the gunnery course as it was realised that his skills and knowledge would be lost had he gone on to complete it.

As the riggers began working in the exposed dispersal the crews drifted toward their hut. Talk at the dispersal with the intelligence officer was of individual duels as combat reports were written up. Two jubilant Sergeants, Maslen and Maconochie, both claimed a Bf110 shot down although these were unconfirmed. Later as the clerk typed up the reports there was a slight flap as concern grew for a sergeant pilot's 'sweet heart' living in Fairlight, near Hastings. A magnetic mine had exploded near her lodgings leaving a crater twelve feet by twenty feet in a field, taking the GPO wires down with it. The sergeant obtained permission from Fletcher and drove the seventy-nine miles in a borrowed Humber to make sure she was all right. When he returned and walked into the dispersal through the tobacco haze he found those on readiness sleeping awkwardly on sofas and on chairs. Sergeant Sydney Hobbs slept fully dressed, having fallen straight to sleep after the de-briefing, still with his Mae West around his neck.

For now the killing was over, but the threat of invasion grew. Yellow air raid warnings at 235's Hampshire aerodrome during August 11 began as the day started. Vital intelligence was urgently required on the invasion ports of Le Havre and Cherbourg by the Royal Navy. In the dispersal hut Flying Officer Peacock and Pilot Officer Wakefield played darts with Sergeant Wilson. Draped over the battered sofa Sergeant Harold Sutton read the *Daily Mail* while outside Sergeants Parsons and Newport played draughts and drank mugs of tea. Sergeants Harold Naughtin, Davis and Copeland sat in silence, deep in their own thoughts. There was a distinct trill of a telephone and the orderly spoke, "Flying Officer Reginald Peacock – Operations on the telephone". It was not long before he replaced the receiver, "OK reconnaissance escort, Le Harve, take-off twenty minutes". Ollie Wakefield was lead navigator to the section. In daylight the three Blenheim fighters streamed off down the north-south runway and gained height, flying above the cloud base. The R/T was quiet. They had to get the Blenheim in and out of Europe with a minimum of fuss. Wakefield recalled, "The Blenheim bomber went ahead, reduced height over Cherbourg, took photographs then we flew to Le Havre". The bomber dropped four 250 lb GP bombs on the oil storage tanks at Le Havre, results were not observed but photographs were taken using the hand-held F24 camera.

At the border of enemy territory at 15,000 feet the temperature changed. Chilled air whistled through the fuselage, in the glazed nose Wakefield checked the wind speed and recalculated. Near Fécamp on the return leg Peacock reduced height to 12,000 feet. Immediately shouts of "Fighters" were heard, the pilots tightened their formation. They had fortuitously stumbled into elements of JG2 or JG27 returning from combat on their way home. Automatically Wakefield left the nose and positioned himself behind Peacock. He slid the emergency window open and stuck his head out. They had a busy twenty seconds. Wakefield: "Two Bf109Es attacked from astern, one was driven off [damaged] and the other was shot down [unconfirmed] by the concentrated fire of our rear gunners Wilson, Newport and Copeland."

One RAF machine was slightly damaged, and a few minutes after landing the flight sergeant asked the pilot to come and have a look. A bullet had gone through the fuel line and got lodged serving as a perfect stopper. By virtue of its shape it had prevented a fuel leak. Without fuel the engine would have seized.

They then packed up for the day. Celebrations followed as Flight Lieutenant Andrew Fletcher led his men nineteen miles to Southsea's Edwardian baroque Queens Hotel for a pint or three. Transport left the mess at 19.30 hours and for once no one got drunk. Upon their return the duty officer reported that Bircham Newton aerodrome had been bombed. Poor weather swept in during the evening together with air raid warnings at 03.38 hours.

Fletcher was called by his batman at 04.45 hours, as were Wordsworth, Peacock and Wakefield. "One of our batmen had standing instructions to call again at 0455 and remove the layers of bedclothes until one of our officers got up," wrote Wakefield, continuing, "A quick wash and breakfast followed, the mess was in a state – ashtrays full, empty or half empty beer glasses on the tables in the ante-room, whilst plates of fried eggs, ham, bacon, fried bread, sausages and tea were devoured. We found from experience that this is the only meal before dinner one could count on getting."

The ground crew on early morning readiness had prepared N, M and R at their water-strewn dispersals ready for the first operation; to escort a 59 Squadron machine. The wind was blowing in off the sea bringing with it flocks of seagulls which scavenged for scraps near the mess halls, before they could be given to the station 'piggery'. Others squawked from the rooftops of station buildings, until flying started. Trades went about their business whilst in the distance sirens could be heard. In front of the watch office building, a meteorologist checked and noted the amount of rain water and wind speed and the local weather was noted as 10/10s cloud. Elsewhere on the station preparations were taking place as crews began planning their route taking into account the implications of weather on their flight plan as well as their aircraft.

Coastal Command ordered 16 Group to press on, despite the view of the station's senior meteorologist that the weather might change for the worse when flying the anti-invasion reconnaissance patrol of Le Havre. Fletcher, Wordsworth, and Hall prepared their machines, while at 59's dispersal newly commissioned Pilot Officer Richard 'Dick' Wightman (formally a sergeant pilot) settled in his seat onboard R3668. At 11.00 hours, just prior to the operation, Wightman sat in the cramped cockpit finishing his drill to taxi-out and wrongly retracted the aircraft's undercarriage mistaking it for the flap lever. R3668's propellers buckled as his aircraft slammed onto the concrete, warping the fuselage structure. An embarrassed Wightman extracted himself from the crippled bomber. Flying Accident Card Form 1180 was filled out, the last words written being: "Gross carelessness". In the end the reconnaissance was abandoned owing to the deteriorating weather conditions over the English Channel.

Fighter Command 11 Group Hawker Hurricanes had been having a tough time in spasmodic air battles since 06.30 hours. Flight Sergeant Dick Nelson was scrambled flying Blenheim T1869 'P-Pip' and carried out a search and rescue square search for a Hurricane lost in an air battle off Portland. The ditched pilot, Sergeant Eric Seabourne of 238 Squadron based at North Weald, suffered horrific burns when his cockpit hood jammed. After a considerable struggle, he left the crippled aircraft and made a rapid free-fall descent from 18,000 feet, pulling the ripcord at roughly 5,000 feet. His parachute opened just before he plummeted into the sea, which had an immediate cooling effect on his burns. The sergeant was rescued by naval destroyer HMS *Bulldog* whilst above a twin-engine plane described by a naval lieutenant onboard the destroyer as an "unidentified British fighter type" tracked back and forth. All three crewmen strained their eyeballs searching for the fighter pilot over the expanse of the water. With nothing spotted T1869 headed back, passing over Seager House School on Hayling Island before landing.

To those at RAF Thorney Island in Hampshire it was just another day, Tuesday August 13, 1940, yet *Adlertag* – Eagle Day – was six hours old as Nelson and his crew were refreshed with a delicious redcurrant cordial drink from one of the WAAFs assigned to the squadron, described in the unit's periodical as 'intensely flavoured, rich in body and beautiful'. That afternoon more enemy bombers and fighters would intrude into British air space, at twelve noon the eyes and ears of the world were on this length of coastline, to the east of Dover's Shakespeare Cliff. It was festooned with news journalists sitting cross-legged amid ripening redcurrant and blackberry bushes, eyes and horse-

AUG	13ᵗ	HURRICANE	P3664	SELF		SOLO		INTERCEPTED 250 plus RAID OF HE IIIs 109's + ME IIOs OFF ISLE OF WIGHT.
							1	SHOT DOWN 1-ME109 & 1-HE113 BOTH CONFIRMED. MY MACHINE DISABLED & SET ON FIRE. BALED OUT. PICKED UP BY HMS BULLDOG. DID 18000' DELAY DROP.

Summary for	AUGUST	1940	T	HURRICANE
Unit	No 238(F) SQDN		Y	
Date	31. 8. 40		P E	
Signature	E.H. Seabourne (Sgt)		S	

GRAND TOTAL [Cols. (1) to (10)]

296 Hrs. 00 Mins.

TOTALS CARRIED FORWARD

The logbook of Sergeant Eric Seabourne, 238 Squadron North Weald.

racing binoculars strained upwards. Others shielded their eyes when white vapour trails moved in deadly concert with the whirling, snarling machines of war. Eagle Day reached Thorney Island shortly before 15.10 when a yellow air raid warning wailed. On the station men and women took notice, but continued with their duties. A short distance away in 235's dispersal hut the orderly reached for the strident jangle of the telephone then yelled, "B Flight scramble! Airfield protection".

Fletcher, Peacock, Wordsworth, Sutton, Nelson and Hobbs raced for their machines and were airborne within three minutes with the safety catches immediately taken off their gun buttons. Climbing up steeply, they began their defence above the aerodrome and creeks at 10,000 feet taking in Hayling Island to Portsmouth then West Wittering to Selsey Bill, but for the moment nothing stirred. At Fighter Command's operations room at Uxbridge at 16.00 hours reports of raids of over 150 aircraft approaching Poole, Portland and Portsmouth came in. At the same time there was news of other raids of over 150 aircraft in the southeast making for Deal and Dover; this gaggle passed inland into the county of East Kent and were soon active in the area. "I wonder what the bastards are up to", came the remark from Air Vice-Marshal Keith Park.

With sirens sounding around the Weald of Kent, the ancient roman city of Rochester eluded the enemy, to the delight of Mr P. P. Roome, air raid precautions officer in the city. They believed it to be a prime target because of the presence of various naval and military installations. Huddled together Roome and his colleagues watched Hurricanes racing to meet the quarry, but an armada of Huns got through: a large wedge of Junkers 87s beneath a veritable cloud of 109 fighters.

Some ten miles away, Coastal Command's RAF Detling station had endured a relatively quiet day with several air raid warnings being issued with colour codings but none lasting more than half an hour. By 15.00 hours all ranks began to relax. The small telephone exchange on the station was busy and the WAAF operators sat attentively waiting for the calls to clear. The local Royal Observer Corps tried in vain to contact the base for an estimated thirty minutes in order to inform them that a raid was imminent. Unfortunately the only two external telephone lines into the station were both in use. In desperation they dispatched a messenger on bicycle. The Luftwaffe was undeviatingly aiming for the Coastal Command base.

At 15.53 a yellow air raid warning sounded. Eight minutes passed and afternoon tea beckoned. Four miles northeast red air raid warnings could be heard drifting in from Maidstone. These were immediately drowned out when Hptm Berndt von Brauchitsch led eighty-six Junkers 87 dive-bombers out of the clouds. With their sirens screaming IV.(Stuka)/LGI's gull-winged machines dropped their noses. Inside the cramped cockpits Luftwaffe pilots watched for their target indicators to come on; a bright light on the contact altimeter which indicated their bomb-release point. At

1,500 feet their 500 kg bombs dropped from the release gear away towards the intended target. Brauchitsch's accuracy was something to marvel, the Coastal Command aerodrome was dysfunctional within minutes. Since May 1940, RAF Coastal Command and Fleet Air Arm squadrons based at Detling had harried the Wehrmacht, Kriegsmarine and Luftwaffe in the Netherlands, France and Germany and continued to plague them like locusts in their build up to the proposed invasion of England codenamed Operation Sealion using European ports. This was their retribution; Junkers 87 dive-bombers were taking out a legitimate military threat.

As the bombs rained down towards the operations building, the protection afforded by the surrounding compacted earth wall was minimal. When the building was designed and constructed in the early 1930s no one could have envisaged the treatment the structure would be subjected to in 1940. Only the camouflage netting draped over the top inspired confidence. As the ground beneath heaved from the effects of explosions, the debris rained down like hail stones on the men and women in the building. However, together with Group Captain Hugh 'Pat' Davis, a pre-war Wimbledon tennis champion, they stayed resolutely at their posts.

Outside an inferno raged. Amid bellowing smoke two Stukas on perpendicular courses screamed down with sirens wailing to unleash their deadly cargo of 500 lb bombs on the station's operations room, their razor-sharp accuracy hitting the roof of the operations block immediately above the operations room. There were two detonations, a brilliant bright flash and then darkness descended. For one minute or more absolute silence filled the air as bodies lay still like mannequins. A shaft of light threaded its way through the heavy dust, concrete, and twisted metal rods to reveal Davis with a jagged six-inch long piece of concrete through his skull. Above ground toy-like silhouettes of German dive-bombers and fighters were outlined against the dirty sky; they too were swallowed up by the landscape.

Scoring three direct hits in three different positions they demolished the water main servicing the aerodrome and one of the petrol installations. WAAF Josephine 'Josie' Fairclough remembered:

"I was doing a spell in the parachute section, we heard noise and a fellow said 'Move! Those are Jerrys!' and we went like hell into the nearest shelter. There was a terrific wallop just as we came down the brick steps and a lot of black smoke, earth and dust came up. The other end of the shelter had been hit. I began clawing away at the earth with my bare hands to get to the injured buried in the blast. Following this raid most personnel never again entered a shelter during a raid."

A direct hit wiped out sixty-seven airmen and women who were taking tea in the airmen's mess as the first bombs tumbled down. Cherry-red patches of flame flickered and fused along what were once the foundations. Stretcher bearers and first-aiders moved gravely amidst the pandemonium. Letters, newspapers and photos fluttered limply or floated away on the blood-stained water that flowed from burst pipes. Here and there haggard men and women leaned stolidly over one of their wounded or dead companions collecting their papers and identity discs.

With the aerodrome's domestic sites wildly dispersed, the first some WAAFs knew of the raid was when two Messerschmitts raced in with cannon and machine-gun rounds pumping out continually. A WAAF billeted out in the large house called 'Woodlands' on the Sittingbourne Road wrote: "I looked out of my bedroom window at about four in the afternoon and saw a khaki-clad soldier running. We take very little notice of the noise of aeroplanes for they are about continuously, but to see a soldier running I realized there was a raid right on us – we had no warning. I dashed into our dugout only just in time. The noise was terrific and I was deaf for two days afterwards. When I came out I shall never forget the sights which met my eyes. I was a cook by trade, but I became a first-aider for many hours after the raid."

Damage caused by exploding bombs had dramatically transformed the station scene. Not one hangar remained, now only a series of blackened bricks and metal support arches stood among the twisted wreckage of burning motorcars and aircraft. Overhead hung low clouds of smoke, nothing existed but mounds of military rubble and shattered buildings. The officers' mess had been hit by two well-placed 500 lb bombs which landed in the middle of the complex. Surrounded by tree stumps the new camp accommodation, part of the current expansion plan, was completely wiped out too. Not one building remained intact, only mounds of soil interspersed with brick and fragments of wood showed where buildings had formerly stood. It appeared as if the whole aerodrome had been liberally sprayed with machine-gun rounds. This was not confined solely to Detling Hill, according to locals there was much damage to property within Detling village. Flight Sergeant John Hearn wrote:

"As the raid diminished it was broken suddenly by Blenheims blowing up with their entire petrol and bomb loads. They were intended to be used on a raid for invasion barges in a French port."

The Tunbridge Wells deputy controller of air raid precautions and the civil defence begin to give assistance. The deputy controller quickly appreciated the severity of the situation: "The number of casualties could not be definitely stated, but they are certainly between fifty and 100 and considerable damage has been sustained." Shortly afterwards a telephone call was received at Tunbridge Wells General Hospital which had been requested to arrange for a reception of injured and to provide ambulances. Mr Turner drove one of the four ambulances with four first aid parties to Detling up through the gap where once the main gates stood. He carefully picked his way around the bomb craters, wrecked vehicles and shattered Blenheim aircraft. He noted how accurate German Bf109E cannon and machine-gun fire had been, particularly when dealing with men, women and dispersed aircraft. Various contract workers with minor and serious injuries lay or sat waiting for help caught in the devastation with the station works engineer Mr Nugent suffering extensive head injuries. An Australian officer reconnoitring with a first aid party reported:

"I passed on carefully to the operations block. They were huddled up close and in the last stages of exhaustion and fear. The wounded, numerous unattended, and the weak groaned and moaned all over the place, damaged by flying fragments and debris as more ambulances shambled in."

As men and women treated by these mobile emergency units were removed, local army medical teams arrived and the civil defence ambulances and first aid parties were withdrawn whilst civil defence rescue parties continued and assisted in the collection of the dead to a central point. They were instrumental in the recovery of several more bodies that otherwise may not have been found because of the precarious nature of building structures. They used flares for lighting until it became impossible due to darkness and blackout procedure. A rescuer wrote:

"Some of the bodies had parts missing, we made a small pile of the oddments that we found and left it to the Maidstone undertaker to sort them out if they could. All these dead people were lifted by hand to a piece of land near the main gate, covered with a brown blanket, including the oddments. We departed for the NAAFI or WI utility van to replenish our thirst with a mug of hot Horlicks and a sandwich."

Casualty Clearing Officer Wallace Beale, a Maidstone undertaker recalled, "Many dead needed the five-foot coffins reserved for unidentified remains. Ninety-four seriously injured personnel were taken to Preston Hall Hospital in Aylesford. It was chaos on a grand scale."

Blenheim casualties consisted of T1938, R3849, R3677, R3819, R3632 and L9460 of 53 Squadron together with a visiting Blenheim from Andover Station Flight. Loss of personnel included operations and signals officers, Squadron Leader Dennis Oliver and Flying Officer Harold Aspen among others. Eight of the squadron's diligent ground crew were killed and a further eight seriously injured as had two observers, Sergeants Douglas Roberts and Kenneth Vowles.

Smoke and dust rose high into the warm Kent evening air. The survivors reflected on the prospect of RAF Fighter Command losing control of the skies over the southeast as they had temporarily over this Coastal Command aerodrome. The results would be catastrophic. Above on the hilltop lay a bare RAF Detling. A few survivors sought solitude away from the stench of death in the quiet lanes where rabbits and hedgerow birds moved in the stillness, walking along the green bridle path of the Pilgrims' Way as night gave way to day. As they walked, smoking cigarettes they could hardly grasp that sixty minutes earlier it had been an RAF station.

In true air force spirit officers shared dining accommodation with the WAAF in their dining hall and the section officer arranged for an extra Aga cooker to be fitted immediately to augment the cooking facilities. Although the airmen's cookhouse was badly damaged, its cooks said that they were "able to cope with the cooking amongst the debris". Two seventy-two-inch ranges from RAF Manston were dispatched to Detling. Two steam traction engines dragged the remains of the hangars to the ground. The Ministry of Works requested the Mid-Kent Water Company to renew the damaged pipe work to the station with immediate effect, as no further piping was available at the Southern Railway depot at Ashford because of recent blast damage. With a water supply it was hoped that the water pressure would allow 'Warren' cookers to be used. Cooking for the vast majority of sergeant pilots was being carried out under restricted conditions.

The grass runways were repaired by men of the Royal Air Force, Royal Engineers and Royal Navy, filling in craters with rubble which had been dumped around the aerodrome for just such a contingency earlier in June. The Royal Engineers continued to deal with unexploded bombs. Engineers from the GPO soon repaired and re-laid telephone lines and the operations room was cleared with the help of a mechanical digger. Electrical services were also being re-laid.

With the continued expansion resuming fifty temporary huts awaited permission to be re-sited near Friningham Manor, the works manager noting that "although somewhat distant they will be naturally camouflaged by trees in the surrounding woods". A war committee note reads: "Detling in its congested layout lent itself easily to concentrated attack. It suffered the most severely to date, and for the moment Fighter Command have ceased to use the station as a refuelling point for their fighters."

Poles from 303 Squadron at Northolt wanted to seek vengeance for the loss of 'their girls' in blue at Detling. Coastal Command's commander-in-chief made reference in 1942 to the bombing when interviewed for the *The Montreal Gazette*: "If Detling had been a sector station for Fighter Command serious questions would have been raised at the highest level but, because it was deemed a Coastal Command airfield it didn't seem to matter in the wider context". The Ministry of Works' repair bill for RAF Detling after this one raid totalled £80,000. The base was hit a further four times by the Luftwaffe in the coming weeks, as further raiding parties against barges and shipping by the Royal Air Force and Fleet Air Arm using Detling as a forward operating base were sent out.

Earlier, before the Luftwaffe had arrived two Coastal Command Blenheim fighters five miles out skirted Detling. By 16.05 they had crossed counties into the Hampshire skies. Flight Lieutenant Frederick Flood in N3531 and Squadron Leader Ronnie Clarke in P9261, came straight into Thorney Island at full throttle during a yellow air raid warning. Flood and Clarke directed their aircraft toward two waiting figures clad in tin hats who guided them in. With engines running at reduced speed, two men in Irvin jackets and flying helmets sprinted in from the rear, buffeted by the propeller back wash. Both these air gunners clambered aboard their respective machines, closing the hatch behind

The only known view of the burial of those lost during the attack on RAF Detling Kent, in August 1940 taken by a *Kent Messenger* photographer. (*Detling Parish Council, Kent*)

the turret. On N3531 Sergeant Alfred Maconochie squeezed into the turret. Both machines immediately scrambled back into the air, eventually formating on the seven 235 Squadron aircraft already patrolling. Pilot Officer Hugh Wakefield recalled that "from our vantage point it looked as if the RAF were throwing everything in".

Fletcher received word from the 11 Group fighter controller, "Trade near Selsey, Buster, Angels One-Five (1,500 feet)". All changed fuel tanks to 100-octane and pulled out their throttles. As they increased speed a single Junkers 88A of 8./LGI was flying in the direction of Selsey Bill heading for its base. Coastal Command's pack of hounds closed in for the kill. The Junkers was observed at 16.17 hours flying at 1,000 feet in and out of thin cloud against the backdrop of blue. The cry went up "Tally ho!" after which they slanted towards it purposefully, eight against one, huddled together as if for warmth. This time 235 couldn't miss!

South of RAF Tangmere, high above at 7,000 feet Blue and Red Section of 257 Squadron were also after the same quarry. Squadron Leader Bill Harkness spotted the Ju 88 above the cloud. Blenheim crews watched as two Hurricanes butted in. Such was the superior speed that their air turbulence caused two of the Blenheims to wobble about like a spinning top. The enemy bomber evaded the Hurricanes, with return fire hitting one, but Pilot Officer Cardale Capon brought his eight guns to bear. With rounds striking the Junkers it was forced into an almost vertical left hand turn. "I noticed that its port engine was on fire and flames were coming out of the wing root starboard side." The Luftwaffe pilot was now down to 500 feet and moving slowly across the sky. A third Hurricane attacked just west of Selsey – flames engulfed both engines, a crew member jumped but the parachute only half opened. The Junkers 88A touched the ground, exploding into a mushroom-shaped ball of flame at 16.35 hours at Sidlesham.

Dejected, the Blenheim fighters dived away back towards base. A further airfield patrol made a total of fourteen flying hours for B Flight. Undisturbed for the next six hours, men caught up on their sleep as cups of tea grew cold on tables or the floor. Before dawn 235 Squadron continued with reconnaissance flights and became embroiled in an encounter over the North Sea. On Thursday August 15 the Luftwaffe launched an attack using the German-based Luftflotte 5 in Norway, against aerodromes at Usworth near Newcastle and Dishforth, north of Leeds utilising Heinkels of 8./KG 26 and I/ZG 76 Messerschmitt Bf110s carrying drop-tanks. German Luftwaffe officers had counted on tactical surprise, with a decoy raid by Heinkel 115 seaplanes heading for the Firth of Forth, before aborting forty miles from the Scottish coast. When the main force steamed in, all was going well until a catastrophic navigational three-degree error saw sixty-five Heinkels and thirty-four Messerschmitts tracking towards the Firth of Forth.

Realizing their mistake the formation turned south, flying at 15,000 feet across the grey-green water like lambs to the slaughter. Spitfires from 72 Squadron pounced off the Farne Islands. Positioning themselves 3,000 feet above, they rolled in from the seaward side out of the sun. Pilot Officer Robert Deacon-Elliott known as 'The Deac' with eleven of his fellows reported over one hundred aircraft. Despite these heavy odds the Spitfires fought for over five minutes and claimed several destroyed, when just north of Blyth, Hurricanes of 605 Squadron who had been scrambled into the air at 12.25 hours joined the fight. Shooting down four more bombers the enemy then split into two, one group edging towards Newcastle. 41 Squadron scrambled from Catterick and a third unit arrived from Northumberland. 79 Squadron caught them just off the Tyne coast. More enemy bombers fell earthwards between Sunderland and Bridlington before the survivors turned for home. Several were pestered over south Yorkshire before exiting British airspace between 13.00 and 13.20 hours.

By 13.45 hours this ramshackle formation were in full retreat across the North Sea. Inside some of the bullet-riddled machines were broken pieces of equipment and wounded bodies, with pilots straining to keep in touch and airborne. Individual aircraft reduced speed to conserve fuel while others fell back because of battle damage. Nearly all were flying at 3,000 feet, one was wobbling from side to side as an injured pilot tried to regain control nearing Horns Reef, west of Denmark. Their day of reckoning was not over yet.

In the afternoon someone at 16 Group had the bright idea to send three Blenheims out on a shipping raid – they must have had some notion that there was some mischief brewing in the North Sea. Running out over the Norfolk coastline at 13.40 the controller told them to be cautious as some Hurricanes and Spitfires had been reported in the area. The pilots, Laughlin, Hall and Jackson-Smith sat up and took more notice of their surroundings. They had been airborne over an hour when Jackson-Smith's observer Pilot Officer Donald Howe handed him a scrawled message, "Eighty miles to Horns Reef off Denmark". Leading the arrowhead Laughlin in L9404 carried out a personal search of the water, dipping his wings slightly as he led T1803 and T1804 with the sun glinting off the North Sea.

At 14.55 hours on the port side T1803's pilot Jackson-Smith spotted black specks moving like ants across the skyline. "Heinkels" came a muffled shout in Jackson-Smith's headset from Howe then "over on the left, about one and a half miles away". Concentrating, he watched, "I don't think they'd seen the three of us. I then called to Bodsie that they were well spread out. I'd already applied the nine plus boost and Howe stood beside me. In anticipation I gently eased the stick and rudder 'let's try and get them' came over the R/T to which I motored off."

Singling the outer flight of six which were in a ragged V formation near Horns Reef, Jackson-Smith manoeuvred into a position of attack. "Being underneath them we must have been difficult to see." He climbed like hell, his throttles were almost at full stretch. Now within shooting range, Jackson-Smith fired. There was a noise of shredding calico as rounds were dispensed, before he pushed the stick forward and swooped 100 feet underneath one enemy aircraft and broke away to starboard. "I pulled up sharply towards one, but stalled then instinctively as my nose dropped away, I immediately opened fire with the belly pack on another. Below me tracer streaked into the top fuselage and enemy gunner's position." At the same moment while breaking away to starboard, his rear gunner emptied a full magazine into the enemy aircraft with unknown results. Jackson-Smith was instantly 100 to 90 yards astern of another, "he was going bloody fast". Immediately opening fire, bits of their Heinkel flew into the air which made off, its starboard engine alight and the port engine streaming white glycol towards the landmass of Denmark. Suddenly rounds shred the edge of T1803's port wing, and with shouts of "Watch out astern!" Jackson-Smith pulled away from the engagement muttering "Bloody Moths". Checking the fuel state he headed for base, evading contact with a further six as all his ammunition was spent.

Flying Officer Laughlin in 'A-Ace' L9404 and Sergeant Hall in 'E-Edward' T1804 waded into the mêlée with unconfirmed results, finding fifteen He 111s at 3,000 feet. Both RAF fighters had been flying at 1,500 feet when they saw a further three struggling some way behind the main formation. Bodsie made quick hand gestures to Hall and both climbed, wheeling in from the stern. Picking one out they fired and manoeuvred. The He 111's engine spluttered to a halt, L9404 broke to port, with Hall taking up position astern. Rounds were seen to prize open the rear fuselage and no return fire was experienced. Further attacks ensued on a second big fat Heinkel. Laughlin raced in as it began to jinx; "he started turning one way and then the other as the gunner loosed off wildly. I would hardly need my sight. Fired longish bursts then whitish smoke came from one engine. It went down to sea level making for Denmark."

Then he was pulling out. Hard. And searching upwards the Heinkels were going like hell now. Turning for base, the strain was lifted as they flew over the expanse of sea, but at 15.40 both received incoming fire from an unidentified ship travelling at 4 knots. The sea state was fairly calm but there was still enough movement for it to wobble. Those manning the machine guns remained steadfast and continued to track the RAF aircraft with accurate tracer fire as Laughlin and Hall yanked their Blenheim fighters around 180 degrees to hit back with a salvo of six 20 lb GP bombs and two incendiaries from each. Explosions rocked the vessel and a deluge of seawater rained down on its wheelhouse and deck. The machine-gun fire ceased. As they got back on course their troubles were still not over for they flew straight into two trawler-type auxiliary vessels (TTA) known as flak ships to the air force. The flak ships pumped out defensive fire of all calibres but it had little effect. "Stupid Hun were firing blanks!" Laughlin's observer Pilot Officer Bill Martin onboard 'A-Apple' also noted, "Very inaccurate bursts of black smoke observed".

Nearing the Norfolk coast, they passed over Titchwell Marsh. Birds took flight and fortunately none struck either aircraft. With Bircham Newton in sight a calm voice from the watch office guided them in over RAF Docking. Both landed at 19.00 hours and taxied in. Martin climbed down wearily and walked off to the dispersal hut closely followed by Laughlin and Sergeant Leo Ricks. During de-briefing the number of rounds used was noted by Jamison: "In the combat 2,250 rounds were fired from the front guns of each Blenheim 'A' and 'L' and 1,700 from rear guns." After a flurry of activity Pilot Officer Norman Jackson-Smith was credited with one Heinkel 111H-4 of 8./KG 26.

Indications of the activity against the northeast were still much in evidence as one of the RAF's Y Service stations picked up enemy wireless transmissions, which were then sent to Bletchley Park on paper by motorcycle courier: "An S.O.S. was sent by an aircraft going down, a second aircraft sent an S.O.S. at 15.18 hours and from a corrupt message received it appears that the crew were taken aboard a Danish vessel."

On the base they were "all very cheered as everyone had a share in the job". There was a celebratory drink in the officers' mess. Refuelled they headed for bed shortly after 10.00 hours. News travelled to Bircham Newton that some of 236 Squadron had been caught at Middle Wallop just after 16.00 hours the previous day. It was now barely operational with numerous unexploded bombs. Leading Aircraftman Tom Wilkinson: "Men wondered how their luck would hold, many seemed to wait with equal indifference for death or deliverance; there were twenty-four wounded men with minor lacerations inside one building, two dead on the floor. The stench was dreadful."

The following day it was more of the same as Heinkel 111s dropped bombs but only a Junkers 88 succeeded, diving out of cloud cover and dropping a stick of four bombs. The Ministry of Works reported that the Middle Wallop aerodrome had been bombed again and was badly cut up. Lorries from Andover transported and helped in the general clear up. One bomb hit 609 Squadron's hangar. Leading Aircraftman Joe Roddis:

"A string of four bombs unleashed from a Junkers 88 came through a large metal corrugated hangar and the hefty sliding door lifted off into the air as it was being closed, and plummeted like a child's kite onto a crowd of airmen and WAAFs who were running past. Myself and other airmen ran down to see if we could do anything. We could not but I saw a WAAF's arm sticking out of the debris with a wristwatch on, still going."

Three Blenheims and several mangled Spitfires were written off and three dead airmen and one WAAF were found crushed to death underneath the hangar door, having been struggling to close it to protect the aeroplanes. Another was injured and also three Department of Works civilian contractors lost their lives with two seriously injured. The Department of Works report continues:

"This one bomb has caused extensive damage – No 5 hangar is practically unserviceable, also due to numerous flying fragments considerable damage has been done to roofs and buildings, difficult to enumerate."

As they emerged from their quarters in Hampshire before dawn on Sunday, August 18, a light haze greeted Peacock, Wordsworth, Sutton and Nelson, as they were transported to 235's dispersal hut at 05.30 hours. Dry shaves were the order of the day, either electric or hand-operated, and there was a busy whining noise as individually they took it in turns to get spruced up. Pilot Officer Hugh Wakefield commented, "It was a great life, and we all gradually came to understand each other's idiosyncrasies". All had been up since first light, on readiness. Suddenly, the operations room telephone rang. Instantly, Peacock, Sutton and Nelson took off, climbing to 9,000 feet searching for dark silhouettes, during a twenty-minute local fighting patrol over Thorney Island which passed without incident. Missing from the congregation this morning was Sergeant Sydney Hobbs, having been nocturnally flying as part of the fighter escort to re-activated Fairey Battles of 12 and 142 Squadrons for a devastating night raid on Boulogne the previous evening. Hobbs' machine 'X-X-Ray' N3540 burnt out at 21.35 hours after overshooting in the blackout, earlier he had the misfortune of damaging P4833 at 06.00 hours, on the same day. Thankfully in both cases Hobbs, Sergeants Herbert Ricketts and Thomas Maslen escaped with slight injuries. He now faced a court of enquiry, having earlier been torn off a strip by the intimidating station commander sighting his inexperience! Hobbs had consistently flown on B Flight's sorties, his flying hours totalling 300, but such a high rate of attrition could not be endured. The twenty-four year old was granted leave and was waved off by his colleagues, in a car heading towards Chichester railway station. His journey began to see his wife Joan Hobbs at their Clapham home in southwest London. Eleven months later newly promoted Flight Sergeant Sydney Hobbs lost his life whilst flying with 143 Squadron.

Proper breakfast had now been missed. Hours passed and the NAAFI tea wagon did a lively trade, as the young coastal boys lined themselves with strawberry jam sandwiches. By midday the haze had cleared. Sutton, Nelson and Peacock prepared for lunch. On the menu was rabbit soup followed by a plate of all the nicest bits of beef and the cook's best roast potatoes, vegetables, mustard, salt, and pepper. As people filed from morning service at Chichester Cathedral and St Nicholas church on Thorney Island at 1300 hours, one hundred and nine gull-winged dive-bombers from Stukageschwader 77 and I./St.G3 on the Cherbourg peninsula were ready for battle. The low-flying cloud over their base had lifted and the ceiling was now clear and with this their spirits soared too. Thirty-minutes later this airborne armada raced across aerodromes, the Stukas' slipstream flattening

These invasion barges assembled for the proposed invasion of England were a priority target by day and night during the Battle of Britain. (*Royal Air Force Museum, London*)

the sheaves of grass. Nearby cut straw was tossed into the air by the backwash of propellers. Airborne they were hustled into place, protected by thirty-two Bf109Es of JG53 and seventy from JG27. Fifty-five Bf109Es from JG2 flew ahead of the force on a freelance sweep.

At Uxbridge, 11 Group Fighter Command's duty controller, Lord Willoughby de Broke, hardly knew where to turn. Squadron Leader H. W. Hickey DSO, commanding officer of RAF Coastal Command at 16 Group, heard his duty controller was at the end of his tether. It was like a gigantic game of chess and communication between both was almost at melt down. Lord Willoughby begged Fighter Command's filter room for information, wading through incoming details from the radar stations but by 13.00-13.30 no one could be certain as to how many enemy formations might be mustering just outside radar range. For the plotters in their confined space the boredom of the previous month suddenly gave way to bustling urgency, fifteen WAAF plotters hovering over the map table holding sticks to push the marker blocks into position. Instead of plotting one raid, they were now going to be following two or three raids at the same time.

In one of the smallest parishes of Hampshire named Poling a curious herd of heifers stood staring over the low flint wall watching as auxiliary territorial service member Joan Hearn-Avis made her way for duty with a fellow operator to Poling Radio Direction Finding (RDF) station. Upon entering through the door her sergeant told them there was no need to change over quickly. He wanted one of them to man the line from Truleigh Hill, an RDF station that did not have a direct link to Fighter Command's filter room at Uxbridge. Hearn-Avis volunteered, she relieved the single WAAF on duty and began working on the switchboard with two headsets, feeding the information through to the filter room. She was on her own, the officer and NCO on watch at the time were located in the receiver hut, a timber-framed shed in the same compound. Hearn-Avis knew from the plots she was hearing through her headphones and from the squared-off map in front of her that a raid was imminent.

Just before 14.00 hours Poling had picked up the first warnings. Now Hearn-Avis was reporting plots rapidly increasing in number and frequency. Initially reporting "eighty plus" travelling north, with the Bf109Es this estimate rose to 150 plus but the true figure was 264. At 14.15 hours the Stukas separated into four as they passed the Isle of Wight. Observers on the ground assumed that Tangmere was the target and red air raid warnings were being sounded when within Stukageschwader 77 and III Gruppen thirty-one dive-bombers peeled away from the main formation detailed to attack the Poling RDF site.

Slung underneath their fuselage was a single 500 kg bomb with four 50 kg bombs under the wings. Major Helmut Bode led the first attack of three Stukas coming in from a northeasterly direction unopposed. The whining shrill got deafening as the dive-bombers unleashed their ordinance at 1,500 feet. The foundations were literally shaking as the bombs detonated, its walls cracked making a mosaic as Hearn-Avis diligently stayed at her post, relaying information unaided. As more bombs exploded the building swayed like a pendulum threatening to collapse at any moment. But nothing distracted the WAAF corporal. On the wire down one set of headphones Truleigh Hill RDF station came through.

"Poling? That block's right on top of you!"

"I know, I can hear them, the bombs are nearly dropping on my head!" replied Hearn-Avis who noted "the noise of the explosions was terrific". The raid had lasted about twenty minutes, with eighty-seven bombs being dropped. One hit the telephone cables; her headphones immediately went dead. There was nothing else Hearn-Avis could do, so she extracted her four-feet ten-and-a-half-inch frame from the hut to seek shelter. It was a scene of devastation when she emerged:

"I don't think I thought about danger. I was defending my country. Junkers 87s dropped bombs around me and I went on transmitting information to the filter room. It was a long way from what I'd originally been doing sewing curtains and loose covers before joining the WAAF and having a purpose. I became one of only six women awarded the Military Medal in the war."

Stukageschwader 77 was visually first reported by the local Observer Corps near West Wittering who estimated "150 plus aircraft" at 14.23 hours. Less than one mile away across the peninsular on Thorney Island two airmen on an observation post situated on Hangar No 1 watched heavy black smoke billow into the blue skies inland some distance away using a naval telescope. Whilst airmen and women could scarcely bear to look in land gazing out to sea they were greeted by a vision described as "a swarm of bees" rapidly coming in for the sting.

When the air raid siren began its banshee wail in the surrounding parishes and on the aerodrome, competing with the telephone's strident jangle their order to scramble came. HQ 16 Group was on the line: "We think there may be some bandits bound for you". Flying Officer Peacock in L9446, Pilot Officer Wordsworth in N3533 and Flight Sergeant Nelson in N3540 raced across the bumpy grass at full throttle. Wheels up, he was airborne at 14.25. Peacock's headset crackled "Patrol base". Climb! Climb! They couldn't climb any faster. Then, *aircraft*! On a converging course which would take them directly into the enemy's path. Oh, God! Masses of them!

Boost was applied and Peacock glanced down to check his safety catch was off. L9446 flew straight for the leader of the I Gruppe pack who rolled away, followed by Peacock who closed within 200 yards, pressing his gun button in on the right hand side of the control column. 1,500 rounds were unleashed in seconds, flashes dancing around on the enemy aircraft's engine cowling. It burst into flames and dropped into the sea, a white smoke swirl marking the spot.

N3540 'Q-Queenie' downed a second Junkers into the sea (unconfirmed) and Wordsworth in N3533 'P-Pip' fired several well aimed bursts into a third Ju 87, but was hustled out of the way by the greater speed of Hawker Hurricanes of 43 Squadron who burst in forcing the Blenheim to break away, sharply buffeted by their turbulence, streaking low over the creeks. Below on a peninsular opposite Thorney Island a herd of heifers fled into the river in panic as the crescendo fell from the cobalt blue skies.

Three dive-bombers slipped through the fighter screen, pouring their lethal loads onto Hangar No 3 and surrounding buildings, being met by little resistance. The once tranquil coastal aerodrome

Hurricane Mark I, P2728, parked outside a hangar at Gosport, Hampshire, whilst on the station strength. This aircraft was a frequent visitor at Thorney Island and Detling before serving with 607 Squadron RAF. It was shot down over Kent by German fighters on September 9, 1940.

had taken on the appearance of a battlefield. Debris showered the area, corrugated metal sliced into the earth or buckled on the concert apron. The ground shook with a second explosion. The tremors reached a nearby shelter where personnel were covered in a shower of concrete dust. Twenty-year-old WAAF Elizabeth Rowdean remembered, "The noise was deafening, I gripped my tin helmet as if my life depended on it". Another report mentions, "A few of us stood and watched what was happening, bombs hit a hangar and as debris was flung up the massive hangar doors toppled onto one or two airmen who were running to a shelter as theirs was full! That was a great shock."

In the seemingly endless procession was Stuka pilot Hans Rudel. "As we came out of the dive I was at a great disadvantage, enemy fighters hemmed us in on all sides. Bombs jettisoned and combats took place while my gunner Hans was firing continuously." Two of the Stuka dive-bombers were still maintaining their trajectory as they pulled out. With his eyes glued to them Wordsworth latched onto a Junkers 87. The enemy aircraft filled the fixed ring sight and rounds hit the gull-winged dive-bomber in a running fight, shooting him down into the sea. He turned slowly to the left while on the R/T a high pitched voice said: "We've been hit Red Section, but we're all right – I think?" Wordsworth looked over. Thorney Island aerodrome was hidden beneath a huge, spreading black pall of smoke and dust. "They'd bombed us! The buggers had bombed our airfield!" It never occurred to Wordsworth that they might not be able to land on it.

Then, to his surprise, directly near them Wordsworth sighted a pair of German airmen in the water swimming about off the south coast. Both men had ripped off the yellow scarves that Luftwaffe aircrew wore for recognition purposes and were waving them wildly. In a chivalrous gesture Wordsworth ordered Sergeant Maconochie to jettison N3533's dinghy. "Just for luck," he said, "Wouldn't want them to drown!"

Meanwhile further dogfights took place over the wide area. Nelson was making an acquaintance with a Junkers 87, unleashing all 2,000 rounds but later lamenting "I failed to bring him down". He then turned the gun button to 'safe'. Over Thorney Island 43 and 601 Squadrons in five minutes accounted for ten Stukas destroyed with half as many damaged. In the aerial battle the Junkers 87 of StabI/StG77's Gruppenkommandeur Hptm Herbert Meisel and his air gunner Obergef Jakob was shot down. Others were caught fleeing south. At 14.45 152 Squadron found the Germans at fifty feet near Ventnor. Also joining the battle was Exeter-based 213 Squadron which pursued the retreating Bf109Es across the Channel, low on fuel. Magically the 'pancake' instructions came. Back in the circuit, the jubilant trios returned at 14.40 hours, much of the smoke and dust having disappeared. Odd holes were dotted around, which looked as if a mole had burrowed to the surface on the grass. There had been other damage too.

Hangar 3 was wrecked and the station photographic building damaged, with the photographic equipment burnt out and beyond use. Many window panes were broken. 59 Squadron C Flight's armoury was rendered unserviceable, as the building was in a precarious state. One of the 59 Squadron's flight dispersal huts had taken a beating; next to it was an upturned lorry, its four tyres pointing skywards. It reminded personnel of a dead hippopotamus! Two Blenheims had been destroyed; T1815 (Thorney Island) and R3835 (Manston) of 59 Squadron along with their communication hack a Miles Magister. The interception of the superior force by Hurricanes was crucial to saving the Coastal Command aerodrome. Ably assisted by the station's 'local fighting patrol' flown by Peacock, Wordsworth and Nelson it meant that Thorney Island had sustained relatively little damage, unlike T1805 flown by Wordsworth which was beyond repair and struck off charge. Peacock recalled in the squadron periodical: "After we returned from this operation, the intelligence officer wanted all the details. We were not all that bothered or interested, it was over. Finished. But Spy needed the information. I believe I'd shot down the Stuka leader because of the markings, [not confirmed] but the local fighter boys made a claim. It was a hard day for B Flight."

Flying Officer Reginald Peacock's claim stood, the Junkers 87 Stuka was his fifth victory, which made him in the annuals of Royal Air Force Coastal Command the first and only pilot to ever achieve 'ace' status in a Bristol Blenheim Mark IV Fighter. The squadron's efforts did not go unnoticed, the next day RAF Bircham Newton's station commander Group Captain William Primrose DFC received No 1035 – Order Of The Day, a dispatch from the Rt Hon Sir Archibald Sinclair, Secretary of State for Air: "Congratulations to your Blenheims on their exploit yesterday". This recognition gave everyone associated with the unit great pleasure. It was noted:

"Group Captain William Primrose DFC also extended his congratulations – '235 under Squadron Leader Neville Clarke has developed into a real fighting unit. Although officially named Fighter Blenheims', the opportunity to fight comes infrequently, and the utmost vigilance is required so that every opportunity should be seized. Recent air combats show that our pilots are not slow to get right down to it when the fleeting chance arrives."

StG77's Kommandeur, von Richthofen, confided in his diary "the Stuka Gruppe has had its feathers well and truly plucked". I Gruppe that had attacked Thorney Island, had seen ten of its machines shot down, and one damaged beyond repair. Of the fifty-six pilots and navigators, seventeen had been killed or seriously wounded with five others taken prisoner.

As battles raged in the skies over England, north of Hadrian's Wall 248 Squadron in Scotland were on protracted duties. For weeks and months their sole link with the war was the never-ending shepherding of convoys or naval craft along the Scottish coast, or reconnaissance flights to Norway that became irksome. According to Flying Officer Sam McHardy they were "a complete waste of time. We had been hearing that 235 Squadron had had quite a number of casualties and 248 were all eager to go south and take their place – back into the fight. But, our future operations would still be off the Norwegian coast. Oh, those lucky bastards."

Soon after breakfast on August 19, Squadron Leader Victor Streatfield, the commanding officer warned his 'young brood' that intensive reconnaissance and shipping strikes would commence, but first intelligence had to be gathered. The crew chosen to be first off was Warwickshire-born Sergeant

James Round, together with his crew Sergeants William Want and Maxwell Digby-Worsley. Shortly before midday, Want stowed a flask of hot tea within L9457 then Round and Digby-Worsley clambered aboard. After last-minute checks two Mercury XV engines coughed in the chilled air; adjusting the throttles the engine's pitch changed and with that Round waved to the ground crew. Two ran in from behind and pulled the chocks away. As they exited Digby-Worsley waved from his position in the turret. L9457 taxied out and with the throttles wide open they disappeared over the hills then did a wide circuit, gaining height. Norway beckoned. Below them was charcoal grey sea, with occasional white ripples and the odd sighting of puffins and gannets. The crossing of two hundred and thirty-five miles was uneventful yet scenic. Round guided his machine down the southern Norwegian coastline checking the leads. As he passed over Flekkefjord anti-aircraft fire streamed up from Kvinesdal. At the same moment four Bf109Es of 4./JG77 scrambled on a 'Flyalarm'. With no adequate cloud cover the Blenheim was intercepted by 4./JG77. As the contact began Round went down to the sea's surface and steered west. In a one-sided aerial duel Oblt Wilhelm Moritz dispatched the three RAF sergeants into a watery grave for his second victory at 14.47 hours having made consecutive beam attacks. Despite Digby-Worsley's brave effort to stem the enemy's fire he was unable to save those aboard L9457. "Jamie never turned up": no longer would Sergeant James Round's beaming smile grace the wooden shack that served as a bar at Sumburgh. "Good men the three of them; we would miss them greatly."

The crew of L9396 flew back over Hampshire totally spent. Since 05.40 hours they'd been in the air more than four times. There was talk of invasion, which was shrugged off. Crews were sent off in a hurry as fighter escort to seven Fairey Battles of 12 and 142 Squadrons to bomb Boulogne harbour. A reconnaissance photograph indicated that more barges had been drawn from the canals of Holland and Belgium and these craft were being modified to enable easy shipment of Panzer and other armoured units. Haze and glare from the searchlight batteries rebounded off the Perspex, temporarily blinding four pilots and rendering them unable to locate the targets. One returned with engine trouble and another because of a bomb-release/bomb-rack malfunction. "We saw the searchlights a long way off, crossing like a seamstress's scissor blades. Then flashes of tracer, going out." One Fairey Battle from 12 Squadron failed to return, its crew becoming prisoners of war.

On the following day the rains came. Jackson-Smith did not fly at all during the day, but did a spell in the ops office where he had a long and meaningful conversation with a pleasant WAAF on the other end of the line at group headquarters. There were no major raids but Britain was still subjected to air raid warnings and attacks to a minor degree although this day, Monday August 19, was to become memorable as Sir Winston Churchill delivered his speech praising the airmen fighting the battle in words that would echo through the decades:

"The gratitude of every home in our island, in our empire and indeed throughout the world, except in the abodes of the guilty, goes out to the British airmen who, undaunted by odds, unwearied in their constant challenge and mortal danger, are turning the tide of the world by their prowess and their devotion. Never in the field of human conflict was so much owed by so many to so few. All hearts go out to the fighter pilots, whose brilliant actions we see with our own eyes day after day."

As the echoes of Churchill's speech were resounding the fate of two Coastal Command aerodromes, Bircham Newton and St Eval, unravelled. The weather was much the same the following day and scattered raids started. 235 rotated B Flight back to Bircham Newton, whilst Queenslander, Flight Lieutenant Frederick Flood led A Flight to Thorney Island. The ground was boggy as they hauled their steel monsters into the air; Z5725, L9450, T2035, T1804, Z5730 and L9396 at 0600 hours. The squall continued with no sign of letting up. In low cloud twenty-four men headed south wending their way slowly through the shires in the direction of the aerodrome. They were all in good spirits, Jackson-Smith:

"My crew usually consisted of Pilot Officer Raymond Kent as air gunner and Pilot Officer Donald Howe as observer, today I had Sergeant Leo Ricks in the turret for the one-hour fifteen-minute trip to Thorney Island, with just our wash bags and a single pork pie for nourishment as company."

826 Naval Air Squadron Fleet Air Arm received their first Albacore aircraft in March 1940; these first examples were shore-based, and were used to patrol and attack German shipping in the English Channel during the Battle of Britain. The Albacore offered the crew an enclosed and heated cockpit, but remained less popular than the Swordfish, however, as it was less agile, with the controls being too heavy for a pilot to take effective evasive action. (*Royal Air Force Museum, London*)

Elsewhere small groups of raiders pressed inland.

Little notice was taken that grey morning of a twin-engine discordant droning as a Junkers 88A-4 of Kampfgeschwader 4 slipped across the Norfolk coastline unseen and was skillfully hedge-hopping its way at 100 feet across the countryside towards its target, Bircham Newton. Nipping in over the boundary hedge, at 08.55 it unleashed four bombs, two demolishing one of the married quarter's buildings, with windows blown in from the blast. There was extensive damage to rooves from the flying masonry. One exploded into the rain-sodden earth amongst 826 Fleet Air Arm Squadron's dispersed Albacores damaging seven and also two Whitleys from Bomber Command's 5 Group. The enemy bomber merged into the moving clouds as quickly as it had come. Casualties on the ground numbered twenty-two, with one very seriously injured, and arrangements were made to move them to King's Lynn Hospital. The RAF Wireless Intelligence Service picked up a large amount of enemy radio traffic from the group carrying out these offensive operations in East Anglia; "A message from one aircraft stated that Bircham had successfully been attacked with buildings burning".

Lord Haw-Haw, the treacherous broadcaster, gloated over St Eval's impending doom. In the far west of England at 13.50 the air raid warning red sounded. Then two minutes later [13.52] three

236 Squadron's hangar after a low-level attack by 2 Ju 88s, St Eval, August/September 1940. (*Gerry Holder*)

Junkers 88 struck the Cornish aerodrome dropping ten high explosive and incendiary bombs on the airfield. Their gunners randomly machine-gunned the vulnerable hangars, stores, administration and domestic blocks, motor transport, offices and supplies. One bomb destroyed hangar No 4 where six of 236 Squadron's Blenheim fighters were damaged with R2776 and T1944 being written off. Suddenly from above two of 236's Blenheim fighters was involved in a skirmish over the airfield; "Looking up from the ground it was an exquisite piece of shooting on the pilot's part". While forming up on their leader Russell before proceeding to Calshot to escort a Short Sunderland, shouts of "Bandit" resounded over the R/T. Searching the skies, a pair saw an enemy aircraft, possibly a Junkers 88, diving over the hangars. "Innis and Nunn pulled out the throttles and attacked from 400 yards astern climbing to 2,000-3,000 feet before the Junkers disappeared, out pacing him into cloud over Land's End." Nunn reported: "I got one burst of ten seconds duration into the enemy aircraft's fuselage." As the escort left for Calshot, smoke billowed into the sky, and their thoughts wandered to those poor souls below.

Some airmen, helped by Mr Edwards, an old country gardener who cared for the station garden and vegetable plot, were already digging fiercely to reach those entombed in a shelter. Aircrew leaped in to help too. Ambulances and stretcher parties were standing by. Everyone braced themselves for the horror within as the all clear sounded and one-by-one the bodies were brought out. Some were hardly recognizable through the dirt, blood and twisted limbs. In the evening the WAAF cooks magically produced a delicious meal of sausages and mash with redcurrant sauce for a cheerful queue of men and women of all ranks. Later on the radiogram they heard how Lord Haw-Haw was delighted that the Luftwaffe had destroyed one of its hangars and killed twenty-one personnel in a shelter. They shouted back in fury.

As these nuisance raids continued, Flight Lieutenant Frederick Flood was instructed to lead three machines herding a single 59 Squadron Blenheim. In the layers of cloud over the English Channel all became separated, but the fighters persevered on to Le Havre. Just off the harbour, Flood found a Henschel 126 skimming a few hundred feet above the wave tops. Attacking, his fire entered the fuselage and after breaking away the Henschel dived into the seawater. No survivors were seen.

There came a brief lull in the fighting for A Flight, with no operational flying, which gave them some small respite from the undoubted strain of all the air raid warnings. The squadron diarist noted: "Local fighter patrols over Thorney – 'Red' warnings come more and more frequently".

Over the coast of Kent dogfights took place with 11 Group fighters attempting to discourage Bf109Es on freelance sorties. The Spitfires did well, as the light faded Coastal Command officers lounged in the anteroom settling down further into their chairs and listening to the BBC broadcast *Air Log* on the wireless. One of their own colleagues Flying Officer Reginald Peacock was interviewed:

"I pressed the gun button, first one short burst of less than one second's duration, then another and then another, and very finally a fifth short burst. All were aimed very deliberately. Suddenly the Junkers' port wing dropped downwards. The starboard wing went up and then in a flash his nose dipped and he was gone. He simply vanished."

Pilot Officer Norman Jackson-Smith explained: "It was a Coastal Command Special *Air Log*, the programme usually being on the Hudsons and Sunderlands. Everyone seemed to forget that Coastal had Blenheim fighters." The excitement was over for the moment.

Between the bright intervals on August 23, fighting flared up. Three crews were put at fifteen minutes readiness, and were prepared for a busy afternoon. Once they had donned their Mae Wests there was nothing else to do but wait. "It was wretched waiting for the telephone to ring", recalled Jackson-Smith. After six hours forty-five minutes air raid sirens sounded and the surrounding area went into a red air raid warning. "I heard the telephone ring and instinctively knew that the word to be uttered was 'scramble' and so without waiting, nine of us sprinted in shirtsleeves to our Blenheims. I clambered up onto the wing then hoisted myself into the cockpit and dropped onto my seat. We were off."

Jackson-Smith led them out. All three formed up on the ground as they prepared for take-off. The Mercury's engines roared as all three accelerated over the grass, wisps blowing up into the air, showering onlookers. Once airborne the creeks and Bracklesham Bay unfolded below. An RAF fighter controller interjected "Local Patrol, Bandit to southeast". Jackson-Smith increased his speed as they tried to sight the enemy. The brief combat report reads: "About 19.07 hours sighted a He 111 approaching, three attacked and enemy aircraft turned away and in so doing opened bomb doors and dropped two bombs into the sea half way between Selsey Bill and East Wittering. Streaking off in pursuit, two of them used up all their ammunition. Enemy banked into cloud after firing bursts from rear gun." The rear gunner ceased firing and rounds also entered the starboard engine as Jackson-Smith flying L9450 finished his ammunition using 2,000 rounds from the front belly pack and 200 from rear in this one-sided duel. After the trio landed, they were congratulated and a celebratory drink beckoned. With the pressure off, 'Skipper' Naish, Dave Woodger, Jackson-Smith, Daniel Wright, Raymond Kent and Donald Howe pooled their earnings together to order hackney carriages for a night in Southsea. Stopping off at The Cut Loaf Night Club (a café that turned into a night club in the evening) "you presented a card and one of the waiters went to the bar and got what you ordered". They had a pleasant evening even though the place was thronging with men and women in uniform 'living for the moment' with heavy clouds of pipe tobacco and cigarette smoke moving across the room every time someone swung open the door. For the six young enthusiastic college drinkers and hard players it was a good evening, "no one spilt beer down their uniforms". At closing time there was only Naish, Woodger, Jackson-Smith and Wright remaining, as the doorman stepped out and flagged a hackney carriage down. Jackson-Smith described the return journey:

"We left the nightclub and were on the way back to Thorney. I was sat next to Dave Woodger, who began to say he'd had a premonition that on his next operational flight he'd get the chop. Skipper Naish said don't be wet. It was totally out of character, I had known Dave Woodger since his arrival on the squadron in '39. We'd been through some scrapes, but he broke down, and sobbed in the back, asking for forgiveness. He was just flagging, a young man who had reached the limits of his courage. On our arrival at the station, Skipper and Wright walked Dave to his accommodation. I went to our dispersal hut. Dave's name was on the flying roster for the next day. Rubbing his name off the blackboard, I then spoke to the duty officer pointing out that Flying Officer David Woodger should be rested from operations and the impending problem. Unfortunately we arrived at our dispersal early in the morning just after five o'clock to find Dave's name had been chalked up on the available list."

A conversation with the adjutant Charles Pinnock got no further. Naish tried but he drew a blank too. Pilot Officer David Woodger had a beaming smile on his face, confident that his determination to fulfill his part of being one of Churchill's 'few' would see him and his crew through. As the sun began to rise, things were fairly quiet on the aerodrome. Flight Lieutenant Frederick Flood briefed his crews on the ever-changing situation remarking, "I'm sure they'll give us plenty of notice so you can get aloft in good time". Minutes faded into hours. Despite the chaotic conditions and increasing threat outside ground crew filled sandbags and played an impromptu game of cricket using the spade as a bat as someone tossed a cricket ball. Elsewhere on the station new panes of glass were being fitted. The smell of cut grass mingled with the stench of 100 percent high-octane fuel and oil, interspersed with the salty sea breeze.

Out to sea the first specks were picked up and their numbers multiplied. At 15.40 hours 10 Group in the southwest received reports into Rudloe Manor from Ventnor RDF of a large enemy formation approaching the Isle of Wight. Upon being notified RAF controllers at 11 Group ordered Squadron Leader Ernest McNab to scramble his fledgling Canadians of 1 (RCAF) Squadron, some of whom had less than twenty hours flying experience and only a limited number of hours on aircraft recognition. Their orders were to intercept the German formation over Selsey Bill, at the southernmost point of the West Sussex coastline. Twelve headed west, racing towards Chichester harbour.

The enemy force consisted of fifty Junkers 88s of Lehrgeschwader 1, escorted by Bf110s of a similar number and they appeared earlier than the RDF and the RAF controller's calculations. An anti-aircraft barrage was put up over Rye, Isle of Wight. 609 Squadron was the single squadron patrolling at 5,000 feet and was caught in the middle of this barrage and directly below the enemy fighter escort. Undeterred Lehrgeschwader 1 continued on track for Portsmouth.

Nine miles northwest was Coastal Command's RAF Thorney Island. Amid the piled up debris from the devastating raid seven days previously rays of sunlight lessened on the horizon. The silence was broken by the noise of the phone. Clarke, the telephone orderly took the call, a muffled voice could be heard at the other end. "Ops confirm 'air raid warning red' – Scramble . . . Air raid imminent!"

Lloyd Loom chairs and an assortment of others were pushed back as they leapt out, making for the door. Running for their machines the adrenaline took over. Six young airmen sprinted as a slight wind began sweeping in from Longmere Point. Their fighters awaited them. Riggers, fitters and armourers had worked continuously with only a few hours sleep between shifts to make T1804, Z5730 and N3531 serviceable. Discoloured water trickled past Z5730 whilst two individuals hoisted themselves rapidly up mechanically placing their footing into the footholds on the left side of the fuselage. One entered through the inward hatch on the roof slightly behind the gun turret, whilst the other continued forward and climbed onto the fuselage just behind his cockpit and lowered himself through the sliding hood over the pilot's seat. Fortunately the Irvin or parachute didn't snag and once he was sitting in the bucket seat he reached up and used both hands to pull the hood shut, clicking the catch lever into place, rechecking making doubly sure it was secure. Instinctively he began strapping in, switching on petrol, starting the engines, checking oxygen, instruments and engine revs. The routine was automatically repeated onboard T1804 and N3531. Rolling forward their speed increased and all lifted off and climbed away. Three minutes had lapsed since the alarm. Controllers had spotted the enemy's intentions; a massive raid on Portsmouth. The pilots Flight Lieutenant Frederick Flood, Pilot Officer David Woodger and Sergeant Kenneth 'Skipper' Naish were ordered to intercept the German bomber stream.

With a sense of urgency the defenders levelled off at 6,000 feet in line astern, their machines silhouetted against the sun, whilst ahead ack-ack blossomed in the sky. Below there was a little haze giving a copper colour to the sea. T1804 was arse-end Charlie. Onboard Sergeant Daniel Wright gave the magazine on the single Vickers K gun a reassuring slap to make sure it had been properly fitted, glanced at his wristwatch and moved into a more alert attitude, scanning the sky and occasionally rotating the turret. Their machines continued to head for Portsmouth to help the beleaguered city and port.

At 16.39 hours black puffs hung stationary in the sky to the west then dispersed watched by Squadron Leader Ernest 'Ernie' McNab. With the altimeter reading 10,000 feet the Canadians swung towards Portsmouth. Instantly fear grabbed hold. "My mouth dried up like cotton wool", McNab recalled. Since the scramble Flying Officer Blair 'Dal' Russel of Montreal had rhythmically chewed gum, but the taste of mint had disappeared altogether. Then McNab's fear rescinded, ahead of him at 6,000 feet three miles northeast of Thorney Island were three aeroplanes flying in line astern. He saw them as Junkers 88s through the shifting sunlight and smoke. Flight Lieutenant Gordon 'Gordie' McGregor saw the black shapes too. At 16.40 McNab leading his vic called, "Echelon, starboard – go, go!" and for every pilot the horizon tilted sharply as they put their Hurricane's nose down and their right thumbs took the first light pressure on the push-button on their control column spade grips. Diving at 300 miles an hour, specks appeared in their reflector sight.

Suddenly, Wright caught sight of single-engine machines diving at extreme speed towards them, cocking his Vickers and talking calmly into the intercom as their range dramatically decreased second by second. Their shape looked familiar, they were Hawker Hurricanes! Three thousand feet above

Squadron Leader McNab led the ill-fated Canadian Squadron into combat on August 24, 1940. Unfortunately his warnings went unheard. Here he is photographed at Northolt, September 1940. (*The Department of National Defense, Ottawa, Ontario, Canada*)

in the silhouetted monoplanes, Ernie McNab and Pilot Officer Paul Pitcher identified gun turrets, which Junkers 88s lacked and the broad white flash on the aeroplane's fins, marking them as RAF. On impulse McNab flicked the R/T microphone switch on his face mask and with an electrifying scream shouted twice, "Break, break, break! Don't attack!" Unfortunately with the Hawker Hurricanes flying at over 300 mph not all his pilots heard their leader's call, their concentration focused on the 'Junkers' and the excitement of the chase. McNab's section broke violently to port away from the field of battle and didn't attack. He cursed repeatedly at what was about to unfold, yelling a third time "Break, break, break!" But his attempts were futile and he couldn't save his men from the impending situation. "Why didn't the sector station at Tangmere or whoever say there were other RAF machines in the area?" he later asked.

As the Canadians streaked in, it became a chase. These aircraft were not turning to fight they were simply continuing on their course. Inside the lead Blenheim Z5730 Sergeant Henry Owen above the deafening roar of the radial engines shouted a warning to Skipper Naish. His voice was heard through the headphones shouting "Hurricanes, Hurricanes!" This experienced pilot clicked the Bakelite R/T switch on his mask, "All aircraft fire recognition signals". The Blenheim's gunners began frantically firing off colours of the day: yellow and red flares, which were the recognition signal for Saturday August 24. They cascaded out with a crescendo of colour and blossomed in the fading light.

From within their cockpits the Canadian pilots didn't realize that recognition signals were being fired but rather saw "long yellow and red spears" of tracer arcing towards them. They applied full pressure on their gun buttons and within seconds rounds sped away. High velocity 0.303 rounds ripped through the thin metal skin of the RAF fighters, shredding all that lay in their path like hailstones on a tin roof. N3531's starboard radial engine took rounds which tore through panels inches away from its fuel pipes, puncturing its vital organs and causing thick oil blotches to appear on the Perspex windscreen.

All three reacted to the threat by breaking, splitting to starboard and port while Flood dived steeply away for the deck. Two of their pursuers, Flight Lieutenant McGregor and Flying Officer Jean-Paul Desloges curved slightly in. McGregor concentrated and fired while Desloges tightened his arc and fired towards Pilot Officer Woodger in Blenheim T1804. Incoming rounds punctured the hydraulic system in the starboard wing and the rear power-operated gun turret instantly became useless. Inside the turret's confined space eighteen-year-old Sergeant Daniel Wright, a proud former miner's son, sat motionless, speechless and praying that these air force pilots would realize their error. Within a breath his young life was snuffed out. The rear fuselage was in bad shape, bullets had shredded the control wires, the dinghy and first aid box and smoke emanated from the tail plane. The starboard Mercury radial engine was ablaze, glowing from the intense heat. Desloges shouted over the R/T "My God he's on fire".

Suddenly T1804 rolled to the right. Inside the cockpit Woodger was struggling with the unresponsive controls or trying to escape, when another two-second burst of 0.303 rounds scythed into the cockpit as the coup-de-grace; Pilot Officer David Woodger died instantly. His machine continued in an uncontrollable spiral heading towards the water east of Thorney Island, over Bracklesham Bay. The fighter Blenheim was enveloped in flames, disintegrating as it tumbled. All was consumed by seawater in the bay, leaving only a wisp of smoke.

The jubilant Canadians, McGregor and Desloges rolled away claiming their first kill, losing sight of their victim after watching it briefly burn. Their fellow combatants Flying Officers Arthur Yuile and William Sprenger followed their section leader Arthur Nesbit into an attack at 16.41, firing at point-blank range. Z5730's air gunner fired a second set of cartridges as bullets rained in from Hurricanes, hitting the hydraulic system, tyre, undercarriage and starboard engine cowling. His attackers pulled away convinced the 'enemy raider' would not be returning to France. Once out of harm's way Skipper Naish guided his battered and scarred fighter Blenheim back, crashing unhurt in a wheels-up landing. Training took over recalled Naish: "I throttled down the good engine to

Canadian pilots of the 1 RCAF Hurricane Squadron. Their operational record book would be wiped clean of the friendly fire incident on August 24. A full account of this would not reach the Canadian defense department until 1947/1948. (*The Department of National Defense, Ottawa, Ontario, Canada*)

almost the minimum required for a Mark IV Blenheim to nurse it and avoid the radial overheating". Flood was lucky too. With his starboard engine holed, his Perspex thick with opaque blotches of oil making it extremely difficult to see forward, he crash landed at Thorney Island having glided in at less than 80 mph.

As the Hurricanes wheeled away with their fuel gauges reading almost empty, McNab and his entourage got clearance from the watch office at Tangmere to land and refuel. McNab drew a careful bead across his young flock as the tentacles from the petrol bowser refuelled their aircraft. Within half an hour they were flying into the Northolt circuit over the hawthorn hedges before landing. At dispersal the Canadian Air Force officers got down from their fighters as fitters and riggers swarmed in pleased that "some had got a Hun". McGregor and Desloges together claimed a Junkers destroyed and Nesbitt, Yuile and Springer claimed hits on another Junkers 88. The Canadian press was quick to latch onto this success story; Harold Fair wrote the copy in 4B pencil: "Roaring into action together as a unit for the first time the first Royal Canadian Air Force fighter squadron to reach England proved itself on Saturday by downing two German bombers." This was wired to Canada and run under the heading 'Group of Canadians Goes Into Action First Time as Unit'. As the journalist's departed in Humbers bound for London, away from watchful eyes First World War veteran and station commander Group Captain Stanley Vincent took Squadron Leader McNab aside, breaking the news to him as gently as possible. McNab, a former prize-fighter buried his head in his hands appalled and cried out, "My God, what have we done? What can I do?" Vincent was compassionate, "My dear boy, there's nothing that you can do, these things happen in war, but the one thing I recommend you must do is to fly down and see them and explain". In the evening a solitary Hawker Hurricane arrived in the local circuit. Upon landing a short man with a thin moustache got down and walked over to the watch office in flying kit. He was greeted by Flight Lieutenants Flood and Naish. Once in the dispersal hut the Canadian apologized to the assembled Blenheim fighter crews and ground crews. If David Woodger had such a premonition, it was fulfilled! Later in the small hours the adjutant wrote up the unofficial diary:

"David Woodger was one of the few surviving original pilots and much liked by all of us. He was a steady quiet type and his loss is a personal one to those of us who knew him well. Daniel Wright was the gunner in Woodger's machine and an extremely keen lad whose loss under such circumstances is greatly deplored. An enquiry is being held about this torrid affair."

The station subsequently received a telephone call from a war reserve constable saying a man had been recovered. In the late afternoon the body of an airman had been found by a boat, and put in a lane-side shed to await collection with a police constable present. The adjacent farmer's cows had to pass the shed on the way to be milked and there was immediate consternation. They could obviously smell death.

A detail arrived in an RAF ambulance to recover the body. The adjutant identified the body as one Sergeant Daniel Wright. He wrote: "The gunner's body was recovered riddled with bullets". The limp body was wrapped in blankets and placed on a stretcher. The medical orderlies bowed their heads as the adjutant Flying Officer Charles Pinnock said:

"I can't give you a hand;
you're for the Promised Land,
my comrade good and true."

In the cool and peace of the evening, men and women in air force blue walked to church, a few flowers nodded in the breeze as if bowing their heads for the departed and the smell of salt drifted inland from the creeks that meandered into Chichester and Bosham. The solitude inside Thorney Island church had a calming effect, albeit temporarily.

The fighter patrols began in earnest on Sunday, August 25, patrolling four or six times daily. At the Air Ministry in London an account of the previous day's engagement was typed up:

"Blenheim aircraft F, A1 and E of 235 Squadron circled Thorney Island aerodrome for fighter protection from 16.15 hours at 8,000 feet during an air raid. At 16.40 hours E of 235 was approached by a Hurricane. All Blenheims fired recognition cartridges. Hurricanes attacked and shot aircraft E down in flames. E went down southwards and fell in the sea off Wittering. One body picked up by boat, the other occupant may have bailed out. Six Hurricanes attacked A1 of 235 Squadron at 16.40 hours. First attack hit wings, fuselage, starboard engine and holed Perspex. Avoiding action taken and another cartridge fired. Second attack made without result. Crash landing on aerodrome, wheels and flaps out of action. Pilot and gunner unhurt except for scratches and bruises."

On the same day at Northolt these unpalatable facts were overlooked, the writer of the Canadian Operational Record Book (ORB) erasing this clash against the Coastal Command Blenheim fighters. The rooms of Pilot Officer Woodger and Sergeant Wright were cleaned, polished and nothing left to chance as Squadron Leader Clarke brought in reinforcements on August 27. He then promptly led, in his usual charismatic way, Pilot Officers John Coggins and Norman Jackson-Smith on a sortie, followed by another at 15.55 hours with Flight Lieutenant Flood, Pilot Officers Wickings-Smith, Coggins, Jackson-Smith and Sergeant Hall. They took off against the red air raid warning sirens as the Luftwaffe sent Heinkel 111s of KG55 against Portsmouth. It was one of those afternoons which seemed drab and charcoal grey on the base but from above the observers looked upon the beauty and tranquillity of the countryside and the raised finger of the Chichester spire.

Meanwhile their sister squadron, 248, found one of its aircraft was missing, having taken off at 10.50 from Sumburgh. Pilot Officer Charles Arthur and his crew put up a spirited fight just west of Egersund, Norway in L9449 but fell to Ltn Heinrich Setz of 6./JG77 at 13.40 hours. Thorney Island aerodrome protection patrols continued until the end of the month which closed on a sour note at Bircham Newton when L9262 crashed in a flying accident involving Pilot Officer John Priestley and Sergeant Edward Graves. Blenheim L9262 was carrying out dogfighting practice when the machine went into a spin from which the pilot failed to recover fully. At 11.15 hours they crashed at high speed at Barwick Farm, Bagthorpe, instantly killing both. The investigating officer stated on the accident card that Priestley "had not pushed the control column forward enough to ensure full recovery". It was Priestley's first and sadly his last sustained spin on this type of RAF aircraft. The squadron diarist noted: "Pilot Officer John Priestley was a New Zealander from Wellington recently posted with twenty hours on the Blenheim and looked a promising type. Sergeant Edward Graves was also a recent posting, hailing from Eastbourne, Sussex as an air gunner with real aptitude."

On the same day Daniel Wright's body was repatriated to Staffordshire's Hammerwich railway station with the help of an escorting RAF officer. On arrival the coffin was placed on a large LMS barrow and transported out of view by a porter. The RAF officer packed his pipe with Barney's tobacco, while a junior employee cycled off to notify the sergeant's parents in Burntwood. Unfortunately William and Mary Wright were unable to pay for its release and Wright's coffin was placed in 'lost luggage' until money was found to repatriate him with his family. Daniel Wright's funeral took place in August at St. Anne's Church in the Wrights' home parish just a short distance from his home. Wreaths from his brother sergeants and the officers' mess were laid by a representative of 235 Squadron.

B Flight went off to escort a convoy but returned after forty-five minutes. As their wheels locked into place and they came in over fields to land sheep scattered and took shelter under an oak tree. Flood and Naish had recovered from their earlier ordeal and flew again. They had been lucky, very lucky. Debate about tactics grew at Northwood, Uxbridge and Whitehall as did the need for replacements as Blenheims continued with their daily tasks. There were always more jobs to be done. It was now September 1940.

In Loving Memory of

Sergt. Daniel Leslie Wright, R.A.F.

The beloved Son of Mr. & Mrs. W. Wright,

Who was killed in action 24th August, 1940.   Aged 18 Years

Interred at St. Anne's Church, Chasetown, August 29th.

———

Peace perfect peace ! in this dark world of sin,
The blood of Jesus whispers peace within,
It is enough ; earth's struggle now has ceased,
Jesus has called him to heaven's perfect peace.

15 Bank Crescent,
Chasetown,
Walsall, Staffs.

The Death Card of air gunner Daniel Wright who died in the friendly-fire incident. (*The Wright family*)

Pilot Officer David Woodger was born in Old Coulsdon, Surrey. He joined the RAF on a short service commission in July 1939. After training on De Havilland Tiger Moths and Miles Magisters, he found himself posted to 235 Squadron. Christened 'Dave' by his fellow pilots, he was a well-respected member of the squadron and of A Flight. He piloted Blenheim T1804, which was shot down by Hurricanes of 1 RCAF Squadron on August 24, 1940. The aircraft fell in Bracklesham Bay. The twenty-year-old was reported missing presumed dead. (*Andrew Bird via Pat Woodger*)

CHAPTER EIGHT

Household Music

For the third consecutive day RAF Detling was in the Luftwaffe bombers' sights. In some places the hill resembled the Somme, as "an estimated fifty enemy aircraft were reported to be heading towards their objective. Probably Detling!" A communiqué from September 1 reads: "Attack 15.32 – 17.00 hours". During these hours it was attacked twice. Nevertheless, Coastal Command Blenheim bombers' raids on the ports that evening went ahead at 20.00 hours. On September 2 the first Fighter Command Hawker Hurricanes making 'pit-stops' came down at 11.00 hours. As they took on fuel recently filled in bomb craters were clearly visible on the aerodrome, with patches of light earth and fresh green shoots pushing through. In the dispersal areas sat an eclectic mix of machines. Pilots sat in monoplane cockpits or cleaned their windscreens. Raids were becoming an everyday occurrence. Not wanting to get caught on the ground, 249 Squadron Hurricanes took off northwards for North Weald after waiting an hour to be refuelled.

Skirting West Thorney village, fighter Blenheims arrived back from their fifth alarm that day. "It soon became obvious that 11 Group had sent us off as an insurance measure." The sky was clear, whilst the pungent smell of seaweed drifted in from the shore. In the dwindling light figures worked methodically. "We learnt that one of B Flight 59 Squadron's kites had run into heavy ack-ack, which had poor 'Shorty' crashing off the runway." The machine had been severely damaged by accurate defensive fire over Lorient, where there had been a long struggle above the empty expanse of water. Hewitt had lay on the floor using his hands to help Shorty move the rudder pedals, while the pointer of the altimeter slid back and T1880 slowly lost height. Arriving over the aerodrome 'P-Pip' crashed on the southeast runway, careering off the edge with a jolt near Stanbury Point and heading into a creek. Three dazed crew escaped. Station padre Squadron Leader Albert Hollings reported: "Short, Hewitt and Burney suffering from severe shock, aid being administered".

Another twenty-four hours passed. Two months of hard fighting had taken an appalling toll and placed an intolerable strain upon the experienced men on whom the nation depended. Sergeant Walter Garfield watched locals enjoying the sea breeze at Banff. Herring boats crowded in the sheltered harbour bow to stern and rose and fell in the tidal water. Walter wanted to shake them from their complacency as L9451 flew over them and back to Sumburgh from Lossiemouth on the bully beef run. They presented such a contrast to the life and death struggle over the European skies, Norwegian fjords and English Channel. He motored on. Sumburgh aerodrome appeared ahead and to port, Garfield curved towards it then went around the hill. All clear.

He flicked the flaps down, L9451 slowed, wallowing in protest to this sudden incursion, and then steadied. Moving the air screws to fine pitch, both Mercury engines raised their noise level to soprano as Garfield cruised in over Virkie. The bay was cordite blue, then there was a green blur underneath

RAF Coastal Command station Detling was used as a 'pit stop' by many RAF squadrons throughout the Battle of Britain. One being recorded by twenty-year-old Pilot Officer Tom Neil of 249 Squadron on September 27, 1940 after shooting down two Me110s. (*Detling Parish Council, Kent*)

as the runway appeared. Garfield held off but the port wheel struck and the aircraft bounced off the ground. Not much of a bang but enough to knock Sergeant Bertram Mesner's head against the Perspex. With a second touch and a slight vibration on the control stick everything was rumbling along. He held her straight then taxied in, parking in the southwestern corner of the airfield. A cluster of Blenheims were roughly dispersed and refuelling equipment and heaps of cases and baggage lay on the grass. Builders had begun digging the foundations for hutted accommodation. "Our operations officer that day was Pilot Officer Sam McHardy. After signing in, we trooped off to the mess for lunch." A letter reads: "The following morning found Bertram and Archibald (Kay) climbing out of their bell tent, plodding through the wet grass in their bare feet. Bertram still said it was wonderful sleeping in the open but rivulets of dew were on the canvas of his bed, everything running and dripping, it was getting most of us down."

Despite these conditions in Scotland and the Western Isles 248 and 254 Squadrons carried on. "The appalling conditions weren't confined to those on the ground, in the air they were more extreme", recalled Flight Lieutenant Roger Morewood. Pilot Officer Archibald Hill had just completed a five-hour and fifty-five minute flight and was now squelching across the grass strip away from 'L-Love'. His machine looked dejected. Pinging and hissing noises came from the Mercury engines as they cooled. It had been a terrible and frightening trip across the North Sea. Low cloud had materialized, just as the met officer had said it would, but during the flight Hill and his 'two bods' had also endured "fog, icing and bad visibility. The visibility in places at just thirty yards". Labouring on with cold feet and hands they carried out a reconnaissance of Trondheim and the River Nidelva where it meets Trondheim's fjord. "We felt our way along then turned the aircraft around, the temperature was minus ten degrees Celsius, or it felt like it." Returning early they landed away at Wick. Once the formalities with the watch office had been completed the three bedraggled aircrew fell into three black leather armchairs that formed a ring around a large blazing fire. Hill, Schollar and Kay thawed. It was wonderfully snug and for thirty minutes the serenity gave the impression that the aerodrome was unruffled by war.

In a fever of enthusiasm during an action-packed twenty minutes an error saw N3529 and N3608 collide, killing five members of 254 Squadron. "I was greatly saddened. Poor Pilot Officer John Laidlay hadn't lasted long trying out new tactics with such earnest enthusiasm", said Pilot Officer Bill Sise. "The dispersal hut seemed empty without Laidlay that night." Meanwhile a different emptiness was being felt in the Shetlands. Sam McHardy explained:

"By Tuesday [September 3] we had run out of all forms of refreshment in the mess bar, with the exception of Drambuie. After a period of ten days of this liqueur everything about the place and one's self was sticky and horrible. The only way to overcome the situation was to borrow the station commander's car and take a bunch of fellows to Lerwick, some twenty miles away. Stopping at the Queen's Hotel to have a bath for one shilling and six pence, we then proceeded to have a large fish supper. This hotel was much frequented by junior officers and squalls of gentlemen in black suits. I set off on my next patrol on September 5 in 'J-Johnnie' R3626."

New Zealander Edric 'Sam' McHardy farmed pre-war with his parents at Waipawa. In 1938 he applied to join the navy but was too late to sit the entrance exam. McHardy then applied for an RAF short service commission and after provisional acceptance, he sailed for the 'motherland' on February 1, 1939. After training at Yatesbury and Sealand, in October he joined 248 Squadron at RAF Hendon. One year later he would be appointed A Flight commander. McHardy completed a third tour of operations in December 1944. (*Sally Goldsworthy*)

Overcast weather hindered them during a trip in which no U-boats or enemy aircraft were spotted. Pilot Officer Clarence Bennett landed at 10.47 in 'Z-Zebra'. Garfield reported: "8/10 cloud, 2,500 feet, visibility six miles with patches of rain". Finally spotting land off to starboard McHardy and Garfield dashed into Sumburgh with completely empty tanks. The New Zealander felt lost. Everything seemed disorganized and confused as some of the new buildings were ready to use. The new officers' mess was comfortable and a world away from the all-pervading sand and the bully beef.

By early afternoon in southeast England however, the sun came out. Crumpled on a chair lay a copy of *The Daily Express* with the headline 'Hitler Screams Threats'. B Flight were called to readiness then scrambled at 17.00 hours "to search for enemy aircraft and a ditched bomber". They thundered across the sea. The German assault was far from over. Veteran Flying Officers Richard Westlake, Douglas Wordsworth and Sergeant Harold Sutton (between the ages of twenty to twenty-five) saw an aircraft skimming along the water off Calais and gave chase. Sutton recognized it as a Dornier 18G. Westlake leading the vic brought his face mask up with his left hand and flicked the switch; "Tally Ho!"

Uffz Heinrich Thiermann saw them in good time and opened his throttles; two Jumo 250C engines edged the machine across the wave tops at 165 mph. In seconds Westlake (N3524), Wordsworth (Z5724) and Sutton (N3523) employed their boost, firing quick short bursts in line astern. Breaking to starboard they wheeled around again but in a fever of enthusiasm all three got in each other's way and broke off, tumbling after Westlake in the lead. Thin streamers of white were curling in their direction. Observer Sergeant Owen Burns noted that the "return fire was spasmodic" as the enemy zigzagged over the water, leaving a slight wake and heading for the French coast. Westlake drew a bead and fired 200 rounds. Tracer ate into the machine like a tin opener, wounding Thiermann and his observer Olt.z.S. Max Dietrich. Dietrich's leg was sticky with blood and he looked for an exit wound but couldn't find one. The assault continued, with rounds whizzing through the aircraft's thin aluminum skin.

An official photograph taken for recruiting purposes. A Flight 254 Squadron, Aldergrove, May 30, 1941. Left to right: Sgt Foster; F/Lt Randall (A Flt commander); Sgt Tyson (Wop/Ag); Sgt Peak (2 Wop/Ag); F/O G. A. Sise (pilot). (*Wing Commander Randall*)

Sutton got a good steady burst off and saw hits striking the fuselage and the central push-pull engines. Wordsworth and Westlake followed in with a quarter attack. Its engine seemed to be smoking. The attackers broke off once all their ammunition was expended. Heading away Sergeant Thomas McCarthy in the turret saw the Dornier still forging ahead. The wounded Thiermann laboured towards the Calais port, which was less than three miles away.

The Blenheims resumed their search for P4973, the missing Armstrong Whitley of 51 Squadron, but they failed to locate the Bomber Command machine which was one of twenty-two lost on the scattered raids over Europe. It had been reported ditched off the Dutch coast near Noordzee, off Texel. Sutton recorded: "Our interrogation by Spy that evening was a quick affair". All three claimed a probable. Combat reports were written and individual logbook entries made: "18.06 hours – Do 18 found, attacked, driven off". Their day's total: one probable.

Friday dawned all too soon and engines burst into life. Sleep was out of the question. The clamour died away. B Flight waited. Their insulated boxes containing breakfast came at 08.00 hours. Six lined up and took their share, always two rashers of bacon, hard-yoked eggs, a slice of fried bread and a scoop of baked beans. For ten minutes they ate without interruption, until the telephone trilled. Wordsworth and Westlake were scrambled at 09.30 hours on airfield protection. They climbed over Bracklesham Bay, but both were back within half an hour. The second engagement of the day took off at 09.55 hours to "search for a missing bomber". John Coggins DFM led but as with the previous day he found nothing and turned and retraced his path.

Watching them land at 13.50 was a member of the Woodger family. They completely disintegrated with grief and could not be consoled. For a long time afterwards they were still in tears, it was more than an hour before they felt fit to take a taxi to Chichester railway station. They had the squadron's deepest sympathy. Families were being asked to accept their fate but the Woodgers felt that their sacrifice was one of the many not being recognized.

During the course of the following morning Ronnie Clarke learnt that Commander-in-Chief Frederick Bowhill had shuffled his deck of cards rotating those of 235 at Thorney Island with crews at Bircham Newton, Norfolk. Flight Lieutenant Andrew Fletcher, Flying Officers Frederick Flood and Reginald Peacock arrived from the burial of New Zealander Pilot Officer John Priestley at St. Mary's Church, Great Bircham, on September 2. He had been buried with full military honours and their Canadian flight commander read from John 11.25.26: "I am the resurrection and the life, says the Lord. Those who believe in me, even though they die, will live, and everyone who lives and believes in me will never die."

As the congregation of mainly air force blue left, the procession of mourners filed past the vicar, the reverend John Waddington and the RAF chaplain who shook their hands, clenching with a reassuring grip. The sun beamed down. With no relatives of the Priestley family present, off to one side Sergeant Edward Graves' family were joined by two representatives from 22 Squadron with whom he had flown on Beauforts prior to his attachment to 235 on the same airfield. They were treated to tea in the officers' mess. Above, three Blenheims locked their retractable undercarriages into place and made off over the top of the hawthorn hedges until they were invisible to the naked eye. The Graves family then walked along the untidy road towards The King's Head Inn before catching an omnibus to King's Lynn. Both accompanied the coffin of Sergeant Edward Graves who travelled in the brake van to Liverpool Street Station, London then onto Eastbourne, East Sussex, where he was later buried.

Shortly afterwards these aircraft were midway to Denmark. Ahead of them in the swell an observer sighted three white fishing boats believed to be "Danish fishing smacks", their distinctive colour standing out against the grey/green sea. He noted their position as "sixty-eight miles off Horns Reef, one tied up to a buoy, but men were seen to cast off when our aircraft approached", also recording, "all three vessels had W/T aerials between masts, and flocks of seagulls were seen swarming around them". Hudson 'R-Robert' of 220 Squadron later reported: "All vessels flew Danish flags and also had the flag painted on the side".

Relaxing to the point of indulgence, Peacock lay back on the grass and gazed into the sky. Quelch had obtained permission to take their jackets and ties off. Basil recalled his previous encounter on September 2:

"It had been another manganese blue sky whilst protecting a Royal Navy destroyer escorting a convoy. At 18.04 two merchantmen opened fire on 'H-Harry'. Twenty-three minutes later 'J-Johnnie' sighted nine enemy aircraft approaching from the west, which fell away and disappeared into the mist. Our shift continued, escorting two motor torpedo boats (MTB) to within forty-eight miles north of Texel until 20.00 hours, while keeping an eye out for a ditched Wimpy crew."

Flying at 2,500 feet one of the three machines, P4835 crewed by Sergeants Basil Quelch, John Merrett and Colin Chrystall, stumbled upon a Dornier 18G of 3./KFlGr406 (K6+DL) fifteen miles off Texel, North Holland bearing 270°. The other two stayed aloft as Quelch prepared for action. He changed the fuel to 100-octane, flicked the safety-catch to 'fire' and automatically kicked the rudder to get him at right angles. Wildly excited, he shot off after the Dornier, urging his aircraft on like a clockwork locomotive, faster, faster. The Dornier was now in his ring sight. Quelch fired, discharging 600 rounds from close quarters. Like sparklers they struck. For a brief moment the enemy aircraft hung in the air motionless then it dropped into the water. On impact it was lost from vision amid a deluge of sea spray, which looked as if it might swamp and sink the machine. The water cleared, its rear engine was unserviceable but the "front engine was still ticking over". John Merrett recorded: "Pilot was seen standing up on the gunwale. Rear gunner lay dead."

The Dornier was rocked back and forth in the swell. Inside two bodies lay drenched in seawater; Fw Dietrich Christensen and Lt zur See Dietrich Logier. Turning and escaping, Quelch formed up with Sergeant John Fenton and John Coggins DFM and they were back on the ground by 20.40 hours. To get all their aircraft back on-line servicing went on until 23.30 hours. Sergeant Arthur Robinson hurried around with the Blenheim fighter serviceability state for the next morning. Flood fixed who should be called early; Naish, Laughlin and himself. Outside the roar of engines could be heard.

Other units were off to cause irritation to the enemy: four Fairey Albacores of 826 Squadron in a coordinated attack on barges in Flushing with three Beauforts of 22 Squadron. All landed away at North Coates with Beaufort 'C-Charlie' crashing upon landing at 22.15 hours. Naval crews patiently waited until midnight to see if Albacore 'B-Bertie' would materialize, but the all too familiar words were chalked up; 'Failed to Return'.

Between midnight and dawn reports had increased of shipping activity which could be related to the invasion. Coastal Command men and women in the photographic section pored over reconnaissance photographs calculating and detailing every image: "Barges are still arriving at Ostend exceeding 110, Veere sixty-five with twelve moving through canals towards Flushing, a further twelve moored with forty at north entrance. Nil barges at Boulogne, fifty E-boats, one with Red Cross, six E-boats at Le Havre." The stills of continental ports and information gleaned by

Oxford-born Basil Quelch worked as a clerk for Simonds Brewery in Reading before the war. As an accomplished sergeant pilot, he added to his tally this Dornier 18 that crashed down in an enormous flurry of white spray. (*Andrew Bird via Basil Quelch*)

The wreck of a Dornier seaplane after a good day's hunting.

RAF W/T stations of heavy air traffic from Norway to France gave the strong suggestion of invasion. Pilots, observers and air gunners waited for the call.

At Bircham Newton aircrews sat outside their dispersal. Blackbirds darted in and out of silver birch trees that continued to reach for the skies. Nearby personnel went about their regular daily routines. A brown and green RAF monoplane towed across the sky with the noise of an old four-and-a-half-litre Grand Prix Bentley was followed by another more aggressive sound; Lockheed Hudson T9276 piloted by Flying Officer J Davis. Davis instinctively hauled the control column into the pit of his stomach as he tried to avoid a collision with the monoplane which flashed across his flight path. The Hurricane pilot was totally unaware of the catastrophic event about to unfold. The two Wright Cyclone 9-cylinder radials were starved of fuel and faltered. The machine stalled and plummeted earthwards. A local farmer tending his fields in the area recalled: "The RAF machine made a piercing cry, I was too earnest to look but jumped out of my skin when the explosion came".

T9276 crashed amongst four armed Blenheim fighters and immediately burst into flames. Flight Lieutenant Flood, accompanied by Flying Officer Laughlin and Pilot Officer Coggins DFM dashed out of their armchairs, adrenalin pumping, and sprinted to the parked Blenheim fighters.

Dragging the chocks clear, it was instinctive; scrambling up onto the port wing, pulling back the canopy, leaping into the cockpit and immediately starting the engines, then taxiing to a safe distance. During these vital minutes two 250 lb bombs detonated on the blazing Hudson, sending shards of hot lethal metal in all directions. Knowing that the remaining 250 lb bombs were in the sparkling, sizzling heat and likely to explode at any second, Flood ran back through the searing noise of burning steel to the fourth Blenheim fighter, its rudder and tail unit in the furnace and its camouflage paint already bubbling as the heat ate into the fin. He clambered up, the heat sapping the air from his lungs, and plummeted into the cockpit gasping for oxygen. He had enough energy to start the engines and taxied the smoldering machine away as finally the station fire wagons came on to the scene.

'The Three Musketeers' were that evening royally treated by senior pilots of 206 Squadron to beer and more beer. One of the three wrote: "Finally got to bed at 24.30 hours or really 00.30 hours tomorrow!" in the squadron periodical. Group Captain John Grey, the station commander at RAF Bircham Newton, stated in the citation for recommended awards:

> "Throughout these officers showed complete disregard for their own personal safety in the face of the greatest danger, and it was due to their prompt action, especially of Australian Flight Lieutenant Frederick Flood, that three Blenheim fighters were taken to safety without major damage and the fourth with only minor damage."

Flight Lieutenant F. W. Flood (RAAF) was recommended for the award of the George Medal while Flying Officer J. H. Laughlin and Pilot Officer J. Coggins DFM were recommended to be appointed Members of the British Empire. Frederick, Bodsie and John had little time to dwell on the matter, as all three would soon be engulfed by the Battle of the Barges.

Between stand-bys and stand-downs the number of vessels in harbours from Flushing and Le Havre mounted steadily. Ostend held 205. Concentration was so dense along the French coastal ports to the Flemish waterways that a preliminary invasion alert was issued: "Attack probable within the next three days". Notice boards in the British countryside were pasted with new posters over the fading 'If the Invasion Comes' by Private Morris Prior. Intercepted messages revealed all German army leave had been revoked from September 8 onwards. Meteorologists said "the conditions in the English Channel would be 'particularly favourable' for seaborne landings between September 8 and 10".

As people tuned in to the BBC it was scarcely necessary to assure listeners that "Hitler may at any hour give the order for the invasion to begin". There was thunder in the air. When the storm broke on London Heinkels and Dorniers were droning through an almost cloudless sky over the capital. The Joint Intelligence Committee expressed in no uncertain terms to the chief of staff and their principal advisers gathered in Whitehall that the German invasion was imminent. Air intelligence reported that the scale of operations by the Luftwaffe had risen by day, while attacks on London were targeting communication networks.

The decision weighed heavily on their shoulders. Despite being awarded medals on the field of battle in forgotten campaigns it was now a matter of King, Country and Empire, and that of the free world. Pewter ashtrays filled with cigarette stubs and tobacco as they deliberated. In the circumstances the chiefs of staff may be forgiven for neglecting their agenda and gazing out of the taped windows. They had come to listen and see all the evidence that the invasion might be launched at any moment. The spectacle they now witnessed, or more specifically, the noises they now heard, reinforced what they were being told. The chiefs of staff completed their deliberations and with Churchill's blessings decided to bring the country's defences to alert. The consequences of this decision were greatly to enrich the folklore of the period, for this was the afternoon on which the official alert 'Cromwell' was issued, creating much excitement and confusion.

Although the natural light diminished with so many fires over the city there was an orange glow in the sky as hundreds of frightened Londoners besieged Underground stations. The locked gates soon gave way to the throng of people, bowing like the local authorities to the inevitable. In these dangerously overcrowded stations there were occasional flashes of humour, which undoubtedly relieved the tension.

This was London's first experience of total war. Lady Dorothy Bowhill, a WAAF cypher officer and wife of the commander-in-chief of Coastal Command looked across towards Hendon and saw nine miles of London was burning. The following morning the country awoke to *The Times* reporting the discovery of a great crested grebe in a public air raid shelter in Euston. Field Marshal Viscount Alanbrooke wrote: "September 11, evidence of impending invasion has been accumulating all day, more ships and barges moving west down the Channel."

In the early hours of this Wednesday morning mist hung over the coastal airfield, with the meteorological officers promising fine weather to come. All had been at thirty minutes readiness since 03.30 hours. The morning passed without a fuss and only one sortie. Pilot Officer Raymond Kent strung several models of German aircraft from the ceiling, Peter Wickings-Smith re-read a recent letter from his guardian aunt Miss Hilda Wickings-Smith as his parents were living in Upper Assam, India. Jackson-Smith watched Peter pick up a copy of *Punch*, "there was immediate laughter I recall, a drawing of an elderly lady confiding in her friend: 'These raids give me the feeling that Hitler appears to be a great deal more worried than he seems.' *Punch* summed up our general mood of confidence on the squadron."

At midday lunch beckoned and everyone was brought to 'one hour availability'. Sergeant Basil Quelch's crew stepped into the dispersal hut having flown a reconnaissance over Terschelling, north Holland. Barges had been sighted travelling westwards. Basil said: "Myself, with Sergeants Kenneth Blow and Colin Chrystall in our Blenheim (P4835), were in a flurry of haste. Ken was looking about urgently through the binoculars." With some success! He sighted a Dornier 18. Fortunately this enemy machine could not retaliate. It had turned turtle 'in the drink' with only the floats showing and was being harried by a strong wind.

Arriving back inside the dispersal there was a lot of chatter as plates of food arrived. In the background the gramophone played 'September Song' by Walter Huston. Sergeant Reginald 'Little' Watts acknowledged Basil as he walked past clutching three white mugs of tea for himself, Pilot Officers Peter Wickings-Smith and 'Bill' Green. Watts had flown with William Goddard the previous day, this would be his third trip with Peter and Bill, their original air gunner Dawson had recently got in an awful flap and Watts hoped that he could become a regular member of their crew. Everyone mooched about whilst outside the weather became steadily better. Chairs were placed outside, Bill thumbed through a book entitled *Games for the Young and Old* as others started or restarted games of chess or draughts. Someone then switched on the radiogram. Churchill was making a broadcast in which his grasp of German preparations for invasion were philosophical: "the next week or so . . .he may come". He compared this time to:

> "the days when the Spanish Armada was approaching the Channel and Drake was finishing a game of bowls; or when Nelson stood between us and Napoleon's Grand Army at Boulogne. We have read the history books; but what is happening now is on a far greater scale and of far more consequence to the life and future of the world and civilization than those brave old days."

On this tense day the RAF photographic reconnaissance flights had been taking in the French coastline since 05.00 hours. Spitfire P9453 set off from Heston at 11.15, tracking between Flushing and Calais and sighting and photographing an array of shipping: "seventeen ships, average tonnage 1,500, steaming line astern eight miles off Dunkirk". P9453 landed at 13.15. The interpretation of these photographs was as follows: "Our general impression is that large shipping units in considerable numbers are moving west from Flushing to Boulogne and beyond". 16 Group was requested to mount an immediate strike against these vessels. With 22 and 59 Squadrons already earmarked for raids elsewhere, it fell to 826 and 235 Squadrons. Planning for the operation got underway. Everyone was brought to 30 minutes readiness. They all knew the form and twenty-four sat and listened: "145 barges and fourteen auxiliary vessels were sighted within Calais and our job was to provide long-range fighter escort to Fairey Albacores on this daylight raid". Seemed easy enough . . .

Stepping outside, a tractor could be heard trundling along. This sound was drowned out as engines started up. Red Section comprised Flood leading in his usual steed Z5725, Wickings-Smith flying L9396 and Wordsworth in L9446. Jackson-Smith flying P3523, Laughlin in L9404 and Coggins in P4835 made up Blue Section. Everything was in order. All climbed away between 15.45-15.55 hours and the sound of radial engines drifted down to the fields and villages, crossing into the Weald of Kent. "It was somewhat surreal to see overloaded horses and carts with the occasional car making for the hop fields below us, reminiscent of Dunkirk." With tension mounting, calmly Wickings-Smith heightened his seat a notch to allow him to see that little bit more. Dark specks blossomed ahead, six naval Albacores of 826 Squadron could be seen circling over Detling Hill. Far below the changing tones of green mapped out their path. With R/T silence the two formations ambled towards Folkestone. Jackson-Smith flying

235 Squadron Pilot Officer Peter Wickings-Smith was a former pupil of Bloxham School, Banbury. He applied for pilot training and was selected. With training completed he joined 235 Squadron, teaming up with Irishman William 'Bill' Green. Their usual steed was L9396. (*Paul Wickings-Smith*)

A Blenheim flies over newly stacked hay in the summer of 1940. (*Andrew Bird*)

'A-Ace' recalled: "There was a slight difference in speed. The Albacores trudged along at 152 mph, 100 mph slower than our machines. I was constantly watching and adjusting my speed." Despite this, there was cohesion in the combined effort. Between Faversham and Canterbury the Albacores' altitude was adjusted to 10,000 feet. Flood organized his escort fighters 1,000 feet above and slightly astern. They etched their own progress over Folkestone, admiring the long stretch of coastline spread out below. France was now in touching distance. It was 17.00 hours and they had five minutes before being due over the target. Faint strands of smoke could be seen. Only this and the constant roar of Sub Lieutenant Anthony 'Steady' Tuke's own Albacore's engine gave evidence of life as he led his men looking down over France.

The enemy convoy had travelled 21.1 nautical miles. Three vessels put into a local port, the fourteen remaining were now sailing eight miles off Calais. Intelligence received from 'a reliable source' said cargoes of military supplies included artillery shells, bridging equipment and Tauchpanzer III amphibious armoured tanks for operation Sealion. This panzer was unique; instead of floating it drove on the seabed while a rubber hose supplied the engine and crew with air. It was a vital piece of equipment for the invasion. As they steamed along they were joined by flak ships and E-boats, with the Luftwaffe on readiness waiting and calculating.

Pilots of Jagdgeschwader 52 (JG 52) discuss tactics and scores in September 1940. (*Operation Dynamo War Museum, Dunkerque*)

One minute remained before kick-off. In the formation was Naval Airman Robert Matthews: "I caught sight of three machines in a vic, 1,000 feet or so above us, their light-blue undersides blended in with our surroundings." Then within seconds hundreds of black puffs from exploding anti-aircraft shells met the force. Albacore 'M-Monkey' L7114 dropped its nose. "For a moment I thought we had been hit, but looking sideways showed me that the rest of the squadron were with us in our descent, though the formation was somewhat loosened to go through the flak", Matthews reported. A shout through the headphones compelled him to raise his eyes, "Fighters". His pilot, Sub Lieutenant Anthony Tuke, reported: "we descended from 10,000 feet. Through the accurate flak we encountered at 8,000 feet I could see a cloud of Messerschmitt 109s rising to meet us from Pas de Calais. At the same time the anti-aircraft fire ceased as quickly as it had started."

Two dozen of Jagdgeschwader 52's yellow-nosed Messerschmitts climbed, immediately bringing their guns to bear on the much slower Albacores in a classic head-on attack. The naval machines split in all directions. Albacore 'P-Pip' fired a long burst from the single wing-mounted 0.303 at a 109 which was seen to go down in flames (unconfirmed). With shouts of "Fighters coming down now!" over the intercom, Flood watched the battle unfold. Instructing the second section over the R/T to deal with the 109s above and look after his tail, the Australian put 'G-George' Z5725 into a forty-five degree dive at a speed of 150 mph, altering the throttles to one-third open. Wickings-Smith and Wordsworth followed their leader. Within eighteen seconds their height loss was 3,000 feet, Flood glanced at his air speed indicator which read 280. They'd gone through the eye of the storm pulling out so hard that they could feel their eyes being forced out with the G-force. Fortunately he did not black out. This confusing air battle was spread out over two miles of sky, it was particularly savage and began to unfurl in seconds between heights of 8,000 to 1,000 feet.

Seeing a Bf109E in pursuit of an Albacore, Wickings-Smith caught up. It seemed enormous as it filled his gun sight and he went surging towards it. He began to fire. The Blenheim's five Brownings made a noise that shook the aircraft and vibrated the length of the fuselage. Ahead bullets splayed out like an octopus's tentacles. All hell broke loose when Blenheim L9396 took a hammering from another 109 coming in from his right as Wickings-Smith tried to knock the Messerschmitt off 'M-Monkey's tail. The Hun then curved away as Green and Watts shrieked over the intercom. Peter broke right then reversed direction, before tearing after the same 109. As the Albacore took fire Tuke in 'M-Monkey' jinxed and slowed to out-manoeuvre this aircraft, while Matthews stood in the rear of the cockpit firing his single 0.303 Vickers machine gun until a 7.92 mm round punched a hole in one of his shoulders, knocking him off balance and onto the floor of the machine. Rounds zipped by "so close you could reach out and grab them". The cockpit was riddled with bullets and the main spar shot away. The upper aileron jammed and Tuke's observer, Sub Lieutenant Edward Brown was badly wounded in the head. His flying helmet was shredded and blood streamed from an open wound. Matthews, although dazed, got to his feet. Pieces of his sheep's skin flying jacket had been blasted into the entry wound with the high velocity round, which had stemmed some of the bleeding but he later reported: "my shoulder hurt like hell". Matthews caught his breath. He was still alive. Through severe pain he checked his weapon, methodically making sure the mechanism was in working order and replacing the magazine with a fresh one. Both were instantly back in action.

Elements of Jagdgeschwader 53 returning from operations over southeast England had stumbled upon the air battle and sat just above the three Blenheims. Then the rascals dropped down, making the most of their height advantage. Jackson-Smith recalled: "our section was passed by the Messerschmitts so we three joined the mass of swirling machines and vapour trails". 'A-Ace', 'J-Johnnie' and 'C-Charlie' half rolled and started to come down into the fray. All the while the R/T was full of chatter and cries. Jackson-Smith was weaving about the sky in 'A-Ace' with tracer buzzing over the gun turret.

Pilot Officer Raymond Kent had never seen a Bf109E close-to before. "Suddenly I had one within yards of me giving short steady bursts." In reply Kent expended 200 rounds. "Unwaveringly this Luftwaffe pilot kept on until at thirty yards it seemed he was intent on ramming us, when suddenly his nose dropped and he was gone out of sight." Jackson-Smith declared: "God was looking after us. Our aerial duel and my constant zigzagging had brought us back towards the English coastline."

Sergeant George Southorn was memorized, his eyes arrested by the sight of Blenheim L9396 ten miles off Folkestone, 3,500 feet below, going down into the sea. Before there was time to watch for the crew's escape his attention was diverted, to a 109 still taking fire.

Emboldened and wildly excited, Wickings-Smith shot after him having disengaged from the naval machine, and urged his aircraft on. Faster. Faster. Had he seen them? He fired again. The 109 broke hard upwards and came around slightly above. Watts pumped out rounds towards their attacker as his pilot jinxed from side to side. Cannon and machine-gun rounds ripped into the port wing. Bill Green watched as a few bright flashes struck, then there was a brief puff of dark smoke, a thin plume at first, then a slightly thicker trail of darkening grey.

The Blenheim suddenly looked tired. Further rounds of both calibres penetrated the aircraft skin. It just sat there. The Bf109E fired again. Then a small puff of debris exploded into the air. It was dying, Wickings-Smith's fight was lost. Like an animal mortally wounded and with its air gunner still firing L9396 fell away, the angle steepening, the trail thickening. 'E-Edward' headed towards the sea. The whole cockpit had been ripped apart and the dashboard instruments had dropped out like cricket bails. The pilot's seat was vibrating loose from its mounts. There was little movement from its pilot who was slumped over the controls. Observer Bill Green was motionless too. Past the main spar, in the rear turret Sergeant Reginald Watts was fighting off their pursuer, with fuel pouring from both engines, ablaze like roman candles. Watts fought back gallantly though it was an unequal exchange, which must have been utterly terrifying for him.

A final blast of tracer bullets streamed into the inferno and the dying Blenheim descended in a shroud of flames and drowned. Albacore 'M-Monkey' passed, dipping one of its wings. 'Steady' Tuke glimpsed air gunner Reginald's face staring upwards helplessly, water lapping over his new fly boots and Irvin jacket while the flames edged closer. His first aerial combat wasn't meant to end like this. Tuke made a rough mental note, "time – 17.40 hours".

The demise of his friend Peter was also witnessed by Douglas Wordsworth: "I saw another Bf109E attacking a single Blenheim 'E-Edward', 1,000 feet below. It crashed into the sea with its engines on fire." Wordsworth immediately eased his stick forward, dropping after the Bf109E and increasing speed to latch onto the monoplane. Keeping the machine in his ring sight was a strenuous effort but Douglas, through the cracked Perspex, got a fleeting glimpse of rounds striking. Bullets thudded into Oblt Jakob Stoll's Messerschmitt. Tuke watched Wordsworth's pursuit; "It was a good steady burst and I saw hits on his fuselage and there was a large puff of black smoke from somewhere, after which it went into a dive beyond vertical". Stoll and his Messerschmitt survived, whilst below there was a huge patch of flames on the sea.

Immediately on the R/T a voice said; "We've been hit, but I'm all right". Naval Officer Sub Lieutenant A H Blacow piloting L7097 had survived a second encounter. Fortunately with

235 Squadron Sergeant Reginald Watts. Known as 'Little' Watts, he joined the RAF as an airman under training WOP/AG. The thirty-five year old completed his training and was posted to 235 Squadron in July 1940. This heroic air gunner from Far Cotton, Northamptonshire was one of the three crew reported missing on September 11. (*Andrew Bird*)

their slower speed the 109s crossed over, dark smoke coming from their exhausts. Blacow was mortally injured, blood splattered onto the canopy and cockpit instruments. In the rear his air gunner nineteen-year-old Leading Aircraftman Frederick Lowe was surrounded by debris and shards of Perspex. The airframe was butchered by bullets and cannon rounds and their radio operator lay unresponsive. With speed slackened L7097 turned for home.

All the remaining naval aircraft nosed down and made for the sea, the smoke trails evidence of the power being demanded of their engines. Blenheims 'D-Dog', 'A-Ace', 'J-Johnnie' and 'C-Charlie' manoeuvred in an effort to draw the Messerschmitts on to themselves as the remaining naval aircraft made a break for home, travelling as fast as their battle-damaged machines would carry them over the dark grey water against a dark blue sky. Pilot Officer John Coggins DFM wrote:

> "The remainder we shepherded along, getting the Albacores home badly knocked about. Four had extensive damage, one of which ditched near Dover."

Visibility was good, the sea flat and calm. As an MTB of the 11th MTB Flotilla returning from a fracas with E-boats approached Dover harbour it was orbited by an aircraft. "It's one of ours!" a shout went up. It appeared to be in a distressed state. L7117 'K-King' then put down on the water at 17.50 hours and was engulfed by spray. "It looked like Niagara Falls", one naval rating observed.

Lieutenant Allan Downes and Sub Lieutenant Conrad Mallett survived the crash-landing, however their air gunner Naval Airman James Stevens died of the injuries sustained during or after the air battle. The senior officer of the motor torpedo boat extricated these two airmen in a skillful manner and within the hour they were ashore at Dover.

Remnants drifted across the British mainland, 'L-Love' L7098 was barely able to stay aloft. Sub Lieutenant T Winstanley and Sub Lieutenant J D Watson were wounded. Glancing down at his temperature gauge Winstanley saw the needle was nearing the hottest limit. Out front, the Bristol Taurus XII engine began to struggle, then as he passed over the railway line to Adisham it coughed and spluttered and finally it packed up entirely. Now horribly low, there was no chance of reaching Detling. He was going to have to crash land. The ground was rushing ever nearer. Houses, cottages and hedgerows flashed by as the Albacore touched the field. Its undercarriage was ripped off and the right wing dropped which took the force of their landing. After a bumpy ride it finally came to a halt, jolting the two sub lieutenants forward. Fortunately their Sutton harnesses held. L7098 had come down at Staple, Kent at 17.55 hours. Civilians had seen their plight and alerted Staple home guard.

Meanwhile Steady Tuke nursed his crippled machine along despite a holed petrol tank and both tyres being punctured, reaching base together with Albacore L7097. 'F4M' L7114 nosed over, Steady unbuckled his harness and clambered down as the ambulance came to the scene. As they were helped into the 'blood wagon' the bouncing and jouncing made some of the men wince or cry out in pain.

The Blenheim observers picked out the landmark of Chichester's cathedral, which could be seen for many miles across the flat meadows. Calling up the watch office as they entered the circuit they began their descent. With speed dropping away, throttle closed, stick back to almost stalling point and nose slightly high, two propellers ticked over. Each machine sunk over the boundary and touched the rutted grass runway, wheels then tail wheel. Running along the pilots eased the brakes, stopped, turned and checked left and right. Bodsie stopped twenty yards from the opposite boundary, his brakes finally working! Somewhat relieved he opened the right window and undid his oxygen mask, perspiration leaving its mark. A waft of air was blown into the cockpit, cooling his face.

Ground crew surveyed 'A-Ace'. "There were so many bullet holes you could have strained spaghetti through it." All walked away thankful of surviving another face-to-face meeting with death. Jamison, the deputy adjutant, came hurrying over to meet them, his face a picture of relief. "'Thank God you're back old boy', he said to me 'You're one of the last founder members, wouldn't do to lose you!'" recalled Pilot Officer Jackson-Smith.

The dispersal hut was a mass of pilots, observers and air gunners. There were searching glances between the intelligence officer and his two WAAFs as combat reports were sorted out. John Coggins DFM claimed two Bf109s as probable (unconfirmed) and Wordsworth one probable (unconfirmed). As the squadron Spy fired off questions he inquired; "Anyone see Freddie Flood?" There was a shaking of heads as they held mugs of tea, a cigarette or pipe, whilst trying to recall the events. Flying Officer Robert Jamison wrote: "His machine Z5725 was not actually seen to go down by any of the others, but there was little hope as to Flood's [Shorrock's or Sharpe's] safety".

The evening was a subdued affair. A stove was lit and the flames danced around as they roared up the chimney pipe while Jamison tapped the typewriter keys, typing nine letters under a dampened lamplight. Paragraphs to Peter Wickings-Smith's aunt read: "There is, in my opinion, no hope that any of the occupants of this aircraft could have escaped with their lives . . . May I express my sympathy to you in the loss of your nephew, which has also been a great loss to the squadron." Later the fallen's attributes were transcribed into the unofficial unit diary:

"Flight Lieutenant Freddie Flood, known to all on the squadron as 'The Negus', had a very successful career in the Australian Air Force to which he proudly belonged. He was a first class flight commander and popular with us all. His attention to detail and gallant conscientious leadership inspired his Flight in a grand way. Shorrocks was a most useful officer and though labouring under the handicap of visual impairment nevertheless became a reliable observer and navigator. Air gunner Sergeant Sharp, a resourceful fighting sort, is also a considerable loss to 235, he'd been with us since July. Peter Wickings-Smith recently joined the unit. He was a good amateur crooner and an all-round athlete, following two generations of his family to play rugby for Blackheath. Pilot Officer Alexander 'Bill' Green, a young Ulsterman, was the first observer to join the squadron. He had a shy and retiring disposition yet Bill had developed into a cool, fearless and impeccable observer. He flapped continuously on the ground, but this subsided immediately he was airborne. He was remarkably keen and was pursuing his ambition to become a pilot. 'Little' Watts, the air gunner thirty-five years young, behaved with the greatest gallantry. He continued firing for some considerable time after his machine had burst into flames."

Laughlin, Wordsworth and Coggins got some food off base; homemade bread, local cheese and pickled onions, washed down with a pint in honour of those that got 'the chop'. "You couldn't dwell on it. We left, shaking hands with the publican, and wished each other luck . . . we knew we needed it!" Heading back Laughlin was ill in a ditch near the airfield before Leading Aircraftman Harold Allonby on sentry duty challenged them coming through the main gate. "Everyone was yelling in unison 'Two Thirsty Five!' at the top of our voices." Ambling to their quarters it was quite impossible to sleep. "God, what a day!"

"The attack", said the Air Ministry news service, "was unexpected and devastating". The convoy was later sighted steaming at reduced speed. As midnight struck, the loss of fifteen RAF aircraft over the Channel ports from Bomber and Coastal Command more than balanced the day's losses in Germany's favour. Suddenly flying didn't seem at all dare-devil, like the pre-war shows of Sir Alan Cobham's Flying Circus.

Aircrews read about their exploits in copies of *The Daily Express* and *The Guardian* whose headlines read 'Nazi Supply Convoys Bombed In Channel' with more lineage given to the attack on barge concentrations. The effect was unremittingly upbeat. Spirits rose further despite the losses, with a signal of congratulations from the secretary of state for air, Sir Archibald Sinclair, and Lieutenant Commander William Saunt DSC for the unit's work:

"To the C-in-C Coastal Command. Please convey to the squadrons concerned in yesterday's fighting in the Channel my congratulations on their exploits. I deeply regret the losses sustained but to have carried out their tasks in spite of being attacked by three times their number of fighter aircraft of which they destroyed three was a splendid achievement. Archibald Sinclair. End."

"Had it not been for the magnificent support given to the Albacores by 235 Squadron it is extremely doubtful whether any of our aircraft would have returned as the enemy were in greatly superior numbers, and there was little cloud cover to take advantage of. Lt/Cdr William Saunt DSC. End."

There was another scramble in mid-afternoon to attack a similar convoy. Pilot Officer Wordsworth and Sergeants Sutton, Hobbs and Nelson followed their leader off at 15.40-15.45 hours. Led by Wordsworth in 'M-Mother,' Sutton in 'P-Pip' and Nelson in 'R-Robert' escorted three 59 Squadron machines; 'B-Beer', 'E-Edward' and 'C-Charlie'. They had been briefed to bomb fifteen motor vessels one mile west of Cap de la Hague. "Composition two tankers of 1,500 tons, one M/V [merchant vessel] of 2,000 tons, plus nine smaller merchant vessels closer in shore." On arrival the three Blenheim fighters strafed the vessels and tore up the decking prior to bombing. At 16.20 hours bombs rained down from 200 feet. A single tanker was hit and caught fire. There were a mixture of hits and misses as heavy flak interrupted their observer's aim. Flying Officer Anthony Fry's 250 lb bombs did not explode due to their low altitude. There was also a very near miss for 'C-Charlie', its

Lt Alfred Zeis flew Bf109E4 1./JG53 'PikAs' White 3 from Étaples France. On October 5, 1940 he was shot down possibly by 1 RCAF Squadron Hurricanes and became a POW. (*Chris Goss*)

pilot recording, "as soon as our bomb load had been released in the appropriate direction (towards a Hun), we headed for clouds and the English coast". Smoke drifted from the tanker's bows and deck and acted as a beacon. A single Bf109E immediately pounced on 'B-Bertie' of 59 Squadron but its alert air gunner Sergeant West drove off the Messerschmitt with concentrated fire of ninety rounds. Luftwaffe pilot, Lt Alfred Zeis of I./JG53 recollected:

"I was flying along the coast and reached Le Havre. I saw some fountains of water on the edge of the harbour basin and saw three aircraft heading into the clouds, one after the other. I opened up my throttles to try and intercept before they could reach the cloud, and just before the end one disappeared. Opening fire I expended all of my 20mm ammunition against him without success, the distance was too great. I was now flying on my instruments alone, in cloud and came up behind the three now flying close together. I took aim at the engines of the left hand Blenheim and then latched onto the right hand one before they disappeared into further cloud but not before my Messerschmitt had received several hits. Before they vanished I saw the effects of my fire – black smoke coming out of one."

Flying Officer Anthony Fry's Blenheim 'B-Beer' had been struck on the propeller and fuselage. Then a second brief encounter took place, Zeis continued: "I turned back, using my compass, towards Le Havre between two contrasting layers of cloud. Suddenly, a second flight of three Blenheims appeared in front of me on a reciprocal course to me. I dived and shot at them."

Sutton, Nelson and Wordsworth climbed with throttles wide open, engines straining. Sergeant Douglas Newport's combat report reads: "The 109 attacked from above and was met with a wall of cross fire". Aboard 'Weiß 3' the rounds slammed into the Messerschmitt; "I saw dark shapes – tracer appeared in front of me – then I was hit again and it was high time I reached Le Havre/Octeville airfield. Within seconds the enemy had disappeared enveloped in clouds, the convoy below in no resemblance of order." The German's ordeal was not over.

> "When I arrived the visibility was extremely poor and my forward vision was zero because my Emil windscreen was covered in oil. I did manage to land and had to leave weiß 3 there as the engine had to be changed and battle damage repairs carried out. Two days later, I flew back to join the rest of the Staffel. In my report I said that at least one Blenheim had been damaged and when asked, I did not completely rule out a kill. However, it is probable that none of the Blenheims received severe damage because I did not have any cannon ammunition left. A victory was therefore questionable."

Two witnesses aboard the convoy said that they had witnessed the duel above but could not confirm whether any of the RAF Blenheims had crashed. Strangely Alfred was allowed to claim a Blenheim as his tenth victory. All RAF machines were down between 17.15-17.20 hours. Douglas and his two fellow air gunners from 235 were convinced that they had driven off the Messerschmitt and had damaged it and their intelligence officer marked it down.

Later in the evening two omnibuses took relays of personnel the seven miles into Chichester to watch a performance by local artists for the benefit of those on the station, "it really was nice to watch – damn good show", wrote 'Pappy' Papworth. Others worried about loved ones staying in Eastbourne, which had experienced a German bombing raid. "Ordinance had fallen at the junction of Gildredge Road and Hyde Road causing extensive damage where some wives lodged, further bombs fell into the sea yards from the Cavendish Hotel. One of our colonial pilot officers was going out with a girl working in service nearby at the time," said Pilot Officer Joseph Chamberlain.

The Belgians had witnessed battles and carnage, but were tearing their hair out with immense frustration. Training continued at Bircham on C Flight, known to the senior staff at Coastal Command Northwood as 'The Continental' flight after the hit song by Fred Astaire and Ginger Rogers in 1935. Air Vice-Marshal David Donald, director of organization, recalled: "it was decided irrespective of their Belgian Air Force service that they had to be conversant with their equipment".

That afternoon on Friday September 13, the decision would be no different. Flying Officer William Goddard who commanded the flight was determined to push on with their training. With great enthusiasm Sergeant Olivier Le Jeune grabbed his parachute and flying helmet and followed two of his fellow countrymen out to their allocated machines for "local formation flying". Pilot Officer James Kirkpatrick took 'O-Orange', Sergeant Rene Demoulin was flying P4833 and Sergeant Le Jeune L9393. All machines cleared the grass strip at 12.10 hours. Forming up into a vic, Kirkpatrick led the arrowhead over the aerodrome before turning on a southerly course.

Below them were fields of barley, as the sun threw down its warmth, the heads hung bleached and bent, surrounded by hawthorn bushes, oaks and cottages, part of Old England. Demoulin sighted St Margaret's Church to the southwest, one of the most dominating landmarks in King's Lynn. Eight miles from there, Le Jeune got into difficulty, mishandling the throttle and mixture controls. Starved of fuel the port Mercury XV engine stopped. The Belgian adjusted the dead engine's propeller to coarse and the starboard propeller to fine pitch, then unfortunately in managing the fuel system the Rootes-built Blenheim suffered a further failure. The engine coughed, stuttered and finally failed as it seized up in mid-air. The pilot immediately put his machine into a moderate glide to maintain control and identified a safe place for an emergency landing. Kirkpatrick and Demoulin stayed with the stricken machine as Le Jeune looked to find a flat piece of land or meadow to put L9393 down in. Silently, five tons of aircraft soared over the hedge at the extreme edge of the landing site and touched down, travelling in excess of 160 mph into a ploughed field between Elder Farmhouse, Elder Lane and the Old Work House in Grimston village. Dejected the Belgian made his way out of the field. Goddard commented: "The difficulty for the Belgians was that flying these machines was still a comparatively new experience". After an interlude training continued on the ground, with the Belgian sitting blindfolded in T1999 going through the flight instruments and controls with Goddard. "His quiet enthusiasm communicates itself to all his subordinates", the diarist wrote. Ground instruction ceased at eight o'clock when isolated scattered enemy raids began.

In Sumburgh earlier that morning Pilot Officer Sam McHardy was woken in his tent; "I had not been asleep long when a runner woke Garfield and told him he was wanted in the operations room. I too arrived with my 'goon skin' clothing over my pyjamas." His observer and air gunner were rounded up and duly briefed, taking to the air in Blenheim L9451 at 05.35 hours.

Sergeant Walter Garfield and his crew were making the daily foray to Norway on their own, searching from the island of Fedje near the entrance of Songefjord then going north to Stadlandet taking in the leads. Out over the North Sea, observer Sergeant Bertram Mesner repeatedly took readings, as the effects of the wind were enormous and he needed to adjust the course accordingly. The weather forecast that the crew received was already four to five hours old and inaccurate. They made landfall near the small island of Norde Tjøholm, Mesner's dead reckoning had been effective. The cold was beginning to bite as the temperature dropped in the rear turret where Sergeant Archibald Kay sat perched. His hand warmers had long since given up and he tried to stay alert. L9451 passed over the rocky outcrop and tall green pine trees on Norde Tjøholm. Looming ahead over the water lay Fedje and Hellisøy lighthouse, a very prominent landmark. Skimming over the water at 600 feet on their port side was Rongevær, its landscape painted in golden colours.

Luftwaffe unit 4./JG77 had been alerted, Fw Olav Dyck was already on a free hunt. At 07.58 hours local time, Fedje fishermen saw a single twin-engine machine; "a Blenheim followed by a Bf109E, which attacked at about 600 feet. The machine dived to sea level. At 300-250 feet the left engine was on fire, there was no reaction." In a brief one-sided flurry of machine-gun chatter L9451 'V-Vic' plunged into the water between Fedje and Rongevær at 08.00 hours.

Fishing boats put out from the shore combing for survivors in the 3.6 miles area separating the islands. None were found. It was not until the following morning, Saturday September 14, that a German trawler-type auxiliary vessel (TTA) crewman sighted movement; a yellow Mae West bobbing in the swell attached to a lifeless body. It was pulled in with a pike pole and the identity tags revealed an RAF airman. Sown on his battle dress tunic were RAF pilot wings with fatigued edges. His tags revealed him to be Sergeant Walter J Garfield. Sea breeze and spray embalmed him on the deck and back in Fedje Garfield's body was wrapped in tarpaulin and later that afternoon transported by a second TTA to Bergen, where the air force officer was buried. Sergeant Norman Stocks confirmed that they had not heard from L9451, typing: "No news from aircraft from the moment of take-off".

Two months previously, on Saturday July 13, 'V-Vic's air gunner Sergeant Bertram Mesner had married a local girl named Jessie from his native Forest Gate, London. Jessie was described as "looking relaxed and extremely pretty" as they said their vows at the altar. Both had looked at each other and understood in that one moment what lay ahead. There was still no news of Bertram after two weeks. No one appeared to know what had happened to the three.

A German trawler-type auxiliary (TTA) known as a flakship to RAF and Commonwealth aircrew. Normally a captured whaler about 250 tons or larger, rebuilt and strengthened. (*Andrew Bird via P/O Len Murphy*)

Air raid sirens sounded and bombs dropped like confetti. German bombing raids increased with an assortment of random raids on south London and coastal resorts, killing quantities of civilians. The Civil Defence registered nearly fifty casualties in the once peaceful suburbs of Kingston-upon-Thames and Wimbledon. Sergeant Sydney Hobbs tried to persuade his wife to leave Clapham. Like other airmen and women he had had a taste of what Londoners were now going through and he was afraid that she might see vehicles awash with gangrenous blood and bits of limbs. "Although the overall sound she remembered, apart from the bombs, was the ringing of the fire engine's bells", said Sergeant Arthur Aslett. Others received scribbled notes through the post; "heavy bombing today, but we're still OK". Sergeant Aslett recalled: "There was nothing we could do except find the bombers on their way home, if the Hun passed near enough". Relentless aerodrome patrols by A and B Flights over Thorney Island continued, scrambling several times till dusk. All passed without incident as the enemy glided away into the starry night. Occasionally there were real signs of concern; servicemen and women running about in tin hats and rushing down to the air raid shelters. Fortunately when bombs dropped in the vicinity no damage was done to the squadron property.

Amid such scenes there was time for celebration too. Flying Officer Reginald Peacock was accosted by a beaming Squadron Leader Ronnie Clarke and informed that he had been recognized and awarded the Distinguished Flying Cross (DFC) for being credited with five confirmed victories (two shared). "Good show, Pissy". Peacock was the only Coastal Command Blenheim fighter ace and it was the first decoration in the squadron, a double celebration! By ten o'clock in the evening three barrels of Simonds beer had been drunk and Fletcher thought perhaps they should be heading back. His main concern was how the flight were going to make dawn readiness.

Woken at 04.00 hours, somehow the pilots and aircrew converged on the dispersal hut, goon skin clothing over blue-striped pyjamas. It was cold and more unsettled weather was predicted. 59 Squadron emerged from their tents around the airfield, still waiting for the works foreman to commence the rebuild of their quarters. Acting Flight Lieutenant Robert Ayres DFC walked across the aerodrome from his temporary accommodation, a cottage on the perimeter. Bristol Blenheim fighters stood silhouetted against the crimson dawn sky and the sound of seagulls mixed with lapping waves around the base. The new day was finally dawning. The stove in the middle of the dispersal hut blazed away until the outside temperature rose to 14 degrees centigrade. For the next couple of hours the crews waited to be scrambled, some tried to sleep. Ollie Wakefield paced the floor, occasionally stopping to admire Kent's handywork on enemy identification models. The dispersal door opened, a breeze blew in ruffling the papers on the telephone operator's desk. Aircraftman Henstock weighed them down with the wood-cased perpetual desk calendar, in the process he turned the day, the Gill Sans-Serif typeface pronouncing it as Sunday, September 15, 1940.

Bertram Mesner was born in Forest Gate, London. He joined the RAFVR in March 1939 as an airman, passing his leading aircraftman exam with 90 percent. He became an observer and completed his training at 1 (Coastal) Operational Training Unit before being posted to 248 Squadron in June 1940. The twenty-year-old was posted missing on September 13, 1940. (*Andrew Bird*)

Amid the chatter Peacock sat in his Mae West when the bellowed cry of "Scramble!" came at 11.10 hours. Peacock followed in the wake of Wakefield and Wilson to 'O-Orange', Wordsworth scrambled aboard 'H-Harry' and Nelson started the engines of 'P-Pip'. Red 1 was leading (Peacock) and all raced into position, turned and took off. They patrolled over the airfield numerous times up a well-worn track, between 15.50-18.25 hours. Flying Officer Charles Pinnock noted: "they were not far from the scenes of heavy fighting, but nothing developed for these Coastal Command fighters hot on the scent of Heinkels and Dorniers. They flew round for some time not catching sight of a plane."

At Bircham Newton it was a quiet day. Sergeant Harold Naughton trundled past in P4833 on a thirty-minute trip to North Coates. On his arrival over the airfield at 18.10, Naughton misjudged his height. Retracting the undercarriage he attempted another circuit, gaining altitude, unfortunately the two Mercury XV engines seemed unable to maintain height and with the possibility of hitting a building Naughton was ordered by the watch office to belly land at 18.15 hours. Nobody was hurt, just Naughton's pride! The diarist closed this auspicious day by writing: "Nothing of importance happened".

The Belgians were assigned a Danish reconnaissance on September 18. Morale was high as Goddard led his section off together with Sergeants Naish, Quelch and Flight Lieutenant Phillip Stickney. An 850-mile round trip saw Demoulin comment: "The most boring thing I have done so far". The group saw nothing of interest. They found it hard to hold their position and had to concentrate hard just to avoid colliding with the other aircraft. The Belgians had been effective in a vic of three over Norfolk and The Wash but they'd not been warned about the difficulties of flying in a large formation. Goddard explained: "This activity was to improve their operational effectiveness", and he also had to reduce the losses through accidents and engines cutting. In the days to come intensive training continued for C Flight under the direction of Goddard. Blenheim fighters were placed around the airfield for wireless transmitter training. In the afternoon they practiced formation flying with a further two hours spent over The Wash chasing a Vickers Vildebeeste pulling a drogue. Crossing back over the coast at just a few hundred feet they followed the Docking Road back, watching an old Morris lorry with farm workers in the back trundle into a field, all waving. It had been a reasonable day.

236 Squadron were still in North Cornwall at St Eval working flat out. Jamaican Pilot Officer Herbert Capstick woke to find the airfield basking in glorious sunshine with not a cloud in the sky, a perfect Indian summer's day. Capstick and Flying Officer William Moore walked around with twenty-year-old Pilot Officer Dugald Lumsden inspecting L6776 'K-King' before going off to breakfast. Lumsden's crew were down on the 'Fly List' and all three sat in the crew room relaxing in Irvin jackets with Mae Wests around their necks. By 06.00 hours they were being briefed; "Reconnaissance. Brest to Guernsey". Sergeant Leslie Ledger calculated it was 113 miles between the two points and also worked out fuel consumption and fuel load. Already there were two further sorties called for that morning to the same vicinity. Something was up. From his vantage point Ledger sighted "three large vessels and six unknown vessels, probably escort vessels, near Ushant at 07.30 hours". A sighting report was sent back. A second signal was sent ten minutes later: "three merchant vessels and six escorts forty-seven miles off Ushant". He watched.

"Like a flock of sheep penned in together with border collies", he thought, "scampering around keeping them in order". Lumsden banked sharply, it was time to go home. He landed at 08.06 hours. As 'K-King's ground crew scampered over the usual noises echoed around the aerodrome. On the far side Avro Ansons were being bombed up, armed and fuelled ready for a theatrical performance in the afternoon. Moore, Capstick and Sergeant Alan Chappell familiarized themselves with the details; "Protective fighter patrol to the Ansons and reconnaissance Brest to Guernsey". The squadron intelligence officer outlined the importance of the target. Crews then boarded into their restricted spaces, Campbell in 'N-Nuts' R3886, Russell in 'P-Pip' T1806 with Moore as lead. They were scrambled at 10.50 hours.

As they climbed to 10,000 feet they passed a bustling St Austell on the starboard side. The dark grey English Channel was spread out before them. Capstick was out of sight in the glazed 'green house'. Moore opened the throttles. Increased vibration sent Capstick's pencil rolling across the plywood navigation table. The pencil came from his days as a boarder at Sedburgh School, Cumbria. Stopping it with his left hand, he replaced it in a chiselled-out groove in the table.

The cloud had started to build up so there was at least some cover. Everyone was watchful as they approached the target. From their vantage point

Born on November 21, 1916 in Barbados, Inniss sailed to Great Britain and joined the RAF on a short service commission in January 1939. After completing training on Tiger Moths and Miles Masters, he was posted to 236 Squadron on September 3, 1939. Inniss took up residence in the officers' mess at RAF Stadishall until the unit was formed one month later on October 31, 1939. (*Captain James Inniss*)

above, Pilot Officer Campbell in R3886 watched a couple of Ansons swoop down through the anti-aircraft fire. One Anson pilot reported: "Dropped four 100 lb anti-submarine bombs on one merchant vessel of 12,000 tons, escorted by destroyer. Bombs dropped 30 yards starboard side of port escort vessel. No hits and no damage estimated." A third Anson struck at St Peter's Port, Guernsey at 13.20, diving out of its cloud cover to release two 100 lb anti-submarine bombs on a single merchantman. "Results unknown as aircraft returned at once to cloud cover." Pilot Officer Frank Tams recalled: "Suffered no losses as all the flak seemed to burst well in front of us. Obviously the German gunners had a total disbelief in our speed! It was scary nevertheless." Pilot Officer George Melville-Jackson flew out in R2799 to report on the damage and to look for barges reported to be moving down the coast.

Pilot Officer Aubrey 'Sinbad' Inniss could not see the spire of St Eval's village church even though it and the airfield were on a high plateau 300 feet above sea level. It really was a foggy morning as he groped his way to the mess for beans and bacon. If it carried on like this everyone would be confined to base. However by 06.00 hours the visibility had increased and within an hour the sun was shining. By mid-morning they had received news of dogfights in the south. At 12.26 one section was ordered out on an offensive patrol following an RAF W/T station picking up a distress call: "Forced landed owing to engine trouble in position approximately 48° 50' North 10° 15' West". In reply to this distress message the operator, Ofw Hans Giermann, was informed that a flying boat was starting at once. Fw Horst Dümcke landed near a small merchant ship. After which no more was heard from him.

The trio were scrambled after a briefing at 12.30 hours. The section was made up of Pilot Officers Graham Russell, Aubrey Inniss and Sergeant Reginald 'Percy' Smith. Initially they saw nothing. They were told however, to continue their patrol out over the Isle of Scilly at 3,000 feet. Part of this cavalry charge hurtling towards the Isle of Scilly included Australian Flight Lieutenant E Courtney flying with 10 (RAAF) Squadron, who had an hour earlier received a signal from Group: "Enemy aircraft in sea 48° 50' North 10° 15' West another aircraft [Walrus] proceeding to attempt rescue, investigate. Blenheim fighters dispatched." Courtney steered Sunderland P9605 to the given co-ordinates. Sergeant Mahon sighted an enemy aircraft, which he initially thought was a flying boat, but then recognized as a new Focke-Wulf 200 Condor. "It was on reflection a low-wing four-engine monoplane", with grey/green paint, logged at 14.16 hours. Their W/T operator sent an immediate report hoping that the Blenheim fighters would intercept this message. Nine minutes afterwards they signalled "enemy aircraft out of sight". These messages were re-sent from Plymouth on 6480 kilohertz instead of 6666 kilohertz and not received in time to allow the orders to be carried out.

The 236 aircrews did as they were ordered but to the great frustration of Inniss they had seen no enemy aircraft except the odd fishing boat since 14.00 hours. Their next encounter was a 'friendly' Short Sunderland, P9605, drawing nearer at 14.54 hours, ahead 12° to starboard. Recognition signals were exchanged between observers, before they took different courses. Then Russell shouted over the R/T at 15.15; "Twelve o'clock!" A bomber's silhouette was roughly on the same level. The WAAF controller's earlier persistence had paid off. Unbeknown to them it was searching for 'shipwrecked' comrades.

Ofw Hans Giermann had transmitted his position and his emergency call had been picked up by the RAF W/T station in plain language. Fw Horst Dümcke had made a perfect ditching on the smooth sea after He 111H-2, RH+NT suffered a sudden loss of power in one of the engines 500 miles west of Brest, alighting near French fishing vessels returning to Brittany from Newfoundland. Immediately after the distress signal from Dümcke's machine was received Staffelkapitän Oblt Rudolf Prasse rushed to prepare He 111H-3 GT+KA, loading a second dinghy for dropping. The crew boarded, manned by Prasse, Reg Rat Dr Hans Reinhart (Senior Met B) Ofw Max Mrochen and Uffz Franz Liebel, for an air search. A French fishing vessel was soon sighted, but the reply was that, it was the wrong one.

Suddenly from the rear Liebel shouted "Fighters". Two Blenheim fighters gained, Inniss from starboard, Russell on the port. Inniss called "Tally Ho!" as they turned towards the enemy. He switched his gun button to 'fire', his euphoria mounting at his first chance to shoot down an enemy aircraft. L6797 continued heading straight towards it. Inniss glanced at his speed, the dial read 255 mph. His observer noted; "position 245° Bishop's Rock 180 miles 15.20 hours". The He 111 was now directly in front of him, lining up the fixed ring sight. Desperately scanning the skies Prasse heard another shout; "They're coming!"

Inniss pressed in the gun button, the calico tore as rounds pumped out at an alarming rate. The Heinkel's frontal structure was penetrated by incoming rounds. Russell opened fire. Smoke burst from the German's port engine. Ofw Max Mrochen said; "Our machine was seriously hit and the port engine set on fire". Prasse dropped his undercarriage and on the altimeter he could see 914 metres (3,000 ft), then 152 metres (500 ft). Within seconds he was inches from the water. Liebel fired a distress signal.

Smith finally arrived and made a beam attack from the starboard quarter. Inniss followed with a No 1 attack and bits of aircraft began to fly off. His final rounds from a five-second burst made their mark, the machine plummeting a short distance into the sea. The sea was calm as the Heinkel impacted the surface. Reinhardt had become a casualty and lay still on the floor, his flying suit pitted by 0.303 bullets. Liebel and Mrochen were busy releasing the dinghy, lifting it from the deck-stand out onto the wing. With the glazed nose already filling with water Prasse left the cockpit through the roof window. Despite the calm, a breeze ruffled their flying overalls. It was a nerve-wracking few minutes, in which they were completely exposed. In the distance aero-engines could be heard, their sound becoming more prominent.

Re-grouped the Blenheims came in at sea level together, as Inniss watched the three crewmen on the port wing of the floating bomber. As Prasse, Mrochen and Liebel tensely waited, Mrochen glanced up and saw gun flashes. Within seconds bullets buzzed in. Liebel was struck in the back and in the arms, their machine was holed above and below the waterline and their aircraft swiftly began to sink. In an instance, the Blenheims were gone. One returned as Prasse and Mrochen helped their wounded comrade, ducking instinctively as it flashed overhead. Inniss ordered his air gunner to jettison 'L-Love's dinghy; "For the benefit of the enemy crew". Inniss was surprised that a sense of elation had swept over him. Rejoining the other two, together they dashed back past Bishop's Rock the sixty-nine miles to base. Innis switched off the motors, breathing a big sigh of relief. He pulled out his R/T leads, released his harness and jumped onto the wing, then slid down on to the ground.

The Luftwaffe crew's fortunes had come full circle with the arrival of a large flying boat, Sunderland P9605. Courtney was surprised to note two collapsible dinghies with survivors in at 15.46. An individual waved, whilst another fired off a smoke flare. The white smoke reached high into the air, whilst below a red beacon glowed. The second pilot, Paddy Mahon, scribbled a note reporting: "Have observed rubber boats in position 245° Bishop's Rock 184 miles. Five enemy aircraft are searching in the vicinity." The message was received back at Mount Batten. Sunderland 'K-King' then accelerated away to starboard and gained height before continuing with its patrol, before becoming waterborne at 17.55 hours.

Ofw Max Mrochen found himself distracted:

"As the sea was calm the British flying boat could have landed, but then it left the area heading towards Brest. We had boarded the second dinghy, well equipped with Verey pistol and emergency packages, and fastened our damaged dinghy, as a spare, to our new boat. Prasse pointed out that it was a long way. As the hours disappeared we sighted several distant fishing trawlers and fired flares, but none came to our assistance. As darkness concealed us, drops of fresh water fell from the sky, it gradually became a torrent and we used the empty tins from the emergency pack to collect the water, which we could then drink. The next day, September 24, our situation had not changed, as the dinghies were pushed along. Our Verey ammunition was now almost exhausted without anyone coming to our aid. Liebel's wounds were still bleeding heavily and he slowly drifted into unconsciousness. In the evening the dinghy began to lose air, and was decompressing rapidly and could no longer carry us. We checked the life-vests, Prasse's was damaged. There was nothing we could do. Entering the water, we held onto each other around the flat dinghy and waited for our last hour. Suddenly, Liebel vomited foam and with his nose bleeding died in my arms while we were still drifting.

"And then a wonder! A fishing trawler approached and heaved us on board, even our dead comrade, Liebel, who Prasse said to save straight away. We were fitted out by the fishermen in dry clothing; red linen trousers, roll-neck woollen pullovers and wooden clogs. The trawler sailed eastwards for four days. The captain in a mark of respect to Liebel, flew the French flag at half-mast until we reached the little port of Concarneau, on the southern coast of Brittany peninsula, from where Prasse and I returned to our base at Brest."

Liebel was carried off on a stretcher and later buried with full military honours. The excitement and the bravado with which they had entered the battle had gone, they had suffered their first loss since moving to Brest. This group of men who formed Wekusta 2, part of Luftflotte 3, were tied by a unique bond and were now aware that a long hard fight lay ahead. It was a sobering thought.

It was a sobering thought for the men flying the Coastal Command Bristol Blenheim fighter too. Cold statistics made for harsh reading; 103 aircrew had lost their lives since the invasion of Norway. With the invasion threat still imminent Bowhill's command would be hard pushed to repel boarders. Everyone would be needed.

Squadron Leader Clarke DFC rang through to Coastal Command headquarters and recommended that C Flight be made operational. Bowhill eventually agreed, after all, like the Poles they too desperately needed experienced, motivated and skilled air crews such as these. Six months after their country had been invaded the Belgians were to enter the battle.

The members of C Flight were up at first light and once they were breakfasted they all settled at their dispersal. The operations phone rang and they were sent to the briefing room. Nine men walked over with a spring in their step.

Coastal Command's 16 Group had ordered a search for shipping from 327 degrees Horns Reef, 42 miles to position 324 degrees Heligoland, 24 miles. "The excitement was a progressive one", said Pilot Officer Steve Hebron, adding; "but on September 18 it was definitely going to become more interesting". The met officer had indicated poor weather over the North Sea, despite this at 10.20 hours the keyed-up continental airmen walked out to their individual machines. They stopped and shook hands wishing each other good luck in their native Flemish.

Take-off was ten minutes away. Scrambling aboard 'F-Freddie'

The warm summer of 1940; on board 10 Squadron RAAF Sunderland P9605.

were Pilot Officers Henri Gonay, Steve Hebron and Sergeant Douglas Cooper. Aboard 'D-Don' were Sergeant Rene Demoulin, Pilot Officers Lucien Javaux and Francois Vensoen. The crew on 'B-Beer' were Sergeants Le Jeune, Albert Michiels and Leopold Heimes. It was drizzling and grey for their first operational flight alone as C Flight.

Forming up in a vic Gonay led them up to 3,000 feet, clearing the Norfolk coast and heading towards Denmark. For this occasion the diary reads: "Carried out the Danish sweep quite successfully". During the Belgians' transition Hebron put his linguistic skills to good use as official interpreter, smoothing out the initial difficulties. Sergeant Leopold Heimes recalled; "Steve Hebron was a good gentleman. We had trouble with names, the language, and so on. He translated for us and also interpreted articles in *Aeroplane* periodicals, pieces of the Blenheim manuals and some navigational aids."

They all began to find their feet as sweeps across to the Danish coast continued, some with the disruption of enemy convoys. Even in the coldest weather they somehow managed to coax the Mercury engines back with scars of battle. The sea was calm and edged with white froth. The calm was a good thing, Heimes thought, for the rubber dinghy they stowed behind him was not designed to weather a gale. Edging over into Norfolk he glanced at the little fishing boats floating askew like burnt matches on a bar floor.

Walking into the dispersal hut Heimes slumped into an armchair, as Le Jeune perched on its arm. There was a rattle of a coffee cup as Michiels poured from a battered enamel French cafetière which one of his compatriots had brought with him. As the smell of coffee lingered and mixed with pipe tobacco, twenty-one-year-old Leading Aircraftman George Osborne on telephone duty opened the window. Goddard entered; "Ops want to send one aircraft off to search for a bomber that's reported down in the North Sea". The peace was broken as coordinates were relayed. "Over a rectangular area from position 005 degrees Lowestoft 5 miles, thence 35 miles south and 30 miles east." It was just after 07.00 hours in the dawn light. Pilot Officers Henri Gonay, Steve Hebron and Sergeant Douglas Cooper rose to their feet and got the gen off Goddard. Maps were drawn and calculations worked out; the show was on. Also entering the fray was a host of other squadrons. "It would not take hours but days to find these bomber boys", wrote Flying Officer Charles Pinnock.

The Bomber Command aircraft had got into difficulty two hours earlier out over the North Sea. Sergeant Dudley Allen was wireless operator/air

The first group of Belgians to join Costal Command, July 1940. Back row from left: Sergeant Demoulin (235); Pilot Officer J. Kirkpatrick (235); Pilot Officer A.L. van Wayenbergh (236); Pilot Officer C.L. Roman (236); Sergeant O. Le Jeune (235); Sergeant. L. Defosse (1 OTU). Front row from left: Pilot Officer G. Dieu (236); Pilot Officer L. Dejace (236); Pilot Officer H. Lascot; Pilot Officer H. Gonay (235).

gunner aboard Whitley P5046, sent with his crew to bomb Berlin. In his small space Allen was sandwiched next to a switchboard with thirty-three switches, a plywood desk, batteries, a priming pump for the aircraft's engines, amplifying valves, oscillating valves and a pipe conducting hot air for heating, lagged with material to conserve heat. Although it was useless in its present state, the bullet-ridden machine had 'copped a packet' over Germany's capital city with the wind whistling through the holes. In the front office Dunn was moving fuel across in an attempt to conserve every drop, as petrol spewed out of one tank, holed by shrapnel. P5046 was nursed 350 miles to the Dutch coast, inch by inch the battle damage took its toll. The faint glow of light on the altimeter needle showed Dunn the loss of height. Throttling back their engines to near stalling speed he changed the trim once more then checked his fuel state. It was getting critical. He glanced at the dwindling reserves from the emergency tanks. They had 279 miles to go to the station and too little fuel. As the sky was clear, a fix was taken using a sextent. There was plenty of light from the moon and the features of the stars were easily discernible. Eighty miles out from the east coast of England Dunn ordered Allen to

Henri Alphonse Clement Gonay was born on July 21, 1913 at Theux and joined the Belgian air force in November 1931. After the capitulation of France, Gonay boarded the Dutch ship *Queen Emma* at Bayonne. It sailed for England and they arrived at Plymouth on June 23, 1940. Gonay was commissioned in the RAFVR as a pilot officer on July 12 and went to 5 OTU, Aston Down to convert to Blenheims. He joined 235 Squadron and became known by the nickname 'Moustique' (Mosquito). (*Andrew Bird*)

crank out a radio message to the RAF wireless transmitter station giving them the fix and advising them of their difficulties. At approximately 05.45 hours, a faint message was received from 'O-Orange'. A second distress signal was sent two minutes later, before the power was sapped; "Ditching . . ."

Dunn ditched into the rough sea; "it felt as if we'd hit a brick wall". Sergeants Gibbons, Saville and Riley huddled around the escape hatch just past the main spar and were thrown violently against either side of the flimsy fuselage; instinctively they hauled themselves out of the escape hatch as waves crashed against this new obstruction, breaking over the fuselage. Buffeted by the elements everyone successfully extracted themselves into their dinghy. Stuffed inside Irvin jackets was a Thermos flask, Verey pistol with spare cartridges and a packet of Huntley & Palmers biscuits which Sergeant Albert Gibbons had received from his parents in Slough, Berkshire, and had taken with him for nourishment on the flight. Now this one packet had to sustain five.

Pushing away from the sinking Whitley, in the moonlight Sergeant Colin Ripley pulled back his jacket sleeve to reveal a watch face. It was exactly 05.50 hours on the morning of September 24. The crew had been flying for seven hours fifty minutes and were 100 miles away from the English east coast. Ripley's wristwatch had stopped with the impact. The black of the sea rose and fell as waves tossed them around like a child's spinning top. Nineteen-year-old Allen leaned over the side of the dinghy and vomited. Dunn used the flask's cup to bail out water, but it was a futile task. They tried to lift each other's spirits. Sunrise was an hour away for these seafarers.

By 07.30 hours the first of over four dozen RAF machines had soared into the sky concentrating on their rescue. 'U-Uniform' piloted by 235's Gonay tracked back and forth over the given coordinates. Hebron and Cooper searched with their "eye balls", which required considerable concentration, looking for a yellow pinprick on the black sea below. There was no moment of contact or adrenalin rush. By 09.30 they had covered hundreds of square miles but had seen nothing that resembled a dinghy. Hebron recited, "I have fought a good fight. I have finished my course. I have kept the Faith" from 2 Timothy iv. 7, as their Blenheim turned about gaining height. The weather was noted as "growing worse" at 7,000 feet, with the machine still accelerating away at 230 mph towards The Wash. Height was then suitably lost as they approached the airfield. With the cowling gills almost closed Gonay pushed the hydraulic selector control downwards and the undercarriage value plunger handle to its down position. There was a slight sensation of shuddering before the flaps were lowered. Gonay was in full control of the machine as it slipped over the boundary and landed. Recording a landing time of 10.20 hours the Belgian wrote, "It was a fantastic experience to fly by oneself again".

By midday the sea conditions grew worse and the Whitley crew were being battered. Huge waves broke over them and the dinghy was swamped with water. They used their flying helmets to bail it out but still sat in five inches of water, their battle dress trousers wet through. For some the initial stages of hypothermia set in. Hundreds of square miles of sea were covered. The dinghy was one hundred miles off Hartlepool at 12.35 hours on September 24, but the sea was so rough that the high speed launch (HSL) was unable to withstand the pounding of the waves and fell foul, taking onboard lots of water.

Over the coming days and nights an array of aircraft were flown over the water; Hudsons, Ansons, Walruses and Blenheims from Kent, Norfolk, Dyce, Sumburgh and Hatston. The bunch of men in their yellow Mae Wests and yellow dinghy were not easily seen in the high seas, over which on most days a 30-50 mile an hour storm whipped the tops and them along. The crew was gradually succumbing to hypothermia. With only the faint shimmering of stars for company a second airman dropped into the water and disappeared as the water consumed him.

At dawn on the morning of September 26, after two days of searching, the new coordinates given were off Flamborough Head. The Whitley crew had travelled sixty miles, and as the Hudsons continued their search they encountered pairs of Heinkel 115s forcing them to flee into protective cloud layers, before being engaged again by 220 Squadron's Hudsons. "One rear gunner got off 500 rounds to good effect", was written on a combat report. 254 Squadron entered the search area from the north, sighting the dinghy at 12.00 hours near Flamborough Head. An Anson was then unable to locate the dinghy in the diminishing light. As they dived amongst the peaks and troughs to get a closer look their Perspex got splattered with sea salt.

A single Blenheim flown by Pilot Officer Sam McHardy from Sumburgh on the 'Bully Beef Run' to Dyce was called in to help. He recalled in his diary; "there was nothing but empty sea with big white breakers". Visibility was poor. Below in the dinghy one airman hung on but two bodies were stiff with the first stages of rigor mortis as another wave came crashing down. It looked hopeless. But the RAF found the dinghy on September 27 and from 14.00-17.30 hours the air force was determined not to lose it again, with 220 Squadron's Hudsons standing guard overhead. HMS *Ashanti* and *Bedouin* steamed in. Only Sergeant Ripley survived and was scooped from the dinghy in the stormy North Sea. All his remaining colleagues had perished. They had been drifting for eighty-four hours and had been carried ninety miles.

As units concentrated on rescues, offensive operations continued, stretching the breadth of Europe. Coastal's fighter Blenheims saw a crescendo of activity. Given the codename Bust, 236 Squadron was on a continual relay from 08.15 to 18.40 hours between Brest and Guernsey. Pilot Officer Graham Russell, with Pearson and Goldsmith went up in the afternoon and intercepted a Dornier 18. Thirty-five minutes into their operation, less than two miles away off Brest, Russell had spotted the distinctive silhouette flitting along the sea. He positioned himself for an attack, his observer Pearson recording "20 miles North of Brest at 16.14 hours". Graham approached from the starboard quarter and a burst of smoke rose from the rear engine. It slowed. He made a beam attack and within seconds 2,500 rounds had been discharged. Oblt zur See Hans-Dietrich Stelle piloting Dornier M2+EK lost control "and the enemy aircraft crashed into the sea immediately". Seawater flowed into the interior through the exposed holes. The forward bulkhead door was unable to stem the flow and it began to sink stern first as the four Luftwaffe crew hastily scrambled onto its upper wing. Two of the four began to inflate their dinghy. As the aircraft wing route was swamped by seawater Oblt Johannes Heuveldop and Fw Ewald Brasch used the wooden paddle to steady it as their comrades Stelle and Uffz Kahifeld climbed aboard. Their flying boat disappeared below. Unfortunately no one appeared to know what happened next to Heuveldop, Brasch, Kahifeld and Stelle. It was the shortest battle Graham remembered. Pilot Officer Stanley Nunn commented "it must have been like shooting at clay pigeon". One month later almost to the day the body of Hans-Dietrich Stelle was washed ashore at the sandy Church Cove, east of Lizard Rock, Cornwall.

Low-level oblique photograph taken from a Bristol Beaufort attacking shipping in St Peter Port, Guernsey. The aircraft was passing over St Julian's Pier at its junction with White Rock Pier. 236 Squadron when based at St Eval, Cornwall acted as fighter escort on similar raids against the Channel Islands in the summer of 1940. (*Captain James Inniss*)

At St Eval crews relaxed and sipped their tea. Two A Flight Blenheims of 248 Squadron flew out on reconnaissance to Norway, covering Stadtlandet to Lista. Flight Lieutenant Alan Pennington-Legh with his crew Herbert Sharman and Charles Wilcock climbed through some light cloud, being joined by Belfast-born Sergeant 'Ronny' Wright, who had taken off ten minutes earlier. With no departure from the route they usually took, to overcome the boredom Ronny checked his cockpit for the sixth time: oil pressure, oil temperature, hydraulic pressure, fuel state, oxygen, gun sight, everything was in order. Sergeant Ernest Mckie traversed his turret to make sure it was functioning too. With adrenalin pulsing, it suddenly occurred to his Devonshire observer Sergeant Edwin Watts that he'd never flown further than thirty miles out to sea before! A new challenge.

Then without warning the cloud cover dispersed ten miles from the Norwegian coast. Down below the sea had got greyer. The naval field glasses were pulled out of their blue pouch at the side of the observer's table. Wright recalled: "With our recent losses our observations were made from this distance, later I would edge nearer inland". Nearing Utbjoa Watts sighted a merchant vessel of 1,500 tons, which was stationary, except for the stern flag fluttering in the breeze. Using this as a marker Wright engaged the boost. With a sudden burst of power the Mercury engines propelled the three forward into battle. 'H-Harry' shed four 25 lb incendiary and three 20 lb fragmentation bombs but missed their intended target. "All I can say about this early attack is the seamen probably got a good shower."

Pennington-Legh and Wright both continued flying along a southerly track towards Egersund. Its deep harbour and sheltered location along an otherwise exposed coast made it a natural bolthole for merchant ships. Two vessels were watched sailing on a northwesterly course near Stabbsaedet Island by Pennington-Legh at 07.48 hours, one hour later Swedish fishing boats came into view, with hordes of seagulls trailing behind them. Their height was adjusted to 3,000 feet. They were edging away from Lista when suddenly to their left and approaching at speed came an "unidentified aircraft at 7 o'clock", but it disappeared into the nearest cloud. Pennington-Legh heaved 'Q-Queen' towards it at 08.38 hours but then the Blenheim reversed direction. This was their last sighting and both dropped down on to grass at 10.05 and 10.06 hours after a four-hour trip. Wright wrote in his logbook, "Attacked 4,000-ton ship".

Two days later, after feverish activity, Pilot Officers Sam McHardy, Clarence Bennett and Sergeant Kenneth Massy continued on convoy duty. McHardy covered the northern sector, Bennett the middle and Massy the southern, skirting around the merchantmen like border collies wagging their tails – waiting. Why didn't the Huns come into *our* sector?

Rainwater ran down the side of the fuselage over the RAF roundel and rhythmically dripped off into the abyss. Then, as if in slow motion, Mallah-born Australian Pilot Officer Clarence Bennett ran into a single Dornier 18 flying boat. Both fought it out over the North Sea. Their engagement began at 09.40 and saw 'G-George' dive from an altitude of 1,500 feet. It was like a cavalry charge with weapons bared. Bennett watched the Dornier's tail rushing towards him, it grew in his ring sight until at four hundred yards he fired, closing to within thirty yards; "tracer seen to enter wings and near engine nacelle". Suddenly bursts of black smoke came from the Dornier; "no definite damage observed". Bennett pulled the control stick to starboard and broke away having fired a continuous burst of 600 rounds. But 'G-George' was not out of harm's way and the Dornier's gunner seized the moment. A steady burst of accurate fire ripped through the lower port underside. Bullets splayed into the cockpit, one tearing into Clarence's right trouser leg, grazing his calf. His observer, nineteen-year-old Sergeant Gordon Clarke was hit in the shoulder. There was a series of violent bumps and then they were gone.

Immediately there was a heavy smell of aviation fuel within the cockpit and nose. Bennett made a visual check of the fuel gauges, but noticed nothing out of the ordinary. Height was gained and they levelled off at 4,000 feet. Sergeant George Brash in the rear turret was unable to see fuel flowing from either wing. With an unseen fuel leak there was no use hanging around. It was time to head home.

As he went down to 2,000 feet the Dornier was still flying low along the water's edge. 'G-George' fled in a westerly direction and after some adjustments Bennett, Clarke and Brash crept back to Sumburgh, landing at 10.31 hours. On inspection they found the port tank was completely empty and a right tyre punctured. They landed a little before McHardy and Massy and while 'G-George's' crew were discussing their engagement Massy joined the circle, green with envy at the excited chatter. Bennett claimed a probable. Massy in 'Z-Zebra' wrote, "sighted Do 18 at 10.10 which immediately took evasive action and turned into cloud for cover".

It was during the evening that Bennett learnt that his quarry Dornier K6+JK of 2./406 had become a water-logged hulk and had to be abandoned before it sank. Its crew took to their dinghy and were rescued unhurt. This Coastal Command squadron, flushed with success from the previous day, could not resist another crack, but the closest they came was when Flight Lieutenant Roger Morewood sighted a Short Sunderland.

Most sorties passed without incident, "but interceptions on our 'Tomato Run' did happen", wrote Sergeant Norman Price to his parents in Reading, Berkshire. Sergeant George Spiers scanned the skies, as in the confines of his turret the humidity increased. Pilot Officer George Melville-Jackson brought 'E-Edward' to within 2,500 feet of the water, heading for Lizard Point. So far it had been an uninteresting Bust sortie and they were now on their return leg. Fifteen miles from their destination at 08.58, everything changed. Spiers sighted a Junkers 88 coming up behind and quickly engaged with his Vickers machine gun. Hearing the sound of outgoing gunfire, Melville-Jackson tried to communicate but at this vital moment the intercom failed. The pilot shoved 'E-Edward' into a tight turn, but failed to see the enemy aircraft as he came out somewhat disorientated.

A Heinkel He 115 on fire and trailing smoke, photographed by the observer. He 115s often fell victim to the Blenheim fighter's belly pack four 0.303 Browning machine guns. (*Andrew Bird*)

Fellow combatant Pilot Officer Stanley Nunn in 'L-Leather' was off later, patrolling Ushant to Guernsey. He sighted two large and four small merchantmen travelling at 12 knots near the island of Bréhat, one mile off the northern coast of Brittany. Then a previously unseen Heinkel 115 alerted Nunn, Wild and Sheridan to its presence when its glazed canopy momentarily caught the sunlight. With levers pulled Nunn commenced an attack; 1,000 rounds burst forth and the He 115 fled inland towards Brittany. Stanley commented; "it was an inconclusive result, the bugger ran away".

Two days later 'K-King' had a brief bust-up with nine Bf110s off Ushant at 16.49 hours. Sergeant Percy 'Reg' Smith headed southwest using evasive action back towards the Cornish coast. "It was definitely a game, I managed to shake them off 17 minutes away from our base", Reg said as his report was written up. "Sergeant Arthur Pipper was invaluable, his constant intercom chatter certainly helped me with the evasive action."

The Sunday Express on September 29 recorded Sir Winston Churchill sending a message of congratulations to Fighter Command on the results of the previous day. But there was no respite. With quite diverse roles Pilot Officers Henri Gonay (N3530), James Kirkpatrick (Z5741) and Leon Prevot (L9252) flew a Danish sweep, whilst in the evening on 236 Squadron Flying Officer Bill Moore with his observer Pilot Officer Herbert Capstick in 'P-Pip', Pilot Officer Alan Lees in 'E-Edward' and Pilot Officer Charles Roman in 'N-Nuts' took off at 17.30 to escort "or rather shepherd" the Waterford-Fishguard mail boat. "Despite a sweep back and forth across the water at 1,000 feet the Great Western mail boat could not be contacted." They returned at 19.05 as the weather deteriorated,

235 Squadron Bircham Newton, October 5, 1940. Some of the aircrew pose for the photograph taken from the port wing of N3530. Left to right: Adjutant Flying Officer Pinnock; Pilot Officer 'The Mole' Martin; Pilot Officer Shorrocks; Sergeant Hall; Sergeant Westcott; Sergeant Ricks; Sergeant Naish. (Front) Squadron Leader Clarke; Pilot Officer Javaux; Pilot Officer Kirkpatrick. (*Andrew Pinnock*)

sighting only small commercial traffic travelling towards Clonmel, in County Tipperary, Ireland. Sweeping round the Cornish coast they came in over Portland; "below us, like a model, lay a sunken ship standing in shallow waters, half submerged". It was soon behind them and the aerodrome appeared. That night and all next day nothing much was seen. The sea swell remained high. Like a gull coming to rest the Blenheim fighter glided down and skimmed along the grass.

By the end of September there had been no further news of Peter Wickings-Smith, Bill Green or Little Watts, good men who were greatly missed. There was a car to be sold, believed to have belonged to Watts. Four pounds was the offer, four of the squadron's junior officers put in one pound each. Before buying everyone wanted a test drive. "It was a Standard Ten in very good condition", said Pilot Officer Joe Chamberlain, "we decided on a trip to Southsea and Portsmouth. On the way back we called in at The Crown Inn at Emsworth. For some reason Pimms was suggested. We eventually arrived at The Cut Loaf nightclub in Southsea as time was called." The stove was alight when they returned to the dispersal hut, all agreeing it was thermals and greatcoat weather. Another day completed and survived.

CHAPTER NINE

Fringes of the Fleet

"As our weeks went by one month slipped into another, we carried out more and more sorties across the North Sea to Norway. With the nature of our work," said Sam McHardy, "we were very vulnerable to enemy fighters, therefore we prayed each time we went over that there would be adequate cloud cover available to escape into if it got rough."

An afternoon sortie resulted in 'U-Uniform' climbing into the northern air in excitement. McHardy steered it over the peat-covered hills in the direction of Bergen at 12.20 hours, causing two cyclists below to stumble into a wall. They found there was a fair amount of cloud around above them and occasionally isolated clouds that went higher than 7,000 feet. "I had landed myself the task of photographing Sognefjord on this sortie with Sergeants Sims and Wilcock. Sims' navigation was spot on, making landfall near Askvoll, but I could not get 'U-Uniform' into the fjord as the visibility was down to 100 yards."

McHardy opened the throttle and climbed, flying above the weather. Suddenly a gap appeared with water below.

"I did a steady descent and found myself in Sognefjord. Positioning our Blenheim in the middle of the fjord I then flew right up under the cloud as though we were in a tunnel, until I reached the furthest end. There was barely enough room to do a turn. At one point 'U-Uniform' stood on her tail in the enclosed area doing another turn, by which time my compass was spinning, a couple more probes and I found my flying unimpeded. The compass settled down and I made it and set off towards the mouth of the fjord."

Turning to port 'U-Uniform' flew down towards Bergen, hugging the contours of the leads that afforded them cover. Sims sighted one merchantman of 3,000 tons one mile from Bergen at 15.00 hours travelling in a northerly direction. It was very distinctive with two masts, a funnel and a German flag. Twenty minutes later the crew came face to face with an armed merchantman perched on the rocks with its cargo being man-handled to a waiting tender. It didn't look half as menacing, holed and dented as it was. In fact it was rather pathetic, its weapons dismounted with barrels drooped in a defeatist way.

"The weather was getting filthy and we had an excruciatingly uncomfortable journey back to the Shetland Islands in pouring rain and hail stones. Back in the mess I learnt that my friend Alan Pennington-Legh was departing to take up a new command. We had formed a close

Aircrew 'scrambling' towards three Blenheim Mark IVFs of a 236 Squadron Royal Air Force detachment at Aldergrove in August 1940. Take-off was within three minutes, a similar time to their monoplane counterparts the Hurricane and Spitfire. (*Andrew Bird via Brad King*)

friendship right from the start at Hendon a year previously, which now seemed a lifetime away. I'd also been fortunate to stay with his parents in Poole, Dorset."

It meant promotion for the New Zealander to lead A Flight. "Our flight office consisted of a tent on a sand dune furnished with a chair, trestle table and a bucket of sand, the latter as a substitute for a fire extinguisher. On the table was the Flight Authorization Book and two wicker trays one 'In' the other 'Out' and that was it!"

For those not on 'state' the afternoon had been spent sitting around, smoking, bathing, reading and feeling frustrated. Pennington-Legh was making plans for his twenty-four hour leave. However, there was bad news to contend with; 'J-Johnnie' R3626, flown by Pilot Officer Clarence Bennett, Sergeants Gordon Clarke and George Brash were 'overdue'. They had flown out on an instruction from Group which had been sanctioned by the commanding officer Victor Streatfield. In view of the weather fellow Australian Flying Officer Lewis Hamilton regarded it as quite incredible that the operation had gone ahead. R3626 went into the murk and on this day they didn't come back. Hamilton wrote to Clarence's family in Torrensville, South Australia:

"Bennett asked me to 'look after things' if he did not come back from one of his flights. Shortly before his disappearance, Bennett had attacked an enemy machine and was injured in one leg by return fire. He had to break off action because of a shortage of fuel. This time he left to do a sticky job by himself, and since then we have heard no more. We in the squadron have great faith that he will be reported as a prisoner of war. So don't give up hope."

Flying Officer Sam McHardy said, "I was greatly saddened, poor Bennett hadn't lasted long, his loss was attributed to the shocking visibility in the fjord. Just as had happened to me, though with more tragic results."

For some there was a break in flying. Two chartered a fishing boat, sailing to the outlying island of Foula to watch puffins. Another dozen officers made their way along the single-track road in a 'Tilly' towards Lerwick. Pilot Officer Elger steered "which wasn't great for those of us in the back", whilst his observer Warren made sure that the transport didn't hit the dry stone walling. The light was fading as they drove along the Sea Road into Lerwick, Warren guiding them to Commercial Street.

The three-storey granite Queen's Hotel was a welcome bolthole, recommended by Hal Randall. All paid their one shilling and six pence and had the regulation five inches of water in the bath. Once refreshed everyone opted for the fish supper, washed down with a glass of shandy.

Just before 04.00 hours on Wednesday, October 2 Flight Lieutenant 'Pam' Stickney's batman had built a welcoming fire in his shared room, with the wooden blackout board held in place by two planks. The flames danced and flickered in the darkened room, its furniture casting large shadows. His batman brought him a hot, black sweet tea in the usual white RAF-crested mug. Washing and shaving using an enamelled bowl, he pulled on his clothes. Barely awake Stickney walked to the dispersal hut, in the distance came a muted sound of a motor launching in the direction of Chichester's bustling marina. Stickney settled down in a chair, glancing at the notice board he read a sign advising that the toilet had broken, someone had scrawled: 'Please use the hedge – for those with tiddlers – beware of seagulls'.

The early hours passed. In the dispersal hut Sergeant George McLeod raised his fork and glanced around. The place was quiet as everyone ate breakfast and McLeod noticed a new face in the crowd. Pilot Officer John Keard from Sidcup, Kent looked about seventeen years of age even though he'd had the seniority since July 21, 1940. Joining 59 Squadron for a couple of hours on the morning of September 11, John lugged his battered brown leather suitcase across the 'drome to join 235, arriving in time for lunch. The adjutant wrote: "A likeable fellow, posted in quickly to fill the gaps in our ranks".

Keard desperately wanted to fight and almost got his chance that afternoon, with McLeod flying 'A-Ace' on a fighter escort job. Flying in an orderly but fairly loose formation 1,500 feet above 'Y-Yorker' of 59 Squadron they had some clouds for protection and reported sighting four destroyers near Barfleur at 14.55 hours with an estimated speed of 30 knots, being escorted by three Messerschmitts. Flying in the second Blenheim flown by Basil Quelch, Keard made further sightings near Barfleur at 15.30 hours. Then a laden merchantman was sighted at 19.00 hours just entering Le Havre. 'Y-Yorker' roared in, totally committed. As Pilot Officer Matthew flew in at 250 mph he realized with masts looming at the same height he was going to be very lucky indeed to make it so with skillful adjustment he made a second run at 19.09 from 3,000 feet, dropping four 250 lb GP bombs. All burst wide. Light flak hosed up into silent blossoms that faded quickly. Soon the formation swept over Thorney Island. After which; "we spread out very slightly and came in, a dark stain was etched on the perimeter" wrote Quelch. "Back at dispersal I learnt about Flight Lieutenant Pam Stickney. He had trundled along in N3838 at 17.44, ready to lead our fighters off." Opening throttles with a flourish of power he roared away smashing into an unseen tractor which had been proceeding down the perimeter track. Within an instant its twenty-year-old driver died of multiple injuries. Stickney and his crew walked away with minor bruising. As a result of this accident the Ministry of Works officer at Thorney erected two further warning boards "to try and discourage drivers from crossing the take-off/landing strip".

In northeast Scotland pilots at readiness were ordered to scramble in the afternoon. As the sound of engines burst into life, convoy protection duty beckoned for nineteen-year-old Sergeant Albert Johnstone. Airborne within three minutes he was soon watching the shoal of merchantmen near Kinnaird Head as his Blenheim R3629 trawled back and forth west to east. In the middle Sergeant Charles Rose guided R3888 back across, whilst Pilot Officer Alfred Tyler cut the corner, edging nearer Rose. Then below at eleven o'clock and six o'clock three faint green smudges appeared: Heinkels. Johnstone raised the alarm at 19.00 hours and minutes later white plumes of water shot upwards as bombs straddled the convoy, falling short of their target "which appeared to be the largest merchantman in the convoy". Rose engaged the 100-octane fuel, flicking R3888 sharply to the left and reducing height, he could see properly now; they were Heinkel 115 seaplanes. With his eyes glued to one flying at fifty feet he latched onto its stern.

The pilot, Oblt Gottfried Lenz, weaved like a minnow. Within twenty seconds Rose fired two bursts. Rounds splayed out as R3888 surged to within 150 yards, dispensing 2,000 rounds. His guns stopped as his 0.303 rounds were seen going into the port engine, which caught alight. Its oil tank exploded as Rose turned his gun button to 'safe'. His vision was then obscured by oil from the seaplane which was liberally spread over the Perspex, "having the consistency of treacle".

With his guns empty, there was no use hanging about so Rose broke away. The fabric of Tyler's four Brownings was ripped open, 250 bullets reached out like exploring fingers but were unable to grasp hold. L9176 was rocked furiously around for a port beam attack, closing to within 100 yards. Tyler began to fire and there was a brief twinkling of lights as 450 rounds hit Lenz's machine which "hit the sea a few seconds later". As the Heinkel became unresponsive Lenz curved away and attempted to land. At 19.14 hours the structure, weakened by gunfire, appeared to break up and the port float detached itself. In its unsteady state it started to sink. Lenz, Uffz R Schweetke and Ogfr H Neuberg were picked up by a naval destroyer escorting the convoy. What remained of S4+BH disappeared below the waves at 20.10 hours.

This air battle was not over. 13 Group fighters joined the party in fevered enthusiasm at 19.24 hours. As R3629 attacked one of the two remaining Heinkel seaplanes "bullets were seen to enter the Heinkel but no definite damage was observed". The naval escort then fired at 'M-Monkey' R3629 but no damage or injury was incurred. Unfortunately between 19.26 and 19.30 hours it was engaged dispassionately by individual Hawker Hurricanes of B Flight Green Section, 145 Squadron believing it to be a Junkers 88. 254 Squadron's diary reads: "Attacked again by a Hurricane, notwithstanding signals with Verey light, Aldis lamp and navigation lights being used", still the three came.

Normally wrongly captioned as 235 Squadron, this is a fine study of 254 Squadron in-flight echelon starboard. (*Royal Air Force Museum, London*)

Johnstone's pilot, Sergeant Albert Tubbs, had everything straining and shaking whilst shrieking expletives as 'friendly' rounds seared through the rear fuselage, one 0.303 going through the air gunner's left hand. Tubbs finally got away from the "lemming-like compulsion" at 19.32 and made for Montrose. The aircraft's undercarriage gave way at 20.25 from damage sustained from the Hurricane attack at 19.26. Sergeant William Constable in a letter to the injured Albert Johnstone described what happened after he had transferred to the 'blood wagon':

"We arrived in the de-briefing room and spent an hour telling our story to an incredulous intelligence officer. How we had all survived was close to a miracle. We walked around the airfield to where our Blenheim R3629 lay in the grass with propeller tips curved, looking a sorry state. Rounds had torn away the struts and radius rods, there were twelve to fifteen bullet holes between your turret and starboard wing. The station commander was there and he shook his head in disbelief surveying the damage."

Amid a lot of chatter 13 Group claimed that Belgian Pilot Officer Baudouin de Hemptinne shot down a He 115. Senior officers with Coastal Command's 18 Group were not happy. An hour later Flight Lieutenant Robert Bungey, B Flight flight commander, confronted him with a stern face: "De Hemptinne, you've just shot down a Blenheim fighter!" The South African tackled John McConnell and Peter 'Stunning Black' Dunning-White who made up Green Section, pale and in distress. The three asked him to explain. Squadron Leader Harold Hoskins joined them and out it flowed.

"A Blenheim fighter of Hoskins' unit had been attacked, the rear gunner wounded and hospitalized and the three of us were up at the time, the obvious culprits. Bungey exploded with Baptist righteous indignation, as if delivering a sermon from the pulpit. The culmination was two hours of aircraft recognition. In the turmoil of events, such incidents were soon forgotten."

Later in the evening as the mist came in, a report was typed on a 1930s Remington Rand: "Pilot Officer de Hemptinne intercepted and is thought to have shot down one of three Heinkel 115 at 19.20 hours, 5 miles southeast of Kinnards Head". Tubbs did not receive an apology from 145 either at Montrose or Dyce and his acquaintance with their senior non-commissioned officers cooled for a time.

Between sorties training continued. 'Bombing practice' was repeatedly penned in flying logbooks as the release, trajectory and placement onto a moving target was drilled into aircrews. An example illustrating ineptitude in this area was brought to the attention of Commander-in-Chief Bowhill at an air staff meeting in Whitehall:

"Blenheim 'Z-Zebra' attacked a small coasting steamer of 800 tons 10 miles off Utvaer Light, speed an estimated 8 knots at 03.34 hours. The steamer was flying the Nazi flag on the aft deck. Aircraft fired 500 rounds from the belly pack. Tracer was seen to enter bridge but no damage was observed. When last seen, the steamer was zig-zagging in an easterly direction. Two merchant ships were then sighted at 08.20 hours off the Norwegian coast, and were dive-bombed from 5,000 feet to 200 feet releasing four 20 lb HE and four 25 lb incendiary bombs. Owing to the angle of attack no direct hits registered, but very near misses."

To help overcome this Bowhill told those assembled around the table: "RAF Catfoss has already transferred from Flying Training Command to Coastal Command. The formation of 2 Operational

Training Unit on the station would train crews for the Blenheim squadrons of the Command." Air Vice-Marshal David Donald commented: "It will be administered by 17 Group Coastal Command, three plus one spare Blenheim Mk I and six plus two spare Blenheim Mk IVs have been procured". As a consequence all Blenheim aircraft had been deleted from the establishment of 1 OTU Silloth. During this intense four-hour discussion it was decided that no Coastal Command Blenheim fighter squadrons would be re-armed with the Blackburn Botha due to its performance. The meeting closed and the officers then dispersed, Bowhill being driven away in an Austin 10 Cambridge, which trundled through the streets passing heavily damaged buildings. The capital was so obviously near the edge. He entered Northwood beneath darkening blue skies, frozen, but in a good mood.

Spirits were high in Sumburgh. There was an ENSA party in the mess and New Zealander Pilot Officer Alfred Fowler that night drank whisky and dark ale, which were the only drinks available. The room started to move around and Hal Randall said that Fowler was talking nonsense. Sam McHardy helped him to retire.

Alfred was on an early show, which took off a little before 07.00 hours. The weather was fair but blustery with enormous cloud formations moving at a steady pace. These dispersed miles out from Norway as 'U-Uniform' of 248 Squadron out on routine reconnaissance made landfall off Fedje. A Bf109E was sighted twelve miles away. Evasive action was taken by the New Zealander, opening up to 250 mph in an attempt to reach land further south, but was prevented by lack of cloud. Alfred set course for base. It was a mundane flight back. Then, ninety miles from Sumburgh Head at 08.54 hours a single Dornier 17Z-2 was spotted flying near to sea level. Diving from 2,000 feet he positioned his aircraft within 400 yards for a stern attack. Tracer entered one of the two Daimler-Benz DB601 engines, fuselage and wing. 0.303 bullets pebble-dashed the interior, injuring Rudolf Heinrich, as the Dornier attempted to extract itself from the battle into cloud cover. The Blenheim's power-operated turret was swung to starboard, Sergeant Rourke brought his Vickers into operation, managing to get off some concentrated fire using 100 rounds whilst the machine was "skirting along the water at less than forty feet".

The remaining Daimler-Benz power unit struggled to gain height. At that moment Dornier pilot Lt Fritz Meinecke realized he was unable to reach the cloud layer, with his pursuer now within 200 yards. Behind him there was the sound of outgoing fire, this resolute return fire found its mark, hitting the Blenheim cockpit.

Instantly 7.92 mm rounds hit the Perspex, splintering into tiny fragments which embedded themselves in Alfred's and his observer Fenn's face and eyes. Temporarily blinded, his pilot fumbled to shut their starboard motor down "fearing an oil shortage". By 09.00 hours 'U-Uniform' was becoming unresponsive. Fearing that he might have to ditch, an SOS was sent out. For twenty-one minutes the fighter was coaxed along in a fragile state, before touching down at Sumburgh. Sam McHardy wrote: "Injuries sustained to pilot and observer – five or more large lacerations, with numerous shards of Perspex removed by Doc with a large pair of tweezers!"

Tuesday October 8 was uneventful in the early hours, until an RAF W/T intelligence station picked up a message that a German aircraft was down. Luftwaffe rescue aircraft had apparently been trying to locate the ditched machine, but were westwards of the site. At 06.20 three Blenheim fighters of 235 Squadron were in the air, dispatched to search for a missing Walrus. They were passed over to 11 Group and on instructions from a controller flew towards the Isle of Wight. They encountered patchy sea fog at 300 feet. With 'V' following the section, machines 'U' and 'S' sighted a Heinkel 59 positioned 240° St Catherine's Point 18 miles at 08.50 hours. They immediately fired but this had a galvanizing effect and the Heinkel turned purposefully towards the lower layer of a massive cloud. From the starboard beam Pilot Officer John Fenton in 'U-Uniform' got nearer; "I fired again, this time from closer range at 150 yards. The rounds hit the engine."

The Heinkel dropped its nose towards the water before it began to level out, then return fire from the rear cockpit came flicking in 'U-Uniform's direction. Pilot Officer Henri Gonay saw John draw away, preparing for a renewed attack, as the Belgian opened his throttles racing in for a head-on quarter attack.

With little protection 0.303 rounds chewed into its engine, radiator and Lt zur See Stelzner, his upper torso collapsing over his control column. The aircraft dived vertically into the sea, smashing up on impact. Like

Telegram wired from Thorney Island to their commanding officer 'Ronnie' Clarke at Bircham Newton, Norfolk October 1940. (*Chris Goss*)

vultures both RAF aircraft circled overhead. In the water below two floats were visible with other debris of TW+HH. Silence followed. Hebron clutched his face in pain, injured during the last engagement when a Perspex pane shattered, a piece embedding into one of his eyes. Gonay headed off immediately.

Pilot Officer Leon Prevot on his lone patrol heard his friend's excitement when in front of him an aircraft was seen moving quickly from left to right, a mile away and slightly below. It took him perhaps half a minute to catch up, by which time Sergeant Albert Michiels was noting down its position as "155° Portland Bill 24 miles". The Heinkel (incorrectly identified as a 59) laboured on across the open wastes of the English Channel, searching for his ditched compatriot. Heightened by the thrill of the chase Leon fired off 250 rounds but his quarry disappeared into cloud. "Were we going to lose the Hun?" Albert and Sergeant George Keel in the rear turret began straining their eyes "in an effort to locate the blighter", the squadron periodical recalls.

Lt zur See Schulz managed to momentarily lose his pursuer and edging out of the cloud DA+MJ dropped until less than fifty feet above the water. Uffz Stargnet shouted a warning and Schulz pushed the stick forward, now about twenty feet above the waves. A wake streamed out behind them which guided the Blenheim in. It was now 200 yards behind and being twisted by the invisible hand of the machine's slipstream.

There was an exchange of fire between the Heinkel 59's rear gunner and Prevot. Pressing the 'fire' button a long burst streamed out from dead astern and the rear gunner fell silent, then all at once smoke appeared. With a growing trail of smoke the float-plane lurched forwards and disappeared into the sea in an enormous flurry of white spray. No wreckage was seen of DA+MJ.

That evening George Keel went to his room and cut from *Flight Magazine* a half page feature on the Heinkel 60 float-seaplane and Heinkel 111. He wrote '8th October, 1940' in black fountain pen

Twenty-year-old air gunner George Keel was posted missing together with his colleagues on the afternoon of October 9, 1940. His body was later washed ashore and buried in Southsea. (*Ray Bullen*)

on a slip of paper and glued all three items into his scrap book before going to bed at 10.00 p.m. He was on the 'fly list' for the next day.

With heavy squalls drifting over southern England on October 9, Fighter Command pilots were at a disadvantage in their continual efforts to harry the Luftwaffe. "We were off at 12 p.m. the next day. Within three minutes the Germans were taking liberties again!" The flight wasn't very long but upon landing after this aerodrome protection patrol Pilot Officers Joe Chamberlain, James Kirkpatrick and Sergeant Rene Demoulin were ordered up to act as fighter escort.

The skies above the Channel and European coast were more dangerous than ever. "Luftwaffe fighters were operating on free hunts", recalled B Flight's Norman Jackson-Smith, " and their numbers ranged from a single 109, to half a dozen or so to a swarm of 200 plus". One Blenheim of 59 Squadron, 'W-William', was tasked to fly an armed reconnaissance sweep off Le Havre. As the bomber began climbing up into the sky the three escorts 'V', 'S' and 'U' left at 16.30 hours, positioning themselves slightly higher and off to starboard. Nearing the French port height was then reduced to 500 feet. Moored in the Bassin de L'Eure at 17.10 hours were six merchantmen with tonnage ranging from 500 to 1,000 tons. Within three minutes four 250 lb GP bombs straddled the deep-water quay, but results were unseen. 'W-William' turned for home but curving in pursuit was a single yellow-nosed Messerschmitt.

The air gunner's eyes in the rear turret focused on the monoplane and registering the 109 he shouted a warning of "Messerschmitt!" into the intercom. Fortunately the pilot managed to escape into a layer of cloud but before the tail was engulfed the 109 was seen to engage their fighter escort. Hptmn Otto 'Otsch' Bertram flying 'Weiß 1' had stumbled upon the escort in a tight vic. Bertram pressed down on his gun button and pumped out rounds astern at 17.23 hours. To his amazement bits of aircraft started to fall off from the starboard machine. Bright flashes sped towards 'U-Uniform' on the starboard side. Sergeant Francois Venesoen seated in the rear turret returned fire but only twenty rounds were ejected before the Vickers jammed; he made hand gestures about his predicament towards Chamberlain in 'V-Vic' on the portside.

Otsch Bertram adjusted his firing position and sprayed rounds liberally towards 'S-Sugar' and 'V-Vic', where Pilot Officer Ernest Phillips, acting as air gunner on this sortie, disgorged 100 rounds at the Messerschmitt, it was then seen to peel off to starboard. All three kept together on the homeward run, with no appearance of trouble but when thirty miles south of the English coast 'S-Sugar' N3530 was seen to lose height slowly from 3,000 feet. He then went into clouds; "the remaining two aircraft

Hptmn Otto Bertram flying 'Weiß 1' claimed 'S-Sugar' N3530 with pilot Flt/Lt James Kirkpatrick and observer Sgt 'Taff' Thomas posted as missing. (*Chris Goss*)

followed him down but lost sight going through the clouds and were unable to find any trace of his aircraft on the sea below the cloud base", said Squadron Leader Ronnie Clarke. "It is difficult to understand how the other two machines failed to locate them after an extensive search." It wasn't easy, as Joe Chamberlain reported; "Hunting in the clouds was difficult, unfortunately I saw nothing".

Both remaining machines were on the ground by 18.00 hours after this difficult operation. Adjutant Charles Pinnock arrived at the dispersal asking for accounts. Within the hour fellow Belgian, Henri Gonay was airborne flying a "20-mile radius around Le Havre", with his observer Pilot Officer Steve Hebron and Sergeant Robert White searching the area for debris or a dinghy. Upon landing at 19.30 hours they reported "no sign of aircraft".

It was a serious blow. Henri went to the room he had shared with James, everything looked exactly the same, James' Ever Ready safety razor tin box next to the hand basin, the white towel hung out the window, polished shoes ready for his evening in the mess. "But he was dead now", noted Henri, "I could not get out of my mind that we had been laughing and joking with Rene earlier and he was now lying in the Blenheim on the floor of the English Channel". Despite the day's events, the letter that Chamberlain wrote home that evening contained no mention of his aerial duel, concentrating instead on the "grand fellows" he flew with.

The next morning Robert Jamison wrote:

"James Kirkpatrick had been a popular, unassuming man. Glamorgan-born 'Taff' Thomas enjoyed choral singing at our Sunday church service."

He was then called to the telephone. It was young wireless operator/air gunner George's mother wondering if there was any news. Robert had to tell her there was no further news and that his commanding officer would be writing to her.

"It seemed awful", said Sergeant Geoff Brazier. "I'd just arrived and being in the same room as Jamison I was seeing for the first time the distress and unhappiness that casualties caused."

It had been a miserable two days for Mrs Gertrude Keel in Trevor Road, Southsea, following the delivery of a postal telegram confirming her eldest son was missing. On Friday, October 11 she received a sympathetic letter from his commanding officer Squadron Leader Ronnie Clarke;

"All aircraft carry a rubber dinghy for use if they are brought down in the sea. There is a small chance that this crew may be safe and picked up . . . George Keel had not been with the squadron for very long and this was one of his first trips into the danger area . . . Although he had not been with us long, your son, with his quiet, unassuming nature and cheerfulness, had become popular with all who knew him."

Sergeant Geoff Brazier BEM, in front of Blenheim IVF of 235 Squadron, Bircham Newton, December 1940. (*Geoff Brazier*)

But by dusk there had been no news from the Royal Navy MTBs who were operating near the position. They later learnt that George Keel had been found. Poor George. Someone said his body was washed ashore at Fishing Beach, Selsey just before 14.00 hours on October 21. Later a telephone message from the local police constabulary to Ronnie Clarke notified him that one of his airmen had been found. Ronnie later identified the body of Sergeant George Keel and informed his mother, signing the death certificate to release the body. Seven days later the twenty year old was buried with full military honours at Highland Road Cemetery, Southsea. The quiet, charming, courteous George, so gentle and un-warlike in nature and appearance.

For several days after October 11 there was constant aerodrome protection over Thorney Island. The Flights flew two or three times, but intercepted nothing. During the same period 236 Squadron, under Fighter Command operations, continually scrambled and were vectored from St Eval and Aldergrove where 236 Squadron now operated a flight of Blenheims on rotation, only to find the enemy had flown. Their diarist recorded: "once again no enemy aircraft seen, so returned to base in failing light".

Three Blenheim fighters, T1811, T1806 and R3886 scrambled to intercept enemy Dornier 17s. After wandering about over Land's End for some fifteen minutes Pilot Officers Leonard DeJace, Graham Russell and George Melville-Jackson of Blue Section grew thoroughly bolshie with their controller. The sea mist came in and DeJace flying 'W-William' decided everyone should return and spent the next seventeen minutes trying to find St Eval. Eventually the watch office got everyone landed safely. A German meteorological flight westwards of Ushant reported having seen an English Blenheim fighter plane. It was flown by New Zealander Pilot Officer Joseph Watters; 'V-Vic' T1945 pursued the Dornier southwest of Lizard, but no contact was made "due to the enemy's greater speed".

248 Squadron's activities remained the same as the poor weather in the northwest marked a change of temperature. "We continued as before, in no way disheartened or lacking in confidence", Simms wrote. "Our colleagues were off between 07.00-07.55 hours on the morning of October 20, in fine weather conditions." These colleagues were Pilot Officers John Dodd in 'L-London', Archibald Hill in 'Y-Yorker' and Maurice Baird in 'X-X-ray'.

Dodd, a former chartered accountant, did one circuit of the 'drome before setting off for the routine patrol area known as 'S.A.1(e)'. Dodd took the north track, Hill flew the middle track and both had returned within five minutes of each other at 09.45 and 09.50 hours respectively.

Still out covering the Norwegian seascape was 'X-X-ray' P6952. Visibility was fair at fifteen miles when a Dornier 18 popped up in front, its two-tone green camouflage scheme rendering it hard to see. The Hun was no doubt horrified by the sight of the Blenheim fighter. After some persistent stalking Baird "reported engaging enemy aircraft at 09.00 hours" from astern with flashes all over the wing like fairy lights from long bursts. Suddenly there was a puff of dark smoke and pieces fell off. Six minutes later the enemy aircraft was reported to be in the sea in position "264° Utsire Light 84 miles" with the crew in a dinghy. Baird took his thumb off the button and swiftly moved the rudder to the right. At roughly 09.35 hours all communication ceased from P6952. 18 Group WAAF radio operator Ellen Watts did not intercept any more R/T traffic, her controller writing: "uncertain as to what has happened".

One hundred and thirty-five miles away, one of three Bf109Es half rolled down towards the single Blenheim fighter. Lt Heinrich Setz began playing a fascinating game of cat and mouse. For a further thirty-five minutes the Blenheim stayed aloft. Air gunner Sergeant Stanley Wood tried to keep him at bay but his "single pea-shooter was useless". Briefly he felt a dull pain "like a punch in a boxing match", then he saw his flying boot turning red. In spite of having a bullet go through one foot he kept up a steady rate of fire. Baird, with his compass swirling, instead of heading for Sumburgh, flew in the opposite direction. There was no escape now, at roughly thirty-seven miles west of Haugesund P6952 presented itself as a target and was shot at several times.

At 10.07 Lt Heinrich Setz fired a volley of rounds into the starboard engine setting it alight. Flames licked from the cowling, Baird feathered the propeller. Smoke billowed along the inner wing, entering into the central fuselage. Conditions worsened and impeded the New Zealander's visibility, despite Sergeant Richard Copcutt opening the sliding windows. Baird pushed the stick as hard forward as it would go, levelling off at about sixty feet. They were now flying blind at 150 mph in a bullet-riddled machine. In the rear Wood placed their dinghy nearer the escape hatch for a quick exit. Getting lower, Sergeants Copcutt, Burton and Wood got into their crash positions as their pilot felt for the surface.

Then they hit the water; "it was like being slammed into a brick wall". The airframe came to a grinding halt and the force of the impact caused Copcutt and Burton to be thrown about, knocking themselves out and rendering them unconscious. Instantly the Blenheim began to fill with cold green water through the nose and countless bullet holes: "I remember sitting in the cockpit and everything was turning bright green. I was fascinated by the stillness of it all." Baird freed himself of his Sutton harness and parachute. Stretching up with both hands he forced the hatch open above his seat. Further down the

Douglas Burton together with Baird and Wood was plucked from the sea by a Heinkel 59. (*John Burton*)

machine Stanley had acted quickly; "just as we'd done countless times in practice drills". The escape hatch swung open. Gasping for air he pushed out the dinghy, then himself. His foot hurt like hell.

Suddenly three 109s hurtled past. Hunched on the starboard wing with the dinghy Stanley raised a hand. Lt Heinrich Setz of II./JG77 had finally got his second kill. Then there was complete silence, except for water lapping against the side as the dinghy was launched. Inside the machine Baird pushed himself into the darkening water, reaching out and grabbing hold of Douglas. In his efforts he swallowed a great deal, yet his mind in this crisis worked clearly and calmly in the confined space. He succeeded in easing and floating the New Zealander out but his struggle to save his crew was by no means over. It was torturous. Baird tried to retrieve his observer Richard who was still unconscious but was unable to rescue him before the whole aircraft was submerged. Richard's thick flying clothing were completely saturated and weighed him down, and he disappeared into the blackness.

Maurice Baird's efforts to help his crew escape the sunken machine had naturally used up much of his strength. The waves kept washing over him, as he quickly climbed into the rubber dinghy and Stanley pushed away. Douglas Burton regained consciousness as the other two paddled. Seated in the flooded dinghy they were all wet through and freezing cold as they paddled against the current. Looking up at the sound of an approaching aircraft they were greeted by the vision of a Heinkel 59. The open cockpit biplane did one circuit then landed, the backwash from the floats nearly causing the rubber dinghy to flip over. Baird, Burton and Wood were plucked from certain death by He 59 BV+HH of Seenotflugkdo 5 and then landed at Stavanger. Wood and Burton were taken away to a Stavanger hospital for treatment of their wounds.

Two-hundred and thirty-one miles away 18 Group ordered a "search for the crew of an enemy aircraft", led by Flying Officer Sam McHardy. Three crews were briefed to "fly a thirty-mile radius about position 278° Utsire Light 73 miles". At 10.40 hours 'V-Vic', 'H-Harry' and 'B-Beer' took off with instructions from headquarters of Coastal Command to "shoot up dinghy". An SOS message had been intercepted, an attempted rescue by seaplane was expected.

Pilot Officer Herbert Sharman rechecked the co-ordinates: 59°-10N /02°-10E, as his pilot McHardy in 'V-Vic' Z5956 led them toward the Norwegian coast. At 11.15 R/T silence was broken and with a crackle of static they heard: "Return to base, repeat, return to base". The operation had been rescinded. The plan to shoot up the dinghy had been countermanded by Air Vice-Marshal Charles Breese. There was an hour's pause in the proceedings.

Co-ordinates and calculations were worked out on a table, led by Squadron Leader Victor Streatfield. Their coverage was between position 060° Sumburgh 36 miles – Utsire Light 18 miles – 107° Utsire Light 9 miles – 251° Utsire Light 88 miles – 090° Fair Isles 30 miles.

Sam McHardy, Victor Ricketts and Anthony Garrad took off at 12.50, 12.55 and 13.00 hours. The Blenheim fighters split up. McHardy took the middle track with Ivor Sims in 'Y-Yorker', while former *Daily Express* aviation correspondent Victor Ricketts took Frank Thompson in 'B-Beer' on the northern track and Anthony Garrad was paired with Sergeant Ernest Bayliss in 'H-Harry' and flew the southern track. "There was no cloud cover on the run to the Norwegian coast, I felt quite naked in the beaming bright sunshine in hostile territory", said McHardy. Blinking into the sunlight 'Y-Yorker' and 'B-Beer' L9455 cruised around maintaining a high degree of alertness as the minutes dragged on. They returned without success.

Whilst heading back from the Norwegian coast Garrad saw off to port at 14.39 two Bf109Es 2,000 feet below. Instinctively the Luftwaffe machines curved upwards to attack on the port quarter. L9450 was engaged by two Bf109Es near Stavanger "255° Utsire Light 50 miles" at 14.40 hours. Taking evasive action both Mercury engines picked up speed but they seemed to be standing still. Garrad pulled the control stick back, putting both feet on the instrument panel to help the proceedings while behind him Bayliss opened fire from a range of 400 yards. Eighty rounds were discharged.

Thick white smoke was seen coming from the cockpit of one of the Bf109Es. Finally 'H-Harry' reached the cloud layer and their cover held for half a mile, until Garrad broke cover. Behind them a single enemy fighter piloted by Oblt B. Jung, quickly caught up and commenced an attack from 200 yards. Two short bursts were fired at the Blenheim before returning to the clouds. In the cockpit, Anthony Garrad's eyes flicked regularly over his instruments, surveying fuel amounts, temperatures and pressures. Crossing the North Sea the visibility was up to twenty miles and soon the Shetland Islands came into view. Joining the circuit 'H-Harry' came straight in at 16.45 hours.

After the excitement of the last seven months, October was proving to be mournful and miserable. Blenheim L9453 had also been lost. Pilot Officers 'Paddy' Gane, observer Maurice Green and air gunner Sergeant Norman Stock had not been heard from since taking off at 07.16 hours. Their fate unravelled. 'Z–Zebra' had flown out on reconnaissance

Pilot Officer Sydney 'Paddy' Gane had already been mentioned in despatches whilst on 248 Squadron. Then on October 20, 1940, he and his crew were shot down over Ballen Hemnefjord, north of Stamnesøya, Norway. He was brought ashore and buried at Stamnes farm before being moved to Trondheim in 1945. (*Castle House Museum Dunoon, Scotland*)

from Stadtlandet to Trondheim. As they reached the leads between Hitra and Snillfjord an eclectic mix of trees interspersed with brightly painted houses on either side. On a southerly course the Blenheim fighter was immediately pounced upon by two Bf109Es of 4./JG77. With both the element of surprise and favourable weather conditions Uffz Ludvic Fröba dispatched 'Z-Zebra' at 10.23 hours. The Blenheim spiralled earthwards. Gane managed to extract himself and bailing out proved to be no problem as he pitched clear. Pulling his ripcord ring the canopy blossomed and he began floating towards the water, but suddenly there was gunfire. An eyewitness recorded: "he was shot in the air". His limp body continued on its course as the pilotless Blenheim L9453 with Green and Stock still onboard impacted and broke up in Ballen Hemnefjord, north of Stamnesøya.

Erling Karlsen, living in the Stamnes area at the time, watched from the shore line as the two Messerschmitts raked the fjord with machine-gun fire: "they both continued flying around firing at plane parts in the sea". Minutes later they were gone. Peace and stillness descended upon the fjord. The sixteen-year-old, having witnessed the Blenheim crash, rowed out with some friends to try and salvage a remnant of a wing. Tying rope around a jagged piece of metal they began rowing back to the shore; "unfortunately the part filled with water and we had to cut the rope to save us and the boat". Elders of Stamnes village then rowed out to retrieve a body floating in the water. A shocking sight greeted them. "The body of Gane was salvaged in a terrible state, torn to shreds, and there was no way he could have parachuted if those injuries were inflicted while he was still in the Blenheim plane." Villagers brought the lifeless body of the twenty-year-old British pilot ashore and German soldiers unhinged a nearby boathouse door to carry him up to the Stamnes farm. The farm owner objected to having the British pilot buried near the farmyard so he was lugged up the hill behind the barn. Pilot Officer Paddy Gane was buried later that day. "We had lost seven of our most experienced men in the space of a day" said Fowler.

At 07.42 hours Flight Lieutenant Roger Morewood was in the air. One hour later while patrolling near Utsire Light he reported "unidentified aircraft" flying in a northerly direction at about 7,000 feet. Suddenly, and to his great surprise, a raft appeared below. "The improvised raft looked like something from Robinson Crusoe and contained four men in position 233° Utsire Light 76 miles rowing toward the Norwegian coast." The Blenheim went down to fifty feet but the men did not wave or make any recognition signals. "They appeared to be in a state of utter exhaustion" said Morewood after landing at 09.55 hours in 'C-Charlie'.

In Scotland Pilot Officer Kenneth Mackenzie in L9046 with Pilot Officer Hal Randall flying N3609 toiled back and forth from 3,000 feet watching naval minesweepers with two destroyers sweeping ahead of a large convoy. Above were several layers of cloud. At 18.00 hours the Royal Navy were happy to let them go. Back on the ground and with winter approaching, they spent more time in the mess where life was orderly and pleasant, with the occasional appearance of a WAAF to take ones thoughts away from aerial warfare.

The pattern of recent Luftwaffe activity over Aberdeen and Glasgow meant that Fighter Command requested 248 Squadron to provide three fighters, 'V', 'A' and 'D', for night-fighter duty. The diarist recorded: "There has been some unusual activity off Aberdeen during the afternoon and early evening, apparently German shipping reconnaissance shadowing naval destroyers".

Under a Fighter Command controller they were sent off after the Huns just after 17.00 hours. It was not a very satisfactory sortie. Sam McHardy was unable to contact the destroyers due to darkness. "I was off again on October 27 in the early morning, just before breakfast was being served. With Easton, Ricketts and Garrad as my companions, we roared through dense cloud between 3,000 and 4,000 feet above the North Sea for almost four hours and twenty minutes before returning." McHardy picked over the remains of a congealed breakfast before catching up with A Flight administrative work.

Pilot Officer Archibald Hill had headed to the crew room fully dressed, not in the custom 'goon suit', his Mae West round his neck. He waited until 08.00 hours when they were scrambled and

Aircrew of B Flight 248 Squadron January 1941. (*R.I. Mowat*)

ordered to patrol from Trondheim to Stadtlandet. Passing over one fishing boat he maintained a steady course and sighted a further forty merchantmen in various positions off the coast from 12.50 to 14.35 hours between Trondheim and Alesund. Pilot Officer Edward Schollar photographed some of them; "which the Germans took exception to". Heavy flak opened up, bursting behind Blenheim 'V-Vic' at 4,000 feet. Using the F24 camera, he also took still photographs of Kristiansund. Archibald heard the word "fighter" at 14.35 hours as a Messerschmitt screamed towards their tail. Hill said: "I took successful avoiding action and obtained cloud cover". The Messerschmitt did not follow and vanished, but then the crew's trouble came in a different form amongst the clouds: ice!

Ice began to accumulate and the lift of the wings deteriorated. Z5956 faltered. Hill dropped down to 2,000 feet as the Mercury engines hesitated and pieces of ice fell from the propellers. Meanwhile the speed mounted rapidly and things quietened down. Hill, Schollar and Proudman were all in one piece and landed at 16.00 hours. The weather for the next few days was "fair" with "nothing seen". Life was becoming boring again. Patches of rain were the only interruption when shepherding a convoy on its slow progress from Lervick to St Magnus, Orkney Isles. 'C-Charlie' flew backwards and forwards along the line of ships and Sergeant Eric Holmes tried desperately to keep warm. Ahead out of the murk rose St Magnus Cathedral – Great Britain's most northerly cathedral. It was well past 6 p.m. when Holmes landed from this convoy sortie.

"Over recent weeks 248 Squadron had been busy", said Flying Officer Sam McHardy. "I was fortunate to fly on the last day of October in 'Z-Zebra' just after 4.00 p.m., it was as uneventful as it was interesting, my regular observer Sergeant Ivor Sims who was a quiet and unassuming man and a solid type did an excellent job." HMS *Berkshire* (FY 183) and her flock of twenty-two merchantmen with one auxiliary trawler stayed steady on course. Sims was kept busy by signal flashes from HMS *Berkshire*, one read, "believe we are still being shadowed".

'V-Vic' was forced to leave the convoy at 18.45 hours, as a foreign language was picked up on R/T; "thought to be German". They were told by their controller to land away at Lossiemouth. The airfield was serviceable but with extreme caution when landing on the northeast corner. Finally the Blenheim managed to get into Wick short of fuel.

At Northwood there was talk of Blenheim fighters flying in pairs or as a trio when dispatched on armed reconnaissance to Norway, and the European coast was a consideration. This produced some bitter comments from St Eval as 236 Squadron had already undertaken to do this as part of their continual fighter escort to Empire flying boats to Lundy Island throughout October. Their detachment at Aldergrove had patrolled over the *Empress of Britain* which had been bombed by Oblt Bernhard Jope, only to see it sink days later northwest of Bloody Foreland. What a disaster!

Sergeant Norman Price described events on October 31:

"mist, low cloud, dull and miserable. Total inactivity since 04.30 hours. I was happy to be sent off shortly after 06.50 on the 'tomato run' out over the English Channel on a Bust armed reconnaissance from Ushant to Guernsey. I named it the tomato run because a family friend in Reading owned a fruit and vegetable shop and his tomatoes came from Guernsey."

About five miles from the French coast the cloud was a lot thinner than he expected. The lack of suitable cloud cover prevented Price from going any further, which proved disappointing. 'X-X-ray' returned at 08.30 hours. The rest of the morning passed uneventfully and by lunchtime their commanding officer decided to release one of the Flights. An Austin 7 trundled along to St Agnes Railway Inn public house to see one of Norman Price's relatives who was visiting North Cornwall.

Fuel of a different kind was being consumed as 235 Squadron celebrated the reformation of the unit. Robert Jamison wrote in the squadron diary:

"The party took the form of a Christmas affair, aircrew serving and entertaining the ground crews in the NAAFI dining hall. There were light refreshments in the way of savoury and sweet biscuits supplied by Huntley & Palmers, a leg of ham was given too by a local farmer, washed down by copious draughts of beer (In all 109 gallons were consumed!). Music was supplied by the recently formed squadron band, ably supplemented by various individual vocals from within the station community. The C.O., Ronnie Clarke managed to get to his feet to make a speech, but had some difficulty owing to the prolonged appreciation by one and all. He began tracing the early First World War history of the squadron documented by Major Allan Robertson at Newlyn, Cornwall. Ronnie then talked about the unit during the first few months of training, he paid tribute to the work and leadership of Wiggs Manwaring and Dick Cross, our first flight commanders, and the keenness of those who worked under them. Then onto the splendid record of the past few months under Flight Lieutenant Andy Fletcher, now a squadron leader and the late Freddie Flood. He thanked the ground crews for their sterling work in extreme conditions at Detling under canvas.

"He made reference to the work carried out by the armoury, the wireless section, parachute packing section, and the orderly room, B Flight and their magnificently consistent work under difficult conditions – particularly 'Lelly' 'Smugger' and 'Tiny'. Altogether, a most enjoyable party for all hands."

It was dark when they arrived back at their rooms. It was the last day of October and winter was setting in. The turn of the month passed entirely unnoticed. 235, 236, 248 and 254 activities remained the same; the only change was the temperature, for some at least. The shorter days and poorer weather marked the onset of winter as November beckoned. With the continuation of British Summer Time by parliament's edict it was noted in 236 Squadron's journal that even dawn readiness was now at an extremely civilized hour.

Pilot Officer Norman Jackson-Smith had been with 235 for six months, six turbulent months which seemed a lifetime. He was one of the few survivors of the original squadron of May 1940. He had watched as his friends and colleagues were killed, wounded or disappeared without trace, either permanently or temporarily.

"The battle was over. It is with a sense of sorrow that we remember so many of the 'Few' who died during the battle. Of those still living in November 1940, close on half did not survive to see the final victory for which they fought. For their bravery and sacrifice in defence of our freedom, we will never forget them – indeed, we will remember them."

Blenheim fighters sit ready at Bircham Newton whilst crews sit or lay on the grass awaiting the scramble. In the background can be seen a visiting 19 Squadron Spitfire and in the distance a 115 Squadron Wellington. The photograph is taken from the water cooling tower next to the squadron's flight office. The Blenheim circled is the one in which Flying Officer Reg Peacock became an ace whilst flying against the Ju 87s on August 18, 1940. (*RAF Hendon Museum, London*)

APPENDIX I

Confirmed claims by Coastal Command
Blenheim Fighter Squadrons in 1940
(Courtesy Chris Goss)

Date	Time	Aircraft/Sqn	Claim	Location
10 April 40		254 1	Ju 52 Dest/He 111 Dam	Stavanger
01 May 40	08:00	J & L/254	Ju 88 Dam?	Romsdal Fjord
05 May 40	15:50	K & M/235 3	Bf 109s Dam?	15 miles N. Nordeney
12 May 40	08:00	235 1	Bf 109 Dest	Hague & SE Hook.
13 May 40	12:05	L & O/254; S/248	1 Ju 88 Dam	CPOX 5947
17 May 40	09:35	G, D, C/254	Bf 110 Dest	Bergen
18 May 40	16:30	248 2	Bf 110 Dest (Potez 631s/AC 2)	w. Blankenberg;
29 May 40	11:30	N, Q, E /235 1	Bf109 Dest	Dunkirk
01 Jun 40	18:32	235	1 He 111 Dest	VXDN 1040
04 Jun 40	15:35	P/254	Do 18 Dest	LKZS 4330
20 Jun 40	19:37	J, A/254	He 115 Dest	Norway
21 Jun 40	06:55	N,R,Q/254	He 115 Dam	XKND 3030
27 Jun 40	15:15	T, E/235 1	Bf 109 Dam	CPOX 2056
27 Jun 40	16:20	T/235	He 115 Dam	CPOX 5840
30 Jun 40		B, T/235	Do 17 Dam	KLWS 2728
11 Jul 40	11:58	236	Ju 88 Dam	ZJEK 0030
11 Jul 40	15:26	236	He 111 Dest	Bishops Rock 180m
17 Jul 40	14:35	D/236	Ju 88 Dam	SRVD 345
27 Jul 40	20:55	X/248	He 111 Dam?	DNXG 2000
03 Aug 40	16:20	W,T,S/235	He 115 Dam	NLMF 3505
04 Aug 40	16:50	H,D,F/236	Bf 109 Prob	15m off Brighton
08 Aug 40	16:35	N,K,M/235	Bf 110 Dest	SRVD 2351

Date	Time	Aircraft/Sqn	Claim	Location
11 Aug 40	13:25	X,Q,U/235	Bf 109 Dest	Le Havre
15 Aug 40	1455	D/235	He 111 Dest	80 m off Horns Reef
15 Aug 40		A,E/235 2	He 111 Prob	70 m off Horns Reef
18 Aug 40	14:25	N,P,Q/235 2	Ju 87 Dest	Thorney island
21 Aug 40	13:52	O,L,M/236	Ju 88 Dam	Trevose Head
22 Aug 40	11:09	F,G/235	He 59	
23 Aug 40	19:07	D/235	He 111 Dam	Thorney Island
26 Aug 40	09:05	W/248	Ju 52 Dam	Norway
02 Sep 40	18:10	235	Do 18	Off Dutch coast
05 Sep 40	18:06	R,H,Q/235	Do 18 Dam	Kent Coast
11 Sep 40	17:30	6 Albacores /826 + 6/235	3 Bf 109s Dam	English Channel
23 Sep 40	15:20	L/236 1	He 111 Dest	Bishops Rock
25 Sep 40	16:14	E/236	Do 18 Dest N.	Finisterre
26 Sep 40	16:19	L/236	He 115 Dam	Guernsey
28 Sep 40	09:40	G/248	Do 18 Dam?	Norway
02 Oct 40	19:15	Q/254	He 115 Dest	North Sea
03 Oct 40	08:54	U/248	Do 215 Prob	SE Shetlands
08 Oct 40	08:50	U,S/235	He 59 Dest	St Catherines Point
08 Oct 40	08:55	V/235	He 59 Dest	24 m off Portland Bill
16 Oct 40	07:38	Q/235	He 60 Dest	English Channel
20 Oct 40	14:40	H/248 1	Bf 109 Dam	Norweagian Coast
20 Oct 40	09:00	X/248 1	Bf 109 Dam	Norwegian Coast
30 Oct 40	17:30	L,N/235	– Dam	Fecamp
31 Oct 40	11:55	L/254	He 111 Dam	Norway

APPENDIX II

Variations of the Bristol Blenheim Fighter
Bristol Aeroplane Company Limited, Filton, Bristol

Blenheim Mark IF (Fighter)

In 1938 the Bristol Blenheim Mk IF came into service. Some 200 were converted from Blenheim bombers by the Royal Air Force on a contracted 'special order' from the Bristol Aeroplane Company Limited and the Southern Railway Ashford Locomotive Works factory supplied conversion kits.

The Mk I had its forward armament of four 0.303 Browning machine guns in an enclosed cradle below the fuselage. Gun packs were fitted at Royal Air Force maintenance units. In February 1940, Coastal Command's newly formed trade protection squadrons started receiving the Mk IF.

Manufacturers:	Bristol Aeroplane Company Limited, Filton, Bristol Sub-Contracted by Avro and Rootes
Horizontal gun tray manufacturers:	Southern Railway, Ashford Locomotive Works
Powerplant:	Two 840hp (630 kw) Bristol Mercury VIII engines
Weights:	Maximum take-off: 1,975 lbs Empty: 8,025 lbs
Dimensions:	Span: 56ft 4in Length: 39ft 9in Height: 12ft 10in
Wing area:	469 sq ft
Performance:	Maximum speed: 255 mph at 7,000 ft 230 mph at 18,000 ft
Climb rate:	11 minutes 30 seconds to 15,000 ft
Service ceiling height:	27,280 ft
Armament:	One fixed forward 0.303 Browning machine gun located in port wing (500 rounds) One Vickers 'K' machine gun in dorsal turret (100 rounds per pan) Under fuselage horizontal gun tray (special order) Four fixed forward 0.303 Browning machine guns (500 rounds per m/g)

Blenheim Mark IVF (Fighter)

The Mk IVF fighters entered service in April 1940 with the Coastal Command trade protection unit nos: 235, 236, 248 and 254 Squadrons.

Some 125 were converted by the Royal Air Force on a contracted 'special order' from the Bristol Aeroplane Company Limited and the Southern Railway Ashford Locomotive Works factory supplied conversion kits, overseen by Mr Oliver Bulleid, chief mechanical engineer at Ashford.

The Mk IVF had its forward armament of four 0.303 Browning machine guns in an enclosed cradle below the fuselage. Gun packs were fitted at Royal Air Force maintenance units.

A further eighteen new aircraft were ordered from the Bristol Aeroplane Company Limited, arriving in July 1940. Eighteen gun packs were assembled at squadron level amongst 235, 236, 248 and 254 Squadrons, when their aircraft arrived. The type also saw service with Fighter Command as a night fighter, the first being delivered in the summer of 1940 to 23 Squadron.

Manufacturers:	Bristol Aeroplane Company Limited, Filton, Bristol Sub-Contracted by Avro and Rootes
Horizontal gun tray manufacturers:	Southern Railway, Ashford Locomotive Works
Powerplant:	Two 920hp (690 kw) Bristol Mercury XV engines
Weights:	Maximum take-off: 15,800 Ibs Empty: 9,790 lbs
Dimensions:	Span: 56ft 4in Length: 42ft 7in Height: 12ft 10in
Wing area:	469 sq ft
Performance:	Maximum speed 255 mph at 7,000 ft 266 mph at 11,800 ft
Climb rate:	11 minutes to 15,000 ft
Service ceiling height:	22,000 ft
Armament:	One fixed forward 0.303 Browning machine gun located in port wing (500 rounds) One Vickers 'K' machine gun in dorsal turret (100 rounds per pan)
Sept/Oct 1940	Modified at squadron level fitting dorsal turret with two 0.303 Browning machine guns Under fuselage horizontal gun tray (special order) Four fixed forward 0.303 Browning machine guns (500 rounds per m/g)

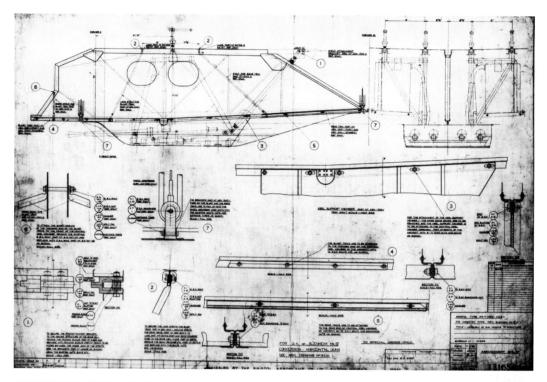

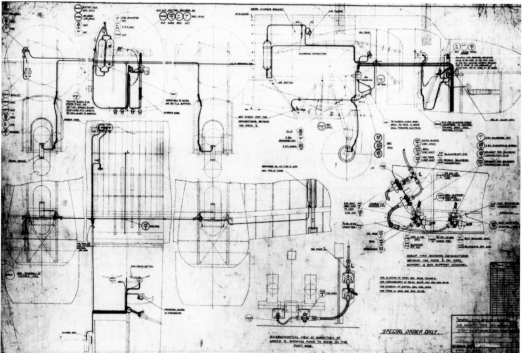

Two views of the original Bristol Aeroplane Company 'special order' drawings for the Blenheim fighter Mk IF and Mk IVF four 0.303 Browning gun pack. The production of components and manufacture of this belly pack was carried out by the Southern Railway Ashford Locomotive Works factory at Ashford, Kent. Overseen by Mr. Oliver Bulleid, chief mechanical engineer at the Ashford works. (*The Aircraft Restoration Company*)

APPENDIX III

Known production figures in Great Britain of the Bristol Blenheim Mk Is and Mk IVs

450 Blenheim Mk Is delivered between February 1938 and March 1939 by Bristol Aeroplane Company Limited, Filton, Bristol.
Contract No. 527111/36 and 529181/36
Serial Nos. L1097 to L1546

34 Blenheim Mk Is delivered between March and June 1939 by Bristol Aeroplane Company Limited, Filton, Bristol.
Contract No. 529181/36
Serial Nos. L4187 to L4822 and L4907 to L4934

84 Blenheim Mk IVs delivered between March and July 1939 by Bristol Aeroplane Company Limited, Filton, Bristol.
Contract No. 529181/36
Serial Nos. L4823 to L4906

250 Blenheim Mk Is delivered between August 1938 and March 1939 by A. V. Roe at Chadderton, Lancashire.
Contract No. 588371/36
Serial Nos. L6594 to L6843
(Serials L6696 to L6708 exported to Romanian Air Force; L6819, L6821 to L6834 exported to Royal Yugoslavian Air Force)

250 Blenheim Mk Is delivered between November 1938 and August 1939 by Rootes Securities at Blythe Bridge, Staffordshire.
Contract No. 551920/37
Serial Nos. L8362 to L8407, L8433 to L8482, L8500 to L8549, L8597 to L8632, L8652 to L8701, L8714 to L8731
(Serials L8619 to L8620, L8624 to L8630 exported to Romanian Air Force)

130 Blenheim Mk Is delivered between September and November 1939 by Rootes Securities at Blythe Bridge, Staffordshire.
Contract No. 551920/37
Serial Nos. L8732 to L8761, L8776 to L8800, L8827 to L8876, L9020 to L9044

220 Blenheim Mk IVs delivered between November 1939 and March 1940 by Rootes Securities at Blythe Bridge, Staffordshire.
Contract No. 569202/36
Serial Nos. L9170 to L9218, L9237 to L9273, (Built as Mk Is but modified to standard Mk IVs before delivery) L9294 to L9342, L9375, L9422, and L9446 to L9482

100 Blenheim Mk IVs delivered between March and June 1940 by A. V. Roe at Chadderton, Lancashire.
Contract No. 588371/36
Serial Nos. N3522 to N3545, N3551 to N3575, N3578 to N3604 and N3608 to N3631

100 Blenheim Mk IVs delivered between April and August 1939 by Bristol Aeroplane Company Limited, Filton, Bristol.
Contract No. 774679/38
Serial Nos. N6140 to N6220, and N6223 to N6242

70 Blenheim Mk IVs delivered between August and October 1939 by Bristol Aeroplane Company Limited, Filton, Bristol.
Contract No. 774679/38
Serial Nos. P4825 to P4864 and P4898 to P4927
(Serials P4910, P4911, P4915, P4916, P4921 and P4922 exported to the Royal Hellenic Air Force; as G-AFXD, G-AFXE, G-AFXF, G-AFXG, G-AFXH and G-AFXI)

62 Blenheim Mk IVs delivered between September 1939 and January 1940 by Bristol Aeroplane Company Limited, Filton, Bristol.
Contract No. 774679/38
Serial Nos. P6885 to P6934 and P6950 to P6961

30 Blenheim Mk IVs delivered in June and July 1940 by A. V. Roe at Chadderton, Lancashire.
Contract No. 588371/36
Serial Nos. R2770 to R2799
(Serials R2800, R2805, R2825 to R2864, R2877 to R2926, R2939 to R2963, R2995 to R3040, R3076 to R3128 and R3140 to R3144 were cancelled A. V. Roe built Mk IVs under Contract No. 588371/36)

250 Blenheim Mk IVs delivered between March and June 1940 by Rootes Securities at Blythe Bridge, Staffordshire.
Contract No. 1485/39
Serial Nos. R3590 to R3639, R3660 to R3709, R3730 to R3779, R3800 to R3849 and R3870 to R3919
(R3877 contracted to Free French Air Force)

400 Blenheim Mk IVs delivered between June and October 1940 by Rootes Securities at Blythe Bridge, Staffordshire.
Contract No. 1485/39
Serial Nos. T1793 to T1832, T1848 to T1897, T1921 to T1960, T1985 to T2004, T2080, T2031 to T2080, T2112 to T2141, T2161 to T2190, T2216 to T2255, T2273 to T2292, T2318 to T2357, T2381 to T2400 and T2425 to T2444
(T1867, T1875, T1935, T2077 and T2079 contracted to Free French Air Force)

800 Blenheim Mk IVs delivered between October 1940 and May 1941 by Rootes Securities at Blythe Bridge, Staffordshire.
Contract No. 1485/39
Serial Nos. V5370 to V5399, V5420 to V5469, V5490 to V5539. V5560 to V5599, V5620 to V5659, V5680 to V5699, V5720 to V5769, V5790 to V5829
V5850 to V5899, V5920, V5969, V5990 to V6039, V6060 to V6099, V6120 to V6149, V6170 to V6199, V6420 to V6469 and V6490 to V6529

420 Blenheim Mk IVs delivered in July 1940 and May 1941 by A. V. Roe at Chadderton, Lancashire.
Contract No. B119994/40
Serial Nos. Z7121 to Z5770, Z5794 to Z5818, Z5860 to Z5909, Z5947 to Z5991, Z6021 to Z6050, Z6070 to Z6104, Z6144 to Z6193, Z6239 to Z6283, Z6333 to Z6382 and Z6416 to Z6455

Both A. V. Roe (Avro) and Rootes Securities would build more Bristol Blenheims than the Bristol Aeroplance Company Limited by the time they had completed the orders for Mk IVs in November 1941.

A. V. Roe built 1,005 Blenheims between August 1938 and October 1941

Rootes built 3,419 Blenheims from November 1938 to October 1943 when the production of the Blenheim Mk V was cancelled.

Bristol Aeroplane Company Limited built 955 of the Blenheims.

The total number built is recorded as 6,185 Blenheims.

BIBLIOGRAPHY

Ashworth, Chris. *RAF Coastal Command 1936-1969.* Patrick Stephens Limited 1992
  Battle of Britain Then and Now, The. The Battle Magazine, Mk V 1989
Bader, Group Captain Douglas. *Fight for the Sky.* Doubleday 1973
Boiten, Theo. *Blenheim Strike.* Air Research Publications 1995
Bonnard, Brian. *Alderney at War.* Alan Sutton Publishing Limited 1993
Brooks, Robin J. *Kent's Own – The History of 500 (City of Kent) Sqdn RAuxAF.*
  Meresborough Books 1982
Bungay, Stephen. *The Most Dangerous Enemy.* Aurum Press Ltd 2001
Churchill, Sir Winston. *Their Finest Hour.* Houghton Mifflin 1949
Collier, Richard. *Eagle Day.* E.P. Dutton 1966
Colville, John. *The Fringes of Power – Downing Street Diaries 1939-1955.*
  Weidenfeld & Nicolson 2004
Cornwell, Peter D. *Battle Of France Then and Now.* The Battle of Britain International Limited,
  Essex 2007
Donnelly, Larry. *The Other Few.* Red Kite 2004
Dudley-Gordon, Sqn. Ldr. Tom. *Coastal Command at War.* Jarrolds Publishers 1944
Franks, Norman. *Air Battle Dunkirk.* Grub Street Publishing 2006
  Fighter Pilot A Personal Record. B.T. Batsford Ltd 1941
Fleming, Peter. *Invasion 1940* Rupert Hart-Davis 1957
H.M.S.O. *Coastal Command 1939-1942.* H.M.S.O. London 1942
Hillary, Richard. *The Last Enemy.* MacMillan & Co. Ltd 1943
Levine, Joshua. *Forgotten Voices of the Blitz & Battle of Britain.* Ebury Publishing 2007
Mason, Francis K. *Battle over Britain.* Aston Publications Limited 1990
Parker, Matthew. *The Battle of Britain: An Oral History of Britain's Finest Hour.*
  Headline Publishing 2001
McNeill, Ross. *RAF Coastal Command Losses of the Second World War 1939-1941.*
  Midland Publishing – Imprint of Ian Allan Publishing Limited 2003
Neave, Airey. *The Flames of Calais.* Coronet Books, Hodder & Stoughton 1974
Newton, Dennis. *First Impact – Australians in The Air War of World War 2 Volume 1: 1939-1940*
  Banner Books, Australia 1997
Prien, Jochen. *Geschichte des Jagdgeschwader 77: Teil 1.* Struve Druck, Eutin.
Prien, Jochen. *Geschichte des Jagdgeschwader 77: Teil 2.* Struve Druck, Eutin.
Rawlings, John D. R. *Coastal, Support & Special Squadrons.* Janes Publishing Company Limited 1982
Ross, David. *Richard Hillary.* Grub Street Publishing 2000

Spaight, J. M. *Blockade By Air – The Campaign against Axis Shipping.*
Geoffrey Bles Limited 1944
Walker, Ronald. *Flight to Victory.* Penguin Books Limited 1940
Warner, Graham. *The Bristol Blenheim A Complete History – Second Edition –.*
Crécy Publishing Limited 2005
Webb, Gordon. *Epics of the RAF – The War in the Air.* Withy Grove Press 1940

Logbooks: Aircrew

Gallway, Ian.	3 GR Unit (attached to 235 Sqn) June 1940
Jackson-Smith, Norman.	235 Squadron, Coastal Command 1940
Morewood, Roger.	248 Squadron, Coastal Command 1940
Quelch, Basil.	235 Squadron, Coastal Command 1940
Wakefield, Hugh.	235 Squadron, Coastal Command 1940
Powers, Charles.	236 Squadron, Coastal Command 1940

Auction Notes:

Peacock, Reginald.	Medals
Sutton, Harold.	Medals

Air Ministry:

Daily Reports	April, May, June, July, August, September, October 1940
Daily Air Ministry Summary	April, May, June, July, August, September, October 1940

Unpublished Private Papers:

Jackson-Smith, Norman.	Holland, Dunkerque and The Battle of Britain
Lancaster, Albury.	To Amsterdam and Back
McHardy, Sam.	Someone on my Shoulder
Neville-Clarke, Ronald	Notes June 1940
Wright, Daniel.	Letter/photograph
Bowhill, 'Ginger' Frederick.	Letters to AM Hugh Dowding 1941
Sutton, Harold.	Diary extracts (anonymous private collector)
235 Squadron Magazine	*Chocks Away.*
Flood, Frederick.	Letter
Wickings-Smith, Peter.	Letter, Bloxham School, Banbury, Oxfordshire School Publication, Bloxham School, Banbury, Oxfordshire

National Archive Ottawa, Canada

1 RCAF Squadron ORB   24 August 1940 (Version 2*)

*Note: The Royal Canadian Air Force Headquarters senior staff did not tell the National Defense Department in Ottawa until after the war of this tragic event until February 27, 1947 and then only after an official enquiry. Subsequently two versions of the ORB of No 1 RCAF Squadron for the month of August 1940 are in existence, version one describing the attack although it implies it is broken off before any harm is done. This also omits the victories on August 26 and 31, 1940. Version two omits text from August 24 but includes text from August 26 and 31 victories and describes the action.

It is version two which is at the UK's National Archive, Kew, London on microfilm. The National Archive Ottawa historical department also has version two.

INDEX